The OECD and Transnational Governance

Edited by Rianne Mahon and
Stephen McBride

The OECD and Transnational Governance

UBCPress · Vancouver · Toronto

20 19 18 17 16 15 14 13 12 11 10 09 08   5 4 3 2 1

Printed in Canada on ancient-forest-free paper (100 percent post-consumer recycled) that is processed chlorine- and acid-free, with vegetable-based inks.

Library and Archives Canada Cataloguing in Publication

The OECD and transnational governance / edited by Rianne Mahon and Stephen McBride.

Includes bibliographical references and index.
ISBN 978-0-7748-1554-3

1. Organisation for Economic Co-operation and Development. 2. Political planning – International cooperation. 3. Economic policy – International cooperation. 4. Social policy – International cooperation. 5. International cooperation. 6. International organization. I. Mahon, Rianne, 1948- II. McBride, Stephen

HD82.O33 2008   320.606'01   C2008-903465-1

Canadä

UBC Press gratefully acknowledges the financial support for our publishing program of the Government of Canada through the Book Publishing Industry Development Program (BPIDP), and of the Canada Council for the Arts, and the British Columbia Arts Council.

This book has been published with the help of a grant from the Canadian Federation for the Humanities and Social Sciences, through the Aid to Scholarly Publications Programme, using funds provided by the Social Sciences and Humanities Research Council of Canada.

UBC Press
The University of British Columbia
2029 West Mall
Vancouver, BC V6T 1Z2
604-822-5959 / Fax: 604-822-6083
www.ubcpress.ca

Contents

Acknowledgments

We would like to acknowledge financial support from the Social Sciences and Humanities Research Council of Canada, Carleton University's Vice-President Research, the Institute of Political Economy at Carleton University, and the Centre for Global Political Economy at Simon Fraser University. We also thank Matthew Lymburner and Frank Richter for their thorough and painstaking work in preparing the manuscript for production.

The OECD and Transnational Governance

Introduction

Rianne Mahon and Stephen McBride

This book brings together a diverse group of students of public policy and international relations (IR), working from different perspectives within these fields to understand the role of the Organisation for Economic Co-operation and Development (OECD) in transnational governance. The contributors avoid the constraints of "methodological nationalism" (Taylor 1994; Brenner 2004) and posit that although nation states still make policy, they do so in the context of an increasingly dense web of transnational networks, operating at different scales. International organizations such as the OECD function as important nodes in these networks, which, taken as a whole, constitute an uneven (and contested) system of transnational governance.

Why focus on the OECD, a little-studied international organization that has been variously described as a "rich man's club," an international think tank, or even a "shared state apparatus" (Dostal 2004)? After all, in contrast to the International Monetary Fund (IMF) and the World Bank, the OECD lacks the power to enforce compliance with its decisions. The OECD does, however, operate as an important site for the construction and dissemination of transnational research and policy ideas embracing a wide range of contemporary issues, as the chapters in this volume indicate. More broadly, the OECD is a "purveyor of ideas," and ideas play an important role in contemporary transnational governance. Institutions and interests (of nation-states, international organizations, and social forces) are important, but ideas also play a critical role. In the broadest sense, transnational norms identify what a modern state "is," and thus sanction appropriate modes of internal and external conduct. In policy terms, the ideas sanctioned by international organizations help to identify problems and to map out the range of "best practice" solutions. Yet, as the chapters in this volume show, this is by no means an uncontested process.

Unlike the United Nations' or the World Trade Organization's large membership of predominantly states from the global South, the OECD's membership is small, currently limited to thirty countries.[1] Its membership includes the United States and Japan and the other advanced capitalist states, to whom the nature of its membership – "rich nations' club" – makes it attractive as an alternative forum for dealing with contentious issues, in comparison with international organizations with a broader membership base. The OECD played a significant role in the construction of the postwar world order, helping to lay the basis for the economic unification of Western Europe and also to constitute the North Atlantic bloc. As this postwar order unravelled, the OECD altered its horizons geopolitically through the expansion of its membership, incorporating former members of the Soviet bloc and a leading "Asian tiger" (South Korea). It also intensified its "outreach" activities, especially to the major economies of Asia and Latin America. The current Secretary-General aims to make the OECD a "globalization hub." Accordingly, at the 2007 meeting of the Council of Ministers, the OECD extended an invitation to Chile, Estonia, Israel, Russia, and Slovenia, while recommending increased engagement, as part of the Group of Eight (G8) Heiligendamm process, with Brazil, China, India, Indonesia, and South Africa.

Transnational Governance

In both international relations and policy studies, and much of modern social science,[2] the dominant approaches have long been rooted in a "methodological nationalism" – the assumption that "all social relations are organized at a national scale or are undergoing processes of nationalization" (Brenner 2004, 28). Increasingly, however, policy studies have come to recognize the importance of international and transnational policy transfer and policy learning. The increased incidence of policy transfer is seen partially as a product of advances in the ability of information communication technologies to diffuse information rapidly across time and space, and partially as a consequence of the increasing coordination of policy through international arenas. As Dolowitz and Marsh (2000) suggest, policy transfer involves "a process in which knowledge about policies, administrative arrangements, institutions and ideas in one setting ... is used in the development of policies, institutions and ideas in another setting" (2000, 5). The policy transfer literature draws attention to the ways in which seemingly closed national policy routines can be "disrupted" by the policy prescriptions of international and supranational organizations, as well as the expertise supplied by transnational consultants (Stone 2003). In some accounts, lesson drawing is considered a rational, voluntary activity, in which learning "starts with scanning programmes in effect elsewhere, and ends with the *prospective evaluation* of what would happen if a programme already in effect elsewhere were transferred here" (Rose 1991, 3). Dolowitz and Marsh, however, raise the important question of the extent to which transfer is always "voluntary" or even necessarily "rational."

For students of international relations, nation-states have operated as the core organizing principle since the Treaty of Westphalia (1648) sanctioned the organization of the world into territorially exclusive, sovereign nation-states. For neo-realists, the state remains the central actor in a largely anarchic state system, and power, understood primarily in military and diplomatic terms, is seen as the most important factor in world politics.[3] "Neo-liberal institutionalists" within international political economy (IPE) posit that international organizations are necessary to assist states in achieving their ends (Hobson 2000, 102-3), a perspective retained even by those versions of the approach that emphasize a networked world order (e.g., Slaughter 2004). Mainstream IPE has been increasingly challenged by neo-Gramscian and social constructivist approaches. While the power of transnational capital is highlighted by neo-Gramscians, they, along with social constructivists like Keck and Sikkink (1999), recognize the importance of social movements that increasingly operate beyond the national scale. Nor is the contemporary world (dis-)order understood as consisting simply of nation-states and trans-national social forces.

The twentieth century witnessed the proliferation of international organizations, and these are more than "empty shells or impersonal policy machinery to be manipulated by other actors" (Barnett and Finnemore 1999, 704). As a result, interest has grown in "global" (Wilkinson et al. 2002; Wilkinson 2005), "transnational" (Djelic and Sahlin-Andersson 2006a), or "multi-level/scalar" (Hooghe and Marks 2001; Jessop 2003) governance. The term "transnational" will be used in this volume as it captures the complex patchwork of networks, operating at variable scales, that together comprise the contemporary system. As Djelic and Sahlin-Andersson argue, "'transnational governance' suggests entanglement and blurred boundaries to a degree that the term 'global' could not ... Organizations, activities and individuals constantly span multiple levels, rendering obsolete older lines of demarcation" (2006b, 4). Similarly, Robert Cox has argued that "the old state system is resolving itself into a complex of political-economic entities: micro-regions, traditional states and macro regions with institutions of greater or lesser functional scope and formal authority" (2005, 149). In other words, transnational networks, whether supranational structures like the European Union or the much more limited North American Free Trade Agreement, define a new porous and variable territoriality, (macro-)regional in scope. At the same time, cities and other subnational governments have gained a new international visibility as centres of important "micro-regions" or as "global cities." Nation-states still matter, but their boundaries are increasingly recognized as permeable.

The choice of the word "governance" is deliberate. It refers to "governance without government" (Cox's famous "*nébuleuse*"): that is, the development, at multiple scales, of a variety of mechanisms of regulation, operating in the absence of an overarching political authority. The absence of formal hierarchy, in turn, suggests the utilization of "soft" as well as "hard" (i.e., formal laws and directives) regulation. Thus, in addition to classic regulation, with formal laws or directives backed by penalties for violation, the emergent system of transnational governance includes *inquisitive* and *meditative* modes of regulation (Jacobsson 2006), in which the OECD is heavily involved. Inquisitive regulation involves the surveillance or monitoring of the actions of states: "member states are not obligated to follow up specific policies, but they are required to 'open up' to others to examine and critically judge what they are doing" (2006, 207). Accordingly, practices such as establishing benchmarks and the organization of peer review processes entail the auditing, comparison, and ranking of state practices. In contrast, meditating activities "are mainly framed as discussions among experts about what is the best way or ways of doing something" (Jacobsson 2006, 208). Jacobsson suggests, in fact, that it is from such "meditative" fora that hard regulations frequently emerge, and from which the standards or "benchmarks" that constitute the stuff of inquisition are derived.

Formal international organizations play an important role here and are supplemented by the work of quasi-formal networks such as the G8 and private actors such as international bond rating agencies and international cartels (Murphy 2005). "Epistemic communities" (Haas 1992) or networks of knowledge-based experts, sometimes operating through international organizations, other times through informal networks, are also engaged in identifying state interests and/or common problems to be tackled in a co-ordinated fashion. In addition, "social forces" (Cox 1987) or "transnational advocacy coalitions" (Keck and Sikkink 1999) contribute to the construction/ transformation of structures of transnational governance.

This does not mean that nation-states have disappeared. They remain key decision points, though they make policy in a context increasingly shaped by multiple and overlapping transnational networks. While some forms of "policy transfer" entail direct or indirect measures of coercion, transnational governance, especially as it is applied to advanced capitalist countries, more typically takes the form of "policy learning." It should not be assumed that such learning is simply a rote exercise (though it may be), through which policy and program models are simply imported from elsewhere and applied in procrustean fashion. Rather, as Djelic and Sahlin-Andersson suggest, "the travel of ideas is an active process and ideas are shaped and translated differently in different settings. Carriers are active in structuring flows and patterns of diffusion but they are also translating the ideas they mediate, reflecting in the process their own projects and interests" (2006b, 15-16).

Nor does the emphasis on "soft" instruments of governance and transnational networks mean the absence of power and contestation. Clearly, meditative activities channelled through international organizations involve the power to classify, fix meanings, and diffuse norms (Barnett and Finnemore 1999, 711), while inquisitive processes such as peer review entail the exercise of the power of surveillance/monitoring, creating pressures on states to conform to new standards and practices. Thus, in this volume, Tony Porter and Michael Webb argue that the transnational "knowledge networks," orchestrated by international organizations like the OECD, help to define what it means to be a "modern" state. States participate in the construction of shared understandings of appropriate behaviour and, through inquisitive activities like peer review, generate "socialization processes" that encourage states to adopt behaviours identified as appropriate (Chapter 2). In the sphere of economic policy, such processes link the OECD with domestic agencies (e.g., ministries of finance) and actors (such as business associations) likely to share its views. The OECD's advice may help to strengthen the latter's position in domestic debates.

For Finnemore, the dominant norms and ideas are decidedly "Western" – such as individual human rights and modern bureaucracy as the paramount form of political organization (Finnemore 1996, 332). To this, Porter and Webb would add liberal economic theory and its definition of efficient economic organization (market economies). The terminology of neo-Gramscians may be different – bourgeois individualism, capitalist relations of production – but it points in the same direction. Power needs to be understood in relational terms, however. For Finnemore, the existence of deep tensions in globalized Western culture leaves ample room for contestation over "the logic of appropriateness" (1996, 342). Drawing on neo-Gramscian theory, Arne Ruckert argues that "hegemonic power cannot be imposed on subordinate social forces but must be secured in a process of negotiation in which consent is engendered through material incentives and social compromises ... Hegemony is thus in constant flux, never complete, and as such is always open to multiple contestations" (Chapter 5). It is important, therefore, to recognize the implications that such contestation holds for international organizations.

The OECD in the Emerging Structure of Transnational Governance

The OECD's work does not focus on classic foreign policy issues. Although its biographer could boast that, in the 1960s, "it stood as a colossal, and colossally successful, challenge to Soviet and Chinese Communism" (Sullivan 1997, 33), this came about through its contributions to the postwar liberalization of trade and investment and, more specifically, the consolidation of the North Atlantic as the centre of the world capitalist economy. The OECD does not possess the budgetary or sanctioning powers enjoyed by the main economic international organizations, the IMF and the World Bank. Unlike the International Labour Organization (ILO), whose conventions have to be submitted to parliaments (Armingeon 2004, 227), governments can choose simply to ignore the OECD's advice. Nonetheless, the OECD did play an instrumental role in developing the "inquisitive" and "meditative" modes of (Western) governance in the postwar period. Furthermore, the OECD Secretariat[4] enjoys a certain autonomy vis-à-vis both transnational social forces and member states, including the most powerful among them (the US). That autonomy, however, is only relative.

While the IMF and World Bank were charged with provision of short-term loans to relieve balance of payments difficulties and longer-term loans for "development," the OECD initially focused on surveillance of economic policies and outcomes in the North Atlantic, with an eye to harmonization. As Cox notes, "such procedures began with the mutual criticism of recon- struction plans in Western European countries (the US condition for Marshall Plan funds), continued with the development of annual review procedure in NATO ... and became an acquired habit of mutual consultation and mutual review of national policies (through the OECD and other agencies)" (1986, 231). In fact, it was the OECD's predecessor, the Organisation for European Economic Co-operation (OEEC), that was created to manage this process. As Robert Wolfe argues in Chapter 1, the OEEC was unable to play the role – allocation of Marshall Plan aid – initially envisaged by the Americans. From 1948 to 1958, however, the OEEC successfully worked to remove quantitative trade restrictions in Europe. Moreover, it helped lay the founda- tions for the European Economic Community and the European Free Trade Association (Salzman and Terracino 2006, 315), while the European Payments Union it formed worked to secure currency convertibility in Western Europe (Chapter 2).

Formed in 1961, the OECD went on to develop and refine techniques for surveillance of member country economic performance and assessment of their policies across a growing range of fields. Article 3 of its convention contains a commitment by member states "to furnish the Organisation with the information necessary for the accomplishment of its tasks" (Chapter 1). This commitment formed the basis for the routine collection of statistics from member (and sometimes non-member) countries, and their assembly into regular reports such as the Economic Outlook (Economics Department) or "Society at a Glance," produced by the Directorate for Employment, Labour and Social Affairs (DELSA). Such activities are routine, however, only in the sense that they form one of the organization's regular, ongoing activities. As Porter and Webb argue, these seemingly mundane activities constitute the basis for intersubjectively meaningful comparisons of national experiences (Chapter 2). The OECD Secretariat plays an active role here, identifying "ap- propriate" indicators and developing common ways of measuring in order to permit cross-national comparison and ranking. The "league tables" thus constructed make visible each country's performance relative to that of its peers, putting pressure on the "laggards" to improve their performance.

Sometimes inquisition involves more elaborate activities. For instance, the Programme for International Student Assessment (PISA) student performance assessments require participating countries to administer a specific examination procedure, designed by a network of experts coordinated by the Directorate for Education (Morgan 2007; Chapter 13). The biennial country surveys produced by the Economics Department involve a deeper, ongoing engagement of OECD staff with their national counterparts. As this methodology is applied, more or less systematically, in other OECD studies, it is worth considering in greater detail.

The production of a country report begins with the design of a questionnaire, prepared by the country desk in the Economics Department of the Secretariat. The questions posed "direct their attention to a set of problem areas that the OECD finds interesting. The questionnaire also provides a vocabulary introduced by the OECD, which conceptualises the problems and limits the margin of manoeuvre for member countries" (Noaksson and Jacobsson 2003, 32). The country under review is obliged to answer the questionnaire, and thus to enter into the mental framework established by the Secretariat. The next step is a visit by the OECD mission, which involves meetings with key ministries, the central bank, appropriate domestic experts, and relevant civil society representatives. This, as Marcussen notes, "might help raise important questions and ideas in the minds of the political and administrative actors in the national polity" (2004a, 29). In addition, it enables the OECD team to establish/reinforce links with like-minded domestic officials, creating a potential basis of support for the recommendations to be contained in the final report.[5]

Up to this point, the process is led by the Economics Department, which engages in a "bilateral" dialogue with its member country counterparts, especially the key economic ministry (usually the department of finance). The completion of the next draft launches the peer review process, drawing in representatives of other member states. The draft report, which "can be quite explicit with pointed recommendations and detailed case studies" (Salzman and Terracino 2006, 319), is distributed four weeks in advance of the meeting of the Economic and Development Review Committee (EDRC). Two peer reviewers are appointed to lead the discussions, which can involve quite sharp debates, with the country under review seeking to blunt criticism, especially in domestically sensitive areas. The whole debate takes place under the rule of "derestriction": that is, no publication can be released until all – both the country under review and its peer-critics – agree (Salzman and Terracino 2006, 319).[6] The final report that is released to the public thus typically represents a compromise, which the Secretariat often plays an active part in reaching (Noaksson and Jacobsson 2003).

The production of the country reviews thus constitutes a classic example of the inquisitive mode of governance in operation. A similar procedure is followed by other parts of the OECD Secretariat in conducting other reviews or special thematic studies, such as the regulatory review launched by the Directorate on Governance and Territorial Development (GOV) in 1997 (Lodge 2005). Just how effective is this process, however, in inducing conformity on the part of the member states?

The Armingeon and Beyeler volume (2004) examines the impact of OECD country reports on the social policies of its Western European members. Armingeon (2004) concludes that the OECD's advice enjoyed "low efficacy." Even where there appeared to be a strong link between OECD recommendations and member country policy, as with the United Kingdom, there was little evidence that the OECD set the agenda for change (Manning 2004, 209). Several chapters in this volume also address this question. Stephen McBride and colleagues' cross-national assessment of the impact of the Economics Department's Jobs Strategy[7] (Chapter 8) indicates that a significant group of countries did not follow the OECD's prescription for "liberalization" of domestic labour markets – and prospered. Holly Grinvalds' in-depth analysis of the Danish case (Chapter 10) suggests that transnational policy learning may involve a more subtle – or creative – process, in which the pupil applies the lesson in original ways, or is inspired by the OECD's definition of the problem to focus on an area but finds its own solution through domestic debate.

The OECD's main contribution to transnational governance may, however, be its meditative function, as Marcussen (2004a) has emphasized. Here its formidable research capacity is brought into play. Its research enables it to highlight certain trends, to identify common problems, and to map out a range of appropriate solutions. This can involve complex technical work, which enables the broadening of the range of statistical surveillance by factoring new data into the equation. Sometimes the concepts thus produced facilitate the coordination of member country activities vis-à-vis non-members. Occasionally, practical concepts originating at the OECD migrate into agreements sanctioned by other international organizations.

Thus, for instance, Sullivan (1997a) credits the OECD's Environment Directorate with devising the concept of "polluter pays." In this volume, Wolfe argues in Chapter 1 that the Trade Directorate and Trade Committee's work on the concepts of producer and consumer subsidy equivalents laid the basis for the "aggregate measure of support" breakthrough at the World Trade Organization (WTO). In Chapter 5, Arne Ruckert notes the role played by the OECD's Development Assistance Committee (DAC) in the formation of codes of best practice in the implementation of development assistance, and goes on to discuss the OECD's work on international development targets, which subsequently formed the core of what has become known as the United Nations "Millennium Development Goals." In Chapter 6, Russell Williams traces the OECD's impact on guidelines for the operations of multinational corporations, including the aborted negotiation of the Multilateral Agreement on Investment (MAI) in the late 1990s.

Such meditation does not, however, take place in circumstances equivalent to that of the proverbial ivory tower: "ethnographic studies of IOs describe a world in which organizational goals are strongly shaped by norms of the profession that dominate the bureaucracy and in which interests themselves are varied, often in flux, debated, and worked out through interactions between the staff of the bureaucracy and the world in which they are embedded" (Barnett and Finnemore 1999, 706). This accurately describes how the OECD performs its meditative function. OECD staff conduct research and produce a range of background studies and reports. In this they draw on their disciplinary knowledge, supplemented by what Dostal refers to as an "organizational discourse" – "claims encapsulating long term political projects as defined by the organization in question" (2004, 445). The latter reflects the effects of organizational learning. An ethnographic account of a directorate thus would map the way key studies and policy documents produce important themes and concepts, which infiltrate and modify the "pure" disciplinary discourse. The "Jobs Strategy," discussed in several chapters, became such a key document/learning experience for the Economics Department, while *New Orientations for Social Policy* (1991) and *A Caring World* (1999) arguably played a similar role in terms of DELSA's social policy staff (Deacon et al. 1997).

Nor does such learning occur purely in-house. Research directions and priorities are set by the managing committee to which each directorate reports; below this is a myriad of subcommittees and working and expert groups that regularly bring OECD staff into dialogue with national officials and other experts in their field (Salzman and Terracino 2006, 324). In Chapter 11, Lisa Drouillard and E. Richard Gold provide a good example of the organizational learning such working groups facilitate, and in Chapter 7, Neil Bradford illustrates the way the OECD's extensive research networks enabled it to produce a new, hybrid urban paradigm.

Elsewhere, Sahlin-Andersson (2000a) has examined the way in which the Public Management Committee (PUMA) of the Governance Directorate helped codify and disseminate the themes of "new public management," an amalgam of public choice theory, principal-agency theory, and transaction cost economics, given practical significance by the public sector reforms instituted in the Anglo-Saxon countries, especially New Zealand, during the 1980s. She argues that PUMA's actions involved the editing out of country-specific experience to produce generalizable conclusions: "Reforms and experiences were generalised and assembled as a reform agenda or policy package, and a common logic and common explanations were ascribed to the reforms. The reforms were described and justified as responses to a common set of problems facing all OECD countries, and they were labelled as a coherent and consistent package" (2000a, 16). In Chapter 3, Leslie Pal suggests, however, that PUMA provided a forum for ongoing learning on the part of OECD staff and committee members, such that the diversity of national experiences has been "edited" back in.

The OECD's "policy learning networks" also include representatives of civil society. From the outset, the OECD has been involved in regular dialogue with the Business and Industry Advisory Committee (BIAC) and the Trade Union Advisory Committee (TUAC).[8] Both regularly consult with the OECD Secretariat and the various committees and working groups. The two associations can also discuss OECD agenda items through the Labour/Management Programme, which is partly financed by the OECD (Salzman and Terracino 2006, 329). In Chapter 4, Richard Woodward charts TUAC's waning status, relative to BIAC, as the OECD abandoned Keynes for monetarism in the late 1970s. As he notes, "increasingly BIAC's agenda was in vogue and it progressively assumed a privileged ideational position within the OECD."

More broadly, while the Committee for Agriculture and the Environmental Directorate have long had relations with civil society groups, it was the MAI fiasco that spurred the OECD to develop what Woodward calls complex multilateralism, "where states remain the main arbiters but have to coexist with a cacophony of civil society voices" (Chapter 4). While the OECD has exhibited real leadership in this regard, Woodward finds that there are clear limits. It is the more conservative non-governmental organizations (NGOs) and business interests that are favoured interlocutors. Moreover, not all parts of the OECD are equally engaged in dialogue with civil society representatives. Thus, while the Agriculture, Environment, and (now) Investment Committees have been actively engaged, the Economic Policy Committee (EPC) remains aloof from such civil society consultations. Yet, as Sullivan suggests, it is the EPC – and its highly influential Working Party 3 (WP 3) – that is in charge of key routines, including the working out of common policies in advance of the annual G7 (now G8) summits (1997, 62).[9] This suggests that the "inner sanctum" – the sites where the most important economic policy issues are dealt with – remains relatively insulated from civil society.

What of the OECD's relationship with non-member states? From the outset, the OECD functioned as a key node in the construction of the North Atlantic alliance (to which Australia, Japan, New Zealand, and Finland were later admitted) against the Soviet bloc in Eastern Europe. With the latter's disintegration in the late 1980s, the OECD joined other international organizations in facilitating the transition to market economies. According to Sullivan, "a key element in the program ... [was] SIGMA – Support for Improvement of Governance and Management in Central and Eastern European Countries, run jointly by the OECD and the European Union" (1997, 45). Through SIGMA, the Economic Development and Review Committee prepared reports on Eastern European countries, "essentially bringing those non-member states into the OECD surveillance process" (Chapter 6). These reports focused on issues of appropriate forms of public sector management for the emerging market economies. In the 1990s, the Czech Republic, Hungary, and Poland were admitted to the OECD, with the Slovak Republic following in 2000. Their admission to the club marked their progress towards the establishment of market economies and liberal democracies.

It is in its relation to the global South that the OECD especially stands out as a rich nations' club. In contrast to UN agencies, the OECD has offered its member states a "safe" forum to explore common interests of the (capitalist) North vis-à-vis the South. Chapter 5 documents the way this has allowed the OECD to play a role in coordinating aid policy and, later, in mapping out the core of what was to become the UN's Millennium Development Goals. Yet the states of the global South are not monolithically composed of equally poor countries, a point driven home in the 1980s by the performance of the "Asian tigers." Since 1992, the OECD has permitted the participation of non-members in its work and one of the Asian tigers – South Korea – was admitted to the organization in 1996, following Mexico, admitted in 1994 after it became a signatory to the North American Free Trade Agreement with Canada and the United States. The OECD is currently involved in active outreach activities in East Asia, Latin America, and Africa. More broadly, one of the key issues concerning its future is the effect of the expansion of membership to include the large and booming economies of China, India, and Brazil.

Nor are the OECD's original member states equal in wealth and power. This raises the question of whether the OECD is and has always operated as a site for the exercise of "Americanization." For Djelic and Sahlin-Andersson, the emergent system of transnational governance represents a process of Americanization in a double sense. First, they identify the "unique and often powerful role and place of American actors and blueprints in the regulatory process, both at the origins and at critical ... moments" (2006c, 397). Chapter 11 in this volume provides an interesting example of the latter. Here it was not agents of the US state per se, but rather leading scholars and key sites for meditative activities within the US, that the OECD drew on in setting its guidelines for genetic invention. Second, Djelic and Sahlin-Andersson suggest that American power "is particularly linked historically to the post second world war period and is associated in part with the threading of an international organizational network – key nodes being the World Bank, the IMF, the OECD, and United Nations and its satellites, the GATT and the WTO" (2006c, 397). There is evidence in support of this proposition as it applies to the OECD.

The OECD's predecessor, the OEEC, was established to help implement the US Marshall Plan. Its replacement by the OECD brought the US (and Canada) into what had been a European organization. The OECD's budget is based on financial contributions that reflect the size of each member's economy. Hence, the US contributes the largest share of the OECD's budget, followed by Japan. While the Secretaries-General have come from a variety of countries, one of the Deputy Secretary-General posts is normally occupied by an American.[10] More broadly, Dostal (2004) estimated that of the OECD's professional staff of 858, Americans (133) were exceeded only by the French (182).[11] Many of these are economists, trained in neoclassical economics, a discipline where the US increasingly sets the standard. There are also specific instances where American policies clearly set limits to what the OECD could do. Thus, for instance, Webb's analysis of the fate of the OECD's "harmful tax competition" treaty concluded that "the Bush Administration's anti-tax ideology had a huge impact on the OECD project even though that ideology found little official support in any other OECD country" (2004, 815). Elsewhere, Graefe (2006) has argued that international organizations like the OECD have played an important role in adapting and disseminating the (neoliberal) American social policy model.

Nevertheless, unlike the World Bank and the IMF, the OECD's headquarters are in Paris, not the US. The majority of member states remain European, and Europeans constitute the majority of its professional staff. In Chapter 9, Andrew Jackson suggests that this has enabled the addition of social democratic ideas to the policy mix, especially with the victories of Left governments in key European states during the latter half of the 1990s. In addition, there are strong connections between the European Commission and the OECD. The European Union is an active participant in many of its committees and has representation on the Ministerial Council. The two organizations collaborate on various projects, although the OECD's longer research involvement around labour market and social policy issues and larger staff complement means that it is the Commission that looks to the OECD, rather than the reverse.

Perhaps, however, the real question is not which member country dominates the OECD. Such a question seems to fit better with the (neo)realist view of international relations as agents of powerful national principals. It is more useful to focus instead on the networks of transnational governance and the concomitant internationalization of the state. Thus, for Cox, one consequence of the internationalization of the state is that "new axes of influence link international policy networks with the key central agencies of government and big business" (2005, 232). Chapters 9 and 10 lend support to Cox's thesis, that it is principally core ministries, such as finance, that are most strongly linked to dialogue and "meditation" with the OECD, especially its central components, the Economics Department and its key committees. Yet while national states may have been penetrated by transnational networks, they still remain important sites of deliberation and ultimately policy decision. They remain, therefore, more than mere transmission belts for ideas established elsewhere. As the chapters on the Jobs Strategy show, policy learning may be taking place in an increasingly transnational context, but that learning can involve a creative process in which national states draw their own conclusions from the lessons learned.

The OECD as Creator, Purveyor, and Legitimator of Ideas

Thus far, we have stressed the central role ideas play in the OECD's contribution to transnational governance, and the processes through which it develops and disseminates these. We have not, however, closely examined the question of what sorts of ideas the OECD has developed and supported. We can imagine that, like states in relation to powerful interests in their own societies, the OECD enjoys a relative autonomy in constructing ideas, even if, in general, it tends to reflect the ideological tenor of the times. Thus, until the mid-1970s, the OECD reflected the postwar conventional wisdom of Keynesianism. Thereafter, the organization gradually came to adopt a different policy paradigm, generally referred to as monetarism or neoliberalism, contemporary renditions of traditional neoclassical economics. Many observers detect some shift in OECD thinking in recent years. How far it has moved from earlier neoliberal orthodoxy remains a matter of debate and may, in fact, vary by issue area.

The OECD's internal discourse has often been viewed as dominated by Anglo-American–trained professional economists. As such, it can be expected to reflect trends in economics, especially as taught in the Anglo-American universities and popularized by think tanks based in those countries (Dostal 2004, 440, 446). That said, the OECD is not one-dimensional and is not simply a transmission belt for the ideas dominant in economics departments. Different trends within orthodox economics may be utilized by different agencies within the OECD itself. In part, this may reflect their links with different agencies in member states. Thus, for instance, the Economics Department tends to interact closely with national finance ministries, and DELSA with ministries dealing with labour and social issues. In addition, different directorates develop distinct organizational discourses, which are reflected in key documents. To the extent that these transnational networks draw on different trends within orthodox economics, one might expect to see an "inclusive" or an "innovative" liberalism, compared with the hard neoliberal economics perspective of the Economics Department.[12]

The "McCracken Report," written by experts commissioned by the OECD to investigate the relationship between employment and price stability, marked the beginning of the hegemony of neoliberalism within the OECD. Adopting a supply-side approach to the labour market, its analyses and prescriptions pointed the way to a new orthodoxy, based on removal of rigidities and enhanced flexibility within the labour market (OECD 1977, 221-23), themes that would figure prominently in the Jobs Study of the

1990s. Of course, particular member states had already begun the shift away from the OECD's previous discourse. For example, in Canada, the central bank had adopted a policy of "monetary gradualism," prefiguring a gradual shift away from Keynesianism in 1975 (McBride 1992, 71-117). Similarly, British Labour Prime Minister James Callaghan had told his followers in 1976 that the Keynesian era was over: "We used to think you could just spend your way out of recession and increase employment by cutting taxes and boosting spending. I tell you in all candour that option no longer exists" (Hall 1993, 285).

Nonetheless, the McCracken Report formed part of a broader paradigm shift in which the inability of an existing paradigm to explain discordant evidence and advance solutions to problems played a part in its replacement. A new paradigm, or specific policies derived from it, may, however, also rest uneasily on an evidentiary basis. As Cox argued, paradigms, like theories, reflect a particular perspective: "All theories have a perspective ... The world is seen from a standpoint definable in terms of nation or social class, of dominant and subordinate, of rising and declining powers, of a sense of immobility or of present crisis, of past experience and of hopes and expectations for the future. Of course sophisticated theory is never just the expression of a perspective. The more sophisticated a theory is, the more it reflects upon and transcends its own perspective but the initial perspective is always contained within a theory and is relevant for its explication" (Cox 1983, 128).

In this context, it is worth recalling criticisms made of the McCracken Report at the time.

Robert O. Keohane (1978) posed two questions about the use of knowledge and expertise, the foundations of OECD policy influence then and now: "To what extent are the policy recommendations of these OECD economists derived from the findings of economics per se – and to what extent do they stem, instead, from unexamined political or ideological assumptions? Are the analytical accomplishments of economics used to generate sound prescriptions, or do they merely serve (with the reputations of the report's authors) to legitimize an essentially political argument?" (109) Keohane concluded that this ostensibly economic report relied on political and sociological explanations of inflation that were beyond the expertise of the team of economists. The latter, moreover, made "no attempt to specify the importance of those phenomena, or even carefully to verify their existence ... they are quite content to select important variables in a casual, ad hoc fashion and to evaluate their significance impressionistically, without benefit of either information or research" (113). Thus, for Keohane, the report actually owed little to disciplinary expertise. According to him, the McCracken Report's recommendations thus contained a "large dose of ideology, which is neither explicitly defended nor critically examined" (125). Indeed, reading the review leads one to think that this is political ideology being rendered as economic science, and legitimized by the reputations of its economist authors. In stating that economics and economic expertise play a key role in the OECD's success, therefore, we need to be careful in how we interpret this source of power.

A later example of the power of economic orthodoxy is provided by the Jobs Study and Jobs Strategy exercises of the 1990s and early 2000s. The Jobs Study proved to be an important document, especially for the organizational discourse of the influential Economics Department. To a degree, the initial Jobs Study reflected different institutional interests within the OECD, which are themselves reflective of broader interests and theoretical disputes in society. Initiated in response to concerns about unemployment, especially in a number of European member countries, the Jobs Study provided an analysis that involved several directorates under the lead of the General Secretariat. Although there was some effort to recognize that economic flexibility for employers should be combined with economic security for workers, the document was grounded in a neoliberal analysis of labour markets based on the concept of a non-accelerating inflationary rate of unemployment (NAIRU) (McBride and Williams 2001). The significance of this theory is that it locates obstacles to non-inflationary employment growth within the labour market itself, rather than deficiencies in aggregate demand or productive capacity. It therefore provides an economic rationale for deregulated "flexible" labour markets. While certainly mainstream by the early 1990s, the doctrine is by no means uncontested within the economics profession (see Sawyer 2004; Setterfield 1996). The original document evolved into the Jobs Strategy, for which the Economics Department assumed sole responsibility (Noaksson and Jacobsson 2003, 17-18). It typified the department's neoliberal discourse and was strongly reflected, *inter alia,* in the biennial country surveys discussed in the previous section. With DELSA no longer closely involved, moreover, the desire to balance flexibility with security gave way to a more pronounced focus on deregulation and flexibility in the labour force (Noaksson and Jacobsson 2003, 47-48).

The contrast between selective, theory-driven approaches on the part of the OECD, emanating from its Economics Department, and more contextual, interdisciplinary approaches characteristic of other organizations is traced in a comparison of the Jobs Study and the EU's Employment Strategy. Noaksson and Jacobsson suggest that "while the EU attempts to adapt knowledge to fit reality, the OECD attempts to adapt reality to fit existing knowledge" (2003, 10). Similarly, Casey points to the greater influence of social considerations on EU analyses of the labour market: the European strategy reflects greater awareness of the potentially negative outcomes that can result from following through some of its recommendations. Accordingly, it is more willing to counsel caution, and more willing to suggest the need for compensatory actions. That it does so is a corollary of its being influenced by a social model "in a way that the OECD strategy is not" (Casey 2004). This would be one reason for non-compliance with the Jobs Strategy on the part of some countries. The strategy appears to have been perceived as one that was useful for finance ministers in pushing for reforms but, where social partners were in a position to resist, unlikely to be implemented (Chapter 8).

It is not only in the Jobs Strategy that evidence can be found of OECD rethinking. Bob Deacon and Alexandra Kaasch argue in Chapter 12 that DELSA's reflections on social and health policy have clearly broken with neoliberalism. Similarly, Bradford argues in Chapter 7 that the OECD's Territorial Development Policy Committee has produced an "innovative" liberal synthesis. At its 2007 meeting, the Ministerial Council announced plans to develop an innovation strategy equivalent in stature to the Jobs Strategy. It will be interesting to see whether the new strategy adopts the kind of blend that Bradford found in the cities reviews. Since such rethinking is evident in other areas, identifying the source and extent of change is an important element of analysis.

One unresolved issue is whether the change(s) represent a new paradigm, distinct from the neoliberalism that has characterized OECD policy approaches since the mid-1970s, or whether it represents adjustment, modification, and fine-tuning of that approach that responds or reacts to criticisms of the neoliberal model without sacrificing the fundamentals of that approach, offering what Graefe (2006) calls "flanking mechanisms."

The most comprehensive statement of the thesis that the OECD has undergone a paradigm shift is contained in Chapter 14 of this volume. Rianne Mahon's analysis of the growing significance of gender in the OECD's social policy discourse signifies that "the OECD is no longer singing exclusively from the neoliberal hymn book," and its reconciliation agenda reflects an "inclusive liberal" approach. While the latter shares certain features with neoliberalism, it departs from it in important ways. Thus, "inclusive liberalism" is seen as a distinctive variant of liberalism, of equivalent status to classic, new, or social liberalism and neoliberalism.[13] Mahon argues that, triggered by the unpopularity of neoliberalism around the world, electoral results in some key European countries, and the European influence on the Paris-based OECD, the OECD's discovery of the need for state intervention to facilitate the reconciliation of work and family life is consistent with neoliberalism in certain important respects: acceptance of trade and investment liberalization, commitment to non-inflationary growth and fiscal conservatism, a supply-side approach to employability, and acceptance of inequality "in the here and now." It differs, however, in its emphasis on investing in people who demonstrate that they are willing to take responsibility for their own development, providing carrots rather than sticks within a supply-side approach, providing incentives to encourage men to share parental leave, and a range of other "positive" measures.

Clearly, detectable changes are underway at the OECD, but do they amount to the emergence of a new paradigm? DELSA's "inclusive liberalism" is distinct from, but does not pose a fundamental challenge to, the neoliberalism that remains dominant within other sections of the OECD, notably its Economics Department. McBride et al. (2007) argue that the revised (2006) Jobs Strategy belatedly accepts that there is a route to good labour market performance and international competitiveness other than that recommended by the original Jobs Strategy. Indeed, what is remarkable, given the preponderance of empirical evidence on this point, is that it took the OECD so long to formally recognize this. Nevertheless, the new Jobs Strategy primarily reflects neoliberal goals and policy instruments, an indication that any change in direction is one of adjustment rather than transformation. In this respect, the OECD's position has undoubtedly evolved since the early days of neoliberal certainties.

The debate about whether new trends amount to a new paradigm is not merely an academic or scholastic exercise. It is important to assess to what degree of change has occurred and is occurring. In discussing Peter Hall's concept of "policy paradigm," Hemerijck and Visser (2003, 12) make the point that when new paradigms emerge, they contain statements of policy goals, identifications of policy techniques to attain them, and prescriptions about the settings of these policy instruments. This can be classified as "higher-order" policy learning (Hall 1993), which is distinguished from "lower-order" learning by its scope. For the latter, learning and change involves fairly minor, incremental changes in instrument choice or in the settings of the instruments. Typically, a higher-order change would be occasioned by some sort of crisis that intensified the search for new solutions. Evans (2004, 68) notes that the adoption of the neoliberal paradigm had involved five specific types of policy change. At the macroeconomic level, financial orthodoxy, control of inflation, and monetarism had displaced full employment and Keynesianism. More attention was focused on microeconomic policy initiatives such as deregulation and welfare-to-work programs. Internationally, protectionism gave way to the embrace of free trade. New regulatory structures were established to condition the behaviour of states and the promotion of enterprise. Innovation and competition displaced general welfare enhancement as the primary goal of politics. To what extent have these characteristics of the neoliberal approach been eroded or transcended?

There are parallels here with the evolution of policy in the Keynesian era. Starting, at least in the Anglo-Saxon world, as policy made by the big levers of fiscal and monetary policy, the Keynesians gradually became more intrusive and coercive (as the example of wage and price controls in many countries indicates) in response to the contradictions of Keynesian policies themselves, and changes in the internal political economy made old instruments unworkable. For some time, the original Keynesian goals continued to inform policy making, and new instruments were devised to keep the enterprise functioning. Whether this was still Keynesianism was a matter of dispute, and various prefixes were applied – late-Keynesian, post-Keynesian, and so forth. By analogy, one interpretation of the shifts in discourse at the OECD would be that the organization continues to sing from the same hymnbook, but different units are now allowed to select their own preferred hymns. More technically, different instrument choices may be possible within the same overall policy paradigm.[14]

This is the conclusion that Craig and Porter come to in their analysis of inclusive liberalism as practised in contemporary development programs as well as the policies of "third way" governments. Despite greater inclusion of the poor and marginalized, inclusive liberalism ultimately has a "hollow ring," falling well short of the social liberalism of the postwar years (Craig and Porter 2004, 233). Similarly, inclusion can mean greater consultation between international organizations and representatives of civil society (O'Brien et al. 2000), though the results of this engagement, in terms of engineering of real change in the dominant policy paradigm, remain ambiguous. However one reads the degree of shift, the fact of contestation and the development of modified and alternative visions is real and is embedded in OECD processes, relations between the OECD and national governments, and intra-bureaucratic differences with national governments, as well as in the broader class relations reflected in interest group and social movement politics in society at large.

Conclusion

The chapters in this volume explore in more specific ways the OECD's role in transnational governance. Some focus on policies and practices explicitly designed to contribute to the liberalization of trade (Chapter 1) and investment flows (Chapter 6), while others focus on its stance vis-à-vis non-member states in the South (Chapter 5) or its relations with non-state actors that are part of an emerging "global civil society" (Chapter 4). Others focus on matters long considered to be domestic concerns – innovation (Chapters 7 and 11), labour market policy (Chapters 8, 9, and 10), education (Chapter 13), health and social policy (Chapters 12 and 14), and public sector reform (Chapter 3). That an international organization like the OECD concerns itself with domestic issues reflects the growing reach of instruments of transnational governance. Even in the Keynesian era, the need for cross-national coordination of domestic policies was recognized by the OECD, but the very economic liberalization to which the OECD has contributed, and the tensions this has generated, have expanded the scope and intensity of transnational regulation.

Although the authors work from different perspectives, one thread running through all chapters is that the OECD represents an important but underemphasized node in the growing networks of transnational governance. In fact, it has pioneered the inquisitive and meditative forms that other international and supranational organizations have more recently discovered. The studies it conducts feed into policy discussions in other international fora such as the G8 and WTO, but its reports also infiltrate national debates, often from privileged locations within them such as ministries of finance, where the aura of expertise surrounding the OECD may be used by national and subnational actors who seek to advance the broader neoliberal agenda. Nevertheless, in times of transition and marked contestation such as these, the OECD is far from monolithic. Different ideological and policy currents may find expression in, and even result in conflict between, different branches of the organization, opening up the possibility that actors seeking alternatives to neoliberalism may draw on the OECD's prestige for their own purposes.

Notes

1 Australia, Austria, Belgium, Czech Republic, Finland, France, Germany, Greece, Hungary, Iceland, Ireland, Italy, Japan, South Korea, Luxembourg, Mexico, the Netherlands, New Zealand, Norway, Poland, Portugal, Slovak Republic, Spain, Sweden, Switzerland, Turkey, the United Kingdom, and the United States.

2 Some might argue that the "world systems" approach escaped such methodological nationalism, yet the world as imagined by Immanuel Wallerstein and others was still a relatively simple one, composed of said "world system" and core and peripheral states.

3 The authors especially wish to thank Tony Porter for his insights into the main theoretical debates in international relations. We also thank Cristina Rojas for comments on an early draft of this chapter.

4 Staff of some 2,000. Initially, the intent was to recruit middle- and higher-level civil servants on five-year rotations from the member states, but Salzman and Terracino suggest that "many in the secretariat make their careers at the OECD" (2006, 324).

5 There is often a second visit, following the production of the interim report, to enable the team to update information and engage in more protracted discussions with national officials (Schäfer 2006, 74).

6 Sullivan (1997, 491) suggests that some reports have been held up for months, as the country under inspection tries to persuade staff and fellow committee members to adopt a different tone or to change prescriptions, while Salzman and Terracino (2006, 319) suggest that some reports are never published.

7 The original Jobs Study, carried out by the Economics Department and the Directorate for Employment, Education, Labour and Social Affairs, became the basis for the Jobs Strategy, overseen by the Economics Department.

8 TUAC's origins date back to the immediate postwar period, when it was created "to provide advice to the OEEC in its implementation of the Marshall Plan" (Salzman and Terracino 2006, 327). Mindful of the tide of worker revolts in the aftermath of the First World War and fearing the spread of communism, Western leaders were keen to involve unions in postwar reconstruction. BIAC's birth coincided with that of the OECD.

9 It became eight with the addition of Russia.

10 Initially, there were two posts. Now there are four, and one of these is occupied by an American.

11 The US was followed by 90 from the UK, with Canada, Germany, Japan, and Italy accounting for between 51 and 62 professional staff each.
12 On these variants of liberalism, see Chapters 5, 7, and 14.
13 On these distinctions, see O'Connor et al. (1999, 43-65).
14 A good example can be found in Boyle and Roy's comparison (2003) of UK youth labour market policy under Prime Ministers Thatcher and Blair.

Part 1:
The OECD and Transnational Governance

1

From Reconstructing Europe to Constructing Globalization: The OECD in Historical Perspective

Robert Wolfe

The story of the Organisation for Economic Co-operation and Development, created in 1961, begins with the political and economic reconstruction of a stable and prosperous international order after the Second World War.[1] In his famous Harvard University commencement speech of 5 June 1947, reflecting on the plight of Europe after the frightful winter of 1946-47, US Secretary of State George Marshall declared that US policy "should be the revival of a working economy in the world so as to permit the emergence of political and social conditions in which free institutions can exist" (OECD 1978, 227-29). This liberal idealism is still the rock on which the OECD rests.

Two themes emerge from the history of the organization: economic cooperation can serve political purposes, and the way to get to the desired policies is through social learning more than reciprocal obligation. I begin with a description of the origins and demise of the OECD's predecessor, the Organisation for European Economic Co-operation (OEEC), and then outline the evolution of the OECD before looking more closely at the two central aspects of its work, money and trade, and the relationship between the OECD and other international organizations, notably the Group of 8 (G8) and the World Trade Organization (WTO). I conclude with some reflections on the organization's changing role as the European Union expands far beyond the original membership of the OEEC and globalization continues to transform governance. European reconstruction is long finished, but developing the consensual knowledge needed to construct globalization is an expanding work in progress.

Origins: The Organisation for European Economic Co-operation (OEEC)
The Marshall Plan was not in fact a plan but an invitation to the European countries to tell the United States what needed to be done to assist postwar reconstruction, implying that aid would be contingent on their ability to work together. After a failed attempt to negotiate a joint response with the

USSR, on 3 July 1947 the foreign ministers of Britain and France invited all European countries to meet in Paris to draw up an economic recovery plan for transmission to Marshall. The conference created the Committee of European Economic Co-operation to manage the initial phases of the European Recovery Program. As the need for a more permanent body became apparent, the OEEC was created in April 1948. Canada and the United States were soon "associated" in OEEC work. Spain, then still under Franco, was excluded, but otherwise the membership was self-selected: Austria, Belgium, Denmark, France, Greece, Iceland, Ireland, Italy, Luxembourg, the Netherlands, Norway, Portugal, Sweden, Switzerland, Turkey, the United Kingdom, and Western Germany. By 1958, all were also members of the North Atlantic Treaty Organization (NATO) except the neutrals (Austria, Ireland, Sweden, and Switzerland).

By developing the disciplines of cooperation and networks of officials, the OEEC laid the basis for subsequent efforts at European integration (Marjolin 1989). A.F.W. Plumptre, a senior Canadian official, recalled that the OEEC developed

> an elaborate code and procedure for European trade liberalization ... supported by credit facilities provided through the European Payments Union (EPU) ... During the 1950s, the OEEC code of intra-European commercial conduct was supplemented by the introduction of other codes of regional economic conduct dealing with capital movements, shipping and other forms of transportation, and other international transactions ... [each] ... supervised by a committee, and other committees concerned with the problems and possibilities of each of the main European industries were set up. The headquarters of the OEEC ... became a centre for intra-European consultation and collaboration on economic matters. (Plumptre 1977, 129-30)

The Americans had wanted the OEEC to be a vehicle for European integration by requiring that the organization allocate Marshall Plan aid, but the OEEC could not bear this burden. The organization carried on for nearly a decade, but it was undermined by its members' growing preference for discussions in the NATO economic committee, and was finally doomed by structural change in trade and payments. In trade, the achievement by December 1958 of 90 percent liberalization of quantitative restrictions, even by France, ended the value of this role just at the moment when the OEEC's limited role in managing the European payments system ended, when European currencies became convertible. Europeans were also embroiled in debates about how to respond to the creation of a common market among six OEEC members following the Treaty of Rome, signed earlier in 1958 (Griffiths 1997). When the Council of the OEEC met on 15 December 1958, its main business was the question of intra-European trade, and specifically the scheme for a free trade area that was being pressed hard by Britain, which was not a member of the new European Economic Community (EEC). An Anglo-French confrontation about discrimination and retaliation led to disarray (Shonfield 1976, 7-13).

The Council of the OEEC never met again. In Europe, the EEC Commission and many influential French officials felt that the cohesion of the Six, the political purpose of the Treaty of Rome, would be undermined if trade liberalization were pursued either through an OEEC-wide free trade area or a free trade link between the Six and the seven countries of the European Free Trade Area (EFTA). American preferences for liberal global trade rather than European discrimination led Douglas Dillon, then US Under-Secretary of State for Economic Affairs, to propose in November 1958 what came to be known as the Dillon Round of multilateral trade negotiations in the General Agreement on Tariffs and Trade (GATT) (Curzon 1965, 98). The tensions, still pressing a year later, were taken up at a Western Summit (France, the United States, the Federal Republic of Germany, and the United Kingdom) in Paris, where the political imperative of Atlantic cohesion during the Cold War was as salient as economic policy cooperation. Leaders agreed that they should now be "devoting cooperative efforts to furthering the development of the less developed countries," and they elaborated a set of principles for discussion of the commercial problems caused by the co-existence of multilateral and European economic regional organizations. This communiqué launched the process of high-level meetings and drafting groups that ended in the signing of the OECD Convention a year later.

Canada and the United States became full participants in the new body: like NATO, it was to be an Atlantic, not a European, organization. Members believed that commercial conflict led to war; that the GATT and the International Monetary Fund (IMF) were the first line of defence; that regional conflict could undermine this broader objective; and, therefore, that the OECD could help, both by promoting the broad objectives of the regimes for trade and payments and by encouraging the leading industrial countries to work together. The Council of the OECD met for the first time in December 1961, with Donald Fleming, Canada's minister of finance, in the chair.

What the OECD Does
In the early years, the OECD's tasks fell in three groups. The first set of tasks, which involved member countries alone, derived from the high degree of similarity and interaction among the economies of the advanced industrial countries. The next set of tasks, involving third countries, derived from the desire of OECD countries to order their relationship or to coordinate their strategy vis-à-vis other groups of countries. The last set of tasks involved the coherence and effectiveness of the international economic system (Camps

1975, 14). Change in how members understand good policy, and structural change in the world, has altered these tasks. Members now place more stress on good national policy than on coordinated international action, and they spend more time talking to third countries than they spend talking about them. Engagement with the most dynamic global economies is now central to the OECD's role.

The OECD has no regulatory responsibility, no independent source of funds, no money to lend, and no instruments within its control. Where the preamble of the GATT speaks of a desire to enter into "reciprocal arrangements," Article 1 of the OECD Convention says that the organization shall "promote policies" designed to achieve "the highest sustainable economic growth and employment and a rising standard of living in member countries." My focus below will be on two policy areas most relevant to global governance – money and trade – but the OECD is also active in all the substantive domains of modern governments, from the environment, through tax, to public management. Energy was not an original head of cooperation for the OECD, but part of the collective response to the first oil shock in 1973 was a conference that led to the establishment in November 1974 of the International Energy Agency (IEA). Members (which did not include France until the 1990s) decided that the IEA should have autonomy in its operational role but that it should work closely with the OECD on policy.

Article 1 also provides that members will "contribute" to sound economic expansion in non-member countries in the process of economic development. A.F.W. Plumptre recalled that "the Americans hoped to encourage greater participation by European countries in programs of economic aid to developing countries; the United States appeared to have been carrying the greater part of the load and the US administration was anxious, not only to obtain some relief for US balance of payments, but also to reassure Congress that this particular 'white man's burden' was being shared with reasonable equity. Thus D for development became one of the initials of the new organization" (Plumptre 1977, 131). The OECD was never intended to be a development assistance institution, however. Its role, as discussed by Arne Ruckert in Chapter 5 of this volume, was to facilitate burden sharing and policy discussion among donors. Development Assistance Committee (DAC) principles define the structure of national aid agencies; DAC definitions of Official Development Assistance (ODA) and "technical assistance" become national definitions.

Here, too, the OECD has sometimes been used to manage political tensions among its leading members. The first time an American secretary of state led the US delegation to the annual meeting of the OECD Council at ministerial level (or "ministerial") was in 1975 (Camps 1975, 9). The double issue provoking such interest was the problem of the collective response to the collapse of the Bretton Woods system of fixed exchange rates, along with the response to the first oil shock. The result was a declaration on relations with developing countries under which the Americans agreed to the Conference on International Economic Cooperation (CIEC) (Putnam and Henning 1989, 22), which itself was partly a response to problems in negotiations with the Group of 77 (the group that coordinated developing country participation in key United Nations agencies, notably the UN Conference on Trade and Development, or UNCTAD) elsewhere. The initial group was succeeded by a Group on North-South Economic Issues to coordinate the participation of OECD countries in the various instances of the "North-South dialogue." Since the end of the Cold War, the OECD has become a forum for policy consultations with non-members, including the countries in transition, and leading developing countries in Asia and Latin America. Many non-member countries now participate in the activities of OECD subsidiary bodies.

In Article 3 of the convention, members agree: (1) to furnish the Organisation with the information necessary for the accomplishment of its tasks; (2) to consult together on a continuing basis; and (3) to cooperate closely and, where appropriate, take coordinated action. The closer an activity is to the beginning of the list, the more common it is at the OECD. Consistent with the first two items of Article 3, the development and sharing of standardized information is the basis of all the rest. The OECD adds value to national data by coordinating definitions and measurements. In any domain, a single country can conduct comparisons with itself through time, but the OECD helps conduct rigorous comparisons with other similar countries at the same point in time. The UN cannot do this job at the same level of detail and sophistication because of its wide membership; similarly, the IMF and the WTO develop information for the different purposes of their near-universal membership.

Surveillance, sometimes called peer review, has been part of the process of sharing and evaluating information, of developing a common understanding of how the world works with a view to better policy making and better policy implementation. (For more on peer review, see Chapters 2 and 9.) OECD surveillance over macroeconomic policies is two-sided: the coherence between domestic policy objectives and the conduct of policy is examined in the Economic and Development Review Committee (EDRC); the way policies add up and, more specifically, the international coherence of national policies has been the focus of the Economic Policy Committee (EPC) (Koromzay 1991, 164). One of the particular strengths of the OECD is that this surveillance is carried out in a number of policy fields drawing on Secretariat expertise in a dozen microeconomic domains (Pagani 2002a). Each reinforces the others. In addition to the traditional surveillance of economic, energy, development, capital, and investment policies, there are now surveillance exercises of education, employment, science and technology, environment, and regional policies.

The third item of Article 3, coordinated action, is relatively rare at the OECD, although in certain areas its long association with the process of regional cooperation in Europe has made it a useful forum. The legal force of OECD obligations is problematic. In Canada, they rarely even require Cabinet let alone parliamentary approval, and they are not "enforceable" in the usual sense because the OECD has nothing approaching a dispute settlement system. OECD commitments work to the extent that they are subject to surveillance by fellow members whose good opinion of one another is of some value. The Export Credit Arrangement, to take one example, was probably negotiated at the OECD for negative reasons: debilitating competition among the OECD countries needed to be restrained, but no other forum was available involving only this group of countries and having a competent secretariat (Moravcsik 1989, 198). No doubt similar reasons exist for the OECD work on money laundering and for the OECD Convention on the Corruption of Foreign Public Officials, negotiated shortly before the failure of the Multilateral Agreement on Investment (MAI) in 1998. The anti-bribery convention was successful because at the time, the OECD could still be said to encompass the home countries of the major global infrastructure contractors and heavy equipment manufacturers, making it the relevant group of countries for dealing with the problem. The investment story, discussed in detail in Chapter 6, goes in the other direction.

Investment was discussed in negotiations for the Charter of the International Trade Organization (1948), but it did not enter the GATT at all until the 1980s, when the United States challenged the performance requirements imposed on investors by the Canadian government through the Foreign Investment Review Agency (FIRA). In the absence of other fora for negotiations, the OECD played an active role. The Code of Liberalization of Current Invisible Operations and the Code of Liberalization of Capital Movements were important as a focus for an emerging normative consensus. The 1976 Declaration on International Investment and Multinational Enterprises was adopted to forestall efforts by UNCTAD to craft a code on multinationals. The declaration and the codes did not go far enough for some American officials, who pushed first for a Wider Investment Instrument and then, in the mid-1990s, for what came to be known as the Multilateral Agreement on Investment. The OECD being unsuited to negotiation of binding reciprocal obligations, the MAI failed, not least because it would have reduced the flexibility of signatories in a potential comprehensive WTO negotiation with the many significant countries that do not belong to the OECD.

The Organization

The purposes and methods of the OECD imply the need for an unusual organization. It relies on strong participation of delegates from national governments in its subsidiary bodies, as does the WTO. It also has a highly competent professional secretariat, as does the IMF. The committee structure reflects the organization of member governments and the evolution of various policy communities. Officials find the OECD useful for exchanges of ideas with colleagues who face similar problems. Often there is nowhere else for such consultations, or consultations at the OECD provide more and faster information about policy intentions than is available elsewhere. While its importance for officials is undiminished in most sectors, its value to politicians and senior officials appears to have declined.

The ministerial was once the highlight of the OECD year. The Communiqué signalled themes to the public, to markets, to other governments or institutions, and to bureaucrats. It could be a directive to the Secretary-General, a normative statement of good intentions, and a signal of policy decisions to come, depending on the conjuncture. Attendance fluctuated, but, with many more opportunities to meet, fewer senior ministers now participate. (In contrast to the Council ministerial, sectoral ministerials – for example, of the Agriculture Committee – usually attract the relevant ministers.)

When the OECD was created, there was no body that would provide a regular forum for senior officials whose responsibilities touched on the management of the international economic system. The Trade Committee and the Economic Policy Committee do not do much work in common, a fact that reflects the division of labour in capitals more than the nature of the issues. When US President Nixon made his famous statement about a New Economic Policy in August 1971, he called for a new linkage between trade and monetary policies. As at the creation of the OECD twelve years earlier, American fears of a new step for the European Community (EC) (in this case, enlargement) were part of the political context. The only way for the Americans to use the OECD to follow up their president's linkage of trade and monetary policy was to call for a new restricted body, which eventually held its first meeting in December 1972. It came to be called the Executive Committee in Special Session (ECSS) the next year. Its creation did respond to the American interest in having a forum where trade and monetary policies could be considered together, but it is debatable whether the body ever fulfilled its potential. In the 1980s, the ECSS frequently played a role in preparing issues for subsequent ministerial discussion, which allowed it, on occasion, at least, to have an overview of international economic cooperation, but its role gradually declined and now senior officials rarely attend.

The European Community/Union and the OECD
European integration and cooperation have always affected the evolution of the OEEC and the OECD. In 1947, political disarray in Europe was the reason the United States tried to use the OEEC to foster European integration. In 1958, the creation of the Common Market and the end of the

European Payments Union fatally undermined the OEEC. In 1972, the enlargement of the EC contributed both to a sense that the OECD had lost its way and to the creation of the ECSS. In the late 1980s, as the EC appeared to be revitalized by the Single European Act, people began to mutter again about the OECD's being adrift. The European Commission wanted to join the OECD but was ignored. Instead Protocol 1 of the OECD Convention allows the Commission to "participate in the work" of the OECD, something more than the observer status granted other international organizations. The Commission, which has its own delegation in Paris, has practically the same rights as a member, with two exceptions. It has no vote in the formal adoption of acts of the OECD and, not being a member, it pays no part of the general budget (Schricke 1989, 805-7).

Nineteen of the OECD's current thirty members are European Union (EU) states. Many people wonder whether the ever-closer integration of the EU will render the OECD irrelevant. EU enlargement poses a challenge for the OECD because member states maintain their individual voices, yet the range of things on which they can speak without reference to collective decision making is diminishing. If the Atlantic area were still the focus of OECD work, this imbalance would be serious, as it would be if formal decisions of the Council were important, but the continuing relevance of the OECD goes beyond the North Atlantic.

Non-Members and New Members

The OECD has always been a forum for concerting the policies pursued by member countries in other fora, but in the 1990s, the organization began to face pressures to include non-members in its work. The Group of the Council on Non-Member Countries was created in May 1988 to oversee the developing dialogue with what were then called the Dynamic Asian Economies, in recognition of the reality that in a globalized world economy, understanding developments in OECD economies requires a window on their partners. The organization has also applied its standard working methods and analytic frameworks in major studies of non-members (for example, see OECD 2007a). These studies, which in themselves demonstrate the continuing relevance of the OECD, are useful both to members and to the countries under examination. In 1992, ministers agreed for the first time to elaborate principles for the participation of non-members in OECD work, and eventual membership. Debates on who should be allowed to join the OECD have echoed some of the less edifying debates on EU expansion, but the organization had to manage a set of rather delicate questions. On the one hand, the OECD cannot divert human and financial resources to programs and activities tailored to non-members without a loss to existing members. On the other hand, the fundamental goal of the OECD is enlarging the zone of stable peace by spreading the knowledge of how the liberal economy works to a larger group of countries. Many OECD economies did not share these values at the outset, and the postwar pattern of cooperation was aimed at building such a community of values.

The major geographic expansion of the OECD area took place in 1964, when Japan's place in the Atlantic community was signified by its membership, which was followed by those of Australia and New Zealand in 1973. The OECD subsequently admitted Mexico (1994), Korea (1996), and a number of European countries. In 2006, a former Mexican foreign minister, Angel Gurría, took office as the new Secretary-General. Enlargement and engagement with non-members was a contentious theme at the June 2007 ministerial. Ministers agreed first to a process of "enhanced engagement" with Brazil, India, Indonesia, China, and South Africa. (Indonesia was added at the last minute at the insistence of Australia.) Second, they agreed to open accession negotiations with Chile, Estonia, Israel, Russia, and Slovenia. The EU was unhappy that the list included only two of its eight new member states not already in the OECD, but others emphasized the global role of the organization by not making OECD membership automatic upon joining the EU. A higher priority will probably be placed on the enhanced-engagement countries than on accessions, especially after the June 2007 G8 summit, where leaders asked the OECD, together with the International Energy Agency, to act as a platform for dialogue with the major emerging economies of Brazil, China, India, Mexico, and South Africa on issues that included innovation, freedom of investment, corporate social responsibility, development in Africa, and energy efficiency. The OECD's expanding global role complements its traditional role in money and trade.

Economic Policy Cooperation
Under the first head of cooperation in the OECD Convention, members are committed to promoting policies designed "to achieve the highest sustainable economic growth and employment and a rising standard of living in Member countries, while maintaining financial stability, and thus to contribute to the development of the world economy." Assessing OECD performance in this area is difficult because the questions are simultaneously highly technical and completely political.

The Bretton Woods system of fixed exchange rates succeeded only to the extent that the United States supplied the system with liquidity by running a budget deficit. As long as people believed that the dollar was literally as good as gold, the illusion could be maintained. After the European currencies became convertible in 1958, cracks began to appear. The system relied on American balance of payments deficits to provide liquidity, but this chronic deficit over the long run undermined confidence in the system. The first run on the dollar came in November 1960. Some authorities maintain that the Bretton Woods system began to operate in pure form only when the European currencies became convertible. The IMF did not prove to be a useful forum, and consultations among the major countries shifted to the OECD, reflecting both the increase in membership of the IMF and a European desire to meet on more equal terms with the Americans (Fischer 1988, 27). The EPC working party on Policies for the Promotion of Better Payments Equilibrium, known as WP 3, was meant to have a limited membership that would keep financial developments under close and continuous review. Members were senior representatives from the treasuries and central banks of countries most affected by world trade and short-term capital movements – Canada, France, Germany, Italy, Japan, the Netherlands, Sweden, Switzerland, the United Kingdom, and the United States. It was useful both as a place for senior officials to talk freely and for the analytic work of the secretariat (Plumptre 1977, 184-85). Later, the General Arrangements to Borrow (GAB) was created in the Group of Ten (G10), with WP 3 as its secretariat, as part of the process by which the rest of the OECD financed American predominance while putting pressure on the American authorities to deal with the dollar problem.

The greatest public prominence for the OECD probably came with its 1966 report on the balance-of-payments adjustment process (OECD 1966a; for a discussion, see Crockett 1989). But if the OECD was *the* forum for international economic cooperation in the 1960s, did this activity amount to anything? Michael Webb argues that "multilateral surveillance in the [OECD] was supposed to encourage countries to pursue policies that were consistent with international equilibrium, but it had no impact on monetary and fiscal policies" (Webb 1992, 160). In his study of the making of American foreign economic policy in the 1960s and 1970s, John Odell concluded that "coordination certainly took place among central bankers and within the Group of Ten, the IMF, and the OECD. This interaction gave rise to attitudes of professional camaraderie. Even occasional coalition building in this field may have taken place, as in the fall of 1971. But when major new directions were determined, the decisions were made by the President and by senior officials whose attitudes were little affected by these networks" (Odell 1982, 349-50). Barry Eichengreen concluded that resolution of liquidity problems in the 1950s was largely accomplished through the market power of the United States, but this factor was less important than coordination in the 1960s because US political and market power alone was insufficient to ensure the stability of the international monetary system (Eichengreen 1989, 258). Adjustment required strategic action among the largest players, coordinated by communication among them, which often took place in WP 3 at the OECD.

The international monetary system did collapse in 1971, in spite of the existing institutions for cooperation. Reform of the system was discussed at the OECD, but it was also on the agenda of the revived Group of Twenty at the IMF, which became the Interim Committee. When the IMF was reformed in the 1970s, the new Article IV surveillance undermined the role of the OECD. Even as new mechanisms for policy coordination were created, the OECD remained a political forum for consensus building on issues of economic management. This role was evident in the mid-1970s, when stagflation troubled OECD governments. The beginnings of the new sound money paradigm (what other chapters in this volume characterize as neoliberalism) are already apparent in the 1977 McCracken Report on how to achieve both full employment and price stability (OECD 1977; for critiques, see Keohane 1978; Cox 1987, 283).

In the mid-1970s, the OECD was renowned as a redoubt of British economists espousing Keynesian principles (Fratiani and Pattison 1991). Conventional wisdom assigns blame to OECD Keynesianism for the supposed disaster of the Bonn Summit package of 1978, which influenced monetary and fiscal policies to move in the wrong direction (Putnam and Henning 1989, 54-55). The agreement, which began life at the OECD, is a famous example of both the benefits and the disasters of coordination. For a time, multilateralism came to be seen as at most the coordination of national policies as countries concentrated on putting their own houses in order (Llewellyn and Potter 1991, 8).[2] Later, the leading countries became more interested in active international economic cooperation, understood as joint action among the largest economies, but that task was assigned to the Group of Seven (G7), not the OECD.

The OECD has had an ambiguous relationship with the annual economic summits precisely because their tasks overlap. OECD relations have been especially unsatisfactory with the G7 finance ministers, who began work in the mid-1980s, negotiating their Plaza and Louvre accords far from the Château de la Muette. Balance of payments problems were perceived to be severe in the 1980s, especially during the period of concern over the so-called twin deficits in the United States, but accounts of the controversy over the significance of the imbalances and how they came to diminish in importance do not even mention the OECD WP 3 (Krugman 1991).

From the beginning, countries excluded from the summit tried to influence its deliberations (Putnam and Bayne 1987). The custom was therefore established, from 1976 onward, of holding the annual Ministerial Council of the OECD a few weeks before the summit itself. Work prepared for the ministerial was often meant to contribute to summit preparations. Shortly after the summit, the sherpa of the host country would visit the OECD to give an account of what had happened. This process gave the non-participating countries outside the European Community some sense of being involved in the summit process. In addition, the summit declarations often linked the understandings reached by the leaders with the work of other economic organizations, notably the IMF, World Bank, and GATT. These devices helped to render the summits, with their highly selective format, acceptable, or at least tolerable, to a wider circle of influential nations. The use of the OECD and, less directly, other bodies for *reassuring* non-participants was one aspect of the interaction of the summit and international organizations. But the summits also turned to the international organizations to provide *continuity* in the subjects that they addressed only at yearly intervals. Maintaining the OECD link to the summit is therefore important for the effectiveness of the summit. It is hard to imagine a useful summit discussion of issues that involve all OECD members that would not involve some relationship to further OECD work. On the one hand, the summit cannot replicate the analytic work of the OECD. On the other hand, the OECD cannot provide the high-level attention generated by a summit. The difficulty now is that one participant in what has become the G8 is not a member of the OECD – Russia proved unable to draw successfully on OECD resources in preparing the St. Petersburg summit in 2006 – while attention is shifting to what some call the "G8+5" (Brazil, China, India, Mexico, and South Africa now have a side meeting with G8 leaders), four of which are also not OECD members.

Meanwhile the EPC has not talked about "policy coordination" in years. Even by the time of the Plaza Accord in 1985, the centre of gravity in EPC discussion was "get your own house in order." Coordination is still very much on the agenda, but not as collaboration. Discussion of coordination now involves the development of what one OECD official has called a "common policy culture," which ensures that approaches to policy in different countries reflect broadly common objectives and a shared understanding of the ways in which policies should be implemented.

Trade Policy

It is hard to imagine an OECD "common policy culture" that did not include a trade dimension, both as a microeconomic instrument for adjustment and as an element of international economic cooperation. Under the OEEC, closer cooperation in trade was seen as a means to political integration in Europe. Trade conflicts arising over different understandings of integration brought down the OEEC, and so, in reconstituting the organization, states hoped to create the capacity for the political management of trade friction.

Recall that where the GATT preamble speaks of a desire to enter into reciprocal arrangements, Article 1 of the OECD Convention says that the organization shall *promote policies* designed to contribute to the expansion of world trade on a multilateral, non-discriminatory basis in accordance with international obligations. Nevertheless, during the time that the OECD Convention was being negotiated, the GATT was struggling inconclusively with the Dillon Round. Some people thought it possible that the OECD would prove to be a better vehicle for trade liberalization than the GATT. This ambiguity is the reason that, although the Trade Committee is one of the organization's most important bodies, it is surprisingly difficult to assess its work.[3] Cooperation on trade ranges from exchanges of information on trade policies through analytic work on how to conceptualize new issues, to discussions about the management of the trading system. Discussion and coordination of action to be taken elsewhere has been important, though now in decline, but attempts at joint action to remove obstacles to trade liberalization were not successful.

The OEEC had an operational role in trade liberalization through the removal of quantitative restrictions, but it had always left tariffs to the GATT (Brusse 1997), and the OEEC Code of Liberalization was not carried over to the new organization. The Americans would not be bound by agreements others had negotiated, and the Canadians were insistent that nothing be done at the OECD that might usurp the role of the GATT. Some minor operational agreements were subsequently negotiated at the OECD, but it is questionable whether such political actions as the 1974 Trade Pledge have been worthwhile. The early notification process gradually fell into disuse as members made more use of GATT dispute settlement procedures, and it became redundant with the many notification requirements incorporated in WTO obligations after 1995. The periodic reviews of main developments in the trading system withered away as the new WTO Trade Policy Review Mechanism came into use.

In 1961, it was not self-evident that the GATT would have such a bright future. In retrospect, given the Kennedy, Tokyo, and Uruguay Rounds, it is clear that the Trade Committee has been valuable precisely because it was *not* operational. It is the place where the principal trading states could assess the state of the trading system without having to hedge their analysis for fear of being tightly bound by their conclusions. The Secretariat can be asked to conduct studies of issues not yet ready for formal negotiations. Strategy for UNCTAD negotiations with developing countries can be discussed in private. When politics makes trade too hot to handle, the OECD could assess the significance of East-West trade, as it did in the early 1980s as part of US Secretary of State George Shultz's strategy for defusing the Soviet pipeline fiasco.[4]

The committee's strengths and weaknesses are illustrated by an example from the Tokyo Round of the GATT. The OECD had begun discussions on government procurement in 1962, when Belgium and the United Kingdom complained against the US Buy American Act. In subsequent years, the Secretariat and the US delegation produced draft guidelines, and the matter remained under discussion until it was transferred to the Tokyo Round in 1976. Gilbert Winham reports that "this lengthy discussion essentially uncovered the political problems and resolved some terminological difficulties of the subject, but *the major trading powers were unable to reach agreement on the matter in isolation from other areas of international trade"* (Winham 1986, 140, emphasis added).

In the aftermath of the Tokyo Round, states were worried about growing protectionist tendencies and the danger that the move towards greater liberalization might grind to a halt, or at least slow. The response was "Trade Issues in the 1980s," a project involving most directorates, launched after a comprehensive discussion of trade at the 1981 ministerial. Work involved most OECD bodies in a report to the 1982 ministerial, which preceded the GATT ministerial of that year. The proposals in the subsequent horizontal ministerial trade mandate (MTM) work program concerned, first, problems that could result in immediate action (including safeguards, for example); second, longer-term trade and related questions, and systemic problems arising initially in a number of sectors, including high technology; and third, the links between trade and other policies: structural adjustment, investment, and competition. The Trade Study was the foundation for the Trade Committee's invaluable role in the preparations for the Uruguay Round, both on services (Drake and Nicolaïdis 1992) and, in cooperation with the Agriculture Committee, on farm trade (OECD 1987a, 1990a).

The organization had begun its important work on domestic agricultural policies in the time of the OEEC, but the work on agricultural trade really began only in the early 1980s. The well-established domestic agricultural policies of the industrialized countries caused few troubles for anybody but the taxpayers who supported them, until an unhappy conjuncture of factors led to extreme conflict between the principal exporters (Wolfe 1998). The MTM allowed states to work together when the issue was not yet ripe for negotiation and in the absence of a forum in which it could be negotiated. The study demonstrated analytically a point that was important politically, namely, that a multi-country, multi-commodity approach to negotiations was essential. The OECD work also made the negotiation of reform possible, by developing the concept of the producer and consumer subsidy equivalents (PSE/CSE), which was the basis for the WTO Aggregate Measure of Support.[5]

In both agriculture and services, the problem was how to think about the issues to be negotiated. Work at the OECD on the conceptual problems posed by the new issues was not easy, but it was possible only because governments knew that negotiations over binding obligations would take place in another forum. The third part of the MTM called for an analysis of the most appropriate methods for improving the functioning of world agricultural markets. It was not easy to get this part of the work launched. Its fruits were reform commitments in the 1987 Communiqué, which, as demonstrated in the annual monitoring reports, countries ignored until the WTO agricultural agreement entered into force. The Uruguay Round would have been difficult without the OECD's work, but analysis is useful only to a point, and the OECD is not the place for negotiation.

Even before the creation of the WTO, members wondered whether the OECD still had a trade role. When the GATT had infrequent meetings, a highlight of the OECD Trade Committee used to be no-holds-barred discussions in private among senior trade policy people from capitals, but members now have many more occasions to meet at formal and informal WTO meetings, and the people they most need to see to resolve negotiating impasses are their counterparts from Brazil, India, and China. To take the Canadian example, the head of multilateral trade policy in Ottawa attended every meeting of the Trade Committee in the 1980s, often accompanied by a junior official. More recently, however, someone from Ottawa attended one in every three meetings, at best. Senior attendance from other countries has been equally sparse, although the level of attendance has picked up recently under the chairmanship of Crawford Falconer, New Zealand's WTO ambassador and chair of the Doha Round agriculture negotiations. It might pick up more if not for the fact that Trade Committee discussion is dominated by the nineteen countries that are also member states of the EU, who have no competence for trade policy under Section 133 of the Maastricht Treaty. The EU members therefore relish Paris as their one multilateral chance to speak (the European Commission speaks for them in Geneva), but other OECD members are bored by the Eurocentric repetition of arguments they have already heard. EU efforts to work through how they are to be represented in international bodies will become more important as more of their members join the OECD.

The analytic role of the OECD continues, however. Unlike World Bank research on trade, the OECD has tried not merely to provide negotiators with useful background but also to advance the negotiations. It maintains good links with the WTO secretariat, and senior members of the WTO secretariat attend the Trade Committee. The OECD Trade Directorate undertook useful work in the early years of Doha, when WTO members were still scoping out the ambition and range of negotiations. Its ability to contribute declined markedly over time, due mainly to the refusal of OECD members to allow work to proceed in a range of areas for fear that it might negatively influence their interests in the negotiations.

Take three examples. First, Secretariat ideas for work on improving services negotiating modalities were rejected because the Trade Committee thought it too close to the negotiations. Second, the OECD has the best comparative data on the main agricultural exporters, the sophisticated models, and the analytic tools to prepare country studies of the leading developing countries, including calculating PSEs, but members have blocked analytic work that might have developed ideas that they did not want to hear. Third, two members of the committee are "developing countries" in WTO terms: they blocked vital work on "differentiation" among developing countries, presumably because the conclusions might have affected their own status.[6] In contrast to these lapses, the WTO has been particularly appreciative of OECD work on trade facilitation and preference erosion, among others, all areas with a strong development dimension and that have involved close cooperation with non-OECD countries. Perhaps the most valuable work has been on making sure that aid works for trade, and on managing the joint WTO-OECD database on trade-related technical assistance and capacity building. One of the main contributions of the OECD to the Aid for Trade Task Force was to focus the debate on improving effectiveness rather than confine attention to providing additional financial resources.

The OECD's future role depends on its ability to consider where the WTO agenda will be in the next decade, not next week. The OECD can use its unparalleled access to networks of experts in all policy domains to bring new ideas to the consideration of commercial problems. EU member states can participate in such discussions without turning Trade Committee debates into a pale reflection of the WTO meetings from which they are excluded. With ever-increasing trade being one driver of globalization, and the vector by which OECD members are brought into ever-deeper contact with the non-members on the organization's "enhanced engagement" list, trade policy remains a vital aspect of its evolving common policy culture.

Conclusion

The topic of the future of the organization has been indelibly inscribed on the OEEC/OECD agenda since ministers first met in Paris in July 1947. The peaks in interest came in the 1947-50 period, when European integration was first mooted, and again in the late 1950s, after the signing of the Treaty of Rome. The turmoil and uncertainty in the multilateral system of trade and payments provided a dramatic backdrop for the round of soul searching stimulated in the 1970s by the enlargement of the European Community. It is surely no accident that the 1990s round of introspection took place at a time of further European integration and disarray in international economic cooperation. In the twenty-first century, transatlantic tensions persist, but the principal threats to global economic stability are elsewhere. The OECD contributes not by being a political forum but by applying its traditional analytic tools to the new economic powers (OECD 2006a) and by helping its members and its new partners think through the challenges of globalization.

As always, the central OECD challenge is good domestic policy, and the message is about how adjustment to globalization does not always take place at the border, which is why OECD work must still embrace so many policy domains. OECD analysis goes much more deeply into the detail of domestic

policy than do WTO negotiations but with a smaller group of similar countries and no binding obligations, which makes discussion of such intrusive
matters easier. The OECD is more than a think tank because it develops not
merely new ideas but also consensual knowledge about how the world works.
The most important thing that changes because of the OECD might be the
thinking of the people – from technical officials to ministers – who attend
its meetings or participate in its peer review process. The ideas it develops
can have influence far beyond the organization – the "polluter pays" principle, for example, was first developed there. Yet it does not move that
knowledge to joint action. Once issues are well understood, and the likely
positions of all parties are known, it makes sense to move to a table that is
equipped for bargaining. The OECD is not an executive, rule-making body.
Nothing in its convention mandates such a task; little in decades of experience suggests that it would have fruitful results. The OECD contribution lies
in influencing policy by identifying norms and principles for negotiations
that take place in the many other international organizations that use its
ideas, especially the G8 and the WTO.

The OECD began by promoting European integration, which required
collective policy action notably in the domains of trade and money. After
the creation of the EEC, the OECD was not needed for collective action in
Europe but for help in managing the transatlantic tension generated by
European integration. The methods and principles it developed for that task
have proved remarkably resilient. Rather than promoting European integration, the OECD message is about adapting to globalization, but the broad
principles are the same – liberalization and integration are better than protectionism and autarchy. This message is increasingly brought to a wider
group of countries: the OECD is no longer centred in the Atlantic, let alone
Western Europe. Other authors in this volume analyze the different variants
of liberalism manifest in OECD advice, but the underlying belief in open
markets and trade as the basis for peace has never wavered.

Acknowledgments
This chapter is based in part on work by Wolfe (1993), and on more recent confidential
interviews with Canadian and OECD officials in Paris and Ottawa. I appreciate the helpful
comments of Nicholas Bayne, Anthony Burger, Ken Heydon, and Knud Erik Jørgensen. The
many people who helped in both stages of this project are responsible neither for the
opinions expressed nor for my errors.

Notes
1 For an early but comprehensive description of the origins and work of the OECD, see Aubrey
  (1967).
2 For an assessment of the institutional and intellectual changes that have affected the OECD,
  see the historical survey in the fiftieth anniversary issue of the *Economic Outlook* (OECD
  1991).
3 This section is indebted to the admirable work of Serge Devos (Devos 1991; see also Stone
  1984; Blair 1993; and Cohn 2002).

4 The Reagan administration angered Europeans when it tried to use US export control legislation to prevent the European affiliates of US corporations from providing high-tech components for a gas pipeline from the Soviet Union to Europe.
5 On the origins of the PSE in FAO (Food and Agriculture Organization of the United Nations) work, and on other details on the OECD's role, see Josling et al. (1990, 440ff.).
6 Expanding membership may also have undermined the confidentiality of Trade Committee deliberations.

2
Role of the OECD in the Orchestration of Global Knowledge Networks
Tony Porter and Michael Webb

The Organisation for Economic Co-operation and Development presents a puzzle for many conventional theories of international organization. It is one of the largest and most costly international organizations, yet many of the problems it addresses, such as education policy, do not involve the interdependence that characterizes most issues on which states collaborate. It rarely negotiates concrete international agreements that produce measurable benefits for member states, and its policy work is too complex, autonomous, and path-dependent for states to be able to rationally calculate the costs and benefits of their membership in the manner suggested by rationalist theories of international institutions.

We argue that to see the OECD as a largely technical research organization with little significance for world politics underestimates the importance for global governance of the knowledge networks that the OECD helps orchestrate, and the contribution of the OECD's knowledge production to the identities of its member states. The knowledge produced in these networks is not just a summation of data and lessons from the past, but also a guide to future directions in the reproduction and development of the practices that shape an increasingly harmonized global political and economic system. The OECD is also involved in the ongoing development of a sense of identity for members as it develops policy prescriptions appropriate for liberal-democratic countries that see themselves as world leaders, and the aspirations of member states (and some non-member states) to that identity gives the OECD considerable influence despite its lack of formal powers.

To an important degree, states involve themselves in the OECD not on the basis of rational calculation of the material costs and benefits of membership (the assumption made by rationalist theories of international institutions) but because of a diffuse identification with the norms and values it represents. As such, the OECD plays a significant role in the constitution of the identity of its member states in a way that is highlighted by state-centric constructivist approaches. We assess the merits of this kind of approach through a case study of OECD peer review practices. Yet we argue that the OECD's role in social construction goes even deeper, in the sense of helping to construct non-state economic actors and market relations among them. This impact of the knowledge produced by the OECD – its contribution to the construction of social facts that have value because of their links to the sense of identity promoted by the OECD – in conjunction with other coherent knowledge-intensive practices, extends well beyond the control of states, and the effect of this knowledge is much better captured by post-structural approaches to knowledge, such as those inspired by the ideas of Michel Foucault. These approaches can also be treated as a type of constructivism and are assessed through a case study of OECD work on corporate governance. The constructivist approach developed here reveals crucial aspects of the OECD's role that are highly relevant for our understanding of not just the OECD but also global governance in general.

A Constructivist Approach to Understanding the OECD: The OECD, Social Constructivism, and Identity

Social constructivist approaches to international institutions can account for some features of the OECD that make little sense from the perspective of state-centric rationalist theories of international cooperation. Rationalist approaches see international institutions as created and used by states because such institutions are more efficient mechanisms for those states to pursue their self-interest than direct state-to-state interactions. As we will show below, much of the OECD's work is too complex and detached from the immediate application of verifiable practical results to be explained as the result of cost/benefit calculations on the part of rational states. From a social constructivist perspective, international institutions do more than just manage relations among pre-existing states with exogenously determined preferences; they help to define the identity of member states, thereby also helping to define their perceptions of self-interest.

The OECD can be seen as a paradigmatic example of an identity-defining international organization. Its primary impact comes through efforts to develop and promote international norms for social and economic policy (Wolfe 1993). It defines standards of appropriate behaviour for states that seek to identify themselves as modern, liberal, market-friendly, and efficient (March and Olsen 1998, 961). This involves distinguishing member states from non-members, and defining the former as superior. Current OECD documents do not put it quite this bluntly, but in its early years, the OECD was explicit about the superiority of member states and the OECD's civilizing mission in the world. In the words of Thorkil Kristensen, the OECD's first Secretary-General, "the industrial countries with market economies have a definite mission in the world during the present phase of history. They have been the forerunners in economic development; and they will remain for a long time the pioneers in a number of fields because their structures are more refined and their national economies more interwoven ... They can, therefore, develop certain techniques of economic policy-making that can later be transferred to other parts of the world ... that are less highly developed" (Kristensen 1967, 103-4).

While rationalist models of international cooperation operate according to a "logic of consequences" – with international negotiations understood primarily as strategic interaction among actors seeking to maximize exogenous interests (March and Olsen 1998) – constructivists view international negotiations as deliberative processes in which arguments about the appropriateness of alternative courses of action play an influential role. The "logic of appropriateness" sees the process of policy choice as one of determining appropriate behaviour for an actor of a given identity. International discussions are often about what is "right," not just what will most effectively serve state interests (Risse 2000, 6-7, 16-19), and about socializing participants into adopting behaviour deemed appropriate. The OECD appears to do exactly this, with OECD processes shaped by their own distinctive norms and rules.

A great deal of the OECD's work is oriented towards figuring out what policies governments should pursue – hence Marcussen's description (2004b) of the OECD as "ideational artist" and "ideational arbitrator." There are about 200 committees, working groups, and expert groups operating under the OECD umbrella. These committees bring together officials from national governments and experts from academia and the private sector, under the guidance of the Secretariat. The Secretariat consists of approximately 700 professionals – economists, lawyers, scientists, and others – and a support staff of 1,600. This makes the OECD one of the largest international bureaucracies (much larger, for example, than the World Trade Organization [WTO]), and every year approximately 40,000 national government officials attend OECD committee meetings. In the OECD's own words, its committees and working groups provide "a setting for reflection and discussion, based on policy research and analysis, that helps governments shape policy" (OECD 2004c, 4). Persuasive arguments in the OECD are ones that are consistent with its "liberalizing vocation" and that draw on the kinds of expert knowledge incorporated into OECD policy research and analysis.

The OECD Secretariat plays a crucial role in the process of determining appropriate policies, though one should not exaggerate its autonomy from member governments and social forces. Representatives of national governments meeting in the Ministerial Council – the OECD's top decision-making body – identify priority areas for OECD study, and national representatives on the Economic and Development Review Committee (EDRC) (usually Paris-based economic counsellors from member states' permanent delegations to the OECD) provide guidance and oversight on a more regular basis

(Marcussen 2004b, 95, 99). Furthermore, the influence that a national government exerts over the OECD's work clearly reflects the country's general power position in international politics. For example, there are cases in which the United States has used its ability to withhold financial support to achieve specific changes (Martens and Balzer 2004, 12; Marcussen 2001, 9). We return to the issue of national power and OECD norms in the section on peer review.

Even with this political oversight, Secretariat officials have considerable influence on deliberations about appropriate policy – more than one would expect from a state-centric perspective that assumes zealous insistence on national sovereignty. The OECD Secretariat is heavily populated by professional economists, because western societies accord such a high value to this kind of expertise and because economic liberalization is central to the OECD's mission. The professional orientation of the Secretariat in turn shapes the policy analysis it produces and the guidance it provides to meetings of national officials. Thus, OECD advice often takes the form of applying liberal economic theory to policy problems (see, among others, the introductory chapter of this volume; Dostal 2004). In the memorable words of Jim Mac-Neill, one-time OECD environmental official, "the OECD is to classical economics what St. Peter's is to Christianity. I mean it's the keeper of the keys" (Bernstein 2001, 198). For liberal economists such as David Henderson (another former OECD official), the OECD's "liberalizing vocation" simply reflects the fact that liberal solutions are the most efficient and effective (1996, 20).

The power asymmetries and the promotion of liberal ideas noted in the preceding paragraphs are very consistent with the neo-Gramscian perspective that is developed by Arne Ruckert in Chapter 5, and raise the issue of the merit of that approach relative to our own. In the neo-Gramscian view, the OECD is an important forum for the development of transnational class consciousness among capitalists and the promotion of neoliberal hegemony in the interests of this class.[1] As our cases show, the OECD's liberal prescriptions are indeed often consistent with the needs of transnational capital, and the corporate governance case shows that the OECD helps to create social actors that fit the liberal mould. At the same time, the fact that the ideas themselves can have influence independent of powerful transnational social forces and powerful states is apparent in other prescriptions that clash with the expressed interests of those powerful actors, and in the willingness of the OECD to modify prescriptions in light of evidence (as in the Jobs Study, discussed in a number of chapters in this volume).

It is also important to recognize that liberal economic theory is neither monolithic nor unchanging. As various chapters in this book reveal, OECD policy prescriptions do not always conform to orthodox economic liberalism and do change over time in response to changing circumstances and changes in economic theory. Diversity and change within liberalism can lead to a contestation within the OECD between economic models that prioritize growth and other approaches that, for instance, put more emphasis on child care as related to child development and equal opportunities for women (Mahon 2005; Chapter 14), environmental sustainability (Bernstein 2001; Lehtonen 2007), or high-quality jobs and personal security (Noaksson and Jacobsson 2003). Neo-Gramscian perspectives can recognize this diversity to some degree, but they continue to assume that this diversity is either functional to the continued dominance of transnational capital or an expression of a compromise between capital and other social forces. While this view is effective in highlighting political factors, it tends to overestimate the coherence of the interests, actors, and social forces that use the OECD, and to underestimate the independent social effects of the knowledge-producing processes at the OECD itself.

Ultimately, whatever the sources of its prescriptions, what the OECD identifies as good policy or "best practice" becomes part of the identity of the ideal modern state – an identity to which western governments aspire, as do many non-western governments. The OECD engages deliberately in this identity-defining process by, for example, calling attention to "leaders" and "laggards" among countries in their adoption of OECD norms (March and Olsen 1998, 961). The OECD's identity-shaping role is quite explicit in its peer review mechanism, which is central to the work of virtually all OECD committees: "mutual examination by governments, multilateral surveillance and peer pressure to conform or reform are at the heart of OECD effectiveness" (OECD 2004c, 4). We will examine peer review after considering more closely the OECD's deeper role in the construction of social reality.

The International Organizational Effects of Knowledge Production
In the previous section, the identity-shaping role of the OECD was examined mainly at a cognitive level, but the importance of knowledge production in the OECD also operates at a deeper level, that of the transformation of knowledge into social facts that appear to exist beyond the conscious influence of policy makers. Our approach here differs sharply from rational choice or epistemic communities approaches to the impact of knowledge. In rational choice approaches, technical knowledge is usually treated as a costly good, and states collaborate to reduce these costs through economies of scale. In most epistemic communities approaches, experts produce technical knowledge that leads rational state actors to redefine their interests, looking at problems in a new way (Haas 1992). Our approach draws instead on Michel Foucault's work.[2] Foucault argued that bodies of organized knowledge have a profound significance in their ability to produce and reproduce relations of power. Power's most important characteristic was not its ability to influence subordinate actors by external threats and inducements but rather the

way that bodies of organized knowledge produce both a field of action, such as the physical and social structures within which actors act, and the actors themselves, such as psychiatry's capacity to constitute the asylum, the inmate defined as insane, and the psychiatrist authorized to carry out treatments.

Relationships of power are constituted by the process through which problems are identified and technologies mobilized to address those problems: "The techne of government – like all other aspects of governing – is necessary, somewhat autonomous, and irreducible" (Dean 1999, 31). Even without peer review, the process of measuring, data production, and standard setting can make certain activities visible and legitimate and obscure other possibilities, conferring a self-propelling momentum on trends that may have been more consciously initiated through the processes discussed in the previous section.

Part of the effect of the OECD's technical knowledge is also the provision of operational routines that, in being followed, bring into being the types of actors that the OECD has defined as proper, while obscuring the external role of power in so doing. Existing research indicates that something other than convincing scientific proof is involved in the influence of the knowledge produced by the OECD. For instance Sahlin-Andersson (2000a) notes that it is the models, rather than their effects, that are most often communicated. Key aspects of the national experiences that the models purport to represent, which are important in evaluating the models, are left out when the models circulate internationally. For example, Noaksson and Jacobsson (2003, 29) point to the difficulties of evaluating the OECD's Jobs Strategy when countries were not consistent in implementing it. Moreover, improved employment performance could just as easily be the result of the implementation of recommendations from elsewhere (such as the European Union) or cyclical economic upswings. With such uncertainties, it is unlikely that countries choosing to follow the Jobs Strategy did so because they were convinced by demonstrated effectiveness of the OECD's recommendations in addressing employment problems.

The knowledge that the OECD produces has a certain autonomous momentum and logical coherence that initiates ways of doing things that are followed because, once visible, they are easier to follow than alternative practices that have not yet been imagined or articulated. The effect is reinforced by the diffuse sense that the OECD's knowledge is an expression of best practices – the national identity effect discussed earlier. The technical knowledge that the OECD produces and the routines it recommends provide a way whereby individual officials and the state as a whole can display that identity, much as a religious congregation can ritually affirm its identity by echoing the gestures and incantations of priests. The more deliberate and conscious processes of identity formation, in which powerful, wealthy states may be more actively involved in recognizing some standards as appropriate and others as inappropriate, are reinforced by the more technical and less conscious processes.

Peer Review in the Economic and Development Review Committee

Peer review backed by expert analysis from the Secretariat is the most common mechanism by which the OECD shapes policy in member states. Peer review relies on expert knowledge and identity dynamics to shape policy despite the existence of few binding commitments.[3] We focus on peer review of macroeconomic and structural policies in the Economic and Development Review Committee, since these issues and this department are at the core of the OECD's mandate.

The OECD describes peer review "as the systematic examination and assessment of the performance of a state by other states, with the ultimate goal of helping the reviewed state improve its policy making, adopt best practices, and comply with established standards and principles" (Pagani 2002a, 4-5). Identity dynamics matter here in the sense that a shared sense of identity – a "homogenous membership [accompanied by a] high degree of trust shared among member states" – has enabled the OECD to develop the practice of peer review more extensively than any other intergovernmental organization (IGO) (Pagani 2002a, 7). Also noteworthy is the fact that a large number of senior officials from national governments (approximately 40,000) participate in OECD committees, not just diplomatic representatives based in Paris.

Peer review requires standards and criteria against which a member state's policies can be reviewed. In some policy areas, these criteria are stated explicitly (e.g., the Code of Liberalization of Capital Movements), but in the case of core macroeconomic and structural policies, there are no explicit agreed-upon criteria. This reflects the political sensitivity of these issues, which are at the core of national economic policy and for which the domestic political stakes are often high. Nevertheless, "strong implicit guidelines have developed" (Pagani 2002a, 15). In the EDRC, "country performance is assessed in relation to broad economic policy principles and best practices that have been developed over the years, the policy orientations of the OECD Growth Project, as well as specific guidelines such as those contained in the OECD Jobs Strategy" (Pagani 2002a, 8).

In the absence of explicit criteria, the most important guidelines take the form of shared understandings about appropriate policy, and are codified only in the OECD's institutional memory. That memory resides in the Secretariat, and OECD officials take the lead in drafting the initial country report that serves as the basis for peer review (Pagani 2002a, 10-11). The initial list of topics to be discussed in a country study is drawn up by the senior economist assigned to lead the effort. That list reflects the official's "immediate institutional environment" (Marcussen 2004b, 96), which includes institutional norms as well as any relevant political guidance from the Ministerial Council and the EDRC. Not surprisingly, the implicit criteria and guidelines are heavily shaped by the OECD's "liberalizing vocation" – the core belief in the desirability of liberal, market-oriented economic policies (Henderson 1996). Yet the specific content of liberal economic prescriptions has changed over the years, and the Secretariat believes that it is important to be "open to new academic ideas and not to bend with the prevailing view of governments" (OECD 2002a, 13; see also Marcussen 2004b, 92, 98).

A key example can be seen in the OECD's mid-1970s shift away from Keynesian demand management to a neoclassical emphasis on monetary stabilization and supply-side reforms that reduce government intervention in the economy. As discussed more fully in the introductory chapter to this volume (see also Keohane 1978), the OECD appointed eight prominent economists to review the causes of economic stagflation. The resulting McCracken Report, following the shift then underway in the field of macroeconomics, argued strongly for refocusing policies on fighting inflation and reducing government regulation (McCracken 1977). Despite the weak analysis of the causes of inflation provided by the report, it was seen as an authoritative analysis of the problem of stagflation and helped shift shared understandings of appropriate policy norms in the OECD in favour of more market-friendly policies.

The process of peer review in the EDRC begins with a report prepared by the Secretariat that provides the basis for discussions between national government officials, OECD officials, and senior officials (called "examiners") from two other member states. The examiners and Secretariat officials "are also free to consult with interest groups, civil society and academics" in the country whose policies are being reviewed (Pagani 2002a, 11). While the published country surveys do not identify those consulted, it is apparent from the bibliography of the country survey of Canada discussed below that consultations with non-government actors involve primarily economists and liberal economic think tanks such as the C.D. Howe Institute (see OECD 2003a). The Secretariat then prepares a draft of the final report, which is discussed by the full EDRC. Following normal OECD practice, the final report must be adopted by consensus. This effectively gives the government of the country in question a veto over publication of the report, and politically sensitive recommendations are occasionally deleted (OECD 2002a, 3).

Nevertheless, published reports do contain criticism of the government in question. For example, the 2003 report on Canada explicitly criticized the Employment Insurance system because it had "moved well beyond providing income support during unexpected spells of unemployment and has become a major vehicle for delivering family, social and regional assistance" (OECD 2003a, 11). This critique reveals a clear yet implicit and unargued assumption about the appropriate function of this kind of policy, one that is consistent with an orthodox liberal perspective but not, for example, with social democratic understandings of appropriate policy.

Why would a government permit such criticism from an international organization, particularly when the government could veto the publication of those criticisms and when the policies in question have few implications for other states? From a rationalist perspective, this is difficult to understand, especially if, as Nicholas Bayne argued, one of the main things governments want from IGOs is their endorsement of current government policies (1998, 219). One possible motive (OECD 2002a, 10) might be to use the OECD's imprimatur of authority to shift domestic public opinion in favour of policies preferred by the government (or by some agencies within government), but that is not the case for most of the policies criticized in the country survey of Canada. Even if governments do sometimes use OECD reports to influence public opinion among their own constituents, such a strategy reveals something important about the OECD; public and elite opinion pays attention to the OECD because it is viewed as an authoritative source of expert policy advice. The OECD's identity-defining function also helps to explain why member states do not use their veto power to eliminate critical recommendations from EDRC reviews, since this would be widely viewed as inappropriate by their peers and, in many cases, domestic public opinion.

Of course, states sometimes do insist that critical comments be removed from published reports, and states experience peer pressure differently depending on their power in the OECD. The largest member states – the United States, European countries such as Germany, Britain, and France, and Japan – have the greatest impact on the implicit criteria used as the basis for peer review of national policies. The OECD's liberalizing vocation corresponds most closely with the ideological orientations of the American and British governments, and on the basis of extensive interviews with OECD officials, Marcussen identified a distinct pattern whereby ideas flowed within the OECD "from North to South ... [and] from the Anglo-Saxon group of the OECD member countries to all the rest" (2001, 22). OECD officials acknowledge that in the peer review process, "size matters very much – political and military importance are substantial elements in determining which countries can lead or block the process" (OECD 2002a, 5).

Nevertheless, even the government of the United States comes under criticism when its policies deviate from OECD norms. A good example concerns American fiscal policy. OECD reports criticized the Bush administration for cutting taxes at a time when spending was increasing rapidly and the costs of Social Security and Medicare threatened to explode as baby boomers began to retire. The April 2004 *Economic Survey of the United States* challenged many of the assumptions the Bush administration used to defend its fiscal policies, and explicitly called for tax measures rejected by the administration – phasing out the deductibility of mortgage interest payments, and better enforcement of corporate income taxes (OECD 2004b, 13). It is difficult to understand, from a rationalist perspective, why a powerful government would allow an international institution to criticize it in this fashion, especially when the institution in question depends on the government for 25 percent of its funding (OECD 2004a). The OECD's willingness to criticize US government policies suggests that the dominance of liberal economic ideas in the OECD cannot be equated with the power of particular governments. State power matters, but the dominance of those ideas reflects their broader strength in western society and the support they receive from powerful transnational social forces.[4]

This raises the issue of the community (or communities) that judges the appropriateness of national government policy. OECD documents identify two key audiences for the output of peer review. The first consists of senior national policy makers responsible for the policies being reviewed in the OECD. According to one senior official, the "aim is to have intellectual influence on policy makers" (OECD 2002a, 7), while another "regarded the senior policy environment in the individual countries as the key audience of the OECD process" (OECD 2002a, 12). The second audience consists of public opinion in member states. The reports are intended to put public pressure on governments and to shift the balance in domestic policy debates in favour of policies endorsed by the OECD (OECD 2002a; Pagani 2002a, 5-6, 12-13). That said, in many cases, OECD reviews do not attract as much attention in domestic politics as the OECD might like, and this can reduce its influence on national policy (Armingeon 2004, 236-37).

Influence in both communities depends critically on the OECD's identity as an unbiased expert source of knowledge and advice. Officials responsible for peer review stress the need to maintain the integrity and credibility of the process by maintaining independence from the governments of the country under review and from its peers, and by grounding the assessments in widely accepted analytical methods (OECD 2002a; Pagani 2002a). In OECD practice, those methods are the methods of liberal economics, and OECD recommendations draw authority and credibility from their grounding in a mode of policy analysis that has a privileged status in OECD countries (Hansen et al. 2002, 118). Credibility also requires that the OECD not give in to pressure from member states to endorse policies that are considered inappropriate by relevant experts and policy makers in other countries, as in the case of current American fiscal policies.

The process of peer review, therefore, corresponds more closely to social processes of knowledge and identity construction through persuasion and argument rather than to conventional processes of inter-state bargaining: "The peer review process is also a cultural phenomenon ... that ... leads to the development of a new frame of mind" (OECD 2002a, 11).

Corporate Governance

"Corporate governance" refers to the rules and practices associated with the relationships of control within the firm, and involves shareholders, managers, boards of directors, employees, suppliers, and customers. While the focal point of corporate governance is the private sector relationships that define the firm, the public sector also plays a crucial role in corporate governance by legislating and enforcing corporation law – the legal rules within which corporate governance functions – and by a vast array of other laws and regulations that shape aspects of corporate governance, such as laws governing employment conditions, employer liability, human rights codes, and accounting and reporting practices.

Before the 1990s, the OECD's forays into corporate governance dealt mainly with relations between multinational corporations and governments (Chapter 6). In the late 1990s, the OECD began to assume a much higher profile in the private sector dimension of corporate governance in response to the perceived link between problems in corporate governance and the financial crises in East Asia and Russia in 1997 and 1998. The OECD published its Principles of Corporate Governance in 1999 (1999b) and revised it in 2004. It also launched, jointly with the World Bank, the Global Corporate Governance Forum, a wide-ranging global networking initiative that has led to the organization of consultations in various regions. Implicitly, work in the OECD was premised on the idea that capitalist institutions were more advanced in OECD member states than in the so-called emerging market economies. Consistent with the OECD's identity-defining role, this meant that it was appropriate for aspiring market economies to adopt the "best practices" developed in the OECD.

There is no evidence of significant inter-state bargaining in connection with the Principles. Nor is there a strong scientific consensus about best practices in corporate governance that rational states simply endorse. Instead, the OECD's role is to reinforce a particular set of market and investor-friendly practices that are consistent with its enthusiasm for liberalized markets by conferring its authority on these practices. The effects of this are political, since some interests (shareholders and investors) are privileged over others (stakeholders such as workers), but this is achieved in a way that differs greatly from the type of inter-state bargaining that characterizes many international issue areas and that is more consistent with rationalist approaches. Instead, this effect involves an assemblage of practices in which knowledge claims and expert judgments amplify particular routine market practices that empower firms and investors. This is a transnational process that cuts across conventional state and public/private boundaries.

The lack of inter-state bargaining over the Principles is evident in the media coverage of their formulation and implementation stages. A search of ABI Inform and LexisNexis databases revealed fifty-seven articles about the OECD Principles between 1998 and 2006.[5] Only three of these articles mentioned anything that could be construed as involving bargaining among state actors. Similarly, in a report summarizing the key points to come out of twenty-five Regional Corporate Governance Roundtables in eighteen countries between 1999 and 2003, involving thirty-eight non-member countries, various international organizations, and business and other non-governmental actors, there is no mention of inter-state negotiations or conflicts (OECD 2003b). In a 182-page compilation of comments on the re-visions of the Principles received from approximately seventy respondents, all of which are non-governmental, none are framed with reference to inter-state negotiations (OECD n.d.). A number of respondents call for the Principles to better recognize the distinctive qualities of corporate governance in their home countries, yet these comments involve non-governmental actors engaging with a supranational drafting process rather than seeking to convince negotiators from their home states to strike advantageous bar-gains with other states.

There are other indications that the Principles' creation and effectiveness have come from their interaction with existing market practices rather than inter-state negotiation. Millstein (2000), who chaired the OECD's informal Business Sector Advisory Group on Corporate Governance, has noted that the Principles "grew out" of his group's report, which "was based on a series of discussions with international business leaders and institutional investors" (see also OECD 1999b, 9; Gregory 2000, 13-14). The referencing, building on, and further elaboration of the Principles by private sector actors constitute a key component of their effectiveness. These actors include the International Corporate Governance Network (ICGN), an association of institutional in-vestors that jointly are estimated to hold over $10 trillion in assets and that endorsed and supplemented the principles; the Institute of International Finance, the main association of internationally active banks (Institute of International Finance 2002); and Standard & Poor's, which incorporated the Principles into its ratings (Nestor 2001; Chapter 4). Public sector actors also have been engaged in endorsing and promoting the Principles, most notably the Financial Stability Forum, but this complements a more private sector process that is relatively independent of states. The integration of the private sector actors whose behaviour is being regulated into soft regulatory mech-anisms such as this has been identified as a distinguishing feature of con-temporary forms of transnational regulation (Djelic and Sahlin-Andersson 2006a). Soft regulatory mechanisms like this also depend upon the existence of shared normative frameworks and shared senses of identity such as those promoted by the OECD and described earlier in this chapter.

Despite their portrayal as technical statements of best practice that should be routinely adopted, the OECD Principles of Corporate Governance and the process by which they are implemented involve crucially important ethical and political judgments that are made not with reference to the specific text of the Principles but rather on the basis of the authority that the Principles confer on particular individuals, especially those conducting peer reviews. In other words, the Principles are more important for the relations of transnational authority and power they constitute than for the way they express negotiated interests of the states that sponsored them.

This is most evident in the *Methodology for Assessing the Implementation of the OECD Principles of Corporate Governance* (OECD 2006b), designed to encourage international public and private sector monitoring of compliance. The document notes that "a number of individual principles are by themselves unobservable to a reviewer ... perhaps the best approach to assessing implementation therefore is to rely on 'a reasonable assessor' or 'reasonable observer' type procedure" (5). The word "judgment" appears 122 times in the ninety-nine-page document. In other words, the Principles and the methodology do not routinely and scientifically compare particular national and corporate practices with a model that is self-evidently superior due to its empirical validation but rather confer authority on the exercise of judgment by assessors.

Despite the effort in this document to portray the type of judgment being exercised as purely professional and technical, there are numerous indications that there are political and social issues at stake. In the news coverage and the comments on the revisions of the Principles that were discussed above, there are many references to debates over the role of stakeholders, especially employees. Labour organizations called for the role of employees in corporate governance to be increased. For instance, the International Metalworkers Federation stated: "The revised text does not reflect the need to ensure that employees and other relevant stakeholders can play an effective role against corporate abuses" (OECD n.d., 36).

The implicit effect of the Principles is to promote an Anglo-American approach to governance that emphasizes the primacy of shareholder rights (Iu and Batten 2001, 4, 53). This is not, however, primarily and in the first instance an expression of the interests of the US and British states, but rather expresses the interests of investors. To be sure, an estimated 76 percent of the US$24 trillion of financial assets in the world's top five markets are held by US and UK investors (Gregory 2000, 6). Yet Euroshareholders, an organization of shareholder associations from eight European countries, "all agreed that the corporate objective is to maximize long-range shareholder value (notwithstanding the continental tradition of emphasizing employee interests)" (Gregory 2000, 14).

The degree to which the Principles are not an expression of a scholarly evidence-based consensus is evident not just in the prominent role of judgment in the methodology, or in the political conflicts that are managed and suppressed by not acknowledging them in the formulation and implementation of the Principles, but also in the lack of scientific evidence supporting the model that the Principles promote. Two leading authorities on variations in financial structures, which most importantly include the variation between the Anglo-American capital markets/shareholder model and more bank- or state-oriented models, conclude: "Overall financial development matters for economic success, but financial structure per se does not seem to matter much" (Demirgüç-Kunt and Levine 2001, 12). As the Japan Business Federation noted in its comments on the revisions to the Principles (OECD n.d., 58), claims that particular corporate governance practices produce positive economic outcomes "have yet to pass the test of conclusive empirical analysis."

On closer examination, then, the OECD's role has been to reinforce trends that were already present in global markets and to use its authority to frame a potentially politicized and conflictual problem as a best practice. Since the "real" elements of corporate governance themselves do not involve the disposition of material resources but rather involve norms or knowledge – such as the rights of shareholders, the role of stakeholders, the responsibilities of the board, and the role of accountability and transparency – then the OECD's initiative primarily strengthens a set of market-based norms that it chooses to support because they are consistent with the liberal economic models and philosophy of the OECD, rather than because they represent convergent expectations among states. In this respect, the OECD's knowledge production capacity is significant for the way it feeds directly into the constitution of the "reality" of global markets, more than because it directly alters the preferences of the leaders of member states. To the extent that the OECD's guidelines on corporate governance are incorporated into private sector practice and national government oversight, the ideas incorporated in those guidelines are transformed into social facts (in the form of the structure and orientation of private corporations) that appear to exist beyond the conscious influence of policy makers. This is where the OECD's power is revealed, rather than in the conscious conformity of states and private actors to bargains negotiated at the OECD.

Conclusion

In our theoretical and empirical discussion in this chapter, we have focused on the degree to which the work of the OECD involves two types of processes that are best understood from a constructivist perspective. The first process concerns the identity of the states that are members or that aspire to be members of the organization. The OECD provides a mechanism for selected states to engage in a process of mutual recognition of the superiority of the social and economic policies that are central to their identities. We focused especially on peer review in the Economic and Development Review Committee as an example of this process. The second process involves a relationship between the OECD as an international organization and market-oriented practices that are quite independent of inter-state bargaining or rational calculation, but instead involve an incremental reinforcement of particular practices though the OECD's ability to confer authority on them by portraying those practices as unproblematic, apolitical, and relatively routine ways of doing things that are known to be best due to the appearance of consensus that the OECD creates. We focused especially on corporate governance as an example of this process.

Contrary to the view of state-centric realists who might dismiss the OECD because it is not focused on military security or the negotiation of binding international law, there are good reasons to see the OECD's work as very significant. Certainly, the level of financial support provided by states to the OECD suggests that states see it as important. Our case studies provide further confirmation of this. In the case of the EDRC, states devote a great deal of time and they risk damaging their reputations by engaging in the peer review process. In the case of corporate governance, the OECD's Principles have had a significant global effect in the policy field of international financial governance, which, after the financial crises of the past decade, is widely recognized as crucial to the health of the world economy, a policy field that the leaders of the most powerful states, for instance through the Group of Seven (G7), have often characterized as a top priority for them. Similar points could be made about other OECD activities.

The central importance of shared identity to the work of the OECD creates a major dilemma for the institution as it faces a changing geo-economic environment. The organization's effectiveness depended on its members' shared sense of identity and their dominance of the world economy. The shared identity was necessary for the functioning of the OECD's deliberative processes and peer review mechanisms, and member states' dominance of the global economy ensured that the knowledge and norms generated in the OECD would have a powerful impact. Yet the rise of new players in the global economy means that the second fact is no longer true, and this undermines the OECD's relevance to global economic governance (Woodward 2004).

Deliberations in the OECD on how to deal with the new circumstances have identified a core dilemma: expanding membership in a bid to sustain the institution's relevance could undermine the shared identity that was the other crucial condition for its relevance (Noboru 2004). The OECD has identified a number of "significant players" that need to be involved, including Brazil, China, India, Indonesia, Russia, and South Africa. The governments of countries like China and Russia, however, define their national identity partly in opposition to existing OECD countries' western liberal values. Many current member states feel that only "like-minded countries" that share the OECD's democratic political values and market-based economic values could contribute positively to the OECD's voluntary consensus-building and socialization processes (Noboru 2004, 13-17).

The Ministerial Council meeting in May 2007 responded to this dilemma by inviting five countries (Chile, Estonia, Israel, Russia, and Slovenia) to begin discussions for accession and by calling for "enhanced engagement" between the OECD and five other countries (Brazil, China, India, Indonesia, and South Africa) with a view to possible future membership (OECD 2007b). Despite its enthusiasm for membership, the current Russian government clearly does not share many of the values associated with the OECD. Some member states hope that Russia's accession will encourage that country to align itself more closely with western liberal values, but others fear that if this does not occur, there could be an erosion of the OECD's effectiveness and that premature membership could reduce pressure on Moscow to conform to those values (Kanter 2006). The same risk applies in relation to the five countries in the second group, especially China, given its economic importance and its government's sensitivity to threats to its policy autonomy and values.

Regardless of how this dilemma might (or might not) be resolved in future, this chapter offers insights into the contribution of the OECD and similar international institutions to global governance that rationalist approaches cannot. It shows that processes that produce and reinforce identity and knowledge can be located in supranational and transnational spaces that are obscured by rationalist analysis. These relatively autonomous processes interact with other processes, including the more traditional processes of inter-state diplomacy, but also with evolving market practices that themselves may play a key role in stabilizing or destabilizing the global system. Identity and knowledge can to some degree be treated as comparable to the material resources that traditional rationalist approaches to statecraft see states as wielding. *Reputation* and *intellectual property* are concepts that have been used by rationalist theories to suggest that actors can buy, sell, and invest in identity and knowledge just as they can with material resources. Identity and knowledge are much more than these passive, controllable possessions. Their complexity, autonomy, and ability to structure the conduct of actors make it imperative to employ constructivism in understanding them. This is important not just for understanding what is occurring in international institutions such as the OECD but also in designing or influencing the multiple new complex processes that constitute our developing institutions of global governance and that in turn can determine success or failure in bringing about the solutions to global problems that are so desperately needed.

Acknowledgments

This chapter is an extensively revised version of a paper with the same title that was presented at the International Studies Association (ISA) meeting in Montreal in 2004, a workshop at Carleton University in 2007, and the Canadian Political Science Association meetings in Saskatoon in 2007. In revising the paper, the authors benefited greatly from comments and ideas from Susan Sell and others at these meetings, including especially Rianne Mahon and Stephen McBride, who also provided subsequent comments. Funding from the Social Sciences and Humanities Research Council of Canada was important in supporting this research.

Notes

1 In addition to Chapter 5, see Cox (1992, 30) and Gill (2003, 87).
2 Hansen and colleagues (2002) have fruitfully used Foucault's concepts to analyze the impact of the OECD's program on the reform of public administration.
3 For an account of the roots of contemporary peer review at the OECD in its adoption of practices of surveillance, see Wolfe (1993, 21-23). For other accounts of contemporary peer review processes, see Jacobsson and Sahlin-Andersson (2006), and Marcussen (2004b) (on the EDRC); Noaksson and Jacobsson (2003) (on the Jobs Strategy); and Lehtonen (2007) (on environmental policy).
4 Unfortunately, space does not permit us to assess the relative influence of these different forces in this chapter.
5 The search was conducted on 14 December 2006, using the terms "OECD Corporate Governance Principles." The LexisNexis search was in the general news category. Duplicates and records with abstracts but not full text were not counted.

3
Inversions without End: The OECD and Global Public Management Reform

Leslie A. Pal

Reform is a journey rather than a destination.
– *Governance in Transition* (OECD 1995a)

But perhaps the most important lesson from the experience of the past two decades is that reform is continuous. As societies keep changing, governments must keep adapting.
– *Public Sector Modernisation: The Way Forward*
(OECD 2005a)

And so these parties divided upon the midnight plain, each passing back the way the other had come, pursuing as all travelers must inversions without end upon other men's journeys.
– Cormac McCarthy, *Blood Meridian* (1985)

The last fifteen years have seen the rise of a movement around public sector reform and "modernization." The movement is prominently driven by international or global organizations, most iconically the World Bank, the European Union (EU), and the Organisation for Economic Co-operation and Development. This chapter focuses on the OECD and its work on public sector reform. As we note below, the OECD became an early global advocate for the New Public Management (NPM) through its governance committee, the Public Management Committee (PUMA), which has now been renamed the Public Governance Committee and consists of senior officials from OECD members who give direction to the Directorate on Public Governance and Territorial Development, or GOV. Its first injunctions about reform ignored national context and proposed a stylized, NPM model that was supposed to define "modern" states. While that remains broadly true today, the OECD has more recently projected a more complex narrative about the nature of governance and public sector reform than is commonly realized. There are only a handful of studies on the content of this narrative. This chapter will examine the narrative in detail, and its master theme of "modernization under stress." The theme emphasizes the importance of emulation and borrowing among a family of nations that wish to move towards modernity together.

As Tony Porter and Michael Webb argue in Chapter 2, the OECD's work constitutes an important instance of "state identity formation," an invocation of what it means to be an "ideal modern state." At the same time, it has had to invert that theme to respect particularities and avoid the impression that only one model of public sector reform is viable or worthy. The narrative is therefore a series of "inversions without end" as the OECD moves from the particular to the universal, from models to modalities, from reform to redemption.

The sheer scope of the OECD's work on public sector reform – budgeting, ethics, e-government, regulation, social policy – makes it necessary to focus on those documents that have periodically treated the general theme of reform and modernization, or what might broadly be termed "governance." The OECD entered the governance field only after a 1979 conference in Madrid, and PUMA was formally established only in 1990. Since then, it has released a handful of documents on the general theme of governance or public sector modernization. This chapter reviews the narratives constructed in four representative documents: *Governance in Transition* (OECD 1995a), two policy briefs on modernizing government (OECD 2003c, 2005a), and the most recent review, *Modernising Government: The Way Forward* (OECD 2005b).

The OECD and Public Management: Narratives and Inversions

PUMA was established in 1990 as one of the OECD's committees; at the time, the abbreviation stood for Public Management Committee. The name of the committee has now changed to Public Governance Committee, and there are representatives of senior officials from central agencies from all thirty OECD members. PUMA actually grew out of a pre-existing committee, the Technical Cooperation Committee (TECO), which provided financial assistance to European countries to modernize both their societies and their economies (Sahlin-Andersson 2000b). TECO had a large budget but increasingly came under pressure as the OECD faced a financial crunch and financial aid seemed less relevant with the establishment of the European Economic Community (EEC) and eventually the EU. This shift from financial aid and economic policy coordination to mutual oversight and surveillance parallels the broader history of the shift from the Organisation for European Economic Co-operation (OEEC) to the OECD itself (see Chapter 1). PUMA was therefore created to provide not financial aid but advice and analysis around public management challenges and issues. Originally, it was to last five years, and

so its *Governance in Transition* report was the culmination as well as distilla-
tion of its first period of life and activity. It was given an extension and
eventually became a permanent feature of the OECD.

What follows is a textual analysis[1] of the rhetorical devices used in four
representative documents dealing broadly with governance and modernization. The first document, *Governance in Transition* (OECD 1995a) is sufficiently
important that it will be treated separately. The other three (two short policy
briefs and the most recent review of a decade of reform) will be dealt with
collectively. *Governance in Transition* was a unique document for several
reasons. First, it was the culmination of five years of PUMA's mandate and
was intended to be its singular product. Second, it was seminal, since no
such broad review of public management reform or modernization had been
attempted before. Third, it is universally recognized as having been uniquely
influential, particularly in popularizing NPM.

The textual analysis conducted on these documents is not meant to belittle
them simply as rhetorical flourishes without content. There were indeed
realities to which these reports were responding, and which they often describe and analyze faithfully. The point simply is that reality has to be framed
and highlighted, and in the process, some aspects are emphasized and some
are not.

Governance in Transition

Governance in Transition had a tone of naked urgency and radicalism that one
rarely finds in reports by international organizations. Its key premise was
that a combination of fiscal pressures, rising public demands, falling public
trust, and increasing global economic competition was creating a policy environment "marked by great turbulence, uncertainty and an accelerating
pace of change" in which traditional "governance structures and managerial
responses are increasingly ineffectual" (OECD 1995a, 15). Half measures were
out of the question; only "fundamental change" would do. The report acknowledged that countries had responded to these challenges differently,
and while there was no single best model of governance, nonetheless it was
possible to identify "common reform trends." Principal among these trends
was a focus on results and performance in terms of efficiency, effectiveness,
and quality of service, and decentralization of public management.

The environment facing governments is described bleakly, evoking a ser-
mon to dinosaurs on the cusp of the first ice age: "Organizations that do
not learn to adapt themselves to ever-faster, multi-fronted change atrophy
until external forces transform them. Governments no less than business
have to adapt to an environment that is becoming more turbulent, complex
and difficult to predict. Global transformations, caused by, among other
things, developments in technology, communications and trade, demand
new abilities. Flexibility and nimbleness have become key objectives. Inherited

forms of governance appear outmoded and inflexible" (OECD 1995a, 21). The report coyly declined to use the term "crisis" to describe this new environment, but it allowed that current pressures were considerable, and that those to come would be "at least equally impressive and challenging" (22).

The bulk of the report is divided into chapters describing major reform efforts in the following areas: devolution of authority; performance and accountability; development of competition and choice; service; human resources management; information technology; regulation; and strengthening of steering functions. It acknowledged that countries differ at the level of individual reforms, but it strongly asserted that nonetheless there was a "remarkable degree of convergence overall" with "clear patterns of reform" (25). The report had no doubts about the radical nature of these changes. They amounted to a "paradigm shift." The "fundamental, comprehensive nature of the changes described represents a move to a new order" (27). Unsurprisingly, the report noted that change on this scale would inevitably generate resistance, and so devoted a chapter to implementing reform, highlighting the fact that public management reform is "a long haul, not a quick fix" (80).

With this publication, the OECD and PUMA were catapulted to the forefront of the global public management revolution. The typically cited "leaders" in this "revolution" were New Zealand (Boston 1996; Boston et al. 1999; Aucoin 1995) and the United Kingdom (Savoie 1994). Most observers attested the success of the movement: "Since the 1980s, a global reform movement in public management has been vigorously underway" (Kettl 2005, 1). Peters and Pierre noted: "Except perhaps during major wars there never has been the extent of administrative reform and reorganization that has been occurring during the period from approximately 1975 onward" (2001, 1).

Premfors argued that PUMA had developed the dominant narrative of public sector reform and that it had "been very successful in stimulating interest and debate among both member governments and wider audiences and in formulating and propagating a particular mode of thinking about administrative reform" (1998, 142). Other scholars agreed: "PUMA has been one of the nodal points in an international network, bringing together civil servants, management consultants and academics (and occasionally politicians themselves) who are interested in public management. It has helped shape what has now become an international 'community of discourse' about public management reform ... The World Bank, the IMF and the Commonwealth Institute have also been international disseminators of management reform ideas" (Pollitt and Bouckaert 2000, 20-21). More specifically, the OECD at this stage was championing a fairly stylized version of NPM. The academic literature notes several varieties of NPM (Barzelay 1992; Bevir et al. 2003; Hood 1998; Kettl 2005), but *Governance in Transition* made only passing reference to those varieties and to different national experiences. It emphasized "fundamental" trends more consistent with neoliberal, market-ized versions of NPM.

Governance in Transition was the first attempt at a broad overview of public management and governance issues in the OECD countries. From that point on, PUMA concentrated on sectoral policy and administrative reforms, and would not take up the broad theme of governance per se until 2003, when it launched a series of policy briefs that "look at the evolving modernization agenda and how governments can best develop their capacity to achieve, and measure, the desired results" (OECD 2003c). In the series, two publications are of direct relevance: *Public Sector Modernisation* (OECD 2003c) and *Public Sector Modernisation: The Way Forward* (OECD 2005a),[2] which will be referred to below as "PB 2003" and "PB 2005," respectively. These, in turn, both fed into the more detailed study *Modernising Government: The Way Forward*,[3] which will be referred to below as "MG." Since they were written only years apart, and since the first two clearly were drawn upon for the longer report, we will treat them as a group.

Policy Briefs and Modernising Government

It is possible to discern six rhetorical themes that appear repeatedly in the three documents. Each theme is presented and discussed below, with representative examples from each document (each document has multiple examples of each theme). They do not stand alone and isolated from each other, however – their organic relationship, and indeed their rhetorical power, comes from being elements of a larger, master narrative. Each document expresses or reflects that narrative slightly differently, like different translations of the Bible. And yet the main lines of the narrative shine through in all three. It is a complex narrative, since it needs to balance opposing ideas and agendas, not least whether there should be convergence towards some single model or a range of different paths up the mountain. This is an excavation from the texts:

In the past years, all OECD countries have faced major pressures for reform – technological, demographic, budgetary, political. All have undertaken reform, though at varying rates and with varying success. Mistakes were made along the way, particularly with a single-minded devotion to efficiency and to instrumental reform. Certainly, there were major surprises as the pioneers of reform forged ahead on the cold, unforgiving plains of their administrative and political systems. We now know some of the mistakes that were made, principally that not enough attention was paid to culture and the fragility of institutions, or to the diverse paths towards modernity. But the pressures have not subsided, and reform and modernization will have to continue. All OECD countries face the same pressures, and they share the same basic principles; how they respond to those pressures and implement those principles will always be a matter of context. Reformers will face challenges, since change is never easy. They must renew their efforts, develop better tools and better calibration, and move forward, ever forward.

Theme 1: Reform Is Driven by Pressure

The animating theme of all three documents, and indeed of the narrative, is the notion of pressures that have made reform inevitable and unavoidable. PB 2003 mentions the word "pressure" 11 times in 8 pages, PB 2005 4 times, and MG 43 times in 205 pages of text. While there is usually reference to technology, the key pressures identified in the text are budgetary and citizenry. The budgetary pressures are privileged as a historical source of public sector reforms, but clearly cannot be as prominent as they were a decade ago. Nonetheless, MG does refer to continuing budgetary pressures due to "demands on social transfer systems" exacerbated by the challenge of an aging population (21). Clearly, however, the main pressure that is cited in all three documents is a dissatisfied and somewhat truculent citizenry. The dissatisfaction manifests itself in different ways: demands for more services, demands for more efficient services, disgruntlement about high taxation, and a vaguely defined set of inflated "expectations." Though the references are brief, the OECD portrays citizens as somewhat petulant *demandeurs*, whom government officials ignore at their peril. This is not to deny the power of public opinion or public outrage and even demonstrations of violence: the point is the rhetoric and the way it sets up the tone of argument. The nature of the pressure, its legitimacy, and its implacable strength makes reform less a choice than a necessity. Not to reform risks "being out of step" or "not adapting" – in other words, rupturing the harmony that should exist between public institutions and citizens.

> With these new challenges, public management is becoming a major policy issue. It is receiving an unprecedented level of attention in OECD countries and beyond, and the pressures for change will not ease off in the decades ahead (PB 2003, 2).

> Budget worries triggered reform in many countries, but the underlying pressure for change came from social, economic, and technological developments that left governments increasingly out of step with society's expectations (PB 2005, 1).

> The impetus for change came from many different sources, including the social, economic, and technological developments in the latter half of the twentieth century, which put pressure on all governments to adapt to new problems, new capacities, and new relationships between citizens and governments. The public were increasingly concerned

about the quality of the services they received and the choices available to them. Citizens were also increasingly resistant to the government's growing share of the national economy. In some countries, an expectation that taxation would decline became generally accepted across the political spectrum. More and more, governments fell out of step with a changing society and with an educated and empowered citizenry looking to amend their social contract (MG, 19).

Theme 2: Surprises and Unintended Consequences

This is a theme that points largely to the past but resonates with possible follies in the future, and so reinforces a sense of caution about what is possible. It projects the notion of early "pioneers" (PB 2003 refers to "first-generation pioneers" and to "pioneer reformers") who were single-minded in their objectives – building sod huts of reform on the unforgiving prairie of management. They accomplished a great deal but made mistakes – ones, moreover, that in retrospect seem surprising. It is upon their shoulders that modern reformers stand. This manoeuvre accomplishes several things. As mentioned, it exculpates the OECD from its youthful enthusiasm for NPM, but it also builds a platform for departures, and indeed a wider agenda of reform that engages not simply management but governance more widely. The early reformers may have cleared the forest but they neglected the ecology of the landscape. Ecological management is much more complicated and demanding.

> The first-generation pioneers of public sector reform also faced the challenge of adjusting to a rapidly changing world economy. But then the rhetoric of the day identified government itself as the problem. This led to an impression that there was a single generic cause ("bureaucracy") to be addressed by a generic set of solutions ("reform") to arrive at the desired result ("efficiency"). This approach suggested a single change from an unreformed to a reformed efficient state, a coherent task with a specific purpose that would be completed when this goal was reached. Since the primary goal was economic efficiency, the pioneer reformers went to work on reducing public expenditure, freeing up the public sector labour market, and making greater use of market-type mechanisms in government (PB 2003, 2).

> Most public administrations have become more efficient, more transparent, and customer-oriented as a result. Perhaps surprisingly, however, these changes have not reduced governments' influence in society; indeed, government now has a different but larger presence in OECD countries than it did twenty years ago (PB 2005, 1).

Despite these changes, and contrary to the expectations of some reformers, public expenditure did not shrink greatly in most OECD countries (MG, 20).

Theme 3: Reform Involves Multiple Goals
This theme is closely wedded to the previous one: the mistakes that were made, principally in the single-minded pursuit of efficiency, were in part due to the complexity of the reform process and the fact that it cannot focus on simply one goal. Multiple goals have to be pursued simultaneously, and consequently balanced carefully. A wider agenda of reform demands more sophisticated tools and analytical capacities.

> To complicate matters, governments are now under pressure to make more profound changes to meet the requirements of contemporary society. A concern for efficiency is being supplanted by problems of governance, strategy, risk management, ability to adapt to change, collaborative action, and the need to understand the impact of policies on society. To respond to this challenge, member countries and the OECD need better analytical and empirical tools and more sophisticated strategies for change than they have generally had to date (PB 2003, 1).

> And openness in itself does not necessarily improve governance, nor does it override all other public values. It should be balanced against other values of efficiency, equity, and responsibility (PB 2005, 3).

Theme 4: The Importance of Culture/Values and the Organic Nature of Reform
This theme is actually an amalgam of three related aspects of governance reform: the organic nature of government, the importance of taking account of organizational culture, and the role of values in organizations. This echoes the complexity theme cited earlier, that public sector reform cannot be mechanistic or purely instrumental, and that it must take into account a very broad range of potential interaction effects as well as the less obvious dimensions of organizational behaviour.

The documents do not use the term "organic" but prefer the notion of a "whole of government" approach. In PB 2005, this is presented as a "lesson" from two decades of reform efforts – that public administration and governance must be seen as part of an "interconnected whole." This suggests a sort of organizational ecology, where changes in one part of the system will ripple through and affect others. This also reflects stronger appreciation of the constitutional integrity of the state. Whereas the reforms in the early 1990s tended to think in terms of "machinery of government" – that is, mechanistically, and in terms of a machine with parts that could be oiled, interchanged, altered, or even dispensed with – the new view being proposed by the OECD is that states have a constitutional personality that is in part founded in law but that is also an artifact of the integral operation of key systems or "levers," such as the budget process, the civil service management process, and the accountability process. These form interactive cycles, and so disruptions or changes in one will ripple through the others.

An appreciation of the organic nature of government is complemented by an appreciation of the importance of culture within organizations. PB 2003 notes, for example, that "it has long been recognized that the core public service is controlled more by culture than by rules, a situation that is likely to continue despite progress in target-setting, performance contracts and measurement." Moreover, these documents express an appreciation for the historical roots of administrative culture in the OECD countries (e.g., the neutrality of the public service) as something that was achieved over decades, if not centuries. In an odd way, this is testament to both the fragility and the resilience of public administrative systems. They are resilient in the sense that they can resist mere technical interventions that do not address real cultural change. Indeed, the documents are forthright in acknowledging that a great deal of the public sector reform movement in the last twenty years was superficial – that it served the interest of certain groups to announce reforms but not to invoke the pain and resistance of actually following through with those changes. By the same token, reforms that focus on behaviours without addressing the norms and cultures that underpin those behaviours will not be successful. But this notion of culture also signals fragility – if these cultural norms are ignored in the enthusiasm of instrumental change, then what is most distinctive and important about the public sector and how it contributes to modern society may be lost.

Closely related to the idea of culture is the notion of values. The distinction is not clear in the documents, and the terms seem almost interchangeable, but whereas culture appears to be more connected to organizational norms and practices, values appear more closely aligned with specific democratic governance norms, such as a professional civil service, a dedication to the public interest, or leadership practices.

A key consequence of highlighting culture, values, and the organic nature of governance is that public management or "modern governance" is not a goal that will be immediately attainable. It requires long-term commitment, thoughtful implementation, and patience. Moreover, if the interaction effects of an ecological view of governance are taken seriously, then it is likely that reform will be a project without end, since reformation of one part of the system will inevitably perturb other parts, which will in turn have to be adjusted and reformed, which will in turn feed back and affect the others, ad infinitum. Inversions without end.

The second problem was a failure to appreciate that, despite its size and complexity, government remains a single enterprise. Governments operate in a unified constitutional setting and coherent body of administrative law, and their performance is determined by the interaction of a few crucial levers, such as the policy process, the budget process, the civil service management process, and the accountability process, all within the ambient political/administrative culture. Because of that, a reform of one of these levers inevitably involves the others (PB 2003, 3).

The third problem was a failure to understand that public management arrangements not only deliver public services but also enshrine deeper governance values and are therefore, in some respects, inseparable from the constitutional arrangements in which they are embedded (PB 2003, 3).

Traditional thinking on public sector reform has often seen policy, people, money, and organizations as though they were independent components of public management. This study has made it clear that they are closely interlinked. It is important for reform strategies to take account of the interlinked nature of these components of government (MG, 201).

Theme 5: Context Matters; Differences among Countries
As noted above, the OECD is widely regarded to have been a key international champion of NPM in the late 1990s, more so than the World Bank, for example. *Governance in Transition* was a high point in that proselytizing for several reasons. NPM was less than a decade old, and was still a dominant force in the academic literature; the doubts and critiques would come later. The challenge of helping the "transition" states in Central and Eastern Europe rested on the assumption that they would be brought up to "western" (i.e., a single set) of standards in economic structures, policy initiatives, and administrative practices, and it must be said that recipient countries were quite prepared to adopt foreign models in order to have access to donor funds.

A decade later, the OECD was taking a more subtle approach, and indeed highlighting the divergent paths countries might take on the arduous journey of reform, as well as the importance of context for the reform process. Interestingly, the importance of context is only a minor theme in PB 2003, but by 2005 it was a major theme of both PB 2005 and MG. This is listed as the second key lesson of two decades of reform, namely, that modernization efforts must pay attention to the specific characteristics of each country and be tailored to circumstances. Similar reform efforts in different contexts will yield different results. In the MG report, context becomes the major finding of the document: "The main lesson that emerges from this review is that modernization is context dependent" (201). It is in this vein that the report is surprisingly critical of the "best practice" movement, because it usually involves the transfer of some universal remedy to contexts that may not be suited to them.

> Modernization is context-dependent: OECD countries' reform experiences demonstrate that the same reform instruments perform differently and produce very diverse results in different country contexts. This variation in reform experiences reflects the disparate institutional structures and environments that confront the reformers. Modernization strategies need to be tailored to an individual country's context, needs, and circumstances (MG, 22).

> The nature of the problem and the solution are strongly influenced by the national country context. The design of reform strategies must be calibrated to the specific risks and dynamics of the national public administration system and take a whole-of-government approach (MG, 201).

Theme 6: Change Is Difficult/Challenging

This theme is less a single element in the reports than a thread that runs through the entire cloth. The themes of complexity and the organic nature of governance signal that public management reform is challenging at best, and verges on dangerous at worst. The repeated references to past mistakes also highlight the risks associated with reform (these comments are usually balanced with acknowledgments that much was nonetheless accomplished, but the message is clear that despite accomplishments, major mistakes were made). Even the strong emphasis on context found in MG is a backhanded reference to the need for care and prudence in proposing best practices. As part of a narrative, of course, this goes well beyond the simple acknowledgment that change is difficult. It helps highlight several messages.

First, and somewhat paradoxically, the emphasis on danger and challenge reinforces the sense that reform efforts are necessary, like a pep talk to a SWAT team before it launches a mission. Second, it steels the will. The subtext is that resistance to change is understandable but irrational. Reformers have to be prepared to encounter irrational resistance and simply ride it through. Third, it subtly delegitimizes resistance to change, precisely by emphasizing it as a universal reaction. Considering it a universal reaction makes it a thoughtless reflex; it should be dealt with the same way a doctor deals with a patient's flinching before the needle. Finally, if resistance to change is universal, it is unlikely to be easily overcome, and so reform efforts will naturally stretch over time, and perhaps a very long time, before they are successful. Interestingly, the documents make little reference to building constituencies of support or collaboration, though this does not mean that these more cooperative strategies of change are being ruled out. Instead, governance reform seems a lonely vocation, doomed to opposition, fraught with uncertainty, and potentially disastrous if done incorrectly.

Major change is uncomfortable and anxiety producing, and because of this there is a natural instinct to resist it. Dedicated managerial attention can change officials' behaviour, but it is only at the point where this behaviour has been internalized by individuals and groups – the point of cultural change – that it is likely to continue without such attention. So a reform that does not reach the critical point of internalization will slip back to the prior state once the dedicated effort for change relaxes. And that is what happens to many attempted reforms (PB 2003, 6).

Reforms cannot substitute for hard political choices. For OECD countries, improving the cost-effectiveness and performance of their public sectors will help reduce pressure on spending. As the past decade has shown, however, this in itself is unlikely to stem the continued upward pressure on expenditure generated by social entitlement programs and social transfers. Public sector reform is not a substitute for the hard and, in many cases, unpopular choices that politicians have to make in some countries if long-term difficulties are to be avoided" (MG, 21).

Citizens' expectations and demands of governments are growing, not diminishing: they expect openness, higher levels of service quality delivery, solutions to more complex problems, and the maintenance of existing social entitlements. Reforms to the public sector in the past twenty years have significantly improved efficiency, but governments of OECD countries now face a major challenge in finding new efficiency gains that will enable them to fund these growing demands on twenty-first-century government. For the next twenty years, policy makers face hard political choices. Since most governments cannot increase their share of the economy, in some countries this will put pressure on entitlement programs. These new demands on builders of public management systems will require leadership from officials with enhanced individual technical, managerial, and political capacities who think and plan collectively and who can work well with other actors" (MG, 205).

Conclusion: The OECD and Global Governance
The OECD has been actively involved in public sector management reform for almost twenty years, since PUMA was created in 1990. It is important to

remind ourselves that the OECD has no authoritative capacity as such, and cannot order its members to do anything. Accordingly, it has had to leverage its position in this field as an information broker – moreover, a broker with distinct characteristics. First, it is an intergovernmental organization; its members are states. While membership currently sits at thirty, the OECD has expanded its activities to embrace non-members as well. In the field of governance, for example, its is mounting a good-governance initiative with Arab states, is involved with Asia-Pacific Economic Cooperation (APEC) in regulatory reform, has a South Eastern Europe Regional Program, and also has programs with Russia and China. So, despite its small formal membership, it is in fact global in scope and influence. Second, the OECD operates with a special mix of research and country participation. Governments broadly set its research agenda, and governments/members are usually involved in reviewing reports before they are published. But the OECD's comparative advantage is that it can draw on the willing support of its members (and other states) to provide "inside" information about what governments are doing in specific fields, and that information by definition is credible. The key instruments that the OECD uses to exercise influence are research-based, informational ones (see other chapters in this volume for detailed examples).

We agree with Porter and Webb (Chapter 2) that this combination of instruments contributes in important ways to a process of identity formation, in this instance with particular reference to the "ideal modern state." Unlike other subsidiary policy areas (child care, budgeting standards), the work of PUMA and GOV was directed at public administration writ large, the very sinews of the modern state, its broadest capacities to organize itself and deliver its services, however those might be defined. It involved, as Porter and Webb point out, a process of deliberation and norm construction, the identification of best practices, and tools to socialize states into accepting these norms as basic standards of modern governance. The discourse of generalized pressures affecting all states, of some states responding to those pressures and others not, and of a constant horizon of modernization is very much a discourse on what it means to be an ideal state in the twentieth and twenty-first centuries. As we note below, the key identity marker in this discourse was being "modern." This is pre-eminently a discourse of identity.

The OECD used all of its basic instruments in the governance and public management field to exercise influence over "public sector modernization." Indeed, as we noted earlier, its 1995 *Governance in Transition* report was widely discussed around the world because it purported to be the first survey and overview of its kind describing what governments were doing in reforming public management, and because it unabashedly supported the prescriptions of a stylized version of NPM, a version "more market/less government" (Sahlin-Andersson 2000b). Many still characterize the OECD's vision in these terms, but as we saw earlier, the organization's views on public sector reform have matured and become considerably more nuanced. Whereas the 1995 report made ritualistic references to contextual factors and the reality of different reform trajectories, the 2005 report elevated context to a prime theme and indeed a key conclusion. Whereas in 1995 the OECD did seem to be pushing universalistic solutions, by 2005 it was much more cautious, both about context as well as about organizational culture and the ecology of government institutions. From time to time, the OECD will highlight the principles that bind its members and that allegedly form a common foundation of values about good governance (e.g., transparency, accountability), and it will occasionally chide governments for not meeting global standards, but its considered views on modernizing governance are no longer confined to a narrowly neoliberal interpretation of NPM.

There are several reasons for this shift from a single meta-narrative to something more complex. First, some of this is due to learning. As the OECD's own report points out, governments have not shrunk in the last two decades, and so a naïve NPMism would make little empirical sense. As well, experience with the Central and Eastern European transition states in the 1990s, with the EU accession process, and with the consequences of failed states around the world shows that governance is hugely important for economic performance and social stability, let alone key services such as clean water and education. Second, we need to take organizational context into consideration as well – the GOV secretariat of the OECD is operating in the governance "market" and needs to maintain and expand its position in that market in order to survive and thrive as an organization. The themes we saw in the reports, as well as the master narrative that binds those themes together, serve the OECD well from a marketing point of view. The emphasis on the difficulty and the challenge of public sector modernization essentially underscores the point that this is not for the uninformed or the fainthearted. The repeated calls for more research and data and indicators reinforce the point. As well, the emphasis on context and variety, on the differences among governments and hence the different paths to reform, establishes a much wider agenda for the OECD over time than would a one-size-fits-all approach. The mid-1990s emphasis on a single value – efficiency – made for a relatively narrow range of recommendations. The new emphasis on ecology, nuance, contradiction, and feedback loops creates "inversions without end," a potential reform agenda that stretches far into the future. The minute calibrations required to get reform right will almost never end, as one set of interventions or reforms calls forth the need for ever new ones to deal with the ramifications of those past.

A third reason has to do with the complexities of neoliberalism itself. As Mahon points out in Chapter 14, neoliberalism has become too crude a category to capture the ideologies at the commanding heights of the global economy. Indeed, if NPM was supposed to be an expression of neoliberalism (and it was often criticized for exactly that), then even this was too crude. While *Governance in Transition* did emphasize efficiency, NPM intellectual currents even at the time incorporated different notes (e.g., service). The changes in the OECD's vision of governance over a decade can therefore be seen to parallel the evolution in its thinking about liberalism, and in particular its move towards a notion of what Mahon calls "inclusive liberalism." The simple recognition of the importance of human capital for economic competitiveness and growth changes the character of "liberal" state interventions; the simple recognition that the quality and integrity of public administration matters shifts the focus from efficiency.

We close now with some observations on the contemporary nature of globalization and global governance. A first, key point is that the OECD's efforts in proselytizing public management reform is part of a global explosion in the past twenty years in knowledge networks around management and management reform, in both the private (Sahlin-Andersson and Engwall 2002; Kipping and Engwall 2002) and public sectors (Kettl 2005). These knowledge networks form dense matrices of actors and organizations that effectively become the discordant lattices of global coordination and emergent forms of global governance (Stone 2004; Slaughter 2004). While the phrase "governance without government" was coined some time ago (Rosenau and Czempiel 1992), it is increasingly being drawn upon to describe a world where rules of every type, at every level, seem to be multiplying into resilient meshes of control. More and more of these rules, however, appear to be "soft law" – standards, norms, guidelines, and frameworks. States are clearly involved but are not necessarily prime movers or dominant players in respective networks: "Governance in a world where boundaries are largely in flux is being shaped and pursued in constellations of public and private actors that include states, international organizations, professional associations, expert groups, civil society groups and business corporations. Governance includes regulation but goes well beyond it. Governance is also about dense organizing, discursive and monitoring activities that embed, frame, stabilize and reproduce rules and regulations" (Djelic and Sahlin-Andersson 2006b, 7).

The paradox is that that this form of dynamic and loose coupling of actors and organizations in the making of soft rules and non-coercive monitoring and compliance strategies is diffuse, messy, and with a variable geometry – and yet it creates order. That order is fragile, unlike hierarchies of command and control backed up by force and sanctions, and so has to be constantly recreated and recalibrated. The OECD is an important contributor to global governance that occurs without a global government. As an arena and a convener, it ceaselessly connects and reconnects government officials around the world, along with experts, non-governmental organizations, and business. Obviously, these actors do not always agree with each other, but the simple fact of meeting creates discursive spaces and a common language of concepts. More than that, however, the OECD is engaged in standards setting, a key instrument in soft law (Brunsson and Jacobsson 2000). Despite the caution that we saw in *Modernising Governance,* the GOV directorate is not at all shy of articulating "best practices," frameworks, guidelines, and success stories. The master narrative of reform not only tells a story but also lays out a conceptual universe, complete with broad objectives and strategies. This is complemented by league tables, indicators, and roadmaps that encourage self-reflexivity and mutual adjustment. Over time, systems begin to look similar, and the managers of those systems learn from each other, speak a similar language, and ultimately begin to coordinate in policy terms, without a central coordinator.

This is not to suggest that this is an order without conflict or power struggles. As Djelic and Sahlin-Andersson point out, the paradox of contemporary transnational governance is that it combines, dynamically, a "bright" (visible) side of actors that "negotiate, enact, transform, resist, translate or embrace evolving rules of the game" with a "dark" (invisible) side of institutional rules or forces that "shape, constrain and embed both dynamic topographies of actors and surface regulation" (2006c, 394). They make the intriguing point that the two sides are mutually reinforcing and dynamically interacting. In terms of the OECD and other transnational actors like it, this suggests a "bright" side of endless negotiation and renegotiation, discursive reformulations and narrative constructions, debates, standard setting, monitoring, violation of norms ... and a "dark" side that is a gradual reinforcement of institutional meta-rules regarding governance and best practices in public administration and management. Those meta-rules may be resisted and redefined, but they emerge as reference points for "normality."

Nonetheless, this still begs the question of why governments and their officials engage as energetically as they do with a body like the OECD, one that can exercise almost no leverage over them. This is a large topic that will have to be developed in future research, but at this stage we can discern at least four factors that create a receptive audience for OECD governance standards. First, we often underestimate the pressure of "policy search" among modern governments. In most cases, when government officials are asked to develop new policies, their first question is, "What are other governments doing?" This is not only to provide a backdrop for domestic policy but also to search for new ideas, techniques, tools, best practices, and stories of success and failure. Most officials would be considered irresponsible if they did not have some grasp of what other governments are doing with respect to a given policy field.[4] The OECD provides a one-stop shop for comparative policy data.

Second, participation in the OECD yields several practical as well as symbolic benefits for most states. In the complex world of international relations, the practical benefits extend from compliance with standards that are recognized by third parties, to the personal connections with counterpart officials in other countries. The symbolic benefits arise from membership (or participation) in an exclusive and prestigious club. For example, even if the OECD's Anti-Corruption Network achieved absolutely nothing at all in practical terms, countries like Kazakhstan and Ukraine achieve a measure of global respectability simply by showing up.

Finally, the OECD has managed to capitalize on a complex global psychology of modernization, a restless hunt to reach an always-receding horizon of improvement. What works now is never good enough. As *Governance in Transition* put it: "Unchanged governance structures and classic responses of 'more of the same' are inappropriate to this intricate policy environment ... Governments must strive to do things better, with fewer resources, and, above all, differently" (OECD 1995a). To be modern is to be *à la mode*. While the OECD is not as ruthless in defining *la mode* as New York or Parisian *fashionistas*, it has appropriated the discourse of modernity, and has a credible claim to defining what is *à la mode* through its membership and associational ties. Most governments, whatever their real inclinations, resist being labelled "conventional," "backward," or "traditional." Most prefer to be "modern" or to be "modernizing." But to be modern is also to be "of the moment," and as the moment is always changing, so the quest is never-ending.

Acknowledgments
This research was supported in 2006 by an Institutional Research Grant, Carleton University, and in 2007 by Social Sciences and Humanities Research Council grant no. 410-2007-2056. I am indebted to my son, Matthew Pal, for a reintroduction to Cormac McCarthy and for the theme of this chapter.

Notes
1 For the purposes of this chapter, we treat the documents as coherent wholes, as though a single author wrote them. Of course, complex documents of this type, especially ones emanating from organizations as baroque as the OECD, are a combination of hundreds of small, cooperative efforts in research and drafting.
2 Both documents are available at http://www.oecd.org/findDocument/0,2350,en_2649_37405_1_119696_1_1_37405,00.html.
3 This is not available for free on the Web. It can be purchased, or it can be accessed by subscribers at SourceOECD.
4 This observation springs from personal experience. The author has served as a consultant on several federal government policy review projects, and each one without fail has demanded some sort of comparative analysis of other countries' policies.

4
Towards Complex Multilateralism? Civil Society and the OECD
Richard Woodward

The years since the early 1980s have witnessed more active engagement between civil society and multilateral economic institutions (MEIs) (O'Brien et al. 2000). Echoing other literature on globalization and governance, however, surveys exploring the relationship between civil society and MEIs concentrate on the traditional troika of the World Trade Organization (WTO), International Monetary Fund (IMF), and World Bank (see O'Brien et al. 2000; Robertson 2000; Scholte and Schnabel 2002; Scholte 2004) and are largely devoid of references to the Organisation for Economic Co-operation and Development. Yet, there are reasons why the OECD deserves to be part of this research agenda. Almost from the outset, the OECD had institutionalized channels for interacting with civil society through the Trade Union Advisory Committee (TUAC) and the Business and Industry Advisory Committee (BIAC). More recently, especially after 1998, when the outcry orchestrated by civil society contributed to the collapse of its Multilateral Agreement on Investment (MAI), the OECD has sought to bolster and diversify connections with civil society. Inventive mechanisms such as the Annual Forum, its own "civil society summit," have enhanced opportunities for civil society participation in OECD work and cemented its reputation as a "top performer" among intergovernmental organizations in terms of its aptitude for engaging civil society (Blagescu and Lloyd 2006, 37).

Drawing upon the historical and theoretical themes outlined in Chapters 1 and 2, this chapter narrates the story of the OECD's affiliations with civil society and their impact on OECD governance. Hastened by the MAI affair, the OECD has inched away from traditional forms of multilateralism where work is propelled by member states and a restricted number of civil society interlocutors towards the more polycentric features of "complex multilateralism" (O'Brien et al. 2000, 3), where states remain the main arbiters but have to coexist with a cacophony of civil society voices. The OECD, however, has judiciously selected its civil society acquaintances and the domains to which they are admitted. The suspicion persists that this is a deliberate manoeuvre by elites to ensure that civil society acquiesces to their neoliberal agenda.

Civil Society and the Rise of Complex Multilateralism

A colossal debate surrounds the personality and function of civil society (see Anheier et al. 2001, 12-15), but for the purposes of this chapter, it is defined as the realm in which a kaleidoscope of non-governmental actors endeavour to mould rules governing social life (Scholte 2002, 146). Mainstream approaches to international political economy (IPE) marginalize non-governmental actors (and hence civil society), implying that states and state-centric international organizations drive the process of global economic governance. Analytical and conceptual innovations such as transnationalism, interdependence, and regime theory acknowledged roles for non-state actors in global economic governance but clung dogmatically to the belief that they were subsidiary actors with limited autonomy from the states system (Baker et al. 2005b, 6-7). This "top-down" understanding has increasingly been disputed by those who conjecture about global economic governance's being driven from the bottom up by agents operating independently of the state and representing a different set of interests (Falk 1999). Controlled by member states and detached from civil society, MEIs conformed to the top-down rubric until the 1980s. Thereafter, MEI and civil society interpenetration steadily grew (see Anheier et al. 2001, 291-2), yielding a "transformation in the nature of global economic governance" branded as "complex multilateralism" (O'Brien et al. 2000, 3). In contrast to multilateralism, which assumes states as the main actor and lone emissary of the public interest, complex multilateralism connotes a public interest and decision-making environment advanced and mediated by "a proliferating and fluctuating set of intergovernmental and multi-stakeholder arrangements with more assertive and diverse actors" (Forman and Segaar 2006, 205).

It is worth pausing to consider why this situation has arisen and its implications. Gramsci (1971) argued that capitalism retained control via a mixture of coercion and consent, the latter deriving from the propagation of a hegemonic ideology that universalized the values of the bourgeoisie. To achieve this, the dominant class needed to make concessions and fabricate liaisons with social forces opposed to their economic interests. This marriage of social forces fashions a "historic bloc," manufacturing consent with the existing social order and helping to produce and reproduce the hegemony of the dominant class. Hegemony is intertwined with his notion of the state, which he separates into "political society" (a realm of coercion underpinned by political and legal institutions) and "civil society" (a private realm predicated on consent). To preserve its control, the dominant class engages in "passive revolution," perpetually allowing its hegemony to change by permitting specific demands from civil society to be fulfilled in the political sphere. Thus, civil society is not only the sphere in which the prevailing social order is embedded but a fertile soil in which the seeds of a new social order can be germinated (Cox 1999, 4).

Today, the political and civil societies talked of by Gramsci are more transnationalized – the former marked by the growth in the size and mandate of international organizations, the latter by the extraordinary expansion of linkages between civil society groups and activism across national borders (Kaldor et al. 2007, 309-21). Nevertheless, it is possible to gaze upon complex multilateralism through these lenses. An optimistic interpretation sees complex multilateralism chiefly animated from the bottom up, marking the beginnings of a workable counter-hegemony forged by elements within civil society disenfranchised by the present neoliberal settlement. The propensity for engagement between MEIs and civil society is not a devious attempt by elites to engage in passive revolution but marks the beginning of a new fusion of societal forces, a new historic bloc, from which will spring a different global economic governance.

Unfortunately, much of the evidence from the OECD and elsewhere suggests that complex multilateralism is more a top-down phenomenon with MEIs, championed by leading states and corporate interests, employing civil society as an agency for entrenching prevailing philosophies (Cox 1999, 11). First, MEIs continue to act as gatekeepers determining who secures access, where, and on what terms. The multiplicity of civil society actors involved with MEIs is limited and cannot disguise the continued predominance of corporate interests. Second, civil society and MEIs are now institutionally and functionally interdependent (Reimann 2006, 63). MEIs supply resources and political space to civil society, which in return assists MEIs by disbursing funds and administering projects, providing expertise, gathering intelligence, pestering states to enact, and monitoring adherence to, policy recommendations, and marshalling public opinion (Gordenker and Weiss 1996). It would be a mistake, however, to construe this as mutual dependence. MEIs have enormous power to structure civil society's input, especially as the dramatic expansion of MEI missions leaves civil society with little option but to interact with them as they aspire to protect and promote their constituents' well-being. Having gained admission to the inner sanctum, civil society groups may come to owe their exalted position to the patronage of the MEI, inclining "the latter's objectives towards conformity with established order and thus enhance the legitimacy of the prevailing order" (Cox 1999, 11). Rather than securing radical alterations to the trajectory of global governance, complex multilateralism will sponsor incremental policy change and institutional modifications to fortify the existing regime.[1]

Multilateralism at the OECD, 1961-98

Prior to the events surrounding the MAI, the OECD typified top-down multilateralism. The organization remained aloof from civil society (Aubrey 1967, 130), and despite their special status, BIAC and TUAC seldom had a decisive impact. Indeed, the tenor of civil society towards the OECD tacitly acknowledged its state-centrism. Instead of challenging the organization directly, civil society nudged domestic policy makers to induce, manipulate, or stymie its initiatives.

Article 12 of the OECD Convention (1960) states:

The Organization may:

a address communications to non-member States or organizations;
b establish and maintain relations with non-member States or organizations; and
c invite non-member Governments or organizations to participate in activities of the Organization.

This ostensibly permissive posture towards civil society was tempered by an OECD Council decision (OECD 1962) that declared:

Any international non-governmental organization may be consulted by the Organization provided that it satisfies the following three conditions:

a it has wide responsibilities in general economic matters or in a specific economic sector;
b it has affiliated bodies belonging to all or most of the Member countries in the Organization; and
c it substantially represents the non-governmental interests in the field or sector in question.

These provisions constrained consultative arrangements between the OECD and civil society because, with transnational civil society in its infancy, there was a paucity of *international* non-governmental organizations (INGOs). Moreover, the INGOs that did exist were insufficiently sophisticated to meet any, let alone all, of the council's preconditions.

In the event, only a handful of INGOs achieved consultative standing with the OECD. The two best known are TUAC and BIAC. Originally devised to give workers an official voice during the administration of the Marshall Plan by the Organisation for European Economic Co-operation (OEEC), TUAC gained consultative status in 1962 and provides "an interface for trade unions" (TUAC 2006) with the OECD. In the same year, the OECD Council granted approval to BIAC, a new organization purporting to be "the voice of OECD business" (BIAC 2006b), lending the OECD the tripartite traits of its members.

TUAC and BIAC share similar institutional features and working practices, and use analogous means to induce developments at the OECD. Both are independent organizations funded and energized by their affiliates in OECD member states. Nowadays, TUAC's affiliations comprise fifty-six trade unions representing approximately 66 million workers (TUAC 2006), while BIAC's entail thirty-nine business peak groups representing over 8 million companies (BIAC 2006b). Each has small (usually fewer than a dozen people) secretariats headquartered in Paris, and work is undertaken in member-composed committees shadowing those of the OECD. Most interactions between the OECD, BIAC, and TUAC are mundane and technical in nature, with BIAC and TUAC pitching ideas to OECD committees and working groups. Proximity to the OECD allows TUAC and BIAC to utilize informal channels of influence, including chance meetings with ambassadorial staff and personnel from national delegations. Formal dialogue takes place through the Liaison Committee (of the Council) with International Non-Governmental Organisations, chaired by the Secretary-General. Additionally, BIAC and TUAC have separate annual meetings with the OECD, tender submissions to the Annual Ministerial Meeting, and converse with chairs or vice chairs of OECD committees. The divergence between TUAC and BIAC lies in their policy prescriptions. Whereas TUAC has persistently advocated strong social institutions to moderate the excesses of free markets (TUAC 2005, 2-3), BIAC posits that such institutions can be tolerated provided they do not impair economic growth (Farnsworth 2005, 218-19).

In this period, relations between BIAC, TUAC, and the OECD epitomized traditional multilateralism. The parameters within which interactions took place were tightly defined by member states, and while BIAC and TUAC may have exerted a subtle discipline on the OECD's values, policies, and strategic vision, examples of major contributions to flagship policies or prominent participation in policy implementation are rare. The regularly cited example is the 1976 Declaration on International Investment and Multinational Enterprises and its accompanying Guidelines, which sought to promote international investment by enshrining the rights of multinational corporations (MNCs) and their host governments and by establishing voluntary principles for upright business conduct. As well as being intimately involved in the preliminary negotiations, BIAC and TUAC helped monitor the declaration by bringing contraventions to the attention of designated national contact points (NCPs). By the end of the 1980s, TUAC had brought over forty cases to NCPs, but because it lacked any binding force, interpretations of the rules were generally ignored (Salzman 2005, 212-15). Similarly, "an essential feature, *particularly from an administrative point of view, is* strict parallelism of

treatment of TUAC and BIAC" (OECD 2006e, emphasis added). The OECD's
pledge to treat them impartially from an *administrative* standpoint is intriguing because it implies corresponding opportunities for involvement in,
but not influence over, the organization's work. The fortunes of BIAC and
TUAC were intrinsically coupled with the OECD's outlook, something determined by member states. The OECD's obedience to the Keynesian gospel
in the 1960s brought discussions of manpower, prices and incomes policies,
industrial policy, and development to the fore, meaning that TUAC's star
was ascendant. During the 1970s, the "house that Keynes built" was dis-
mantled in favour of market-oriented supply-side models. Increasingly BIAC's
agenda was in vogue and it progressively assumed a privileged ideational
position within the OECD.

Correspondingly, elements of civil society not designated by the OECD
Council applied pressure by petitioning their governments to promote and
defend their views in the organization. The OECD's committee system is
particularly susceptible to lobbying at the national level. Each year, more
than 40,000 officials from national administrations attend OECD committee
meetings, which provides an opportunity to articulate anxieties broached
by domestic constituents (OECD 2003d, 96). The OECD's preference for
consensus means that briefing a national government about the pitfalls of
OECD proposals and stirring up domestic opposition was an effective way
to stall, eviscerate, or thwart negotiations at the OECD, as was the case with
discussions about agricultural trade in the 1960s (Cohn 2002, 150). Conversely, these tactics can launch or further negotiations in the OECD. In the
1970s, the United States' pursuit of trade in services at the OECD stemmed
from the fact that domestic commercial interests awakened the interest of
the administration and the Congress to their comparative advantage in the
services sector and its importance to the US economy (Drake and Nicolaïdis
1992, 46; Cohn 2002, 144).

Some areas of the OECD were more amenable to direct civil society input.
The best illustration was the Chemicals Division of the Environment Directorate. In 1981, the directorate evolved a Mutual Acceptance of Data (MAD)
agreement whereby contracted parties agreed to recognize the validity of
data from each other about the non-clinical safety of products, including
chemicals, pesticides, pharmaceuticals, cosmetics, food, feed additives, and
biocides. This obviated the need for companies to replicate tests in different
countries and prevented the deployment of differential assessment standards
as a trade barrier. For this to work, there had to be consensus on appropriate
experimental procedures and mechanisms to check that they were being
followed fastidiously. Under the auspices of working groups in the Environment Directorate, a 7,000-strong network of experts from industry, academia,
trade unions, and environmental groups have elaborated and policed more

than 100 Test Guidelines and Principles of Good Laboratory Practice (see Salzman 2005, 200-3). Elsewhere, the Committee for Agriculture has routinely consulted the International Federation of Agricultural Producers and the European Confederation of Agriculture since 1962 (OECD 2005c, 3), and, in the early 1990s, the political will engendered by the International Chamber of Commerce and Transparency International (TI) alongside BIAC and TUAC proved crucial to the negotiation of the Convention on Combating Bribery of Foreign Public Officials in International Business Transactions (the OECD Anti-Bribery Convention) in 1997 (OECD 2003e).

Multilateralism under Stress: The MAI Affair
Despite the expansion of foreign direct investment (FDI), states have been unable to devise a multilateral regime to govern international investment activity. The US failed in its attempt to include investment in the Uruguay Round of the General Agreement on Tariffs and Trade (GATT), and the issue was kicked back into the OECD's Committee on International Investment and Multinational Enterprises (CIME). In 1995, after a four-year gestation period, the OECD announced its readiness to commence negotiations to bring a multilateral agreement on investment (MAI) to fruition by May 1997.

Initially, civil society was indifferent to these developments, with only a handful of NGOs tracking the deliberations. Endemic resistance started after a draft of the treaty was posted on the Internet by Ralph Nader's Public Citizen organization. The draft was excoriated as an "investor's charter, privileging the pursuit of profit and eviscerating the ability of governments to pass legislation to protect consumers, workers, and the environment" (Woodward 2004, 120). The anti-MAI crusade gained momentum, and by the time the campaign reached its crescendo, with the infiltration of the OECD's normally tranquil Paris citadel for two days of direct action to coincide with an MAI negotiation meeting, more than 600 groups in seventy countries (Kobrin 1998, 97-98; see also Kurtz 2002) were involved. Shortly afterwards, following France's withdrawal from the negotiations, the OECD announced the effective abortion of the MAI process.

More simplistic analyses ascribe the MAI's disintegration to the pandemonium of October 1998, but a more compelling explanation was that civil society outmanoeuvred the OECD's efforts to secure international consensus by successfully mobilizing *domestic* political opinion against the treaty (Rugman 1998). The initial leak divulged misgivings harboured by OECD members about the MAI, fissures that civil society exploited as they rallied parliamentarians, bureaucrats, and citizens to pressure governments to reject it. Fatally, in an attempt to salvage the operation, the OECD was obliged to dilute the treaty and allow endless exemptions for individual member states. This backfired because it failed to appease elements of civil society prejudiced against the MAI and simultaneously undermined support from elements of civil society that supported the unadulterated agreement. The scarcity of domestic backers sounded the death knell for international negotiations.

The MAI affair marked a watershed in OECD/civil society relations, highlighting to both parties the hazards of eschewing each other and the profitable possibilities of positive engagement. Albeit belatedly, the MAI transformed civil society's perception of the OECD from the peripheral "club," "forum," or "think tank" portrayed by most commentaries to the "crucible in which some of the most important ideas, norms, rules and principles underpinning contemporary global governance crystallized and, via interactions with non-members and a continuous cycle of surveillance and peer review, the vehicle through which they have been disseminated and upheld" (Woodward 2008, 1). Whether civil society yearned to reverse or entrench the tide of global governance, engagement with the OECD was essential. Furthermore, the MAI affair alerted civil society to the OECD's neoliberal credentials. This reputation was sealed by civil society appraisals of other contemporary OECD reports that were also peppered with free market policy nostrums and "the logic of no alternative" language beholden to neoliberal hagiolaters (Marcussen 2001). Neoliberal adornments are sufficient reason for some elements of civil society to passionately support or vituperatively disapprove of a multinational economic institution, but because the OECD legislates across almost the entire economic landscape (see Table 4.1), it has ample opportunity to propagate this philosophy. Less than 15 percent of the OECD's judgments are Decisions, full-fledged international treaties creating binding obligations on their signatories, but they have exercised a tremendous impact over the evolution of the global economy. For example, the OECD Code of Liberalization of Capital Movements and the OECD Code of Liberalization of Current Invisible Operations agreed to in 1961 have inspired the dismantling of obstacles to trade and finance (Henderson 1996). The remaining OECD edicts take the form of non-binding "soft law" enforced through moral suasion, surveillance, and peer review. Nevertheless, as is the case with the inclusion of the OECD Principles of Corporate Governance (2004) among the Financial Stability Forum's 12 Key Standards for Sound Financial Systems (Financial Stability Forum 2006), they are widely extolled as paragons of international best practice.

Those tempted to dismiss the OECD's pontifications because of its emphasis on soft power were dissuaded by the way the MAI affair unveiled the organization's clever use of these tools to mould ideational frameworks and wider processes of global governance. Ideas spawned in the OECD radiate far beyond the institution because its committees are "communities of influence" (Salzman 2000) that cultivate policy agendas elsewhere. Repeated encounters in OECD committees nurture shared normative perspectives and common understandings of policy problems. Judgments reached by OECD committees are imbued with authority because they are colonized by renowned experts in their field, and national politicians frequently invoke their pronouncements to debunk alternatives or justify unpopular measures (Kanter 2006; see also Armingeon and Beyeler 2004). In the case of the MAI, conversations in CIME ironed out discrepancies concerning the legitimate extent of the state's role in regulating investment, demonstrated the virtues of liberalizing foreign direct investment, and established the superiority of a multilateral over bilateral investment treaties. These discussions were a prerequisite for garnering support in member states because they gave governments ideas to "sell" to their various social constituents.

Globally, the OECD's close working relationship with other MEIs, especially the WTO and Group of Eight (G8), is another outlet for its influence. Sometimes the OECD is picked as a pre-negotiating forum (see Cohn 2002) for agreements that later emerge in other MEIs. The OECD's smaller, more homogeneous membership is more conducive to reaching agreement, and because discussions are private and lead to non-binding outcomes, states are more malleable than in formal negotiating contexts. Once compromise is reached, OECD countries can act as a caucus when it resurfaces in a more formal decision-making environment. Its reputation for erudite interdisciplinary research means that the OECD is also customarily chosen to initiate analytical work or to study emergent or difficult issues on behalf of other MEIs (Cohn 2002; Ougaard 2004; Woodward 2008). The MAI exemplifies the OECD's acquaintances with other MEIs. After intractable impediments to a formal agreement appeared in the GATT, the MAI was devolved to the OECD in the hope that an informal agreement could be brokered that would lead to the topic's incorporation in subsequent WTO trade rounds. The OECD's suitability as a forum for pre-negotiating the MAI rested on its expertise and impressive track record in fashioning a framework for governing foreign investment, and on the fact that OECD countries were the overwhelming originators and recipients of foreign direct investment and had more to gain from a multilateral agreement. The MAI taught civil society that engagement with the OECD was often inescapable if they desired to sway developments in more high-profile international organizations. Entrusting tasks to the OECD means that it is often the first intergovernmental organization to systematically interrogate an issue, which confers upon it the power to frame the problem and set the terms of future debate. Furthermore, the OECD offers an invaluable opportunity to wield influence before national positions ossify in the glare of hard-nosed public bargaining.

The MAI affair gave the OECD several reasons to take civil society seriously. First and foremost, it demonstrated to the OECD that it was not immune to civil society. The failure to prevail over civil society opprobrium offered a stark insight into the latent problems facing OECD projects. Worries about the prospect of further embarrassing casualties courtesy of civil society were

Table 4.1

OECD acts by type and subject, as of April 2006

	Decisions	Recommendations	Others	Total
Agriculture	4	3	0	7
Capital movements	1	0	0	1
Competition law and policy	0	10	0	10
Consumer policy	1	7	0	8
Corporate governance	0	2	0	2
Current invisible operations	1	1	0	2
Development assistance	0	3	11	14
Education	0	2	1	3
Employment, labour, and social affairs	0	2	2	4
Energy	1	0	0	1
Environment	14	49	4	67
Financial markets	0	7	0	7
Fiscal affairs	0	15	1	16
Information, computer, and communications policy	0	5	4	9
Insurance	1	9	0	10
International investment and multinational enterprises	5	7	4	16
Nuclear energy	1	4	3	8
Public management	0	3	0	3
Scientific and technological policy	0	4	5	9
Shipbuilding and maritime transport	0	2	4	6
Steel	0	0	1	1
Tourism	1	2	0	3
Trade	0	4	2	6
Total	30	141	42	213

Source: OECD, "Instruments of the OECD," http://webdomino1.oecd.org/horizontal/oecdacts.nsf/subject?OpenView&Count=1000&ExpandView.

exacerbated by a second factor uncovered by the MAI affair, namely, the wider malaise menacing the OECD. Outflanked by geopolitical upheavals and newer or revitalized competitors (Woodward 2006a), the ignominious denouement of the MAI affair lent credence to depictions of the OECD as an expensive, elitist, and unnecessary anachronism, especially to states reining in expenditure on international organizations in the post–Cold War world. From the OECD's standpoint, these two factors were interwoven. Fears that civil society, buoyed by its recent success and the OECD's vulnerability, could inflict further injuries on the OECD, imperilling not just individual missions but the organization's place in the architecture of global governance, were not unfounded. For example, in 1996 the OECD embarked upon its Harmful Tax Competition (HTC) initiative, which aimed to deter tax dodging by improving the transparency of national tax systems and making mandatory upon request the exchange of information about foreign investors. Libertarian think tanks, MNCs, and the tax planning industry rallied to the defence of the status quo, and between 1998 and 2000, utilized techniques analogous to those that vanquished the MAI to extract concessions from the OECD (Webb 2004; Woodward 2006b). Despite being trimmed of its more swingeing clauses, the project survived. In the new millennium, civil society fought the HTC by preying on another OECD vulnerability, namely, the issue of funding. Some of the most strident critics of the HTC came from the Coalition for Tax Competition, an alliance of (mainly US) think tanks, with the Center for Freedom and Prosperity (CF&P) in the vanguard. In 2004, pressure from the CF&P (see Center for Freedom and Prosperity 2004) led then chair of the Senate Budget Committee John Gregg to supplement the spending bill with a provision withholding OECD funding pending the suspension of projects antithetical to US interests. This stipulation was lost, but in February 2006, with the HTC again in the foreground and an OECD delegation rattling the collection plate in Washington, the CF&P wrote to Office of Management and Budget director Joshua Bolten, urging "that the Administration should strongly consider eliminating or at least dramatically reducing funding to the OECD" (Center for Freedom and Prosperity 2006). The US supplies a quarter of the OECD's budget, and with the organization's work program strained by savage cutbacks since the mid-1990s, the wishes of its biggest benefactor cannot be dismissed.

Paradoxically, the MAI affair brought into relief the aforementioned benefits to be accrued by IGOs from constructive relations with civil society. The MAI had its detractors but large segments of civil society were sympathetic to the OECD's agenda and could advertise the organization's assets, correct misunderstandings, and advocate OECD initiatives in domestic polities. Civil society could alleviate pressures on the budget by helping to implement or monitor OECD schemes. Finally, civil society could bring expertise and fresh perspectives to the OECD, inspiring pioneering projects central to the organization's competitive advantage.

Towards "Complex Multilateralism": OECD/Civil Society Relations in the Post-MAI Period

In 1996, the Ministerial Meeting exhorted the OECD's newly anointed Secretary-General, Donald Johnston, "to accelerate the process of structural change in the Organization ... with a view to further enhancing the relevance, efficiency and effectiveness of the Organization" (OECD 1996a). To attain this, Johnston argued, required a reform program involving internal restructuring, possible enlargement, and modifications to the OECD's dealings with non-members, including civil society (OECD 1997a). The MAI imbroglio lent impetus to Johnston's campaign and forced the OECD to shelve anodyne rhetoric about "inclusion" and "reaching out" to stakeholders in favour of concrete action to promote communication, dialogue, and participation with civil society (West 2005). The reforms have not dislodged or seriously challenged states as the main actors at the OECD, but have unquestionably diversified the range of voices involved in the organization's policy processes and bred the novel institutional innovations emblematic of complex multilateralism.

Communication

The OECD already maintained avenues for communicating with civil society through the OECD visits program, parliamentary liaisons, OECD centres in Berlin, Washington, Mexico City, and Tokyo, and the bi-monthly *OECD Observer*. These mechanisms tended to be monopolized by elements of civil society already integrated into the OECD's decision-making circuitry. The poverty of existing approaches was amply exposed during the MAI negotiations. Vibrant and accessible anti-MAI websites sprang up daily, whereas the OECD took fourteen months from the leak of the draft MAI to construct a website endorsing its merits, and when it did, the website was laced with technocratic jargon.

Johnston elevated communications to the heart of OECD operations. In 1997, he inaugurated the Public Affairs and Communications (PAC) Directorate to supervise the OECD's corporate image, media relations, political liaison, and publishing activities. The PAC enunciated a communications strategy to deliver a coherent vision of the OECD "brand" to stakeholders. This ranges from the development of an organizational logo to processes for ensuring that contradictory messages cannot materialize from different directorates. The strategy also entails tailoring communications to specific audiences, such as expanding the availability of country-specific information and the numbers of multilingual publications and Web pages. Guidelines designed to reduce the proportion of classified OECD material and to speed declassification proved less effective (Blagescu and Lloyd 2006). Theoretically, most OECD documents should now be in the public domain, but in practice most documents are available only after six years and many, including those from peer reviews, are never made available.

Greater nuance now goes into *what* the OECD communicates. The inward- and backward-looking approach of the past, whereby OECD missives reported on meetings and publications that had already occurred, has been superseded by a forward- and outward-looking approach outlining how the OECD's efforts are thrusting an agenda forward and impacting on policy debates elsewhere (OECD 2006f). The OECD's primary communications tool is the website. The PAC has revamped the site and introduced a host of new features, including SourceOECD, an online repository of OECD statistics, databases, and publications, subscribed to wholly or in part by 4,700 institutions globally (OECD 2006h, 86); MyOECD, which enables surfers to adapt the OECD website to their needs; additional country websites (including many non-members); and features and resources designed especially for civil society groups, including a civil society newsletter, *CivSoc.*

Dialogue and Participation

The new communications strategy was designed to improve communications *from* the OECD *to* civil society, but if genuine dialogue was to be attained, developing channels for civil society communication *to* the OECD was equally important. TUAC and BIAC's extensive involvement during the revision of the Guidelines for Multilateral Enterprises (1998 to 2000) and the Principles of Corporate Governance (2003 to 2004) emphasized their unrelenting centrality to OECD decision making (OECD 2005c, 2006c). Alone, however, the BIAC/TUAC framework was ill suited to an emergent epoch characterized by issues transcending their class-based agendas. Additionally, engaging the OECD in a manner equivalent to that of BIAC or TUAC required resources and wherewithal beyond those available to all but the most sophisticated NGOs.

The OECD has established the Civil Society Coordinators Network, containing at least one spokesperson from each directorate, to facilitate exchanges and disseminate best practice about civil society dialogue (Blagescu and Lloyd 2006, 43). Nevertheless, each OECD committee can tweak the modalities of dialogue with civil society (OECD 2005c, 2). What follows is therefore not exhaustive, but conveys a flavour of the changes taking place. Arguably, the investment committee, CIME, has done the most to take civil society to its bosom. During the revisions to the Declaration on International Investment and Multinational Enterprises, CIME held the OECD's "first truly public consultation process" (Salzman 2005, 217). A brainstorming session with BIAC and TUAC and selected NGOs – including Oxfam, Friends of the Earth, the World Wide Fund for Nature (WWF), and the Northern Alliance for Sustainability (ANPED) – led to the circulation on the Internet of draft proposals for public comment. Moreover, the final agreement expressly established a monitoring role for civil society, entitling it to bring alleged breaches before NCPs. Connections established between civil society groups during the initial consultations eventually gave rise to a new civil society coalition, OECD Watch. Created in March 2003, OECD Watch is an alliance of 60 NGOs from 33 countries (including 23 NGOs from 16 non-OECD members) that aims to promote sustainable investment and corporate accountability. OECD Watch probes the efficacy of the Guidelines for Multilateral Enterprises through sitting on CIME's Roundtables on Corporate Responsibility and annual meetings with NCPs, and it liaises privately with CIME after each plenary session. Lastly, the organization is a valve between the OECD and wider civil society, disseminating information about the Guidelines to government, business, and NGOs and supplying them with the tools to bring cases before NCPs (OECD Watch 2005).

Elsewhere, the OECD's Trade Committee calendar includes an annual consultation with civil society, supplemented by sporadic invitations for civil society organizations to participate in conferences, symposia, and workshops hosted by the Trade Directorate (West 2005, 5), of which the Trade Committee is the leading body. Building on their links with civil society, the Environmental Policy Committee (EPOC) regularly consults with environmental NGOs. NGO participation is coordinated by the European Environmental Bureau (EEB), whose members include the WWF, Greenpeace, and Friends of the Earth. The EPOC has used the fringe meetings of major global conferences, such as the 2002 Earth Summit in Johannesburg, to get involved in the work of environmental NGOs. Likewise, Transparency International continues to assist the Directorate for Financial and Enterprise Affairs to monitor the Anti-Bribery Convention.

Hospitality for civil society in OECD committees has been complemented by new agencies, most notably the Global Forums initiated in 2001. Operating through irregular workshops and an annual plenary session, Global Forums provide a hub where a diversity of stakeholders from specific policy communities can probe transdisciplinary policy problems whose solutions require contributions from non-members and civil society. Ten Global Forums cover the fields of agriculture, competition, development, education, governance, international investment, knowledge economy, sustainable development, taxation, and trade. The latest Global Forum on Development, launched in 2006, exemplifies the outlook and philosophy. Its members are drawn from think tanks, international organizations, development banks, development agencies, foundations, the private sector, and civil society organizations from member and non-member states. The Global Forum is currently preoccupied with the issue of development finance, and will eventually address possible reforms to the global development architecture. This work is supported by DEFINE, a network of think tanks proficient in the problems of development finance (OECD 2006g).

Lastly, unremitting dialogue in OECD committees and Global Forums is accompanied by "multistakeholder summitry" (West 2005, 10-11) in the form of the Annual Forum, first convened in 2000. Billed as a venue for ministers, heads of international organizations, business, NGOs, and civil society to congregate and "impart and share information, improve communication and foster a climate of enlightened policy making," the Annual Forum precedes the Annual Ministerial Meeting and feeds into its deliberations. Each Annual Forum revolves around a core theme. The eight Annual Forums convened so far have drawn over 10,000 delegates from 100 countries (see Table 4.2) and have been lauded by Donald Johnston as a "landmark in the life of the organization" (Johnston 2001).

Complex Multilateralism in Action: Conclusions and Implications

The designations made under Article 12 are unchanged,[2] but with a more heterogeneous set of civil society actors regularly assuming more substantial roles across a wider range of policy areas (OECD 2005c, 2006d), the OECD conforms ever more to the rubric of complex multilateralism. The rapprochement in OECD/civil society relations is unlikely to set off major reverberations in global economic governance, however. Emulating the conclusions of O'Brien and colleagues (2000) about other MEIs, the changes wrought by complex multilateralism at the OECD are confined to institutional modifications, with few tangible changes in *ideas* or policy.

As was previously claimed, civil society is not only the sphere of hegemony accommodating to the prevailing order but also the sphere in which counter-hegemony can be forged. Moreover, "civil society is not just an assemblage of actors, i.e., autonomous social groups. It is also a realm of contesting ideas in which the intersubjective meanings upon which people's sense of 'reality' are based can become transformed and new concepts of the natural order of society can emerge" (Cox 1999, 10). As several other contributors to this volume attest, ideas are the currency in which the OECD principally deals. At present, far from showing a willingness to engage in this ideational battle, the OECD appears to be shunning it by systematically organizing in civil society groups sympathetic to neoliberal ideas and systemically organizing out those that are not. For example, to mollify opponents of its HTC proposals, the OECD sought extensive consultation with business groups and published a co-authored article with BIAC's leading tax expert. "From the perspective of critical groups which struggle to get any hearing at all in the OECD, this is the equivalent to consulting with the fox about policies to protect the henhouse" (Webb 2004, 812). BIAC is also implicated in defying alternative civil society agendas in areas such as export credits. NGOs have opposed OECD attempts to get non-members to apply its export credit disciplines, but BIAC is aggressively promoting this and its recommendations to the leadership of the OECD Export Credit Working Party have been warmly received (BIAC 2006a, 18). Superficially, the Annual Forum appears to be a radical departure that qualitatively and quantitatively expands OECD/civil society interactions. Scratch the veneer, however, and a pronounced prejudice in favour of Northern, conservative, and corporate social forces promptly appears. Of 914 speeches made to Annual Forums, 811 (88.6 percent) were by those hailing from OECD nations and just 13 were made by delegates from Africa (see Table 4.2). Speakers representing pro-capitalist, corporate interests (227) outnumber those from more socially or charitably orientated organizations (161) (see Table 4.3). These figures understate the bias towards corporate interests, as speakers from the media and, to a lesser extent, educational institutions are overwhelmingly pro-capitalist (*Economist, Financial Times,* and Bloomberg, for example) and the event is perennially sponsored

Table 4.2

OECD Annual Forums, 2000-7: Participants and speakers by country

	2000	2001	2002	2003	2004	2005	2006	2007	Total	%
Participants	1,000	1,500	1,200	1,400	1,250	1,250	1,400	1,550	10,550	
Speakers										
From OECD members	92	112	134	107	102	96	82	85	810	88.6
From non-OECD upper-middle income/ high income countries	8	5	7	3	3	4	5	4	39	4.3
From non-OECD lower-middle income countries	4	4	9	1	4	7	9	4	42	4.6
From non-OECD low income countries	4	6	4	1	1	5	1	1	23	2.5
Total	108	127	154	112	110	112	97	94	914	100.0

Note: Income brackets are those used by the World Bank. Some countries have moved between income brackets over time. The classifications refer to the income group the country was in at the time the Annual Forum took place.
Source: Derived from OECD Forum Speakers List for the years cited (http://www.oecd.org).

Table 4.3

OECD Annual Forums, 2000-7: Speakers by sector

	2000	2001	2002	2003	2004	2005	2006	2007	Total	%
OECD	12	13	17	13	5	6	7	10	83	9.1
National politicians/government officials/ international organization	32	33	40	31	46	35	31	22	270	29.5
Corporations	24	26	20	18	14	19	15	19	155	17.0
Business lobbies	12	12	14	7	3	7	6	11	72	7.9
Media	3	5	10	16	16	17	14	11	92	10.1
Educational institutions	5	9	16	9	9	9	10	5	72	7.9
Social/charitable organizations	19	29	29	18	17	19	14	16	161	17.6
Other	1	0	8	0	0	0	0	0	9	0.9
Total	108	127	154	112	110	112	97	94	914	100.0

Source: Derived from OECD Forum Speakers List for the years cited (http://www.oecd.org).

by corporate entities and business lobby groups. Overall, the Annual Forum is an institutional rather than ideological innovation where choirs of neo-liberal prophets congregate to extol the benefits of capitalist globalization. Those looking for evidence to substantiate Cox's assertion (1999, 12) that there is a "nascent historic bloc consisting of the most powerful corporate economic forces, their allies in government, and the variety of networks that evolve policy guidelines and propagate the ideology of globalization" need look no further than the Annual Forum.

A second factor limiting civil society's impact at the OECD is the discrepancy in levels of civil society penetration across the organization. Directorates concerned with more peripheral issues such as agriculture, the environment, and investment have been more receptive to social forces critical of OECD policies, albeit not stridently opposed to the OECD's overarching philosophy. Even here the sense is that their influence is marginal. Commenting on the guidelines on MNEs, OECD Watch (2005, 15) "believes that the legitimate expectations of civil society groups that participated in the 2000 revision of the Guidelines have not been met." Moreover, more critical forces have failed to pierce the Economic Policy Committee, the place where the real power of the OECD arguably resides. The EPC provides expert surveillance of the global economy and handles economic reviews of member and non-member states, and its reports are keenly anticipated by politicians and economic pundits alike. Its policy process is closed to interlopers, and even groups with more privileged access such as TUAC complain that this opacity and uniform viewpoints result in biased surveys that take insufficient account of the social dimensions of economic policy (TUAC 2005, 3).

Lastly, the executive head of a multinational economic institution is a key variable explaining its disposition towards civil society (O'Brien et al. 2000), and the elevation of Angel Gurría as Secretary-General of the OECD in June 2006 may be an ominous sign for civil society groups seeking to roll back the OECD's neoliberal agenda. During his stint as Mexico's minister of foreign affairs, Gurría was closely associated with the North American Free Trade negotiations. Later, as minister of finance and public credit, he became a financier's darling, attracting the unwanted sobriquet of "scissor hands" because of austerity measures he introduced to forestall a financial crisis. During the election process, Gurría pointedly refused to reply to TUAC's solicitations of his views about labour and social issues (*Financial Times* 2005), and his tenure has received a warm reception from BIAC (2006a, 2006b). Gurría's neoliberal predilections suggest a renewal of the OECD's acquaintance with the neoliberal creed and a continuation of the OECD's strategy of maintaining this hegemonic discourse through highly selective interactions with conservative social forces.

Notes

1 An assessment corresponding to the concept of flanking mechanisms for neoliberalism, developed by Graefe (2006) and used by other contributors to this volume.

2 Confidential correspondence with the Public Affairs and Communications Directorate.

5
Making Neo-Gramscian Sense of the Development Assistance Committee: Towards an Inclusive Neoliberal World Development Order
Arne Ruckert

> Contributing to global development is a key objective of the OECD. Its founding Convention calls upon the OECD to promote policies designed to contribute to sound economic expansion in member as well as non-member countries in the process of economic development.
> – *Making Poverty Reduction Work* (OECD 2000a)

The problem of economic development has been at the heart of the work of the Organisation for Economic Co-operation and Development ever since its establishment as the Organisation for European Economic Co-operation (OEEC) in 1948. From the start, the OECD has been engaged in development issues and has contributed in numerous ways to the ideas and practices that constitute the field of development cooperation. Despite the prominent role of the OECD within development cooperation, the role of its development arm, the Development Assistance Committee (DAC), in development has rarely been critically examined.[1] This chapter uses a neo-Gramscian framework to make sense of the DAC. From this perspective, the OECD, and DAC within it, forms part of an emerging transnational structure of authority (TSA) and, as such, features prominently in the making of an emerging transnational hegemonic power bloc.

This chapter critically examines the role of the OECD in the numerous changes that have crystallized in the field of development cooperation over the past five decades. It retraces the influence of the DAC on development discourse and practice, and argues that, at various conjunctures, the OECD has been instrumental in forging a consensus on international development policy. After illuminating some of the cornerstones in the development of the DAC, the chapter focuses on the role of the OECD in the articulation of a new policy consensus in the mid-1990s, thus contributing to the construction of the global development regime. This new consensus crystallized around three key initiatives: the promotion of international development targets (IDTs), country ownership of development policies, and poverty reduction strategies. The OECD played an important role in the forging of a novel world development order, one characterized by a modified neoliberal development regime with a markedly "inclusive" orientation.[2] As other chapters in this volume demonstrate, this attempt to move beyond traditional neoliberal policy advice is not limited to the field of development but also finds expression in the OECD's policy stance in a number of other areas.[3]

The chapter begins with a critical review of mainstream understandings of the OECD and introduces neo-Gramscian theory to address some of the shortcomings of mainstream approaches. The next section outlines the ways in which the DAC has left an imprint on development cooperation from its foundation in the early 1960s to the crumbling of the Washington Consensus. The bulk of the chapter focuses on the OECD's role in articulating an emerging inclusive neoliberal development regime in the mid-1990s and lays out some of the characteristics and contradictions of this regime.

Theorizing the OECD: From National to Transnational Consensus Formation

Mainstream approaches have adequately identified many of the key functions of the OECD within the global governance regime. As Richard Woodward suggests, the OECD is more than a "rich man's club," "think tank," or institutional body pooling statistical information and economic expertise.[4] Rather, it fulfills a number of prominent tasks in the global governance regime (Woodward 2004, 114). First, and most important, the OECD promotes cooperative solutions to problems by providing a space where governments can interact, discuss, deliberate, and settle on collective responses to identified problems, a practice discussed in the literature as legal governance (Woodward 2004, 115). While the OECD has no coercive apparatus that could be used to enforce common agreements and concords, peer review and surveillance nevertheless represent strong incentives to internalize agreed-upon frameworks and rules.

At the same time, the OECD plays a key role in the development of a shared identity among its member states, a process referred to by Martin Marcussen as "cognitive governance" (2004c, 120-23). The capacity to "enunciate a philosophy that stitches particular states together as imagined communities" thus represents the OECD's second main function (Woodward 2008, 6). As part of this process, the OECD diffuses shared knowledge structures and ideas, promoting converging views as to how policy problems ought to be confronted and thus participating in the formation of consensus. In the language of constructivists, the OECD is a space where intersubjective meanings emerge through the repeated social interactions of its member states, and where social identities and realities are constructed.[5] Finally, the

OECD has played a key role in agenda setting in the international policy sphere. As Woodward notes, the OECD has often been the first international body to investigate pressing policy issues, and many key international policy initiatives originate with the OECD (2008, 10). This can be seen not only in the sphere of development, as demonstrated in this chapter, but also in other policy fields, such as education, health, and social policy.[6]

While mainstream approaches have accurately identified many of the ways in which the OECD participates in the global governance regime, they have not paid enough attention to the kinds of policies and ideas being promoted, nor have they probed who predominantly benefits from the policies pursued by international organizations (IOs). In short, mainstream approaches have effectively assumed that struggles over policy directions within the OECD take place within a level playing field, and thus have been agnostic about the particular interests being promoted though international organizations and the ways in which ideas can be used by social forces in a strategically selective way so as to achieve desired results (Bieler 2001, 96). A neo-Gramscian framework can address some of the shortcomings of mainstream approaches and shed light on the policy shifts within the DAC in the mid-1990s, from the market-radical Washington Consensus towards the inclusive neoliberal Post–Washington Consensus.[7]

Neo-Gramscians suggest that the emergent transnational social forces are engaged in an attempt to promote a hegemonic neoliberal world development order and that IOs are a crucial element in this consensus-making project.[8] Here hegemony is not understood in the realist way, where it amounts to the (generally military) domination of one country over others, but rather derives from Gramsci's usage of the term. For Gramsci, hegemony refers to a political process where domination is not based solely on economic and thus material power but is also a function of its ability to provide cultural and ideological leadership, offering an integrated system of values and beliefs that is supportive of the established social order and projects the particular interests of the dominant social forces as the general interest of all members (Egan 2001, 75-76). Hegemonic power cannot be imposed on subordinate social forces but must be secured in a process of negotiation, in which consent is engendered through material incentives and social compromises, and where the dominant ideology is organically linked to the life experiences and world views of subaltern social forces (Robinson 2006, 80). Hegemony is thus in constant flux, never complete, and as such is always open to multiple contestations.

In periods marked by hegemonic governance, international organizations play a key role in the reproduction of historical structures, and they feature prominently in the organization of consent within non-hegemonic structures. The key functions of IOs in this process have been partly identified by mainstream approaches that highlight the legal and cognitive governance functions. These ignore, however, other aspects that need to be included to provide a more holistic account of the OECD's role in global governance. In his seminal article "Gramsci, Hegemony and International Relations," Robert Cox lists five elements vital to understanding the operation of hegemony through international institutions. International institutions help to (re-)produce hegemony, because "(1) they embody the rules which facilitate the expansion of hegemonic world orders; (2) they are themselves the product of the hegemonic world order; (3) they ideologically legitimate the norms of the world order; (4) they co-opt the elites from peripheral countries; and, (5) they absorb counter-hegemonic ideas" (1983, 172). The last three elements in particular will be used to shed light on the rethinking that went on within the DAC in the mid-1990s.

From a neo-Gramscian perspective, the current neoliberal world order must be seen as a non-hegemonic order, one increasingly characterized by the use of coercion in the reproduction of neoliberal social relations and the resolution of conflicts.[9] In the development field, non-hegemony is best exemplified by the growing unwillingness of developing country governments to voluntarily implement structural adjustment policies (SAPs), and by the rapidly growing opposition to neoliberal restructuring in developing countries, such as in the "IMF riots" and anti–World Bank street marches.[10] The OECD's initiative to promote a more poverty-sensitive neoliberal development regime in the mid-1990s can thus be read as an attempt to produce hegemony around a slightly modified, "inclusive" neoliberal world development order, or, to use Gramsci's language, as an instance of *tranformismo*.

By co-opting counter-hegemonic ideas, such as civil society participation and poverty reduction, the DAC attempts to appease the critics of the neoliberal mantra of commodification and liberalization. More importantly, the DAC members put pressure on developing countries to increase social spending in areas such as health care and education within the context of poverty reduction strategies. Such strategies provide (though arguably scant) material incentives to the subaltern social forces to prop up support for SAPs in the developing world. To put the rethinking that went on inside the DAC in the 1990s in historical perspective, the next section outlines the ways in which the DAC influenced the governance of international development during the hegemonic postwar embedded-liberal order.

From the Beginnings of the DAC to the Unmaking of the Washington Consensus

The birth of the DAC in 1961 marked the beginning of a long process of OECD engagement with development issues. As Goran Ohlin (1967, 235) notes, concerns with development have always featured prominently in the core work of the OECD. In fact, the main mandate of the OEEC, the organizational precursor to the OECD, was to coordinate postwar European development efforts. The OECD's formation coincided with the start of the United Nations' Development Decade. Not surprisingly, the newly created OECD formed a Development Assistance Group (DAG) in 1960, which was renamed the Development Assistance Committee (DAC) a year later. The Marshall Plan's success in Western Europe created considerable (and perhaps excessive) optimism regarding the prospects for helping developing countries catch up to the industrialized countries through external assistance. As Plumptre notes, the US administration also "hoped to encourage greater participation by European countries in programs of economic aid to developing countries" so as to share some of the burdens of development cooperation (1977, 131).

The DAC is the principal body through which the OECD deals with issues related to development cooperation, and it has played a critical role in structuring the development field (Wolfe 1993, 48). Although the DAC has no funds of it own and does not administer any development programs, DAC countries provide over 90 percent of all official development assistance to developing countries. One of the DAC's main achievements has been the evolution of codes of best practice, which member states are expected to observe in the implementation of development assistance. This attempt to harmonize assistance and to build hegemony around a particular policy paradigm is arguably the cornerstone of the DAC's agenda.

It should come as no surprise that critics have pointed to the lack of inclusion of developing country voices in the articulation of development policy consensus within the DAC. In fact, the DAC's foundation was highly controversial among developing countries, who favoured the creation by the UN of an international organization dedicated to development, which would be democratically controlled by all UN member states (Therrien 2002, 454). Following years of negotiation, under the lead of the US, the developed countries nevertheless went ahead and founded a development institution under the auspices of the OECD that would be tightly controlled by the West. This contributed to the consolidation of the asymmetrical power structure on which the international aid regime was erected, one that allowed the US to exert some control over the development policies of other Western states. In short, the DAC became an "exclusive club" where discussion was limited to a closed circle of Western experts, with the primacy of the US among "equals." By virtue of its modus operandi, the DAC put clear limitations on the notion of a North-South "partnership" in development policy making (Therrien 2002, 455).

In neo-Gramscian terms, the DAC was one institutional actor in the postwar embedded-liberal development order, in which a profound policy consensus prevailed regarding the necessary steps to be taken by developing countries to catch up to advanced economies. While this policy consensus integrated the dominant voices in the developed world, it also provided incentives to subordinate social forces in developing countries to acquiesce to the embedded-liberal consensus. International organizations, such as the OECD, were truly inter*national* organizations, but ones that predominantly represented the interests of the more powerful nation-states and the dominant social forces within them. The OECD also coordinated state behaviour on the international stage, thus contributing to the reproduction of the hegemonic embedded-liberal development order.

During the reign of the embedded-liberal development consensus, foreign aid approaches remained largely consistent with modernization theory, including elements of the predominant Keynesian paradigm. Development was equated with industrialization and the expansion of urban-based "modern" sectors at the expense of traditional rural sectors. The state was seen as a key actor in the area of infrastructural development, actively involved in the management of many aspects of the national economy. In turn, much of overseas development assistance ended up in state-directed infrastructural projects. While the market would be institutionally embedded and a strong state would step in whenever market failures would result in socially suboptimal outcomes, it was assumed that the benefits of capitalist accumulation would eventually trickle down and allow the poor to reap some of the benefits of development (Lairson and Skidmore 1997, 278).

In the 1960s and 1970s, numerous DAC publications articulated this view and the DAC was itself an important institutional space where this embedded-liberal consensus was promulgated and consolidated. There are, however, also more technical aspects on which the DAC clearly left its imprint during this period. For instance, in 1969 the DAC spearheaded the untying of bilateral development assistance at a DAC High Level Meeting in Tokyo (Fuhrer 1996, 22). The widely used concept of Official Development Assistance (ODA) was also launched from inside the DAC and, in the early 1970s, figures on ODA as a percentage of GDP were collected for the first time. This allowed the DAC to better oversee development assistance and to scold those governments that were not living up to their financial promises of 0.7 percent of ODA/GDP.

In the mid-1970s, there was a brief counter-hegemonic moment when the DAC showed mild support for the basic-needs approach that had been articulated in the World Bank under the leadership of Robert McNamara, and when the New International Economic Order (NIEO) was seriously being discussed inside the DAC (Fuhrer 1996, 30). These progressive political concerns quickly faded in the early 1980s, however, with the onset of the debt crisis and the ascendancy of market radicalism in the form of the Washington Consensus. Coincidentally, neoliberally minded elites took control of the two leading donor governments, the United States and Britain, leaving their undeniably strong imprints on the DAC and the wider development project.

During the 1980s and early 1990s, the DAC proceeded with a strong sense of certainty in promoting a particular set of market-oriented development policies that came to be known as the Washington Consensus. Proponents of this new consensus, such as the DAC, argued that previous approaches to development had not placed enough emphasis on encouraging markets forces and private enterprise. The basic policy prescriptions of this consensus are easily identifiable: privatization of state-controlled enterprises, liberalization of trade and finance, reduction of subsidies to welfare recipients, private sector promotion, and the elimination of regulations that discourage foreign direct investments. Access to concessional finance through the international financial institutions (IFIs) was made conditional upon the implementation of structural adjustment policies, reforms designed to reduce the state's role in the economy.[11]

Again, the DAC was instrumental in bringing about this shift in development discourse and practice, and, more generally, it participated in the promotion of neoliberal globalization. The committee provided strong support to many highly controversial World Bank publications, such as the *Berg Report* and the subsequent *Toward Sustained Economic Development in Sub-Saharan Africa* (Fuhrer 1996, 39). In these reports, the World Bank blamed African underdevelopment on corruption and government failure, arguing that heavy state intervention stifled economic growth, and prescribed market-unleashing reforms instead, such as the privatization of state-run companies and trade liberalization. Thus, the new consensus completely disregarded international structures of domination as the root causes of underdevelopment identified by dependency theory and acknowledged by the UN system in the 1970s.

It is important, however, to underscore that this policy consensus never achieved hegemonic status (in the Gramscian sense), and, during the 1990s, it was increasingly challenged by a multiplicity of counter-hegemonic voices occupying various social spaces in both developed and developing countries. This is not surprising, given the decline in living standards in many parts of the Third World during the heyday of the Washington Consensus. Between 1980 and 1989, the majority of developing countries actually experienced a drop in per capita GDP, and the overall levels of poverty have increased significantly over the last two decades (Therrien 2002, 457). Consequently, mainstream academics began to question the economic effects of structural adjustment programs on developing country economies, while civil society groups pointed to the immense social costs associated with adjustment policies.[12]

At the same time, previous and current employees began to rebel against "their international financial institutions," which, despite obvious failure, religiously continued to adhere to the policy prescription of the Washington Consensus (Chang 2002). In conjunction with the development of a new academic branch, the new institutional economics (NIE), these alternative voices promoted a profound rethinking of development processes. Once again, this originated inside the DAC and culminated in the publication of a number of key documents that articulate an emerging policy consensus around an inclusive neoliberal development model.

The DAC and the Making of an Inclusive Neoliberal World Development Order

Since the mid-1990s, a new aid consensus has been materializing in the development community, prompting some analysts to suggest that "far more than at any previous time in the last several decades, both donor and developing countries are in more general accord about the broad approaches required to foster sustained, poverty-reducing growth and development" (Sewell 1997, vii). The OECD played a decisive role in forging this new consensus with its 1996 milestone publication *Shaping the Twenty-First Century: The Contribution of Development Co-operation* (OECD 1996a). Expanding on a policy statement made in 1995 at a DAC ministerial meeting, the report stands out for a number of reasons. First, never before had a comprehensive program for action in development been formulated at so high a level. What is more, the degree of political buy-in among key development actors and agencies and the high-profile backing it received are arguably unprecedented in the history of development cooperation (Therrien and Lloyd 2000, 25). Finally, *Shaping the Twenty-First Century* puts forth a comprehensive road map addressing a uniquely wide range of social, economic, and political dimensions of development.

In line with neo-Gramscian theory, this most recent rethinking process inside the DAC needs to be understood in the context of fading support for the market-radical neoliberal project in a non-hegemonic world development order. Non-hegemony refers here, on the one hand, to the growing unwillingness of developing countries to implement structural adjustment policies, and, on the other hand, to the increasing social protests against certain elements of the neoliberal world development order, particularly the privatization of basic utilities and the liberalization of trade. In short, non-hegemony denotes the fact that large segments of world society feel politically and economically excluded, and as a consequence have started to engage in pronounced social struggles to make their exclusion visible. This resentment of neoliberal policy advice has not been restricted to the developing world, however. It has also found expression in significant social protests all over the developed world, such as in the "Battle of Seattle" in 1999, or during the Free Trade of the Americas Summit in Québec City and in the anti-G8 protests in Genoa in 2001.

The introduction of an inclusive neoliberal development model arguably represents an attempt to resolve some of the legitimacy problems and contradictions that neoliberal policies faced, particularly in the developing world. By absorbing counter-hegemonic voices and concerns, and by forging a transnational policy consensus through an inclusive neoliberal world development order, the DAC has managed to take some wind out of the sails of anti-neoliberal protests. Indeed, the inclusion of previously excluded people seems to be part of an effort to make the neoliberal project and its concomitant principles of privatization, liberalization, and deregulation truly hegemonic.

As two DAC representatives have recently put it, "strategies developed without inclusion are inherently weak. It is particularly important therefore to reach out to stakeholders, especially the very poor and marginalized, for otherwise crucial information held by excluded stakeholders may be ignored and implementation may be impeded because they do not feel that they own the strategy" (Smilie and Lecomte 2003, 14). Yet, this emerging inclusive neoliberal development regime also speaks to the power and agency of counter-hegemonic forces in developed and developing countries. These forces have pushed their own concerns for social inclusion onto the DAC's agenda and have been somewhat successful in transforming the world development order. From this perspective, the DAC is a moving target, a "moment of crystallization" of antagonistic social forces pulling in different directions, and not simply an instrument of the emerging transnational managerial elite in establishing a transnational hegemonic power bloc.

Poverty Reduction as Development Imperative
At the heart of the emerging inclusive neoliberal development regime lies a growing concern with poverty and exclusion among the key development agents. Important norms that entered the global development regime under the tutelage of the Post–Washington Consensus, and have consequently left an imprint on the practices of most development organizations, are empowerment and political participation of the poor, partnership and country ownership in development cooperation, and poverty reduction as the guiding principle of all development practice. Together, these norms signify the emergence of a neoliberal project of a markedly inclusive orientation. The Poverty Reduction Strategy (PRS) represents the most visible policy tool of this novel policy consensus.

The DAC was among the first development institutions to explicitly discuss the need for such inclusive development strategies. In *Shaping the Twenty-First Century,* it acknowledged that the number of people living in absolute poverty and despair was growing rapidly, and that "those of us in the industrialized countries have a strong moral imperative to respond to the extreme poverty and human suffering that still afflict more than one billion people" (DAC 1996, 1). The same report marked a milestone in the Herculean task of poverty reduction through the articulation of international development targets (IDTs), later renamed by the United Nations "Millennium Development Goals" (MDGs), while the content of the goals remained largely the same. As Chapter 12 highlights, the DAC showed important leadership in the development of the MDGs because its members thought it was time "to select, taking account of the many targets discussed and agreed at international fora, a limited number of indicators of success by which our efforts can be judged" (DAC 1996, 2). Although the targets can rightly be criticized for not being aspiring enough,[13] it is nevertheless clear that the DAC has performed a crucial task by setting a benchmark in the form of seven quantifiable goals by which the performance of international development agencies can be evaluated (White and Black 2003, 1). These include the following goals, which are to be achieved by 2015: (1) the proportion of people living in extreme poverty in developing countries should be reduced by at least one-half; (2) universal access to primary education should be achieved in all countries; and (3) the death rate for infants and children under the age of five should be reduced in each developing country by two-thirds, and the rate of maternal mortality by three-fourths of the 1990 levels (DAC 1996, 9-11).

Development Partnerships and Country Ownership
The DAC has also proposed a new way of doing business with developing countries, putting forth the notion of an open and mutually beneficial partnership between developed and developing countries: "Acceptance of the partnership model, with greater clarity in the roles of partners, is one of the most positive changes we are proposing ... Paternalistic approaches have no place in this framework" (DAC 1996, 13). This also implies locally owned development strategies that directly address the idiosyncratic and contextually specific problems identified by developing countries themselves. In other words, developing countries are supposed to be in the driver's seat, owning and devising their idiosyncratic development strategies. As the DAC maintains, "these goals [the IDTs] must be pursued country by country through individual approaches that reflect local conditions and locally-owned development strategies" (DAC 1996, 2).

The ideas of ownership and partnership address deep-rooted problems that had been identified earlier by the DAC and other international institutions: the unwillingness of many developing country governments to voluntarily implement structural adjustment policies, and the subsequent failure of policy conditionality, conditions that speak to the non-hegemonic nature of neoliberal development policy. While many Southern governments have paid lip service to structurally adjusting their economies, they have often not followed through with the implementation of many of the most highly contested policies, in particular utility privatizations. Nor have they always met policy conditionalities. As the World Bank elaborated in a statement released to the media in 1999, "conditionality has been unsuccessful:

governments fail to deliver on promised reforms and actually hold back from reform in the hope of being able to 'sell' the reforms to donors for a higher price – or a second time (cited in Cammack 2004, 201).

In this context, the new partnership is seen by the DAC as a way to make development cooperation more effective and efficient, and ownership is expected to contribute to a genuine commitment to implementing inclusive neoliberal adjustment policies. What is unique about the inclusive neoliberal model, then, is that it contributes to the DAC member countries' recognition that a strong consensus around policies in the developing world will make the implementation of neoliberal adjustment policies less contentious and more probable. This realization has been articulated poignantly by the International Monetary Fund (IMF) in a policy paper on country ownership: "Ownership matters because it directly affects program implementation ... When the program is owned by the country, decisions on such actions are likely to be made quickly and in support of the program, which makes it more likely that the program will succeed. Furthermore, ownership will make it easier to generate domestic political support for the program, since it is likely to be seen, at least in part, as an indigenous product, rather than a foreign imposition" (2001, 14).

In a similar fashion, Joseph Stiglitz, former chief economist of the World Bank and the main architect of the Post–Washington Consensus, explained that "policies that are imposed from the outside may be grudgingly accepted on a superficial basis, but rarely will be implemented as intended" (1998, 21). Moreover, "there is likely to be greater acceptance of reforms – and a greater participation in the transformation process – if there is a sense of equity, of fairness, about the development process, a sense of ownership derived from participation, and if there has been an effort at consensus formation" (Stiglitz 1998, 22). Ownership should help to make development aid more effective and efficient. According to the World Bank, the "single most important theme running through the dialogue on development effectiveness is the need to put committed developing country governments and their people at the center of their development process" (quoted in Abrahamsen 2004, 1455).

The inclusive neoliberal model can help to create mutual relationships of trust between donors and developing country governments, which, in turn, translate into growing commitment to reform processes on behalf of developing country governments. This instrumental view of ownership raises concerns as to what are the real intentions behind the introduction of partnerships and country ownership.

The Neoliberal in Inclusive Neoliberalism

The newfound emphasis on poverty reduction and country ownership has been widely welcomed among the development community and within civil society. What is certainly problematic about this emerging inclusive neoliberal consensus is that inclusion concerns continue to be circumscribed by a macroeconomic framework that does not stray substantially from earlier neoliberal ideals. Thus, in *Shaping the Twenty-First Century*, the DAC reminded developing countries that they have the responsibility to "adhere to appropriate macroeconomic policies" and "carry out sound financial management, including efficient tax systems and productive public expenditure" (DAC 1996, 15). This clearly relativizes any notion of country ownership and raises a number of uncomfortable questions regarding the degree to which countries truly own their development policies.

What is more, the DAC members have spelled out in great detail what they expect macroeconomic policies to look like in the *Sourcebook for Poverty Reduction Strategies* (Klugman 2002a, 2002b).[14] The donor community highlights that these are supposed to be guidelines only, representing "technical knowledge" and "best practices" (Klugman 2002b, 2). It is not surprising, however, that most developing countries have closely adhered to these policy guidelines and that Poverty Reduction Strategy Papers (PRSPs) generally portray macroeconomic frameworks similar to those pursued during the era of structural adjustment.[15] Thus, while developing countries are expected to commit to the laudable goals of poverty reduction and civil society participation, this takes place within the parameters of a slightly modified neoliberal macroeconomic framework that is full of internal contradictions and that had been established prior to the development of national PRSPs.

This can best be exemplified through a discussion of the policy advice given to developing countries in areas such as budgetary and fiscal policy, trade liberalization, and utility privatization. When it comes to the budgetary process, the *Sourcebook* highlights the need for government spending to be prudent and anti-inflationary while also poverty-sensitive. Sensitivity to poverty can be discerned in the emphasis given to health and education sectors in most poverty reduction strategies, and the subsequent growth in health and education expenditure in many developing countries (Driscoll and Evans 2005). At the same time, governments are expected to invest in a prudent manner, without risking the resurgence of macroeconomic instability. Macroeconomic prudence is defined in terms of current-account and fiscal balances with low and declining debt levels and inflation in the low single digits, whereas unsound policies are understood to encompass large current-account deficits financed by short-term borrowing, high and rising levels of public debt, and double-digit inflation rates (Klugman 2002b, 5-8).

As UNCTAD has recently argued, this unwavering commitment to tight monetary policy is problematic, as it might translate into lower-output growth and higher levels of unemployment, and therefore undermine the attempt to reduce poverty through economic growth and poverty-sensitive budgets (UNCTAD 2002a, 24). Moreover, inflation targeting substantially reduces the policy options that developing countries can resort to in times of economic recession, such as deficit spending and credit expansion. Finally, there might be a conflict between the goals of poverty reduction and inflation targeting, as the later circumscribes the extent to which governments can spend freely on poverty-related causes.

According to the *Sourcebook,* an important long-term goal for most developing countries in the fiscal realm is "to raise domestic revenue levels with a view to providing additional revenue in support of their poverty reduction strategies" (Klugman 2002b, 13). Growth in public revenues is instrumental in allowing developing countries to increase their overall levels of social spending, particularly as external resources currently used in the fight to reduce poverty will dry up once the Enhanced Heavily Indebted Poor Countries (HIPC II) and the Multilateral Debt Relief Initiative (MDRI) have been fully implemented. Unfortunately, the *Sourcebook* embraces a regressive tax regime with a broad tax base and moderate marginal tax rates in the effort to raise domestic revenue.

The "most efficient tax systems" available generally include "a broad-based consumption tax, such as a VAT, preferably with a single rate, minimal exemptions, and a threshold to exclude smaller corporations from taxation," while "the personal income tax should be characterized by only a few brackets and a moderate marginal tax rate" (Klugman 2002b, 13). As UNCTAD has recently pointed out, the tax regime described by the DAC members as the "most efficient tax regime" is a highly regressive tax system, in which poverty is arguably being augmented through the negative side effects of consumption taxes on the poor (UNCTAD 2002a, 27). Even the World Bank has recently suggested that (generally regressive) indirect taxes tend to increase poverty. This did not, however, lead it to question regressive taxes in favour of higher direct income and business taxes. The latter could play an important role in the progressive redistribution of income and assets in developing countries with high levels of inequality. Instead, the World Bank maintains that the negative effects of regressive taxes should be temporarily offset through the expenditure system (Klugman 2002b, 14).

Here again, there seems to be a contradiction between the goal of poverty reduction and the actual policy advice given to developing countries in the area of taxation. The recommendations emerging in the area of taxation under the inclusive neoliberal development world order, rather than contributing to poverty reduction, have the potential to substantially worsen the situation of the poor, depending on the kinds of compensation policies that accompany the introduction of indirect consumption taxes. Thus, while there is a strong emphasis on poverty-related government spending in the fiscal realm, which arguably distinguishes the inclusive neoliberal from the neoliberal development regime, this extra money channelled towards the poor could be wiped out by increased tax burdens through the introduction of indirect consumption taxes.

The liberalization of trade has been a particularly thorny and contested issue within the development community over the last decades. The DAC and the IFIs have recently acknowledged that previous liberalization efforts have in some cases created unnecessary hardship among the poorest and weakest segments of society during the adjustment process. Consequently, the DAC members now propose that liberalization be accompanied by compensation measures that temporarily insulate the poor from the vagaries of liberalized markets. At the same time, the donor community seems to hold on to the notion that trade liberalization is inherently good for economic growth and development, despite the lack of a substantial consensus on the issue within academic circles. As the DAC suggests in a recent study on poverty reduction: "Studies have found that countries that do the most by eliminating or reducing distortions and discriminatory practices, register larger welfare gains relative to others. Greater efforts to liberalise trade could significantly enhance trade flows and welfare: these include further rationalising non-tariff policies and reducing transaction costs generated by inefficient import and export procedures" (OECD 2000a, 9).

This "technical knowledge" is highly contested, and other international bodies, such as various UN organizations, and numerous academics have come to dramatically different assessments regarding the desirability of the liberalization of trade for developing countries. As critics of the neoliberal wisdom continue to point out, trade liberalization might in fact have contributed to the impoverishment of uneducated workers and concomitantly to growing inequality within developing countries (UNCTAD 1997, 1998; Stiglitz and Charlton 2005). Moreover, the countries that have developed rapidly over the last decades have not followed the standard advice of liberalization given to developing countries in the area of trade (see, for example, Wade 1990; Chang 2002; Stiglitz 2002). More broadly, the inclusive neoliberal regime acknowledges the possible negative side effects of trade liberalization and proposes mechanisms, such as social safety nets, to ameliorate those effects, without, however, granting developing countries the space to truly choose their own trade policy.

Utility privatization has become a key conditionality of development assistance during the era of structural adjustment, and it continues to be promoted under the inclusive neoliberal development regime. Indeed, many recent studies confirm that conditionalities linked to privatization have actually proliferated since the articulation of the inclusive neoliberal development project, despite notions of ownership and partnership (Jubilee Debt Campaign 2006). Nevertheless, there is significant discontinuity in the way in which the topic is being approached by the donor community.

For instance, much more emphasis is being placed on the need for an appropriate regulatory framework as a precondition for successful privatization. Moreover, the likely negative social implications of utility privatizations are acknowledged more openly, and the *Sourcebook* consequently calls for compensation measures if the poor are negatively affected by privatization, such as the cross-subsidization of water and electricity consumption (Klugman 2002b, 286). Nevertheless, developing countries are still pressured to further divest and privatize utility providers. It is unfortunate that such a delicate political issue as utility privatization should be the outcome of a fundamentally undemocratic process of external imposition of conditionalities, particularly given the current environment, in which partnerships and country ownership are touted as a cornerstone of the development regime.

The DAC and the Added Value of Neo-Gramscian Theory
This chapter has argued that the OECD is a significant actor in the global governance regime and has focused on the role of the Development Assistance Committee in the articulation of an emergent inclusive neoliberal development policy consensus in the mid-1990s. This inclusive neoliberal world development order contains a number of fundamental contradictions and constraints. Inclusive neoliberalism tries to integrate and engage previously excluded social forces, drawing them into a more inclusively oriented world development order, while adhering (closely) to the inherently exclusive neoliberal macroeconomic principles. It recognizes country ownership as imperative in achieving sustainable and stable outcomes in poverty reduction, but *ex ante* prescribes a narrow set of neoliberal macroeconomic policies and best practices.

Neo-Gramscian theory represents one possible (and plausible) theoretical tool to make sense of this recent shift in the DAC's development approach. From this perspective, the promotion of the inclusive neoliberal world development order needs to be located in the context of the ascendance of transnational social forces, the political project of neoliberal globalization advocated by such forces, and the different forms of counter-hegemonic struggles and social resistance that it engendered. The OECD is only one agent among a host of international institutions that, in a complementary manner, have participated in the promotion of a neoliberal world order; nevertheless, it has played a key role. The initial neoliberal project ran into serious trouble in the 1990s and counter-hegemonic policies have been articulated and counter-practices carried out at a number of levels, first within civil society and later by those UN institutions not fully subservient to the neoliberal project.

Some of these progressive ideas have been absorbed and co-opted by the DAC and turned into tools of hegemony building in the attempt to engender an inclusive neoliberal policy consensus that deviates somewhat from the OECD's earlier neoliberal policy advice. In this process, a number of welcome progressive policy shifts have materialized that represent important first steps towards moving beyond neoliberal forms of governance in the world development order. These findings are in line with the arguments made by other contributors to this volume, which similarly suggest that the OECD no longer simply adheres to the traditional neoliberal wisdom, particularly in the field of social policy.[16]

In this respect, the DAC is more than just an instrument of transnational social forces in their quest to subjugate the whole planet to the rule of market forces, as some neo-Gramscians would suggest.[17] In fact, neo-Gramscians have arguably exaggerated the coherence of the neoliberal project and overestimated the extent to which international institutions such as the DAC are monolithic entities. As indicated earlier, the DAC itself is part of a larger state/society complex that surrounds it, and thus is not autonomous, nor is it insulated from social struggles that take place in its social environment. Rather, it should be conceived of as a social relation, a moment of crystallization and condensation of antagonistic social forces. This also implies the need to historicize our understanding of international organizations and to acknowledge the contradictions and unevenness that surround the ascendance of transnational authority structures such as the OECD.

As Daniel Egan has accurately noted, there is no guarantee that transnational social forces "have it their way" in the international political arena. The transnationalization of political authority is a highly contested process with no fixed outcome and is possibly reversible (Egan 2001, 92). In other words, the DAC does not lie outside the realm of ongoing social and political struggles and is part of a social reality that is permanently contested and, as Gramsci notes, "a relation of forces in continuous motion and shift of equilibrium" (Gramsci 1971, 172). The recent rearticulation of the development regime by the DAC in the form of a more inclusively oriented neoliberal world development order constitutes but one example of the (open) negotiation process during which social forces struggle over the form and content of transnational authority structures.

Nor is compliance with DAC guidelines guaranteed, despite the fact that DAC member countries control the vast majority of the financial resources disbursed to developing countries, and despite the emergence of a nascent inclusive neoliberal policy consensus. This, however, should not prompt us to underestimate the importance of the DAC in the global development regime. The DAC forms part of a complex web of international organizations that have been essential to the globalization of economic and social relations and whose prescriptions have been tremendously influential, particularly in financially dependent developing countries. It has contributed to the formation of a transnational order despite the absence of coercive mechanisms that would enable the DAC to impose its policies and enforce agreed-upon rules. Indeed, because of this inability to impose its will, the DAC may be the ideal social space within which to articulate and organize a hegemonic development policy consensus and to pass off the particular interests (of transnational social forces and capital) that continue to be deeply embedded in the inclusive neoliberal development regime as the general interest of the majority of the poor in developing countries. The scant material incentives given to subaltern social forces through inclusion processes, and the lack of organic grounding of inclusive neoliberal ideology in the world views of the poor majority, however, make it unlikely that a truly hegemonic inclusive neoliberal development order will materialize on a global scale.

Notes

1   For two outdated accounts of the OECD that discuss the DAC, see Aubrey (1967) and Ohlin (1967). The more recent scholarship on the OECD includes Wolfe (1993), Armingeon and Beyeler (2004), and Woodward (2004).
2   For scholarship on inclusive neoliberalism, see Craig and Porter (2006); Ruckert (2006, 2007); and Macdonald and Ruckert (forthcoming).
3   See, in particular, Chapters 12 and 14.
4   See also Salzman and Terracino (2006).
5   For a constructivist reading of the OECD, see Chapter 2.
6   On the OECD's agenda-setting role in these areas, see Chapters 12 and 13.
7   For the rapidly expanding neo-Gramscian literature, see Cox (1983, 1986, 1987); Gill (1990); Murphy (2000); Rupert (1995); Bieler and Morton (2004); and Robinson (2004).
8   See also Chapter 13, which highlights the OECD's attempt to achieve world hegemony in the education policy field.
9   Stephen Gill (1993, 2000), for example, argues that the current transnational historic bloc is increasingly characterized by supremacy, taking the place of hegemony. Where hegemonic orders are inclusive and intend to incorporate subordinate interests, supremacist strategies rely more openly on coercion and seek to develop domination over apparently scattered and atomized sets of interests. For an argument that stresses the increasing prevalence of coercion in North-South relations, see Soederberg (2006).
10   The growing resistance to neoliberal capitalism is cogently discussed by Prempeh (2006). See also Gills (2000).
11   For the initial formulation of the Washington Consensus, see Williamson (1990).
12   For a discussion of the disappointing results of structural adjustment, see Stiglitz (2002) and Bienefeld (2000). For a persuasive critique of SAPs by civil society actors, see SAPRIN (Structural Adjustment Participatory Review International Network) (2003).
13   The development targets would simply be achieved if all developing countries experienced 3 percent of GDP growth per capita until 2015. Moreover, critics have noted that the original goal of the NGO campaign has been to eradicate poverty completely, not to reduce it to levels that are tolerable.
14   While both volumes of the *Sourcebook* are edited by Jeni Klugman, the individual chapters are predominantly written by World Bank and IMF staff and contain policy advice to developing countries on how to achieve poverty reduction in a sustainable manner.
15   See, for example, Gottschalk (2005), UNCTAD (2002a), and Mouelhi and Ruckert (2007).
16   See Chapters 12 and 14. My contribution differs from Mahon's argument in Chapter 14 about inclusive liberalism, however, in that I conceptualize inclusive neoliberalism as a mutation of second-generation neoliberalism, and therefore see more continuity than discontinuity in the DAC's approach to development. Mahon, on the other hand, asserts that

inclusive liberalism is a new policy paradigm that needs to be treated not just as a hybridization of neoliberalism but as a separate approach, since it departs from neoliberalism in many important ways.

17 For an insightful article that problematizes the neo-Gramscian tendency to totalize hegemony, see Kenny and Germain (1998). For a similar critique, see also Macdonald (1994).

Part 2: Governance and Economies

6
The OECD and Foreign Investment Rules: The Global Promotion of Liberalization
Russell Alan Williams

> From its earliest days, member governments have used the OECD
> as a forum for systematically reducing the extent of their restrictions
> on international capital controls of all kinds.
> – David Henderson, "The Role of the OECD in
> Liberalising Trade and Capital Flows" (1996)[1]

The collapse of the Organisation for Economic Co-operation and Development's Multilateral Agreement on Investment (MAI), which would have seriously curtailed states' powers to regulate foreign investment to serve domestic policy goals, was variously represented as a victory for the "anti-globalization" movement, as a victory for Internet technology–based transnational civil society, or simply as a symbol of the shallowness of international support for neoliberalism (Smythe 2001; Deibert 2000; Wood 2000). Unfortunately, it has also appeared to entrench the view of the OECD as a less important organization in global economic governance. When the MAI is placed in a broader historical context, in which the OECD has devoted decades to a neoliberal campaign to remove domestic barriers to foreign investment, a different picture emerges. This chapter argues that the OECD has contributed to the construction of an international investment regime to promote free movement of capital. The OECD has been at the centre of international activities to remove barriers on foreign investment since its inception.

Theorizing the OECD's role in promoting a global investment regime is a difficult task. Liberal constructivist approaches highlight the role of international organizations in generating identities and norms that affect state policy choice (Chapter 2), while critical global political economy approaches focus on the role of international organizations in transnational class formation (Chapter 5). Both suggest that organizations like the OECD are increasingly important policy sites. In these literatures, the staffers of international organizations, such as the OECD's committees and Secretariat, are variously portrayed as "moral entrepreneurs" or "organic intellectuals," opportunistically redefining the logic of appropriate domestic policy choices via their international surveillance and policy review activities. International organizations are seen to "teach" states to value certain policy goals. Public policy scholarship has similarly grappled with this phenomenon, probing the role of organizations like the OECD in policy formulation and agenda setting. Others are skeptical of claims that "moral suasion" or "norms" affect policy outcomes, arguing that detailed national case studies illustrating how these norms enter and affect domestic decision making are required (see Chapter 10). While the effect of OECD activity on investment liberalization on national policy cannot be explored here, this chapter will detail the way that the OECD has consciously set out to redefine the logic of appropriate policy choices in regulating investment. As a result, it has created a normative framework supporting liberalization and established procedures and principles that help commit states to progressive liberalization.

While in theory the OECD is a member-driven organization whose commitments should be guided by the aggregated policy goals of member states, in practice the OECD's work on investment has been far more political, promoting one set of ideologically driven goals as "best practice" with regard to investment policy. In the broadest terms, the OECD is dominated by economists committed to an organizational discourse of (neo)liberal economics (Dostal 2004). Inured to other viewpoints, the organization has demonstrated a long-term commitment to "selling" its perspectives on global economic governance. As such, it is often out in front of the governments it ostensibly represents.

OECD Institutions and Investment Governance

Since its establishment in 1961, the OECD has supported the development of binding mechanisms to limit states' powers to regulate capital flows. Two of its founding agreements, the Code of Liberalization of Capital Movements and the Code of Liberalization of Current Invisible Operations, were intended to help achieve this, despite the prevailing support for capital controls in the Bretton Woods monetary system (Helleiner 1994) and existing "embedded liberal" support for national policy autonomy in financial arrangements. With the failure of the MAI, these codes remain the world's only truly multilateral instruments for the liberalization of capital movements (OECD 2002b).

The broad connections between a wide array of domestic policy networks and OECD committees strengthen competencies in the OECD and make it perhaps the only international institution capable of dealing with the politically thorny problem of liberalizing investment barriers. Barriers to investment such as sectoral ownership restrictions in key service sectors such as banking and telecommunications are embedded in domestic policy networks with their own complex policy styles. While the trade regime has proven to be less than effective in getting national governments to commit to liberalizing these barriers, the OECD has firsthand knowledge of the complexity of the regulations involved and the political arrangements that have generated them. While OECD investment initiatives have often been overambitious, the OECD is the international organization best suited to handle negotiations on liberalizing barriers like these.

In terms of instruments, the two codes are both, in theory, legally binding, although, as will be discussed, there are practical limitations to how enforceable they might be. Another important mechanism is the National Treatment Instrument, which is a non–legally binding declaration agreed to in 1976. The National Treatment Instrument codified the application of non-discrimination principles drawn from the trade regime with regard to foreign investment. It does not have the same legal standing as the codes, although it does largely clarify principles that exist in the latter.

Oversight and revision of the codes, along with the ongoing OECD surveillance activities of national investment restrictions, have historically been the preserve of the Committee on Capital Movements and Invisible Transactions and the Committee on International Investment and Multinational Enterprises.[2] Despite constant turnover on the committees, perhaps reflecting the selection of committee members from national finance departments in particular, both committees have had a long-standing commitment to more liberal orientations towards investment flows than has been the case in other organizations. In fact, David Henderson, who was head of the Economics and Statistics Department of the OECD from 1984 to 1992, argues in his various "insider's" analyses of the committees' work that they saw the promotion of wholesale investment liberalization as the purpose of their work.

In terms of method, the OECD promotes liberalized investment flows in a number of ways. First, in the "inquisitive" mode of governance (Jacobsson 2006), the OECD engages in policy research and review, codifying restrictions to international investment and censuring states that have been slow to abandon barriers. The purpose is to either pressure individual states into reducing investment barriers or to arm domestic advocates of liberalization with credible arguments supporting their position in policy debates. Indeed, the OECD argues that its research activities and committee work support economic liberalization by providing a forum for discussing common problems encountered by officials, by providing technical information on the policies and strategies of other governments to the organization's members, and by lending support in committee discussions to policy proposals that would advance the economic interests of member states but that are politically difficult to carry out:

The OECD approach does not rely on dogma or political negotiation, nor on detailed prescriptive recommendations for policy implementation. Instead it involves a process of shared, mutually beneficial learning, where both individual and collective stumbling blocks on the path to open markets are inspected and discussed. It has been found that peer pressure in a multilateral setting can provide strong incentives for authorities to undertake policy adjustment. By "benchmarking" domestic regulations and measures against those implemented by peer participants in this process, countries receive guidance and support in the complex area of financial liberalization. (OECD 2002b)

Second, the OECD has also been extremely proactive, displaying a problem-solving, or "meditative," approach to liberalization. Much of the OECD's work on investment has been geared towards exploring and developing policy instruments and international norms that make it easier for states to engage in liberalization. Its leadership in promoting the application of trade regime principles to investment functions is a good example of this approach. Third, the OECD does have negotiated, legally binding rules that require investment liberalization. This will be discussed in the next section, but it is important to recognize that this is somewhat different from other OECD policy areas, where there are no binding instruments and the organization's role in global governance is necessarily more discursive (Djelic and Sahlin-Andersson 2006a). Fourth, the OECD has supported these formal investment initiatives with other projects that also effectively support investment liberalization (see OECD 1998a). Its efforts to combat the risk of double taxation for multinational corporations is a good example of this (Webb 2004).

Finally, when it comes to investment, the OECD has historically attempted to broaden the coverage of its program to non-members. For example, OECD surveillance of investment barriers includes examination of non-members. Also, potential new members are required to bring their investment rules into compliance with the OECD. Starting with the MAI and continuing since, many leading developing nations have opted to participate in OECD negotiations and discussions on investment. The OECD views these efforts as a way to extend the benefits of the organization's expertise and experience to the developing world. It argues that non-members need to understand that when it comes to investment barriers, "there is now fairly general recognition of the distorting effects of such controls, in terms of sheltering financial institutions from foreign competition, weakening discipline on policy-makers, vesting unhealthy discretionary power with bureaucrats and inviting rent-seeking behaviour by privileged interest groups" (OECD 2002b).

These various activities are all valued by supporters of liberalization. Even member governments, often reluctant to implement the organization's proposals, have supported this work because "they simply recognize – though not without reservations of various kinds – that there would be benefits to all their countries, and indeed to the world as a whole, from moving to a more liberal international economic order. They use the Organization both as a means of identifying, reviewing and agreeing on specific ways of advancing in this direction, and as a mechanism by which departures from accepted liberal practice can be averted or kept within bounds" (Henderson 1996, 15).

Early OECD Investment Initiatives: Establishing the Ground Rules
There has been a tendency to treat the founding Code of Liberalization of Capital Movements and Code of Liberalization of Current Invisible Operations as "fluffy." There has been little examination of their provisions, as states were very reluctant to implement liberalized investment rules through the first twenty years of OECD activity (Griffith-Jones et al. 2000). Nonetheless, the codes created a framework for liberalization and clearly specified a mandate for OECD surveillance and "meditative" intellectual activity in this area. Both codes supported the notion that international financial transactions should be liberalized, and that barriers to investment that sheltered domestic economic interests should be removed to support the efficiency provided by a globally integrated financial market. Thus, the original OECD codes laid the groundwork for forty years of promoting the liberalization of investment flows.

It is difficult to explain why member states chose to do this, given the existing "embedded liberal" norms of the era. Since so little was written on the early days of the OECD, there simply is not much evidence to go on. One thing to keep in mind, however, is that while OECD members had previously established the International Monetary Fund (IMF) to actually oversee international finance in the postwar era (along anti–capital mobility lines) the IMF was technically given no mandate to involve itself in normative debates about capital account liberalization.[3] Thus, while the IMF had a direct role in overseeing global finance on an ideologically managed basis, OECD member states seem to have concluded that there was a need for an organization that might at the very least *discuss* liberalization over the longer term – a sort of "policy shop."

The codes were intended to be legally binding. Although members were initially given time to prepare their financial systems for liberalization (Henderson 1999, 63), now all members are bound "to notify the OECD of existing restrictions on foreign direct investment, capital movements and cross-border trade in services, not to introduce additional restrictions (except under specific conditions), to apply any measures without discrimination among OECD countries, and to submit themselves to a peer-review process that aims progressively to remove remaining restrictions over time" (Ley and Poret 1997, 38).

The codes were aimed at all barriers to foreign investment and capital movements. This included explicit capital controls that inhibited currency exchange and monetary flows, general restrictions on foreign direct and portfolio investment (inward and outward), and national sector-specific restrictions on foreign direct investment (FDI).

The OECD now claims that the codes' efforts to promote the removal of explicit national capital controls should be regarded as a long-term success. The codes progressively required the removal of barriers to an array of financial transactions that restricted portfolio investment and currency speculation. In 1961, the codes bound states to liberalize personal capital movements and underlying financial transactions that facilitated foreign investment. By the 1980s, they had expanded to the point where they required states to remove national restrictions on "all other capital movements, such as money-market transactions, operations in forward markets, swaps, options, and other derivative instruments" (Poret 1998).[4] As OECD reviews of its own activity on capital control liberalization note, they have been abolished within the OECD. New members have been required to liberalize existing capital controls upon entry into the organization (OECD 2002b).[5]

The OECD never supported the principles of embedded liberalism with regard to the use of capital controls to ensure domestic monetary and fiscal policy autonomy. Its research supported the ideas behind the founding Codes of Liberalization – that a globalized investment market is good for economic welfare. OECD surveillance and research activities historically lent normative support to the codes, encouraging members to abandon attempts to limit international financial transactions.[6] Its recent work on capital controls has been aimed at convincing developing and transition economies to also abandon these mechanisms (OECD 1993a, 1995c).[7]

Although the codes addressed the organization's desire to remove general restrictions on foreign exchange and financial transactions, they also sought, in a somewhat more nebulous and historically ineffective fashion, to remove barriers to FDI. The codes attempted to promote the removal of barriers to what we would now refer to as "trade in services," and in particular to remove direct national restrictions on certain kinds of FDI. While these efforts were ineffective in the 1960s and 1970s, they laid the groundwork for all subsequent attempts to negotiate the removal of national or sector-specific barriers to FDI.

The codes specify a principle of "progressive liberalization" with regard to investment liberalization that was intended to provide a framework under which the goal was to gradually reduce barriers to FDI over time. Progressive liberalization entailed two norms that were to be adhered to in all investment instruments: the norm of the "standstill" mechanism, which meant that states should not introduce new barriers that violated existing provisions in the codes, and the "rollback" norm, under which states were morally required to negotiate reduced barriers over time. A second major principle of the codes was that states were bound to *transparency* and *surveillance*. States have been required to fully disclose to OECD committees all of their existing restrictions on foreign investment and accept that these reported restrictions would then be subject to OECD criticism through normal OECD peer review activity (Houde and Yannaca-Small 2004). Finally, the OECD explicitly adopted non-discrimination principles drawn from the trade regime (the National Treatment and the Most Favoured Nation [MFN] principles), which it hoped would help states pursue progressive liberalization. The non-discrimination principles required member states to treat established foreign investors the same way that domestic firms were treated and to offer the same market access privileges to investors from OECD states that were offered to their most favoured investment partner (Houde and Yannaca-Small 2004, 5).

These principles, intended to anchor a regime that would progressively reduce the myriad of barriers to foreign investment that existed in the 1960s and 1970s, were not as effective as OECD promotion of the removal of general capital controls. From the outset, member states were allowed to list top-down reservations, or national exemptions, for sectors they were not prepared to liberalize at that time. They had to clearly register these reservations with the OECD so that they could be subject to the critical review of OECD committees.[8] The idea was that these reservations would be negotiated down over time. Many states chose to list widespread reservations, however. Progress in removing these has been slow. It is also the case, as the OECD recognizes, that the codes' efforts to remove FDI barriers are rendered fairly ineffective by the absence of a legally binding dispute resolution system. There was no *investor-to-state* or *state-to-state* mechanism for seeking redress if a state violated its commitments under the codes (Houde and Yannaca-Small 2004, 5). Thus, while the codes are viewed as legally binding, their enforceability is questionable.

Despite the principles of the codes, the project of liberalizing FDI barriers was overly ambitious in 1961. States have always been reluctant to surrender the right to directly regulate FDI, particularly to regulate whether foreign firms can provide domestic services via foreign direct investment in a subsidiary. Historically, the service sector has been protected from the activities of foreign firms, largely through foreign ownership restrictions (Williams 2002). The codes posed serious policy puzzles and potentially involved a wider range of domestic policy networks in their efforts to remove these kinds of barriers. As such, the next forty years of OECD activity on investment rules have revolved around trying to find the appropriate set of instruments to help achieve the ambitious goals of the codes. The OECD recognized that domestic political opposition from protected industries would have to be managed, frameworks for negotiating commitments to liberalizing investment barriers would have to be established, and, most importantly, some mechanism had to be created to make OECD liberalization commitments enforceable.

The principles established by the codes created a kind of OECD investment regime, however, one in which the OECD and member countries bound themselves to the liberalization of FDI over the long term. While the task would be difficult, the original OECD codes created a framework within which work could progress. The application of non-discrimination principles from the trade regime to investment agreements, combined with the principles of transparency, standstill, and rollback, would be subsequently expanded by the OECD both in its efforts to put investment rules into the trade regime and through its own Multilateral Agreement on Investment.

Bilateral Investment Treaties

In the mid-1960s, recognizing the initial shortcomings of the existing codes, the OECD attempted to give investment rules more teeth by proposing a Draft Convention on the Protection of Foreign Private Property that would have more clearly codified national obligations to foreign investors. Ultimately, opposition from both developing countries and member states meant that the convention was never adopted (Tobin and Rose-Ackerman 2003, 6-7). Given the lack of practical support among OECD nations for the widespread removal of domestic FDI restrictions, the OECD chose instead to offer its support to the development of a web of bilateral investment treaties (BITs) as a fallback liberalization mechanism. In effect, while providing a safer and more stable environment in which to pursue FDI as a business strategy, BITs extended to foreign corporations *legally enforceable* rights offered in the abstract by the OECD Codes of Liberalization – such as National Treatment. The OECD has played a crucial role in establishing the basic norms of BITs (Houde and Yannaca-Small 2004).

The most common type of BIT, sometimes described as the "European Model," which drew inspiration from a series of twenty-three BITs negotiated by the US in the 1940s, was recommended by the OECD Council in 1962 as a template for use by member states. The OECD model provided a standard definition for what constituted foreign investment and what the rules should be for admission of investment. Subsequent BITs have been fairly standardized (Tobin and Rose Ackerman 2003, 7).

In practice, the greatest impact of these treaties was the direct legal protections they offered foreign investors, as rules limiting expropriation and the like were legally enforceable through investor-to-state dispute resolution procedures specified in the BIT. The "model" BIT also clearly specified adherence to OECD investment regime principles of National Treatment and MFN in investment rules (UNCTAD 2002b). While there are other templates for BITs, such as the "North American" model developed in the 1980s, these tend to build on OECD investment regime principles. In fact, the major difference is that the "North American" BIT extends more rights to foreign investors in the pre-establishment phase (Houde and Yannaca-Small 2004, 4). There are now estimated to be over 2,200 BITs in place, most of which involve at least one OECD member state. Unlike investment liberalization promoted by regional trade agreements, by the World Trade Organization (WTO), or via the mooted MAI, BITs tend to act more to protect the rights of FDI once it is in place, rather than to remove barriers (UNCTAD 2002b). As such, proponents of liberalization (including the OECD Secretariat) view them as an ineffective stopgap. The OECD has continued to explore alternative mechanisms for investment liberalization.

Subsequent OECD Efforts to Remove FDI Restrictions: Breathing Life into the Progressive Liberalization Principle

While the removal of capital controls promoted by the OECD proceeded rapidly in the 1970s (in large part due to the abandonment of the Bretton Woods system), efforts to remove direct sectoral restrictions on FDI were less effective. In fact, the OECD Codes of Liberalization languished as states simply refused to negotiate binding multilateral commitments to remove these barriers. In its "inquisitive" and "meditative" modes, however, the OECD explored various strategies to get liberalization on the agenda. In the 1970s, the organization began to use its surveillance and peer review activities more aggressively. In numerous reports, the OECD recommended the removal of investment restrictions in the financial services sector, the relaxation of national systems for reviewing proposed foreign investments, and the promotion of privatization to expand the opportunities for global service firms engaged in FDI.[9] All OECD reports shared the same basic assumption, that FDI was "an engine of economic growth and a powerful force for global integration" (OECD 1998a, 6).

While this moral suasion was important, at a deeper level the OECD engaged in a long-term problem-solving program searching for a more effective means to negotiate reduced barriers. One major initiative was the OECD contribution to the development of the "trade in services" concept and its subsequent efforts to promote the inclusion of trade in services within the General Agreement on Tariffs and Trade (GATT) trade regime. The conceptual framework developed by the OECD was essentially that provided by its earlier work on the codes, at least with regard to the investment aspects of trade in services – that GATT non-discrimination principles should be applied to a multilateral mechanism binding states to reduced FDI restrictions. In fact, all efforts to achieve investment liberalization via the GATT and the WTO have "borrowed" from the principles outlined in the original OECD codes.

OECD Investment Norms and the WTO: The Results of the Uruguay Round

OECD investment liberalization principles have found their way into many aspects of the modern WTO. The GATS, TRIMS, TRIPs, GPA, and ASCM all have investment provisions derived from liberalization norms advocated by the OECD, and there is considerable overlap between the OECD Codes of Liberalization and the WTO (Houde and Yannaca-Small 2004, 6). Most important among these agreements with regard to reducing investment barriers is the GATS.

After negotiations, the GATS included three elements originally laid out by the OECD's "Conceptual Framework" developed in 1979-81: (1) a set of general rules that should apply to measures affecting trade in services; (2) specific commitments that apply to those service sectors and subsectors that are listed in each state's schedule to be liberalized; and (3) a set of annexes that allow for temporary exemptions from the Most Favoured Nation (MFN) obligations of the GATT in some sectors. Drawing on the OECD-proposed framework, the GATS creates a four-part typology of "modes of delivery" for services. The agreement treats the liberalization of barriers to each mode separately. Both modes 3 and 4 involve rights of establishment for foreign firms providing services to consumers in other countries; essentially, they require the removal of barriers to investment and establishment for foreign firms (Houde and Yannaca-Small 2004, 6). Since the GATS is subject to all WTO non-discrimination principles and the dispute settlement mechanism (DSM), this means that it extends National Treatment and MFN to foreign investment in service industries in the manner suggested by the OECD Codes of Liberalization. It also means that commitments made by each state are potentially more enforceable because of the existence of the WTO DSM.

Many argue that the GATS represents a significant paradigm shift in liberalizing investment barriers, given prior attitudes towards binding investment rules (Hoekman 1993, 1995). Furthermore, subsequent negotiations expanded GATS coverage of investment rules considerably. This was true of the 1997 WTO Agreement on Telecommunications Services and the WTO Financial Services Agreement (FSA). It was also an important agenda item for the Doha Round of WTO negotiations. While some question the degree to which the GATS has worked to remove existing investment barriers, at the very least it prevents backsliding, as new barriers to FDI seem unlikely once a state has committed to removing them – inserting investment into the WTO has helped formally institutionalize OECD principles of "standstill" and "rollback" via the DSM. Furthermore, progressive liberalization is the entire purpose of WTO institutions. This is clear in the case of the various WTO Dispute Resolution Panel decisions, which have aggressively interpreted the scope and meaning of the GATS to give it wider effect than negotiators may have intended (Weiss 1998; Sinclair 2000).

Nonetheless, the GATS and subsequent efforts at the WTO have not been as effective as advocates of liberalization would have liked. At the structural level, much like the OECD Codes of Liberalization, states were allowed to list top-down reservations of sectors that would not be liberalized. This, in combination with the bottom-up list of exempted modes of delivery (including FDI), means that states had a great deal of latitude to simply exempt their existing FDI restrictions (Houde and Yannaca-Small 2004, 6). This was seen as a major problem with the WTO investment provisions, and was a contributory factor to the decision to go ahead with the MAI (OECD 1996b).

From the OECD's perspective, the problem was that states simply had not agreed to wide enough market openings. The Financial Services Agreement concluded in 1997 illustrates some of the shortcomings. In principle, the FSA required that states create opportunities for foreign financial service companies to establish subsidiaries and remove barriers to FDI in the financial services sector (Porter 2005, 97). The FSA is relatively weak, however. Not all WTO members were required to sign the agreement. The agreement allowed "extensive" national limitations on commitments, national obligations vary considerably, and it is not clear that the FSA maintains the standstill principle, as backsliding is possible (Key 1999).

The bottom line was that while the WTO formally institutionalized OECD norms and principles with regard to investment liberalization, drawing heavily on the existing OECD framework (and generated considerable market openings), to advocates of liberalization it simply did not go far enough in committing states to real reductions in existing barriers to FDI. States were unwilling to agree to deep, binding restrictions on their right to regulate FDI in banking and other sectors. Similarly, regional trade agreements (RTAs) coverage of investment rules also falls short of what had been hoped for. Aside from the controversial Chapter 11, on the investor-to-state dispute resolution system, the North American Free Trade Agreement (NAFTA) can also be seen largely as a "standstill" agreement on investment liberalization rather than one that achieves widespread "rollback" (McKeen-Edwards et al. 2004; Gensey 2003). In the end, the OECD view appears to have been that getting investment into the trade regime helped to expand the applicability of OECD investment norms, but that more binding negotiations were needed and these could be secured only in a smaller forum, such as the OECD itself.

The Multilateral Agreement on Investment
At the annual OECD Council meeting in 1995, the ministers were presented with a report prepared by the Secretariat for both the Committee on International Investment and Multinational Enterprises and the Committee on Capital Movements and Invisible Transactions. Responding in part to dissatisfaction with the WTO agreements on investment, the report proposed

moving forward by negotiating an OECD-based "Multilateral Agreement on Investment," arguing that such an agreement could be largely based on the existing OECD investment instruments – the Codes of Liberalization – and the organization's existing expertise concerning investment liberalization (OECD 1995d). Inside the OECD, the initiative was seen as a natural extension of past efforts to remove barriers to FDI (Henderson 1999, 6-7). It would correct the shortcomings of the WTO's handling of investment (in the OECD's view) and would expand the principles of the Codes of Liberalization into a more tangible set of binding commitments.[10]

The OECD was attempting to place the principles of the existing codes within a fully enforceable legal framework. For example, under the MAI, the principle of National Treatment would have become fully legally binding. Commitments made by states would have been fully subject to a system of dispute resolution, *including* investor-to-state resolution. Furthermore, much of the negotiations focused on trying to bind states to real reductions of existing FDI barriers. The number of national reservations, or sectors exempted from the OECD codes, would be vastly reduced under the MAI's negotiated commitments (Houde and Yannaca-Small 2004, 11). The ambitious scope of the agreement, added to the OECD's existing work on investment, would have made the OECD the central institution in a global investment regime. As is well documented, however, the negotiations were formally abandoned after a promising start (see Chapter 4).

While there are a range of opinions on what went wrong, inside the OECD, Secretariat members complain that the public controversy generated by the agreement was unfair. This is understandable, since to most staff the MAI was a logical extension of existing commitments. Used to operating under very little public scrutiny, and generating vague principles and commitments that were often not broadly understood, the OECD simply underestimated the scope of domestic political opposition to a wholesale investment treaty. In Paris, behind closed doors, member states found it difficult to reach an agreement that touched on such a diverse range of issues and affected so many domestic policy sectors. More importantly, once the scope of the negotiations became public, fuelled by a transnational campaign involving a host of non-governmental organizations, negative public opinion made an agreement unlikely. Many, including those supportive of the MAI and the OECD's work on investment, have argued that it was the "publicness" of the debate about the MAI that ultimately resulted in the decision at the Ministerial Council meeting in 1998 to call a halt to the process that they had initially supported (Henderson 1999, xi).

Contemporary OECD Investment Initiatives
While the failure of the MAI was a major setback for OECD investment liberalization initiatives, the organization has not abandoned its goals but has

continued to pursue other avenues. For a time, it had hoped that the Doha Round of WTO talks might advance investment liberalization, but the recent collapse of the round suggests that in the short term, the OECD must focus on its less regulative modes – focusing more on its traditional inquisitive and meditative approaches, increasing its surveillance/moral suasion, and expanding its problem-solving efforts.

Indeed, the OECD has significantly expanded its surveillance and policy recommendation activities. It has conducted a series of country-specific "Foreign Direct Investment Reviews" primarily directed at member states. The committees involved also chose to review a number of leading emerging economies, such as Brazil (1999) and Argentina (1997). The purpose was to identify barriers to investment. The OECD also paid a great deal of attention to the task of integrating Eastern European states into globalized finance. The Economic and Development Review Committee prepared a number of technical reports advising those countries on necessary policy reforms – essentially bringing those non-member states into the OECD surveillance process. Furthermore, the organization made new efforts to codify and statistically measure existing investment barriers (Golub 2003) in order to bring peer pressure to bear on those that scored poorly for high restrictions.

In 2006, the OECD released its comprehensive *Policy Framework for Investment*. Resembling other comprehensive OECD policy packages designed for the adoption of member states (such as the 1994 Jobs Strategy), the framework is self-described as a checklist of policies for member states designed to attract international private investment flows (OECD 2006i, 3). While the recommendations are far-reaching, affecting everything from labour market policy, taxation, and corporate governance, much of the framework is directed towards removing obstacles to inward foreign investment. The framework was developed through the cooperation of many of the OECD's committees. Jointly, they supported a task force that drafted the recommendations after extensive consultation with private sector groups, the World Bank, and the United Nations Conference on Trade and Development (UNCTAD). Representatives from all OECD member states participated in the process, as well as twenty-six non-member states; indeed, one of the task force co-chairs represented Chile. The recommendations are intended for both members and non-members. It is too early to gauge how this framework may influence domestic policy, but the project is the most serious surveillance effort to date and illustrates that, post-MAI, the OECD has not abandoned its mandate to promote investment liberalization.

The OECD is also involved in a variety of policy-relevant problem-solving activities relating to investment. Much of this work focuses on financial crisis management, as the organization has argued that while investment liberalization is an "inevitable" aspect of modern economic development, banking crises, currency and debt crises, and financial market instability all reduce the willingness of policy makers to embrace liberalization (OECD 2002b). As such, the organization has done extensive research on the need to strengthen systems of crisis management, and has been heavily involved in the debate over reform of the existing financial architecture, particularly reform of the IMF (Armijo 2001). The OECD has also weighed in on the debate over proposed "Tobin taxes" (taxes designed to reduce currency volatility and speculation), arguing that they could stifle liberalized investment flows to the detriment of economic performance; instead, states should work towards more effective monitoring and crisis management mechanisms (OECD 2002b). In 2006, the organization also explored how investor-to-state dispute settlement procedures might be improved to help strengthen the transparency and enforceability of existing investment agreements (Yannaca-Small 2006).

The OECD has also investigated possible avenues for more effectively co-ordinating the provisions of all the existing investment instruments. There is a concern that as the web of investment agreements grows, it is likely that they will overlap and contradict one another. While most of the agreements are based on OECD norms, such as National Treatment and MFN, "textual variations" and the depth of commitments can vary considerably (Houde and Yannaca-Small 2004). The OECD has argued that the principal way to ensure some conformity is to assert the primacy of its own rules and norms in anchoring the system. For example, the OECD asserts a right to "clarify" the interaction between different agreements. The OECD National Treatment Instrument, the WTO Agreement on Government Procurement, and the GATS all contain provisions covering the rights of foreign investors or foreign firms in gaining access to government contracts. The OECD Committee on International Investment and Multinational Enterprises has simply issued a "clarification" on how the relationship between these agreements should be understood by the signatories (OECD 1993b, 33-35). Furthermore, the OECD claims that the existing Codes of Liberalization take precedence over all investment agreements concluded since the founding of the OECD (Houde and Yannaca-Small 2004). In practice, given that a core OECD principle is progressive liberalization, in the event of a dispute over which agreement should take precedence, the understanding has been that the agreement that provides the most liberal support for free investment should prevail.[11]

Finally, the OECD has continued its efforts to get states to make legally binding commitments to reduce restrictions on FDI. The Codes of Liberalization have been recently revised, largely to update their provisions to ensure the rollback principle. The revisions codify and entrench any areas in which states have liberalized investment barriers in recent decades. The codes now explicitly state that the member states are committing themselves to a process where the "ultimate objective is that residents of different Member countries should be as free to transact business with each other as are residents of a single country" (Henderson 1996, 15; OECD 1995b). Along these lines, some, committed to liberalization, see OECD expansion as one possible mechanism for pursuing investment liberalization. For example, China, Russia, and India, the largest non-member economies, all would be required to undertake significant liberalizations on exchange controls and FDI restrictions upon joining the OECD, under the provisions of the existing codes. Membership would also bring them fully under the moral suasion/surveillance umbrella of activities.

Evaluating the Impact of the OECD Investment Work

Since 1961, the OECD has tried to construct an investment regime characterized by progressive liberalization. The efforts are remarkable for their consistency, despite ever-changing personnel and the reluctance of member states to bind themselves to liberalization commitments. Indeed, much of the OECD's work on investment calls into question its basic status as a member-driven international organization. Member governments often have not shared the OECD's end goals on liberalization. As the recent European Union struggle over the European Services Directive reveals, states wish to maintain their prerogatives in regulating investment activity, and yet the OECD opposes state autonomy in this area. Indeed, it does appear that in the case of investment, the OECD has acted as a conveyor of a more "American style" set of policy preferences, in the manner suggested by Djelic and Sahlin-Andersson (2006a), supporting more liberalized rules for finance than most member states are willing to accept.

The crucial question is what the OECD has achieved. Certainly, since its founding capital flows and FDI have grown immensely. In recent decades, intra-OECD FDI flows have grown faster than merchandise trade and investment outside the OECD area, which the OECD argues is the direct result of its success in removing barriers to FDI. Despite the logic of globalization and the competitive potential of Less Developed Countries to attract FDI, over three-quarters of OECD-based FDI activity remains within the OECD area, and this ratio has not changed since 1981. The OECD argues that this is occurring because of the wave of deregulation, privatization, and domestic "de-monopolization" (particularly in the service sector), all of which have been influenced by the organization's efforts to remove restrictions on foreign investment (OECD 1998a). Of course, the OECD could hardly be expected to conclude that its efforts had been ineffective – that states have ignored its recommendations and that its "binding" commitments have been unenforceable. Yet, the organization is right to suggest that it has achieved a great deal. Members' exchange controls have been completely abandoned (Greece and Ireland were the last to do so in 1994), and there has been a substantial reduction in restrictions to FDI.

It is, however, extremely difficult to measure the impact of the OECD's efforts on national commitments to liberalization. The OECD still has no clear enforcement mechanisms and no dispute settlement system, and much of its work has focused on generating norms that will positively predispose states to liberalization and on creating frameworks for negotiation that make liberalization more likely. How are we to measure the impact of such things? Even OECD celebrants find it hard to judge. Henderson (1996), a key player in OECD investment initiatives, argues that even in cases where there has been liberalization (such as explicit capital controls), member states may have wanted to pursue the policies for other reasons; thus, it can be difficult to say that the OECD has "led" states into doing anything. Nevertheless, he notes:

> First governments are sometimes ready to liberalise and to grasp political nettles in doing so, if they are acting in conjunction with others and as part of a wider agreement of understanding; an international agency can help in bringing this to pass. Second, what happens within these agencies, and the evidence and arguments to be found in their publications, may help to tilt the balance within countries as between liberalism and interventionism. All governments are subject to conflicting pressures and internal divisions. In cases where the balance is not too uneven, the various mechanisms of intergovernmental exchange and cooperation may influence what is decided. (Henderson 1996, 20)

That is, if the OECD has achieved nothing else, it has helped domestic proponents of liberalization pursue their goals. In addition, its standstill principle has made it legally more difficult for states to backslide once national governments have made commitments to liberalization. While BITs, RTAs, and the WTO are the principal instruments that bind states in reducing investment barriers, the OECD developed the norms and procedures by which this liberalization could occur, and lent them a great deal of intellectual legitimacy.

Finally, the OECD has not been supplanted by the WTO's increased role in investment. Such a view is too sanguine, both about the success of integrating investment into the WTO and about the general removal of barriers to investment. Many barriers remain and states are still reluctant to fully liberalize rules regarding foreign investment. OECD insiders, ideologically committed to liberalization, are therefore likely to continue seeking new means of keeping progressive liberalization on the agenda.

Notes

1 David Henderson was a long-serving head of the OECD Economic Research Directorate.
2 Other committees have, however, involved themselves in the "investment file." The Committee on Fiscal Affairs' work on international tax issues is a good example of this.
3 Ironically, it remains the case to this day that the IMF Charter does not give the organization a role in promoting investment liberalization (Kapur 1998).
4 For an examination of the various amendments to the codes that bind states to reduced capital controls and restrictions on both direct and portfolio investment, see Griffith-Jones et al. (2000).
5 Mexico had to accede to the Codes of Liberalization upon its entry. As a result, Mexico "disposed of its foreign exchange controls and many of its obstacles to foreign direct investment" (OECD 1994d, 26). Similarly Korean investment restrictions were a topic of serious committee discussion during its accession process, demonstrating that "establishing that the criteria for accession have been met is no formality" (Henderson 1996, 20).
6 The OECD argues that capital and exchange controls are no longer worthy of consideration as a policy option for member states (OECD 2002b). Indeed, summarizing its own research in the area, the organization argues that liberalization of capital controls and investment barriers has been good for member states. It has made them more competitive, provided access to larger pools of capital, and reduced blockages to growth generated by weakness in domestic financial sectors in some of the smaller member states (OECD 2002b).
7 The OECD argues that there was a delay in the relaxation of capital controls required by the early codes because member states had to be given time to upgrade their domestic systems of financial supervision, etc., to meet the challenges of globalized financial flows (OECD 2002b). The fact is that under most circumstances, OECD members have bound themselves not to impose national capital controls again. The Codes of Liberalization prevent backsliding and are therefore an important set of international investment rules.
8 For the current provisions of the codes, see OECD (2006w).
9 This work is summarized in OECD (1998a).
10 The decision to pursue the MAI was a direct result of concerns inside OECD committees that the WTO was going to prove unable to seriously advance agreement on binding removals of restrictions on FDI (Henderson 1999, x-xi).
11 Houde and Yannaca-Small (2004) argue that OECD primacy was confirmed in response to the Canada-US Free Trade Agreement, which contained investment liberalization provisions. In response, the OECD Committee on Capital Movements and Invisible Transactions and the OECD Council declared that the existing agreements made by the two states under the Codes of Liberalization should take precedence in the event of a conflict.

7
The OECD's Local Turn: "Innovative Liberalism" for the Cities?

Neil Bradford

These global trends affect us all but require businesses and governments to adjust their strategies to the specific context of their societies so as to generate the right action on the ground. Hence urban and rural policy, and local and regional policy – what we here at the OECD have called territorial development – have attracted increased attention as the injunction to "think globally and act locally" has taken hold ... Central government policies can be reinforced by measures at the grass roots to stimulate entrepreneurship and innovation.
  – Donald J. Johnston, OECD Secretary-General
    (OECD 1998b)

But cities also fall victim to what is sometimes called the "urban paradox" – alongside high concentrations of wealth and employment, they also tend to concentrate a high number of unemployed and marginalized people. Cities have to deal with the challenges of economic adjustment, poverty and social cohesion, and in many cases with higher criminality.
  – Angel Gurría, OECD Secretary-General
    (OECD 2007a)

Over the last decade there has been growing awareness that many of the most urgent public policy issues are playing out in cities. Geographers studying innovation in the knowledge-based economy now emphasize the importance of localized clusters of economic actors for national prosperity. Analysts of social inclusion focus on the multiple barriers that individuals and families face living in distressed neighbourhoods that limit access to the services and opportunities of the surrounding city-region. Most recently, environmentalists have documented major ecological stresses in urban centres, demonstrating that decisions taken locally about land use, transportation, and development are crucial for global sustainability. Common to all of these perspectives is appreciation of how local geographic contexts – the form and nature of *places* – shape challenges and opportunities. National governments increasingly work from the ground up, tapping local knowledge and connecting central resources with local action to solve complex policy problems (Polèse and Stren 2000; Hambleton et al. 2002).

The "local turn" has not been without controversy, however. While some envision new opportunities for community building and economic innovation, others describe an intentional retreat by government from the universal commitments that remain the foundation of "socially sustainable cities" (Bradford 2007a). Indeed, the policy substance of what has come to be known as the "new localism" remains contested. A host of think tanks, research institutes, interest associations, and social movements have advanced their own interpretations and prescriptions.

This chapter focuses on one such idea generator, the Organisation for Economic Co-operation and Development, which in the past decade has dedicated considerable resources to policy analysis of territorial issues through an urban lens. Arguing that the OECD is a significant player in contemporary urban debates, we explain its influence through analysis of two specific organizational strategies adopted by the Territorial Development Policy Committee (TDPC). First, the TDPC has not sought to impose narrow or overly abstract "solutions" on member states. Instead, through its extensive research networks, we find that it has creatively woven insights from the three most prominent narratives of the new localism into a distinctive urban policy paradigm. Second, in its urban policy dissemination activities, the TDPC has pursued a model of "contextualized learning" that pays close attention to conditions on the ground in different cities (Hemerijck and Visser 2003). In the process, the OECD's urban agenda has remained close to the aspirations of the two Secretaries-General cited above: holistic in its policy attention to multiple urban realities, as Gurría envisioned, and attuned to the need for the "right action on the ground," as Johnston proposed. Of course, whether these research and advocacy qualities have enhanced the OECD's capacity to actually shift member states' urban policies in line with its thinking is another matter. The chapter closes with some reflections on this larger question of influence and the prospects for embedding new paradigms.

The argument is developed in three parts, building on Bengt Jacobsson's description of different modes of "soft policy regulation" that apply to international organizations such as the OECD (Jacobsson 2006). First, in the *meditative stage*, we explore the substantive content of the OECD's urban ideas, identifying a new hybrid paradigm of "innovative liberalism." Second, we track the *inquisitive processes* whereby the OECD monitors the member state policies and practices in relation to its chosen paradigm. The case of Canada is used to illustrate the review process, and especially the domestic institutional/political factors that shape local reception of international policy frameworks. Third, we add to Jacobsson's twofold framework a third mode of soft regulation – *exhortation*. It brings into focus the dynamics of global-local policy transfer. Across each of these three stages, the analysis is informed by the OECD's major urban policy study, *Competitive Cities in the Global Economy*, published in 2006 (OECD 2006j). Taking stock of the OECD's entire urban agenda, it supplies an excellent foundation for our analysis.

The OECD and Policy Learning: Soft Regulation
As other chapters in this volume make clear, the OECD is an international organization that lacks the authority to issue commands or directives compelling member states to act. Its core business is knowledge production and the dissemination of policy frameworks. Its methods are those of "soft regulation," a collective learning process for generating shared understandings that inspire policy change and institutional reform. Member state compliance does not flow from threats of legal sanction but from analysis, deliberation, and review. In exercising such ideational power, the OECD deploys three interconnected modes of soft regulation: meditation, inquisition, and exhortation.

Meditative activities involve research and discussion of international trends and national policies. Organizations engaged in policy meditation "function as arenas where all kinds of experiences can be transmitted and compared, where ideas are generated and shared" (Jacobsson 2006, 208). Meditation involves recruiting experts to map directions and convening dialogue among such experts and policy practitioners in government. Ideally, meditative processes result in new policy paradigms that identify problems and solutions, and that clarify roles and responsibilities for implementation. These ideas provide the templates – standards, indicators, and benchmarks – for monitoring member state performance.

Inquisitive activities occur as OECD officials, in conjunction with member state representatives, apply policy paradigms to assess national policies. The process typically involves production of country reports based on site visits by OECD officials, expert study, and peer-to-peer dialogue over the performance of the state that is the subject of inquisition. The point is not simply to monitor behaviour but to drive change along lines consistent with the paradigm. In addition to detailed country reviews that include specific reform recommendations, the inquisitive activities often generate cross-national rankings that expose gaps in national policies, or outcomes lagging behind the international standard.

Exhortation seeks policy change. It packages the ideas and lessons from the meditative and inquisitive stages into concrete action plans that inform OECD advocacy in specific countries, regions, or cities. This means transferring "experiential knowledge," marketing "good practice," and encouraging appropriate policy reform. As such, this form of soft regulation raises important questions about precisely how ideas circulate. Is the route one of "fast policy transfer," meaning "importation of off-the-shelf program techniques from other locations" (Peck 2002, 344)? Or is the interaction more iterative and reflexive? In the urban field, these issues are particularly salient given that cities have long been the site for a great variety of policy experimentation and demonstrations orchestrated at national and international scales (Beer et al. 2003).

While these three modes of soft regulation are usefully distinguished for purposes of analytical clarity, in practice the interconnections are most important. Meditative work in the realm of ideas establishes a conceptual foundation. Inquisitive activity is the "field work" that bridges meditation and exhortation. And exhortation translates the learnings from meditation and inquisition into actionable recommendations. Jacobsson and Sahlin-Andersson aptly describe *combined modes* of transnational regulation (2006, 256): "Sometimes one regulation mode paves the way for others and sometimes one mode of regulation serves as a means of authorizing and strengthening other modes."

The rest of this chapter tracks the OECD's urban policy work across the meditative, inquisitive, and exhortative stages of soft regulation. To begin, the OECD's local turn must be situated in its larger discursive context. Indeed, the OECD's meditative work generated a new urban policy paradigm that drew ideas from each of the three most prominent new localism narratives.

The New Localism: Three Discourses of Development
The new localism is a discourse resonating across a multidisciplinary literature analyzing how globalization's most important flows – of people, capital, and ideas – now intersect in urban centres around the world (Gertler 2001; Clarke and Gaile 1998). An eclectic body of research advances some basic claims: first, city-regions, with their population density and organizational synergies, are the engines of national economies; second, these same city-regions are also the places with the most concentrated poverty and entrenched socio-spatial polarization; and third, when issues of such national consequence play out in cities, then upper level governments require an *urban lens* to frame their policy making. Urban centres must be recognized as strategic policy spaces where collaboration across sectors of society and between levels of government can tackle the so-called wicked problems, ranging from homelessness and economic restructuring to urban sprawl and distressed neighbourhoods.

While the above three claims represent a shared departure point for the new localism, contributors have gone on to interpret the dynamics of devolution and collaboration quite differently. By the time the OECD formally engaged the urban agenda in the late 1990s, three key discourses of development were contesting the implications of the new localism for economic and social well-being.

The first discourse has been labelled *rollout neoliberalism* (Brenner and Theodore 2002). It views the urban agenda in the context of the capitalist global economy and the associated market-competitive regulatory framework that severely limits the policy discretion of national states. Constrained by the neoliberal nexus of international investment agreements and transnational financial networks, central governments are increasingly hollowed out as authority and capacity shifts upward, outward, and downward. Local actors – both municipal officials and community organizations – find themselves with massive new policy responsibilities, from social service provision to economic restructuring. The new localism signals a belated recognition by central governments and international organizations that local actors require aid if the neoliberal project is to survive. A series of supports are thus "rolled out" from above, helping local actors to cope. The rollout has economic and social dimensions. For the local economy, "urban locational policies" are implemented to strengthen the business infrastructure of global city-regions caught up in the high-technology competition (Brenner 2004). In social terms, local partnerships are mandated for strategic planning in labour force development, neighbourhood renewal, cooperative housing, and so forth. The retooling of localities, however, effectively obscures the wider structural dynamics and macro-level choices that are the root cause of the urban pressures. Rollout neoliberalism is about managing the excesses of globalization manifest at the local scale. It is not about contesting its logic or appropriateness in different places, and local adaptation relies on "off-the-shelf policy fixes" (Peck 2002).

The second discourse finds in the new localism a promising model for the *learning region* (Wolfe and Gertler 2002). Focused on economic development in the context of knowledge-based production, this discourse identifies limitations in both dirigiste and neoliberal frameworks in grasping the "new competition" and the potential of city-regions. Dirigiste planners wrongly assumed that they possessed the expertise to pick winners and the resources to bail out declining regions. For their part, neoliberals naïvely believed that unleashing an investment competition among localities was sufficient to grow the high value–adding enterprises of the new economy. Neither perspective understood the new competition and the potential of city-regions. Economic innovation – the building of new business competencies and connecting them with markets – is now the foundation of prosperity, and it occurs in specific places through social learning that pools knowledge among firms, researchers, financiers, and governments. Urban centres are the critical scale for innovation because their density and diversity generates and, more importantly, rapidly circulates the knowledge – often tacit and informal – that drives innovation. Yet not all cities are learning regions: governance systems must cultivate networks and establish an innovative milieu through appropriate infrastructural investment. While this discourse often showcases the same few high-tech hot spots, its message is different from rapid policy rollout. Learning regions are encouraged to follow the *process* for creating an innovative milieu. This is distinct from trying to replicate the exact cluster profile of global leaders such as Silicon Valley or the Third Italy.

The final new localism discourse is organized around social strategies for *community development* (Amin et al. 2002; Orr 2007). Front and centre is the high concentration of socioeconomic inequality and growing spatial segregation of residents by class and race in large cities. The community development version of the new localism aims to empower residents in order to improve social services, transform neighbourhoods, and open housing and labour markets. Here, the community development narrative identifies three fields of engagement for local action: strengthening third sector capacity to design holistic services, developing labour market intermediaries to address employment challenges from immigrant recognition to social enterprise growth, and giving voice to civil society representatives in urban governance. A range of generic tools and techniques is prescribed – asset mapping, neighbourhood vitality indexes, and collaboration protocols. The community development perspective also insists that local organizing must be supplemented by national governments, investing in social infrastructure and empowering their own "street-level bureaucrats" to work alongside local actors.

Across the 1980s and 1990s, these three discourses of development gained considerable influence among scholars and practitioners of the new localism. When the OECD formally launched its urban project in 1999, the terms of debate were established. Below, we discuss how the OECD created its own discursive space in a crowded field.

Joining the Debate: The OECD's Meditative Regulation

In 1998, Secretary-General Donald Johnston explained the rationale for the OECD's entry into urban policy. The overarching concern was to support effective implementation of the macroeconomic and structural policies that were at the heart of the OECD's work. Rehearsing standard themes from the new localism, Johnston elaborated:

Complementarity among macro-economic, structural and territorial policies is important for several reasons: structural economic changes depend for maximum success on stimulation of regional and local entrepreneurship and innovation; central government policies rely on dynamic communities in which business, public authorities and civic society can establish new partnerships and follow approaches adapted to their circumstances; dynamic communities can strengthen social cohesion by, for example, facilitating "welfare to work" policies to integrate the unemployed and excluded, and by pioneering new forms of democratic participation. (Johnston 1998)

Johnston's invocation marked a turning point in the OECD's treatment of the local scale in policy analysis. Since the early 1990s, an Urban Working Group had been instrumental in drawing attention to particular themes, such as the prospects for local partnerships, the role of women in cities, and the plight of distressed urban areas (OECD 1996c, 1998b). A new program was launched on "Local Economic and Employment Development" (LEED), with a mandate to investigate how decentralized strategies might advance the OECD's macro-level structural reforms in employment and labour market policy. The LEED program produced a series of studies on area-based governance in different countries, concluding that local partnerships could better coordinate economic development, labour market, and social welfare policies (OECD 2001a). It thus explicitly linked the local turn to improved structural policy and introduced a context-sensitive method of policy learning and transfer (OECD 1996c, 2001b).

In 1999, this initial local research was expanded with the formation of a Territorial Development Policy Committee as part of the OECD's Public Governance and Territorial Development Directorate. The TDPC addressed two principal themes – metropolitan governance and urban competitiveness – and their interdependence. As a forum for international research and dialogue on "new territorial development policies," the TDPC was mandated to review approaches and assess progress by partners at national, regional, and local levels. Three working parties were formed: Territorial Indicators, Territorial Policy in Rural Areas, and Territorial Policy in Urban Areas.

Over the next several years, the TDPC published a stream of urban research reports exploring different ways in which increasingly localized dynamics affected member state macro-level policy performance. In 2001, the committee published *Cities for Citizens: Improving Metropolitan Governance,* underscoring the need for balance between urban policies for economic competitiveness and social cohesion. The key was enhanced governance capacity in metropolitan areas, and *Cities for Citizens* developed a number of principles "to define the adequacy of systems of governance for metropolitan regions in the twenty-first century" (OECD 2001c, 18). The animating vision was policy coherence achieved at the city-region scale through vertical collaboration among governments and horizontal networks bridging public and private sectors. Surveying institutional and financial arrangements in numerous metropolitan areas, the report concluded that existing policies were "outdated and not well adapted to the tasks they face" (OECD 2001c, 12). This negative assessment was reaffirmed at the TDPC High-Level Meeting on Innovation and Effectiveness in Territorial Development Policy in 2003. Policy fact sheets for that gathering catalogued the problems when "spatial-economic changes have outpaced institutional reform" (OECD 2003f, 10). Inadequate local governance capacity implied that "even well-designed policies can miss their objectives" (OECD 2003f, 14).

To assist in closing the institutional gap between current policy practices and the new conditions, the TDPC organized four conferences in 2004 and 2005 to specify the links between national competitiveness, urban governance, and quality of life. The series began in Paris, examining central government perspectives on urban fiscal challenges, and continued in Spain, Japan, and Montreal, addressing, respectively, the topics of local economic innovation, city physical attractiveness, and the social dimension of city competitiveness. Each conference featured expert papers from leading urban scholars, and roundtables and panels included the political, bureaucratic, and nongovernmental sectors.

All of the meditative work was drawn together in the landmark 2006 report *Competitive Cities in the Global Economy*. Subtitled a "horizontal synthesis report," this document constitutes the most comprehensive and mature expression of the "organizational discourse" on urban affairs that structures the TDPC's activities (Dostal 2004). As such, it is the authoritative reference for interpreting both the OECD's substantive ideas about the new localism and its advocacy strategy in member states. In *Competitive Cities*, we find a *discursive hybrid* that blends themes and concepts from each of the three existing new localism frameworks. At the *centre* of the TDPC hybrid was the learning region. But it was *framed* by the neoliberal and *flanked* by the community development perspectives.

To begin with the neoliberal framing, established views of globalization's competitiveness imperatives set boundaries on the urban thinking. At the macro level, the appropriateness of the economic and structural policy agenda was a given. National governments act within neoliberalism parameters by embracing non-inflationary growth, respecting existing property rights, and shifting territorial policy from "equitable geographical distribution of resources" to "focus more on mobilizing local resources to build competitive strengths" (Johnston 1998). The same globalization logic reaches down to frame local innovation and restructuring strategies. Local strategies react to trade and investment liberalization, and regional measures should reinforce labour market flexibility through the movement of productive factors from less to more dynamic places. The TDPC's neoliberal framing was explicit: "With the irreversible trend of global economic integration, there is growing recognition among policy planners that the only way that cities can secure competitive advantages over their perceived competitors in an ever intensifying inter-city competition is by pursuing entrepreneurial strategies" (OECD 2007c, 1-2). The goal was always effective adaptation and adjustment to global imperatives, not resistance to, or questioning of, those forces.

Within the neoliberal framing, however, there remained considerable discursive space for adaptive strategies beyond "a pure laissez faire approach" (OECD 2006j, 100). In other words, the neoliberal framing did not extend to the rollout of neoliberal adjustment measures. Instead, the bulk of *Competitive Cities* was devoted to formation of a "public strategic vision" for urban competitiveness *and* livability" (OECD 2006j).

At the centre of the TDPC organizational discourse was the city as a learning region. Competitiveness depended on proactive metropolitan strategies to help firms access research and innovate on the basis of product quality. Government's contribution was investment in both the physical infrastructure of the knowledge economy – transportation, communications, facilities – and the soft infrastructure of human and social capital that cultivates and connects talent. Metropolitan areas were the ideal social space and geographic scale for knowledge creation and diffusion. But only those places that transformed their knowledge resources and competitive assets into an innovation system were learning regions. Such an innovation system supplied "'local collective competition goods' to favour business growth and help clustered activities flourish" (OECD 2006j, 118). These collective goods were typically not available through the market, and they included networks for sharing tacit knowledge about design concepts or sector-specific links between university research and science-based industry. According to Colin Crouch, on whose research the report drew, such public goods "give the firm competitive advantage over competitors who lack such access and either have to go without the good in question, or must pay for it" (OECD 2006j, 320). Context-sensitive policy was the key: "tailor-made cluster development approaches should be adopted to accommodate cluster and metropolitan peculiarities" (OECD 2006j, 115). Reflecting the neoliberal frame, however, *Competitive Cities* emphasized the importance in all learning regions of cultivating export-oriented clusters. Globally oriented local clusters "are what are really fundamental to building metropolitan competitiveness" (OECD 2006j, 105).

At the same time, the report attended to the social consequences of the learning region framed by neoliberalism. It recognized the "urban paradox" whereby "certain characteristics of dynamic post-industrial cities produce increasing socioeconomic inequalities that increase segregation and its consequent discontent" (OECD 2006j, 76). Two dimensions of inequality associated with the cluster strategy were acknowledged. On the one hand, *between* cities, it was recognized that not all places can become high-tech hot spots and that many will struggle with less dynamic niches. On the other hand, *within* cities, it was observed that even the global clusters have large populations in low-end service work. Further, it was noted that exclusion results in spatial segregation of poor people and that distressed neighbourhoods are increasingly home to racial minorities and recent immigrants. Socio-spatial divisions constituted a "drag factor that reduces the competitiveness of the region as a whole" (OECD 2006j, 145). *Competitive Cities* concluded that "metro-regional economic and social development need to be elements of a single coherent strategy" (OECD 2006j, 145). Familiar neoliberal prescriptions for tax-free enterprise zones were rejected on the grounds that the firms attracted by such fiscal privileges were unlikely to stay long, and were almost always engaged in "down-market activities" ill-suited to the learning region (OECD 2006j, 144). Instead, the learning region's menu of collective competition goods could be expanded to include more firms and workers through strengthening of the social economy and employment standards (OECD 2006j, 133, 146).

In sum, the TDPC created a hybrid policy discourse for competitive cities. The synthesis report envisioned integrated local development strategies for globally competitive high value–added clusters *and* labour-intensive community-based development. For each, the public policy formula was the same – macro-level interventions that lined up with locally identified priorities.

Joining vision and practice, this hybrid constituted a new paradigm for policy and governance in cities. Peter A. Hall proposes that policy ideas become paradigms when they announce new policy goals, identify strategies to attain them, and set instruments for their implementation (Hall 1989a). The TDPC's meditative work meets the test. Its goal of the self-reliant learning region departed from both Keynesian equalization and neoliberal adjustment. Its design was based on a novel instrument mix privileging customized interventions in hard and soft urban infrastructures, replacing command-and-control regulation and direct spending with a variety of incentives and supports. Finally, implementation would occur through multilevel negotiation responding more to community rhythms than bureaucratic mandates.

We call the TDPC's urban policy paradigm *innovative liberalism*. Respecting the broad imperatives of the current global order, the paradigm remains rooted in liberal economic ideas about competition and adjustment. At the same time, it reflects substantive engagement with arguments demonstrating significant market failures in relation to urban well-being. The TDPC created from existing approaches to local development a new framework for place-based policy and collaborative governance in a learning-driven economy. Of course, Peter Hall also emphasizes that a paradigm's internal coherence or novelty reveals little about its actual influence over government policy. The power of ideas is always mediated by institutional and political factors, and this is nowhere more apparent than with internationally generated paradigms. The next section takes up these issues, examining how the TDPC's paradigm travelled through the OECD's inquisitive regulation.

Testing the Field: The OECD's Inquisitive Regulation

In the course of preparing *Competitive Cities,* the TDPC undertook a series of territorial reviews at the national and metropolitan scales. The reviews were described as audits of structural and territorial policies for improving competitive advantage and combating social disparities, and assessing the distribution of competencies and resources among different levels of governments (OECD 2002c, 3).

The TDPC inquisitive regulation is typically an eighteen-month process based on quite intensive interaction between the OECD and the territory in question. In the case of a metropolitan review, local authorities make several commitments, including co-financing and arranging a local team with whom the OECD directorate can work. The local team further assumes responsibility for preparing a background report, guided by a questionnaire provided by the TDPC, outlining the main socioeconomic trends, governance frameworks, and particular challenges and opportunities. With this report in hand, the OECD organizes a study mission in the metropolitan region to interview government officials, experts, and business and third sector representatives. An interim report is prepared, including preliminary evaluation of the local policies and practices. The OECD then recruits international experts who use their comparative knowledge to deepen the assessment, provide tailored policy recommendations, and assist in preparation of a report that will be discussed by representatives of all OECD member states at a high-level meeting. Upon their approval, the report is submitted to the local authorities and published in the OECD series, often in conjunction with an international conference to consider its recommendations.

The OECD's inquisitive regulation of cities actively encourages participating governments to adopt the policies and practices generated at the meditative stage. Compliance is neither automatic nor assured, however. In these terms, the recent Canadian experience with OECD territorial reviews is instructive. Long known for Keynesian-style regional development initiatives delivered through complex federal/provincial deals, Canadian policy communities in the early 2000s expressed concern about the absence of any coherent urban strategy or place-based policy thinking (Bradford 2002). The OECD's two territorial reviews in the early 2000s – a country study in 2002 and a metropolitan study of Montreal in 2004 (OECD 2004d) – were timely interventions in an emerging national debate.

The country review asserted that Canadian public policy was in the midst of a "paradigm shift in territorial policies" from redistribution to lagging regions towards identifying growth opportunities based on maximizing local assets in urban settings (OECD 2002c, 12). The review then catalogued the obstacles to such a paradigm shift, declaring that Canada's "whole approach to urban areas and their role in economic growth needs rethinking" (OECD 2002c, 113). Outdated constitutional arrangements that left municipalities without any recognition or standing were compounded by a litany of anti-urban policies. Federal cutbacks in transfers and infrastructure investment had led provincial governments to offload responsibilities to municipalities and impose top-down, one-size-fits-all institutional restructurings. The OECD opined that long-standing Canadian advantages in urban quality of life over their American counterparts were at risk. There was growing evidence of the TDPC's urban paradox: Canadian city-regions with the most innovative clusters also exhibited the greatest income polarization and spatial concentrations of wealth and poverty. A "sharp increase in the number of very poor neighbourhoods" was reported in Toronto and Montreal. The review cited United Nations commentary on the growth of homelessness in Canadian cities, and even referenced "a growing trend towards the development of segregated ghettos" (OECD 2002c, 54, 128). Canada's "disjointed approach" was not sustainable in the new globally competitive context. The country's future prosperity was jeopardized by "a failure to draw up an integrated urban policy" (OECD 2002c, 133).

Of course, the review not only documented barriers to the paradigm shift but also mapped a positive course. Questioning the federal government's long withdrawal from urban affairs, the review called for a new strategy encompassing fiscal, governance, and policy reforms. The magnitude of the change called for concerted federal leadership, and the review emphasized that the "Constitution does not prohibit the federal government from engaging in productive relations with municipalities, while fully respecting provincial jurisdiction" (OECD 2002c, 136). It described "a growing understanding that limited resources can be used more effectively through an integration of strategies, policies, and programs" (OECD 2002c, 131). Clarifying a legal basis and policy rationale for renewed federal urban engagement, the review recommended that Ottawa "set national objectives and provide a national framework for urban competitiveness." It was, however, "essential that the strategy development and implementation be led locally" (OECD 2002c, 137). Three federal/local policy pathways were proposed to balance these principles. First, institutional mechanisms were needed to allow the largest urban centres to deal more directly with the federal government in matters such as economic competitiveness and infrastructure, housing, immigration, Aboriginal people, and the environment. Second, more formal agreements among the three levels of government were needed for "area-based partnerships" to meet the challenges of spatially concentrated poverty or to exploit the opportunities of clustered technology assets. Third, federal and provincial governments needed to negotiate "legislative change that would allow cities to raise revenue beyond the property tax" (OECD 2002c, 137). All three pathways involved new forms of multilevel governance in Canadian federalism, and the review recommended a federal coordinating body to drive reform.

As a national-level territorial study, this review did not address in detail development strategies in specific cities. Of course, the neoliberal framing was familiar – Canadian cities "increasingly compete with one another, and with other cities around the world, to attract investment and knowledge activities" (OECD 2002c, 10). However, it was the second territorial review, in 2004, that explored the details of local economic development and urban governance, focusing on Montreal. This review probed Montreal's efforts to develop a regional innovation system for strengthening its traded clusters in high-technology products. Documenting the city's lower productivity, the review argued that a barrier to Montreal's economic competitiveness was inefficient, or at least overly complex, government. A highly fragmented institutional environment had prevented formation of a coherent plan – or what the TDPC called a strategic public vision – to make Montreal a learning region. A new metropolitan governance framework was urgently required, and the review applauded the recent formation of the Montreal Metropolitan Community as well as the provincial amalgamation of municipalities. Both institutional innovations were seen as better aligning Montreal's administrative boundaries with the functional economic unit. Not surprisingly, concern was expressed about any "disamalgamation" that would recreate the "over-complicated institutional mosaic of the metropolitan area" (OECD 2004d, 4). Similar problems of fragmentation and isolation characterized the existing cluster-building efforts in Montreal. Relationships between knowledge producers and firms were disjointed. Access to venture capital was limited. The city-region lacked a unified brand for marketing itself to global investment and talent.

The review's main message to all levels of government present in Montreal was better coordination and more focused metropolitan economic planning. It recommended improved intergovernmental relations for cluster support and infrastructure investment. Two multilevel governance models were identified as promising. The provincial/municipal "City Contract" signed in 2003 that provided five-year funding for social investments, granting considerable autonomy to the city in implementing its priorities, and the federal/provincial/municipal Urban Development Agreements in western Canadian cities that joined economic innovation and social inclusion activities in a single governance structure were favourably referenced. For maximum policy coordination, the review emphasized the importance of such multilevel governance encompassing the entire city-region, as opposed to discrete deals for particular municipalities or neighbourhoods.

With these two territorial reviews, Canada was a leading site for the OECD's inquisitive regulation in urban policy. The 2002 national territorial review intervened in a growing debate about the problems of Canadian cities. An urban policy coalition of big-city mayors, the banks, community organizations, and think tank experts had mobilized behind a "New Deal" for cities (Bradford 2007b). In this context, the OECD review brought conceptual order to a still quite diffuse national discussion. It described a framework for multilevel urban governance within the federal system and showed how an urban policy lens could work. Moreover, the OECD review arrived at a strategic political moment, as power was passing from Prime Minister Chrétien to Paul Martin. Where Chrétien was wary of the constitutional and fiscal entanglements associated with a national urban agenda, Martin saw the cities file as his "signature issue" (Simpson 2004). He actively sought out ideas for his "New Deal for Cities," which he termed a "national project for our time" (Martin 2005). In 2005, he established a federal department to coordinate urban interventions, negotiated revenue transfers for municipalities, promised a seat at the policy table for big-city mayors, and promoted tri-level Urban Development Agreements as the most promising intergovernmental model for tackling complex, localized problems. Each of these initiatives had been recommended in the 2002 OECD review.

Subsequent implementation of the Martin New Deal, however, also reveals how domestic factors condition the impact of international paradigms. For example, whereas the OECD had recommended a federal focus on large cities (and especially Toronto, Montreal, and Vancouver), the original New Deal for Cities was soon extended to include *all* municipalities. And the OECD's strong call for federal leadership on the urban agenda quickly bumped up against political constraints on the ground: simply put, the provinces asserted their rights in mediating any direct federal engagement with municipalities. Thus, progress on the New Deal was incremental in the two years of the Martin government, and whatever momentum was building came to a near standstill when the Harper Conservatives won power in 2006. Declaring that the federal government had "stuck its nose into provincial and local matters," the new prime minister emphasized that his government's policy priorities did not include urban affairs (Bradford 2007b).

Similar dynamics were at play in relation to the OECD's Montreal review. Certainly, the study conformed to the TDPC's paradigm of innovative liberalism. Competitiveness in the global economy depended on transforming Montreal into a learning region, with some attention to social inclusion through targeted federal and provincial community investments. And the OECD study laid the conceptual groundwork for the city's 2005 economic development strategy – the Metropolitan Innovation Strategy – built around learning and clustering. But the OECD's call for cohesive metropolitan governance to consolidate the learning region fell flat when the new Liberal provincial government supported a "demerger" movement. Further, the OECD's recommendation for tri-level mechanisms like an Urban Development Agreement in Montreal failed to inspire the provincial government in Canada most resistant to an active federal urban policy.

In sum, the OECD's inquisitive regulation in Canada at both the national and metropolitan scales followed a common trajectory. A coherent policy paradigm was elaborated, and specific recommendations were made for reform. But follow-up depended on domestic institutional and political factors, and obstacles surfaced in both cases. This interplay between international ideas and national contexts is central to the third form of soft regulation – exhortation.

Making the Case: The OECD's Exhortative Regulation
The 2006 *Competitive Cities* synthesis report made the case for the paradigm of innovative liberalism, but in so doing paid particular attention to the complexities of transmitting policy ideas. Notably, it identified seven "dilemmas with which policy-makers (either national, urban or both) are confronted" (OECD 2006j, 17). These dilemmas were presented as "strategic choices" that demanded careful reflection on "the scope for creative compromises around them, and also initiatives which have sought to transcend the need for choice" (OECD 2006j, 80). The synthesis report acknowledged that the territorial reviews had not delivered simple or direct answers to the challenges. As such, the TDPC was advancing its paradigm but in a way that recognized knowledge gaps and encouraged "reflexive experimentation" by member states. Case examples were liberally cited but caution was the watchword when it came to borrowing ideas and applying lessons: "Cases are quoted, not because they serve as models to follow, but because they illustrate themes and provide examples. The actual paths chosen in specific contexts will depend on political criteria, the particular balance of issues at stake, and the creativity of individual groups of policy-makers" (OECD 2006j, 80).

What were the specific dilemmas that *Competitive Cities* highlighted? Among the seven, three addressed broad policy design issues and four considered the practicalities of new governance arrangements.

With policy design, the first dilemma involved deciding whether cities, in fact, were the engines of national economies. At issue was whether big cities, on balance, take more resources (people and investment) from outlying regions than they return through "positive spillovers." It was possible in some countries that national urban policies could limit overall growth by hindering regionally differentiated competitive strategies. The second design issue flowed from the first. Recognizing the extraordinary fiscal and infrastructure needs of the large cities, how might these costs be optimally shared? The appropriate mix would balance devolution of revenue streams to the largest municipalities to better meet their special needs with retention of the national policy capacity for investments in lagging regions. However, the territorial reviews demonstrated that "the structures of governance in place in many metropolitan areas of OECD are not well adapted to the tasks they face" (OECD 2006j, 156).

For governance reform, *Competitive Cities* identified four areas of strategic choice. First, tensions were acknowledged between the OECD's preferred metropolitan scale of governance for the learning regions and the democratic need for citizen responsiveness and accountability through local government. A variety of approaches to city-region governance were profiled, with a caution against imposed amalgamations and a preference for "lighter forms of governance" that were more flexible and institutionalized with public support (OECD 2006j, 26). The second governance issue concerned the need to create a "public strategic vision" and planning capacity that still responded to market forces. Appropriate flexibility could be maintained through devolution to arms-length authorities – "competitiveness councils" with a developmental mandate and tools (OECD 2006j, 129). The third governance dilemma arose, however, when the local development bodies become dominated by particular business interests or trade associations. The risk was twofold: emerging clusters might not be represented in development strategies, and civil society organizations might find themselves excluded.

The final governance challenge was central to the entire TDPC urban project. With urban affairs being increasingly critical to national well-being, how can upper-level governments best intervene in cities? Multilevel governance pursues seemingly contradictory goals: local autonomy *and* national standards, innovation *and* inclusion, horizontal networks *and* vertical collaboration, metropolitan planning *and* voluntary cooperation. Effective multilevel governance, the synthesis report strongly argued, required a negotiated rather than hierarchical approach: "The *contract* formula would allow government mechanisms to be adapted to local characteristics and replace traditional hierarchical relationships with contracts based on negotiation and a learning process" (OECD 2006j, 206; emphasis in original). The report went on to list general principles of multilevel governance, such as structured negotiations with clear timelines, incentives for participation among different governments, and specific monitoring and assessment protocols. To illustrate the range of multilevel frameworks, several member state contractual models were highlighted: the French Metropolitan Contracts, Canadian Urban Development Agreements, and Swedish Local Development Agreements. The importance of this approach to the TDPC's overall territorial agenda was further confirmed in a 2007 publication investigating multilevel contractual arrangements in five countries (OECD 2007d).

In sum, the TDPC's exhortative strategy was sensitive to local context and receptor capacity. The main message was that that there is *"no best practice or one size fits all solution"* (OECD 2006j, 191; emphasis in original). In identifying seven urban policy dilemmas, *Competitive Cities* cautioned: "It is important for policy-makers to recognize the reality of these conflicts and tensions and not to avoid them through functionally neat formulae that succeed only in hiding them" (OECD 2006j, 199). This style was evident in its call for cluster strategies that warned against quick-fix solutions based on widely celebrated Silicon Valley or Third Italy successes. Learning regions grew over the long term based on social networking and customized investments in urban infrastructure. Similarly, policies to deal with the social consequences of cluster building would be shaped by country-specific welfare state traditions and local civil societies. Rather than imposing a finished or fixed model on member states, the TDPC looked to inform purposeful and reflexive action around the common dilemmas revealed through its territorial reviews.

Conclusion: Innovative Liberalism for the Cities?
This chapter has interpreted the work of the OECD in urban policy and governance. In the late 1990s, it joined a flourishing debate around the new localism. Analyzing different modes of soft regulation, we argued that the OECD created a new hybrid urban policy paradigm. The Canadian experience was used to illustrate how the paradigm influenced domestic policy agendas but also was reshaped by national and local factors. This attention to the complex interaction across scales in the transmission of policy ideas was fully reflected in the TDPC's exhortative approach. It described a series of urban dilemmas and counselled caution in the face of limited policy knowledge and tentative lessons from the territorial reviews.

What about the future prospects for implementing the TDPC's innovative liberalism? For guidance, we can return to Peter A. Hall's discussion of policy ideas. In addition to providing criteria for identifying policy paradigms, Hall proposed that their effective power depends on securing viability in administrative, political, and discursive terms (Hall 1989a). In relation to the OECD's soft regulation, Hall's three criteria can be tracked along two dimensions. First, *internally* within the overall context of the OECD's public policy work, the question arises as to the discursive fit of the urban paradigm with the larger macroeconomic and structural policies. Second, and *externally*, the ultimate fate of the TDPC's paradigm depends on administrative and political factors particular to member states.

As to the first issue, it is clear that the OECD, in the words of Secretary-General Gurría, recognizes that "the development of dynamic cities depends as much on national framework conditions as on an effective urban policy agenda" (Gurría 2007b). Much less obvious is whether the OECD's preferred macroeconomic and structural policies actually support implementation of the urban paradigm. The TDPC's organizational discourse addresses several market failures in economic development, and calls for flanking social and community development investments. Yet, neither the market failures nor the flanking investments are included in macroeconomic and structural policies celebrating restrictive budgetary measures and labour market flexibility. Moreover, the fiscal and income security policies central to the OECD's macroeconomic and structural discourses are mostly the preserve of national governments (and central banks), with little consideration given to input from below. Without more inter-scalar integration across the OECD's macroeconomic, structural, and territorial policy paradigms, the TDPC's innovative liberalism remains a bounded project.

In relation to the second dimension of viability – implementation in member states – it is clear from the territorial reviews and inquisitive regulation that nationally specific administrative and political legacies are critical determinants. As such, more action research around the seven policy and governance dilemmas should reveal institutional/political configurations that facilitate or hinder innovative liberalism in urban settings. Here the preference for contextualized learning is welcome. It is notable that many of the main ideas that have informed the TDPC's policy work emerged through connections with the urban agenda of the European Union (EU). This cross-fertilization is highlighted in many OECD publications and conferences. Moving forward, the EU/OECD dialogue should include modes of policy transfer. The EU, through its employment strategies and methods of coordination, has pioneered cross-national processes of contextualized learning (Noakson and Jacobsson 2003). As this chapter has shown, the TDPC is well positioned to embed such sophisticated dissemination frameworks into all of its urban policy work.

8
Policy Learning?
The OECD and Its Jobs Strategy
*Stephen McBride, Kathleen McNutt,
and Russell Alan Williams*

The Jobs Study reports of the Organisation for Economic Co-operation and Development (OECD 1994a, 1994b) were produced for member nations' labour, economic, and finance ministers, who sought improved policy responses to rising unemployment levels. The resulting "Jobs Strategy" was championed as a best practices guide for countering high unemployment rates through deregulation, market liberalization, and the removal of labour market rigidities. The Jobs Strategy included a suite of policy recommendations designed to improve key performance measures in the labour market and reduce barriers to competition and growth. Policy ideas associated with the strategy were diffused through a system of peer review, which was assumed to promote learning through processes of policy transfer and emulation[1] (Hodson and Maher 2001; Pagani 2002b).

This initiative provides a useful example in which several of the themes identified in the introduction to this volume can be discerned. The OECD played a role in developing an explanation of 1990s unemployment (meditative role), but was even more visible in proselytizing its conclusions and attempting to hold member countries to account through its reports and country studies (inquisitive role). Further, the OECD recommendations raise the issue of Americanization, since the empirical reference for the OECD's theory of unemployment and what to do about it appears to have been the contrast between the US labour market and that of Europe.[2] Certainly, the Jobs Strategy recommended transformation of labour market institutions towards the laissez-faire US model (Howell 2005, 18). Perhaps more important, though, than any empirical model was the theory-driven nature of OECD analysis of unemployment, particularly that provided by its Economics Department. The influence of neoclassical economists, many trained in Anglo-American universities and interacting with colleagues in the same discipline in national ministries of finance, was paramount. It was, we argue, both a powerful source of policy recommendations and a source of resistance to evidence that contradicted the certainties expressed in OECD publications. That said, the OECD is not a monolithic organization and there were certainly other currents within the organization (see Chapter 14) and between it and officials in other countries, and civil society organizations (see Chapters 9 and 10). The eventual rethinking of the OECD Jobs Strategy in 2006 also enables us to enter the debate about the extent to which OECD thinking has evolved, and to make use of the heuristic categories developed by Peter Graefe (2006) – countervail, flanking, or rollout – in analyzing the process of neoliberalization. The process of rollout refers to the reinforcement and further entrenchment of the neoliberal paradigm in both economic and social policy domains. Alternatively, policy reforms may be used as a "flanking mechanism" to support the neoliberal paradigm by ameliorating some of its social effects while strengthening its core. Finally, some states may adopt countervailing strategies that challenge the neoliberalization process (Graefe 2006).

For over a decade following the adoption of its 1994 Jobs Strategy, the OECD advocated policy activity associated with deregulation, market liberalization, welfare state restructuring, and labour market readjustment. It sought to harmonize labour market strategies, advocating the implementation of neoclassical economic policy to address global economic competition and high unemployment. Eventually, however, it had to admit that "efforts to implement the prescriptions of labour market deregulation did not necessarily lead to an impressive performance regarding employment and growth" (Schneider 2003, 30).

Evidence had been mounting for some time that the OECD Jobs Strategy had little or no impact on labour market performance. McBride and Williams's examination of OECD countries (2001) found no statistically significant correlation between compliance with OECD recommendations and improved labour market performance. Baker and colleagues (2004) found the empirical research inconclusive and, in a subsequent publication (Baker et al. 2005a, 108), concluded that there was a "yawning gap between the confidence with which the case for labour market deregulation has been asserted and the evidence that the regulating institutions are the culprits." Similarly, John Schmitt and Jonathan Wadsworth (2005, 189) argued that "data for the OECD countries, then, appear strongly at odds with the microeconomic model that has guided the OECD's recommendations to member countries and that has informed much government thinking on international differences in unemployment." Paul Gregg and Alan Manning (1997) considered that the blind faith placed in a deregulated labour market is analytically imprisoned in classical liberal orthodoxy, while Michèle Belot and Jan C. van Ours (2004) suggested the analyses failed to fully calculate institutional legacies and interactions into the competitive equation. Jonas Agell's analysis .

(1999) also contradicted the OECD's Jobs Strategy hypotheses, finding evidence that the pressures of globalization and international competition may even require greater labour market rigidities.

Furthermore, empirical evidence supporting the OECD Jobs Study and subsequent Jobs Strategy hypothesis tends to limit evaluation to economic effects, while providing only cursory considerations of the strategy's effects on institutions and social conditions. Indeed, the Jobs Strategy did not provide an adequate policy focus on non-economic objectives of social policy generally, a fact that member states noted when the recalcitrant among them refused to implement the OECD program due to concerns about "social cohesion" (McBride and Williams 2001). Building on these insights, we argue that it was apparent, long before the spring 2006 re-evaluation of the Jobs Strategy by the OECD, that its claim to superiority over other labour market models was unsupported by the evidence. Second, we note that when the re-evaluation occurred, it was half-hearted at best, leaving the thrust of the original Jobs Study in place while making cursory acknowledgments that other models functioned equally well or better. For too long, the OECD was resistant to the evidence that some countries that rejected significant parts of the OECD analysis and policies were doing well on labour market indicators and maintaining social cohesion *and* international economic competitiveness.

To draw out this aspect of the OECD's failure to learn, it is useful to note that patterns of labour market policy continue to conform to a modernized version of the typology of welfare state regimes developed by Esping-Andersen (McBride et al. 2007), and that analysis of the performance of particular clusters can highlight the OECD's rather blinkered approach to labour market issues. Esping-Andersen's now classic three worlds typology (1990) remains a benchmark in comparative welfare state research (Anderson 2001; Hartman 2005). The model identifies three welfare state regimes, with each characterized by a set of social policy variables that influence the state's degree of decommodification and stratification (Green-Pedersen 2002a; Hartman 2005; Patterson and Briar 2005; Ryan 2003). In part, the popularity of Esping-Andersen's model is its ability to explain welfare state resilience (Bonoli 2003; Pierson 1994) and the continued "varieties of capitalism" despite the harmonizing logic of globalization (Hall and Soskice 2001; Pontusson 2005).

Analyzing Clusters

Using Esping-Andersen's (1990) typology as a basis, we construct two contemporary clusters to highlight the point. The "liberal" group of states (those largely compliant with OECD labour market policy recommendations) consists of Australia, Canada, New Zealand, the United Kingdom, and the

United States. These states have embraced the neoliberal policy paradigm and have sought to improve labour market flexibility to nurture competition (Bryan and Rafferty 2000; Cronin 2001; Lloyd 2002; McBride and Williams 2001; Wiseman 1998). The second cluster is the "flexicurity" cluster, a modernized version of the social democratic regimes, which seek a greater balance between economic competitiveness and social protection (Auer 2004; Hayden 2000; Nielsen and Kesting 2003; Sarfati 2003; Svensson and Öberg 2002; van Oorschot 2004). As a result, they are less compliant with the OECD Jobs Strategy model, as a group, than the liberal cluster. Nations included in this cluster are Denmark, Finland, Norway, the Netherlands, and Sweden. The ten states used in this comparison rank among the twenty wealthiest, most globalized economies in the world, and have embraced policy restructuring in the period of globalization.

Neoliberal strategy for improved labour market performance rests on two principles. At the macroeconomic level, neoliberals argue that if inflation is to be controlled, some unemployment is inevitable and central banks and ministries of finance must accept the non-accelerating inflationary rate of unemployment (NAIRU). Neoliberal analysis also rests on the empirical claim that poor European labour market performance in the 1990s was the result of a "European sclerosis" in which excessive state intervention and spending were undermining labour market performance relative to the United States, where wage rate flexibility and truncated employment protection forced workers to adopt more quickly to economic change (Auer 2004). States in the cluster provide minimal standards featuring means-tested assistance, modest social transfer to the working class and poor, and stigmatized benefits: Flexicurity policy is premised on an appropriate balance between labour and welfare priorities. The primary policy objective is to provide social protection for workers engaged in flexible employment relationships and promote greater levels of labour force participation through the provision of state policies supportive of entry into the labour force. The flexibility-security nexus is designed to provide a flexible workforce for employers seeking to enhance competitiveness, while at the same time providing workers engaged in atypical or nonstandard employment with some level of basic economic security. (Klammer and Tillmann 2001, 16). The flexicurity model rests on a series of complex trade-offs:

> The flexibility side of such a model involves acceptance of limited job security (as opposed to employment security), tolerance of job creation in non standard forms of employment, and pro-employment wage bargaining outcomes; while the security side involves relatively equal wages and benefits in different forms of work, access to career ladders, decent unemployment benefits, and swift access to new and higher quality jobs for unemployed

workers. Training, active labour market policies and workplace co-operation all help make equitable labour markets employment friendly. (Jackson 2004a, 4).

Flexicurity countries continue to have significantly higher "rigidities." For example, flexicurity countries tend to guarantee more rights to workers and spend more on labour market programs in which the state intervenes directly in the market. While all countries have seen declines in program spending (as labour market conditions have improved and fewer workers are in need of unemployment insurance, etc.), there is still variation between the two clusters; liberal countries average 1.54 percent of GDP spent on labour market programs, while those in the flexicurity cluster average 2.78 percent (OECD 2004e).

Similarly, the level of "security" that workers enjoy varies between the two clusters. This can be illustrated through measures of union density, collective bargaining coverage, and the "Decent Work Index" of the International Labour Organization (ILO) (see Table 8.1).

The flexicurity cluster's workforce is far more organized, with stronger levels of union density and more collective bargaining coverage. "Decent work" is a concept originally introduced by the ILO, which identified four key components of decent work, including social protection, workers' rights, employment, and social dialogue (ILO 1999; Anker et al. 2003). The employment aspect of decent work encompasses all forms of labour, including unpaid

Table 8.1

Security of employment indicators

OECD nations	Decent work ranking	Union density ranking[1]	Collective bargaining ranking	Aggregate rank
Neoliberal cluster				
Australia	8	7	3	6
Canada	5	6	8	8
New Zealand	9	9	8	9
United Kingdom	6	5	7	6
United States	9	10	10	1
Flexicurity cluster				
Denmark	2	3	3	3
Finland	4	2	1	2
Netherlands	7	8	3	5
Norway	3	4	6	4
Sweden	1	1	1	1

[1] Union density ranked highest (1) to lowest (10).
Sources: Dharam (2003); OECD (2004e).

domestic, self-employment, unregulated, and non-standard. It also considers opportunities for employment, adequate living wages, and the health and safety of workplace conditions. Workers' rights include freedom of association, opportunities for organization and collective bargaining, protection against child labour, and assurance against forced labour activity (Dharam 2003). The importance of social dialogue for achieving decent work standards is also identified as critical, suggesting that workers should have ample opportunities to negotiate with employers free from coercion, participate in activities that directly impact the interests of workers, and provide a public environment in which employees exercise freedom of expression. Finally, social protection refers to the importance of economic security, levels of state-sponsored protection, and human capital investment. The ILO suggests that the concept of decent work is meant to counter the prevailing neoliberal economic model, which fails to provide social democratic accountability and justice for the world's workers (ILO 2003). The flexicurity countries tend to score much higher on the Decent Work Index. Not only do they tend to spend more on labour market programs, but workers tend to be more secure in these national settings.

The question is: do these national labour market rigidities hurt the economic performance of these countries, as neoliberals assume, or are they a source of economic strength, as many have traditionally argued?

The Neoliberal Consensus and the OECD Strategy

Globalization has significantly altered the global market, domestic economies, and the world of work (McBride 2005). Economic policy pundits quickly identified the American model as the "best" response to the effects of globalization, arguing that labour market inflexibility arising from such structural rigidities as employment protection policy and union participation in the wage-setting process were the primary reasons for poor economic performance (Stanford 2003). The rationalization for the global diffusion of the American-style policy approach was sustained economic growth and concurrent low levels of unemployment in the US. In 1994, the OECD Jobs Strategy standardized the neoliberal framework provided by the American experience, often problematically referred to as the "flexibility model" – problematic since it posits a narrow understanding of labour market flexibility. The OECD consolidated the neoliberal labour market policy agendas into a ten-point action framework in its Jobs Study in 1994 (OECD 1994a). The action framework included measures to:

- encourage non-inflationary growth
- support the creation and diffusion of technological know-how
- increase flexibility for employers
- make wage and labour costs more flexible

- reform employment security provisions that inhibit the expansion of employment in the private sector
- strengthen the emphasis on active labour market policies
- improve labour force skills and competencies
- reform unemployment insurance and related benefit systems
- enhance competition within the economy.

The Jobs Study also established a global system of benchmarking to identify a best practices approach to labour market policy. The consensus among policy advisors was to direct states towards a wholesale adoption of NAIRU-based labour policy as the best response to globalization.

Nevertheless, to support the recommendations of the Jobs Strategy, the OECD endorsed eighty specific labour market policy recommendations, emphasizing deregulation and the removal or reduction of the influence of various labour market institutions (unionization, social benefits, and employment protection). Equipped with this agenda, the OECD launched a surveillance project aimed at encouraging member states to adopt the study's specific recommendations. The results were published in the OECD's regular country surveys. As well, special publications dealing with implementation have been issued (OECD 1997b, 1997d, 1998c, 1999c). This represents a major effort to keep the deregulatory labour market strategy on the political agenda in member countries.

From these recommendations, a measure of compliance can be developed, illustrating the degree to which states' labour market policies conform to the neoliberal agenda (Table 8.2). This measure of compliance, originally

Table 8.2

OECD labour market compliance rankings

OECD nations	Number of recommendations	Number of policies monitored	Compliance score	Rank order	Percentage compliant
Australia	5	2	73	1	91.25
United States	7	0	73	1	91.25
United Kingdom	5	5	70	3	87.5
New Zealand	8	6	66	4	82.5
Canada	12	4	64	5	80.0
Denmark	13	5	62	6	77.5
Sweden	23	1	56	7	70.0
Norway	21	4	55	8	68.75
Netherlands	19	7	54	9	67.5
Finland	25	6	49	10	61.25
Maximum possible			80		

Sources: OECD (1997b, 1998c).

produced by McBride and Williams (2001), provides a rough measure of our
ten selected OECD nations' embrace of the Jobs Strategy policy advice.
The number in the compliance score column represents the number of
the eighty OECD recommendations that, in the OECD's view, have been
satisfactorily implemented. As the compliance scores of Australia and the
United States illustrate, these two nations had largely conformed to the
OECD agenda, suggesting that both *should* enjoy growing levels of employment and competitiveness. Alternatively, Finland's lower score shows that
it continued to display significantly higher labour market rigidities.

**Policy Performance I: Neoliberal Compliance, Competitiveness,
and Employment Growth**
The language of flexibility emphasizes improving competitiveness and labour
force participation. Indeed, neoliberals argue that real improvement in labour
market performance can be achieved only by removing the politically generated "rigidities" in the market that create disincentives for adaptation. These
include the presence of strong trade unions, employment protection legislation, social supports, and unemployment insurance, which by this interpretation actually increase unemployment above its natural level, since people
are simply encouraged not to work (Kuhn 1997). To measure competitiveness
among states, we employ the World Economic Forum's Growth Competitiveness Index, which is composed of three "pillars," "all of which are widely
accepted as being critical to economic growth: the quality of the macroeconomic environment, the state of a country's public institutions and
policies, and, given the increasing importance of technology in the development process, a country's technological readiness" (Schwab 2004, xii).
The Growth Competitiveness Index provides a rank ordering of a state's
ability to compete in a globalized market. As Table 8.3 reveals, neoliberal
policy approaches do not guarantee such success, with the flexicurity cluster
outperforming the neoliberal cluster.
If neoliberal analyses were correct and the OECD's policy agenda did encourage growth and enhance competitiveness, then Finland should have
been the least competitive market in these clusters and the United States
and Australia the best. While it is clear that the flexicurity cluster's labour
market rigidities were higher than in the neoliberal states, there is no correlation between the compliance score and enhanced competitiveness.
Finland boasts the best ranking for growth and competitiveness despite its
labour market "rigidities" (see also McBride et al. 2007).
The picture in terms of employment growth is similar. While neoliberals
argue that more flexible labour markets will boost overall employment levels
over the long term, evidence suggest that countries with the most neoliberal
policies were outperformed in employment growth by the flexicurity cluster
(see Table 8.4).

Table 8.3

Growth Competitiveness Index (GCI) rankings and OECD Jobs Strategy compliance

OECD nations	GCI 2004 rank	Compliance score rank
Neoliberal cluster		
Australia	8	1
Canada	9	5
New Zealand	10	4
United Kingdom	6	3
United States	2	1
Flexicurity cluster		
Denmark	4	6
Finland	1	7
Netherlands	7	8
Norway	5	9
Sweden	3	10

Source: World Economic Forum (2004).

Table 8.4

Employment rate change, 1994-2003

OECD nations	Employment rate		Rate change 1994-2003	Ranking
	1994	2003		
Neoliberal cluster				
Australia	65.7	69.3	3.6	7
Canada	67.1	72.1	5	4
New Zealand	67.8	76.1	8.3	2
United Kingdom	68.8	72.9	4.1	5
United States	72.0	71.2	–0.8	10
Neoliberal average	68.28	72.32	4	
Flexicurity cluster				
Denmark	72.4	75.1	2.7	9
Finland	59.7	67.4	7.7	3
Netherlands	63.8	73.6	9.8	1
Norway	72.2	75.9	3.7	6
Sweden	71.5	74.3	2.8	8
Flexicurity average	67.92	73.26	5.3	

Source: OECD (2004e).

Thus, the flexicurity countries, far from suffering from rigidities, actually performed better than the countries that pursued the neoliberal policy mix. This finding is even more provocative when we move beyond evaluating labour market performance in simply economic terms and turn to the question of social reproduction.

Policy Performance II: Social Reproduction

Social reproduction refers to such activities as health care, education, care-giving, and child rearing, and a myriad of functions traditionally associated with domestic labour are included (Bakker 2003). Keynesian-era labour market policy and social protection services were predicated on a model of the male breadwinner, which assumed that a male partner engaged in public sphere labour activities would earn a living wage that could support the female partner and any other dependent located within the household (Orloff 1993). The realities of modern labour markets and family forms are funda-mentally at variance with the male breadwinner model, however. Instead, there is an increasing reliance on co-breadwinning, in which dual-income earners are necessitated by the volatility of flexible employment arrange-ments and precarious work (Forrest 2001). Other things being equal, this will create greater reliance on the state and non-household agencies for performance of social reproduction activities.

Programs during the Keynesian era provided some mechanisms to assist both those whose careers were in the home and those whose careers meant entry into the labour force. Although the programs implemented during this era where structurally paternal and perpetuated sexism, racism, and homophobia, the policies were designed, although certainly not always successfully, to ensure a minimum standard of living. Programs associated with this era were predominantly structured on the family-wage model, in which the state supplemented family income and played an active role in social reproduction in terms of education, training programs, housing, and financial assistance. With the ascendancy of neoliberal globalization, how-ever, there were a myriad of incremental shifts in policy away from the arena of social reproduction in many states. As the notion of the atomized indi-vidual was absorbed into the political fabric of politics, the family-wage model was abandoned for market-friendly policies that did not provide the stabilizers associated with the Keynesian model. During this era, women experienced numerous policy losses and were increasingly forced to partici-pate in a hostile labour environment.

To compare social reproduction performance, we first looked at spending on income security. For example, drawing on the OECD's recent attempts to calculate "net public social expenditure," which measures both gross public social spending and income tax effects on social support, there are consider-able differences between the two clusters (Adema 2001) (see Table 8.5).

Similarly, the number of citizens living in poverty varies, with the flexicur-ity cluster able to limit poverty to less than 10 percent of their populations while the neoliberal cluster experienced poverty rates as high as 15 percent (Adema 2001).

Gender equality is another indicator of the state's role in ensuring social protection, risk diversification, and justice. As economic and financial

Table 8.5

Social reproduction support: Net social expenditures as a percentage of GDP

OECD nations	Net social expenditures as percentage of GDP	Aggregate ranking
Neoliberal cluster		
Australia	17.9	8
Canada	18.7	7
New Zealand	17	9
United Kingdom	21.6	5
United States	16.4	10
Neoliberal average	18.32	
Flexicurity cluster		
Denmark	26.6	2
Finland	24.8	3
Netherlands	20.3	6
Norway	24.4	4
Sweden	28.5	1
Flexicurity average	24.92	

Source: Adema (2001).

openness permeate the post-industrial world, women's engagement in part-time employment and precarious employment increased. To measure gender equality, we employed three specific indicators from the United Nations Human Development Branch and Divisions of the Advancement of Women (Table 8.6). The gender empowerment index is a "composite index measuring gender inequality in three basic dimensions of empowerment – economic participation and decision-making, political participation and decision-making and power over economic resources" (UNDP 2004). The flexicurity cluster clearly provides a greater degree of empowerment.

The ratio of women's earned income to that of men reveals the degree of states' commitment to ensuring economic equality and women's income security. The flexicurity cluster performed better in terms of income equality, with women earning an average of 70 percent of men, compared with 65 percent in the neoliberal cluster. While any variation between women's and men's wages is problematic, the flexicurity cluster has provided a greater degree of equality in wage earnings. Finally, we considered states' commitment to women's rights, emanating from the 1995 Beijing Fourth World Conference on Women and various international laws designed to protect women and girls. The flexicurity cluster and New Zealand have fully complied and implemented policy to advance and protect women's rights. The neoliberal cluster, minus New Zealand, has a varied record on compliance, with the UK and Canada more committed to women's equality than the US and Australia.

Table 8.6

Gender equality: Rank order of indicators

OECD nations	Gender empowerment measure rank	Ratio of earned income women-to-men rank	Compliance with international women's rights	Aggregate rank
Neoliberal cluster				
Australia	6	4	9	7
Canada	7	7	7	8
New Zealand	8	6	1	5
United Kingdom	10	9	7	9
United States	9	8	9	9
Flexicurity cluster				
Denmark	3	3	1	3
Finland	4	5	1	4
Netherlands	5	10	1	6
Norway	1	2	1	1
Sweden	2	1	1	1

Sources: UNDP (2004); United Nations Division for the Advancement of Women (2005).

In sum, the performance of the flexicurity countries falsifies the OECD Jobs Strategy hypothesis that labour market rigidities impede competitiveness and construct obstacles to strong economic performance. The conventional wisdom of the neoliberal labour market response to globalization advocated by the OECD lacks empirical validation. Indeed, some of the most significant positive gains have been accomplished in nations with high social wages, organized labour forces, and active state intervention (Alderson 2004) (Table 8.7).

The OECD Jobs Strategy, by these measures, does not improve labour performance, nor does it appear to enhance competitiveness compared with the flexicurity countries. Jobs Strategy compliance scores were strongly negatively correlated with net social expenditures, security of employment, and gender equality. On the other hand, perhaps unsurprisingly, state support of social reproduction was strongly correlated with gender equality.

What does all of this suggest? First, there is no compelling reason to assume that a neoliberal emphasis on labour market flexibility – flexibility to be achieved by welfare state retrenchment – improves economic performance in a global economy. Second, it does appear that the choice of this strategy will, however, undermine efforts to support social reproduction and gender equality and to reduce poverty.

Conclusion: The Revised Jobs Strategy (2006)

One of the most notable things about the last fourteen years of OECD work

Table 8.7

Aggregate ranking of indicators and OECD Jobs Strategy compliance

OECD nations	OECD Jobs Strategy compliance	Security of employment	Competitiveness	System of social reproduction
Neoliberal cluster				
Australia	1	6	8	8
Canada	5	8	9	6
New Zealand	4	9	10	6
United Kingdom	3	6	6	10
United States	1	10	2	8
Flexicurity cluster				
Denmark	6	3	4	3
Finland	10	2	1	4
Netherlands	9	5	7	5
Norway	8	4	5	2
Sweden	7	1	3	1

Sources: See Tables 8.1 to 8.6.

on labour market policy is that the record of "policy learning" and transfer has been poor. While some member states, those ideologically predisposed to the Jobs Strategy, adopted OECD recommendations, many did not. Despite OECD efforts, existing domestic institutional arrangements, domestic policy networks, and ideological differences made much of the initial OECD program politically unthinkable throughout Europe, no matter how much credibility the OECD lent its reading of "best practices."

The absence of social learning among national policy makers has been mirrored at the OECD. Prior to 2006, despite serious mounting evidence that many of the key claims underpinning the Jobs Strategy were not being borne out empirically (against the OECD's own benchmark measures, such as employment rate growth), the OECD chose to stand by its neoliberal model. Rather than investigate anomalous success stories – those states pursuing the "wrong" strategy but performing well against OECD indicators – the Secretariat's supporting studies went to great lengths to massage the reading of various cases to validate the assumptions of the Jobs Strategy (McBride and Williams 2001). Mounting evidence that the strategy did not necessarily work, or that there were alternative approaches, only stimulated further endorsements of the strategy. Clearly, this continued resistance was linked to the theory-driven nature of advice emanating from the OECD's Economics Department.

Eventually, however, the empirical record of the Jobs Strategy did force a partial re-evaluation. Few could deny the fact that some countries were doing a better job of combating unemployment by ignoring OECD norms. Even the business press has lauded Denmark's flexicurity approach (*Economist* 2006) (not without noting that this approach cannot be copied elsewhere!). Conceding that the evidence of actual labour market performance has not done any favours for the Jobs Strategy, and reflecting the fact that so many OECD member states had rejected the original strategy in practice, in 2003 the employment and labour ministers asked the Secretariat to reassess the entire strategy. This led to the 2006 release *Boosting Jobs and Incomes: Policy Lessons from Reassessing the OECD Jobs Strategy* (OECD 2006k), along with supporting studies in the 2006 *Employment Outlook* (OECD 2006n).

The 2006 Jobs Strategy has been publicly promoted by the OECD as an endorsement of the notion that there is more than one path to good labour market performance:

There is no single strategy for improving labour-market performance. Several successful performers – notably, the United States – combine low levels of social benefits, low taxes and light employment regulations. Others – such as the Nordic countries – offer generous, but well designed social benefits. However, this does not mean that anything goes. The successful performers share some common features, such as an emphasis on macroeconomic stability and strong product-market competition. These make up the four pillars of the 2006 OECD Jobs Strategy. (OECD 2006l, 3).

This was seen as a major concession to critics of the neoliberal emphasis of the earlier strategy, as it appeared to endorse the flexicurity approach as a possible alternative.

While this about-face was important, the revised strategy also suggested a fundamentally new emphasis – that the goal of labour market policy was no longer simply to reduce unemployment but rather to ensure adequate labour supply for the future. Thus, much of the discussion of the strategy revolved around the question of how those outside the labour force (35 percent of the OECD working age population) could be brought into the workforce (OECD 2006m). Additionally, the report placed renewed emphasis on the need to support the knowledge economy through adult skills, and investment in training, which were already pillars of the economic growth platform published in the 2003 *Growth Study* (OECD 2003g). With these concerns in mind, the revised strategy replaced the original ten-point program of the 1994 Jobs Strategy with a new "Four Pillars" of job creation and job demand. (See Figure 8.1.)

While the 2006 Jobs Strategy is certainly a revision of the previous recommendations, much of the analysis and policy advice remains staunchly neoliberal. In fact, it does little to come to grips with the success of the

Figure 8.1

Highlights of the "Four Pillars" of the revised Jobs Strategy (2006)

Pillar A: Set appropriate macroeconomic policy

• Achieve price stability and sustainable public finance

Pillar B: Remove impediments to labour market participation and job search

• Implement well-designed unemployment benefit systems and active labour market policies
  – Set unemployment benefits and social assistance at levels that do not discourage job search
  – Ensure that employment services are compulsory after a certain length of joblessness
  – Regularly and rigorously assess active labour market programs to ensure that inefficient programs are terminated

• Make other non-employment benefits more work-oriented
  – Put in place measures to prevent individuals with work capacity from leaving the labour market through sickness and disability systems
  – Phase out early retirement, and reform pension and welfare systems to remove incentives for early retirement

• Facilitate family-friendly arrangements
  – Increase child care support to remove barriers to employment for those with family commitments

• Adjust taxes and other transfer programs to make work pay
  – Make employment more financially attractive

Pillar C: Tackle labour and product market obstacles to labour demand

• Ensure that wages and labour costs respond to labour market developments
  – Ensure that minimum wages are set low enough so that they do not harm job creation for low-productivity workers
  – Reduce payroll taxes
  – Allow individual firms to opt out of sectoral collective agreements

• Enhance competition in product markets
  – Reduce competition-restraining state control of business operations

• Facilitate the adoption of flexible working time arrangements

• Make sure that employment protection legislation helps labour-market dynamism and provides security to workers
  – Reform employment protection legislation in countries where it is overly strict

• Promote transitions to formal employment

▶

◄ *Figure 8.1*

Pillar D: Facilitate the development of labour force skills and competencies

• Promote high-quality initial education

• Work with social partners to improve labour force skills
  - Improve system for recognizing foreign credentials of immigrants
  - Ensure that training is more demand-driven and responds to firms' skill requirements
  - Expand the scope of apprenticeship contracts by easing age limits and allowing flexible compensation
  - Ensure that some employment programs are targeted to the specific needs of disadvantaged people

Source: Based on the summary recommendations in OECD (2006k).

---

flexicurity countries. Instead, despite its stated acceptance of an alternative approach, the report and its "Four Pillars" recommendations largely support the neoliberal orientation of the 1994 Jobs Strategy. For example, even though the Jobs Strategy (2006) accepts that alternative strategies can work, the OECD Secretariat is clearly skeptical. In June 2006, Human Resources and Social Development Canada and the OECD hosted the OECD Jobs Strategy Forum in Toronto, where the revised strategy was presented for discussion purposes, with a number of leading economists invited to present their views. They proceeded to shift discussion from the merits of alternative approaches to questioning the evidence supporting flexicurity, suggesting that large active labour market programs in Nordic countries "masked" higher real rates of unemployment (OECD 2006l, 4). While this was presented as a "dissident opinion," it is important to note that one major assumption of the revised strategy is that many workers are being improperly sheltered outside the labour market through overly generous early retirement, sickness, and disability programs, all of which should be reduced, according to the new strategy. The target countries for these reductions are those pursuing the successful alternative strategy. Raymond Torres, a member of the OECD Economics Department and one of the leaders of the re-evaluation of the Jobs Strategy, summarized his view in an OECD newsletter, arguing that while the report acknowledged that the programs pursued by countries like Denmark could reduce unemployment, "this approach, however, is not without its own problems. It can be costly to the public purse. Also, people may react to closer monitoring of their job search and benefit sanctions by applying for other out-of-work benefits, such as sickness or disability, lone parent and early retirement benefits. In some countries falls in unemployment have been matched by increased flows onto these other programs" (OECD 2006l).

While the 2006 Jobs Strategy publicly proclaims the existence of an alternative strategy, much of the Secretariat's analysis emphasizes that this is not a good policy to pursue.

More to the point, the substance of the new "Four Pillars" recommendations clearly favour a more neoliberal policy framework than otherwise. For example, consistent with the original Jobs Strategy, the new recommendations seek to remove rigidities from the labour market that discourage adaptation to globalization. The new recommendations suggest keeping unemployment and social assistance benefits low, keeping minimum wages low, and reducing access to long-term disability and early retirement programs (OECD 2006k, 2006m). The proposals also encourage states to remove tax and pension incentives that encourage people to leave the labour market early, while also suggesting that income taxes should be reduced to "make work pay." All of these measures are promoted as vital to ensuring that the labour market is competitive and provides employment even for low-productivity workers. They also act to ensure that the labour market is "flexible" (in the language of the earlier Jobs Strategy) for employers. Furthermore, despite the admission by the OECD in its research that strong levels of employment protection legislation that prevent rapid job shedding do not seem to have the negative effect on unemployment levels that was assumed in the 1994 strategy (OECD 2006l, 3), the new strategy continues to suggest that member states should reduce such legislation "where it is too strict" (OECD 2006k). All of these recommendations fit nicely with the assumptions and "best practices" put forward by the original Jobs Study, and seem to directly attack the underlying structures of the flexicurity approach.

Despite increased recognition that alternative strategies are working, these are deemed risky and undesirable, and so the revised Jobs Strategy continues to promote a set of neoliberal labour market policies. Thus, despite the evidence that many other states have had more successful labour market policies, the OECD continues to promote its own preferred policy framework. OECD best practices remain ideologically bounded, focusing on flexibility as the necessary response to globalization. In terms of Graefe's categories, this looks like a rollout strategy – neoliberalization continues with remarkably little in the way of concession to the countervailing evidence. This is consistent with both an ideological attachment to orthodox economics and a belief in the superiority of the American model. While this may not be the case in all policy areas, in the crucial labour market area, theoretical "push back" by advocates of other and less socially costly routes to labour market success has had limited impact.

Acknowledgments
The authors gratefully acknowledge funding under a Community University Research Alliance grant (Social Sciences and Humanities Research Council of Canada) – the Economic Security Project (Principal Investigators Seth Klein and Marjorie Griffin Cohen).

Notes

1 "Emulation" suggests that one nation borrows ideas, policy instruments, or programs from other nations and then adjusts the design to domestic conditions (Bennett 1991). "Policy transfer" refers to cross-national learning in which one nation adopts "policy goals, policy content, policy instruments, policy programs, institutions, ideologies, ideas and attitudes and negative lessons" based on knowledge garnered through the experience of another nation (Dolowitz and Marsh 2000, 12).

2 Although, as Jonas Pontusson (2005, 9) has pointed out, Europe's unemployment problem seems to have been confined to a small group of states.

9
"Crafting the Conventional Economic Wisdom": The OECD and the Canadian Policy Process
Andrew Jackson

As a case study of the influence of the Organisation for Economic Co-operation and Development on the national policy-making process, this chapter attempts to gauge the influence of the organization and its country review process on Canadian economic and labour market policy in the period from 1993 to 2006.[1] This covers the tenure in power of the federal Liberal Party, and also overlaps closely with the first phase of the OECD-led Jobs Strategy (see Chapter 8). One might have anticipated some tension between a government of the political centre that was a key architect of the postwar Canadian welfare state and a set of policy recommendations that has been widely and justifiably characterized as neoliberal. However, the key priorities of the 1993-2006 federal government led by Prime Minister Jean Chrétien and Finance Minister Paul Martin (who served a brief term as prime minister from 2004 to 2006) were government deficit and debt reduction, achieved by deep cuts to program spending. A major reform of the Unemployment Insurance system was justified, not just by the need for fiscal discipline strongly endorsed by the OECD but also by the supposed need for a more flexible labour market as advocated in the OECD Jobs Strategy.

Canada can be seen as a model student of OECD-led policy learning with respect to macroeconomic and labour market policy. Certainly, Department of Finance officials think that OECD criticisms over the past decade have been relatively minor and *pro forma,* and the major lines of federal government economic policy have closely echoed OECD recommendations in published *Economic Surveys* (hereafter referred to interchangeably as country reviews).

Where major differences do exist, they tend to reflect political choices that would not be endorsed by Department of Finance officials. For example, the 2006 country review was critical of the newly elected Conservative government's decision to cut consumption taxes as opposed to taxes on business. Department of Finance research submitted to the OECD team put forward no defence of the cut in the Goods and Services Tax (GST), and indeed showed that it would have the least impact on long-run economic growth of any major tax cut. As detailed below, the OECD has long been rather critical of some features of Canada's Unemployment Insurance program, but again this is broadly in accordance with Department of Finance views and would be seen by officials as politically motivated policy making.

Of course, broad congruence between OECD recommendations and Canadian policy does not mean that the OECD has been an external disciplining force. The organization has the power only to influence national policy, and the relationship between the OECD and national governments is not reducible to a one-way transmission belt. On the contrary, OECD country-specific policy recommendations arise from a rather intensive two-way policy discussion with national government officials.

Moreover, national government officials play a key role within the OECD itself through its various committees and working parties, and by directly serving on the OECD staff. Canadian officials believe that they play an important role within these structures, which tend to be relatively less important for the United States and other large economic powers. As such, the OECD cannot be seen as external to the domestic policy process.

The main argument here, based on the Canadian case, is that OECD processes have been influential and important in terms of defining the "conventional wisdom" that drives economic policy advice. Seen through the prism of published country reviews and based on information provided by senior Canadian government officials in interviews, the OECD strongly influenced the main themes of Canadian economic and labour market policy over the 1990s – very large cuts to the deficit achieved by cuts in social spending; deep cuts to the Unemployment Insurance program; deregulation and privatization; the pursuit of greater labour market flexibility; formal targets for low inflation; and a major focus on debt reduction and tax cuts as opposed to reinvestment in social programs after the elimination of the federal deficit.

The OECD and the Economic Policy Process

Applied economic policy research at the national level is strongly driven by meta-narratives or frameworks, and by the perceived need for evidence-based recommendations arising from different national experiences. The OECD is well suited to provide both to national officials, who tend to see policy making as a technical and expert process. As argued by Holly Grinvalds in Chapter 10, economic officials greatly value OECD advice and participation in OECD activities as a source of knowledge.

The dominant OECD economic policy narrative as embodied in key documents such as the Jobs Strategy of 1994 is ostensibly "objective" and "evidence-based," but it is also strongly associated with neoliberal ideology and the closely associated mainstream neoclassical economic discourse. A key basis of the OECD's influence is its ability to craft, refine, and effectively disseminate a "conventional economic wisdom" that is based on technical and academic economic expertise, honed through an important, ongoing insider discussion between OECD staff and senior national officials in numerous conferences, committees, and other fora. Key players in this process have been forceful advocates of liberalized markets and a limited role by governments in terms of regulation, social spending, and delivery of public services.

As Chapters 8 and 14 of this volume argue, there is an important internal tension within the OECD and its member countries between neoliberalism and a more inclusive form of liberalism that recognizes the importance of social investment and some forms of labour market regulation to more equitable outcomes than are delivered by a pure neoliberal economic and social model. However, the OECD's Economics Department's development of the "conventional economic wisdom" has been an extremely important contributor to the hegemony of neoliberal ideas in national economic policy. To a very significant degree, at the OECD as in Canada, professional economists who do not adhere to the major tenets of this conventional wisdom are excluded or marginalized from applied policy debates.

To give one concrete but telling example, the forum on the revised OECD Jobs Strategy jointly organized by the OECD and the Government of Canada in Toronto in 2006 featured two leading academic economists speaking to the Swedish labour market model. This model was highlighted as an alternative path to good employment performance in the revised Jobs Strategy, partly due to the influence of the Directorate for Employment, Labour and Social Affairs (DELSA) (see Chapter 8). Both invited academic economists were highly critical of the model, however, as was well known from their research. Attempts by the Trade Union Advisory Committee (TUAC) to the OECD to secure a more balanced panel (including noted Harvard University labour economist Richard Freeman) had been rebuffed.

The OECD is ostensibly directed by a Ministerial Council (usually not attended by a front-rank minister in the case of Canada and larger countries), but it is basically run by and for economic policy officials, and has a particularly close working relationship to ministries of finance and central banks of member countries. Within the OECD itself, the deeply neoliberal Economics Department (ECO) looms very large in terms of internal influence and resources compared with DELSA, which is associated with the "inclusive liberalism" policy agenda. The ECO agenda is in turn strongly shaped by the Economic Policy Committee (EPC), which consists of senior finance department officials from member countries (in the Canadian case, participation is at the assistant deputy minister level). The Canadian Department of Finance views the EPC and its working groups (such as WP 1 on macro-economic policy) as a much more important and serious forum for economic policy debate relevant to the domestic agenda than the International Monetary Fund (IMF) or the World Bank. ECO and the important Economic and Development Review Committee (EDRC), made up of Paris-based national department of finance officials appointed to OECD country delegations, also drive the important process of country reviews that is detailed below. Other OECD departments only occasionally make very country-specific recommendations.

In Canada, as in most OECD member countries, the Department of Finance plays a key role in shaping the overall government policy agenda. Finance officials largely determine the overall level and allocation of government expenditure between departments through the annual budget process, and the department is organized in such a way that policy proposals coming from social and labour market ministers have to be endorsed to have much chance of success. For example, social policy proposals coming from Human Resources and Social Development Canada (HRSDC), which is responsible for income security and labour market policy and programs, will not normally proceed to consideration by the federal Cabinet unless approved by Department of Finance officials responsible for shadowing social policy. Prime Minister Chrétien's senior policy adviser from 1993 to 2005 reports that he and the Prime Minister's Office as a whole worked very closely with senior Department of Finance officials in developing and implementing the government's overall policy agenda (Goldenberg 2006, 120-30).

The very close networked relationship between the OECD, itself dominated by economic officials, and Department of Finance officials is the key mechanism for OECD influence on the Canadian policy process. Similar networks engage DELSA at the OECD with HRSDC officials, but the more inclusive liberal agenda is relatively marginalized by the dominant policy axis between ECO and the Department of Finance (which also engages the Canadian central bank).

It is sometimes argued that the OECD puts forward cookie-cutter, one-size-fits-all policy recommendations. This is true to the extent that broad neo-liberal themes such as the need for labour market flexibility, low and stable inflation, low taxes, balanced budgets, and market deregulation underpin OECD policy advice. At the same time, however, OECD policy advice is based on learning from different national experiences, and is informed by the overall process of country reviews and information sharing. As argued in Chapter 8, the evolution of Jobs Strategies between the 1994 and 2006 versions was partly informed by the fact that the Scandinavian social democratic countries did well in terms of economic and employment performance even though they rejected some important parts of the conventional wisdom, such as the need to cut unemployment benefits and lower the wages of unskilled workers. OECD country reviews also put forward quite specific policy recommendations based on a fairly close analysis of specific national circumstances. In short, the OECD influences national economic policy because it seriously engages with specific national circumstances. Again, this reinforces the view that the policy influence of the OECD arises from its networking of key economic officials rather than from the existence of a transmission belt of ideas from Paris to Ottawa and other national capitals.

The Country Review Process: The Canadian Case

As noted by Mahon and McBride in the introductory chapter of this volume, from the mid-1990s, the focus of OECD economic surveys/country reviews shifted to "structural reform," meaning deregulation of the labour market, product markets, and tax reform (i.e., reduced taxes and a shift to consumption taxes and away from taxation of investment and savings). A major milestone was reached in 1994 with the publication of the OECD Jobs Study, which, on the basis of a major research program and engagement with governments, urged a broad but consistent mix of policies to lower unemployment, with a major focus on macroeconomic stability (sound public finance and low and stable inflation) and less regulated labour markets. The OECD Jobs Strategy called for reform of unemployment insurance systems to promote greater labour market efficiency, and more flexible wages (i.e., wages reflecting individual skill levels as opposed to statutory or bargained wage floors).

While reflective of the prevailing wisdom of mainstream academic economists and the UK and US Treasury Departments, the explicit focus on labour market deregulation as the key antidote to high unemployment was sharply contested. As TUAC argued, supported by many reputable economists and by the influential Employment Directorate (DGV) of the European Commission, the roots of high unemployment in the 1980s into the early 1990s could be just as plausibly seen to be rooted in restrictive macroeconomic policy, reflecting excessive fear of wage-driven inflation, and the solutions could plausibly be seen to lie in active labour market policy and social bargains between labour, capital, and governments, as opposed to deregulated job markets.

Country reviews were subsequently used to systematically monitor and push for implementation of the pointed country-specific recommendations of the Jobs Strategy. Before 1998, *Economic Surveys,* including for Canada, put forward policy recommendations in fairly general terms, but these have since been presented much more systematically with reports on progress made. An analysis of country reports over time thus provides a means to gauge the extent of the OECD's influence on economic policy.

At the OECD, ECO supports the EDRC, made up mainly of finance depart-ment officials from national delegations, and drives the country review process. DELSA, which has provided an internal OECD counterpoint in the labour market flexibility debate through many published studies in the an-nual Employment Outlook, is not involved in the process (though it has helped produce thematic chapters on social policy themes, such as the chal-lenges of an aging workforce and the need for lifelong learning, in recent country reviews). *Economic Surveys* of Canada are primarily the result of a sustained engagement between ECO and the Department of Finance, and relatively exclude DELSA and its Canadian counterpart, HRSDC, despite the focus of many reviews on labour market policy.

The draft Economic Survey is prepared by the OECD Secretariat starting about one year before the final survey is published. The work is carried out by a team consisting of two economists, sometimes in cooperation with additional specialists, and supervised by a head of division. ECO has a "desk" for each country, which is also responsible for preparing the semi-annual Economic Outlook for the country. The desk interacts with the cross-country analysis undertaken by the Economics Department. At an early stage, the team from the OECD Secretariat visits the country and meets with a wide range of government officials, some academics, and the "social partners" to collect information and responses to a detailed multi-page questionnaire. In the case of Canada, the labour movement is consulted at this stage, but has no access to the draft report and recommendations. (In rare cases, the social partners in corporatist European countries have been consulted on draft recommendations.) Civil society organizations other than labour are not normally consulted in Canada, and the emphasis is on meetings with federal and sometimes provincial government officials. Later on, the same team, but now headed by a director, goes on the policy mission to discuss the Secretariat's tentative conclusions with senior officials.

The country assessment and recommendations process is finalized in the Economic and Development Review Committee, which has one member from each OECD country delegation. Canada is represented by an economic counsellor appointed from the Department of Finance to the Canadian delegation to the OECD for a term of about three years. This person assumes responsibility for leading EDRC reviews of other countries. The final draft of the *Economic Survey* formally reflects the OECD countries' joint conclu-sions, published under the responsibility of the whole committee. Two EDRC members lead each examination and often draw in experts from their gov-ernments at home. The examined country is represented by a delegation of high-level officials from across government departments. This is formally supposed to create common ownership for the policy recommendations. However, "the committee's conclusions as summarized by the chairman at the end of the one-day meeting do not necessarily mirror the wishes of the country being reviewed. Indeed the value and integrity of *Economic Surveys* rests on the sharpness of the pen with which they are written, and their assessment and recommendations often introduce new perspectives to the national policy debates" (OECD 2006o; see also Pagani 2002a).

The Canadian side of the review process is coordinated through the Department of Finance, with the Bank of Canada also playing an important role. It engages bureaucrats, not ministers or political staff. Other departments may or may not be invited to participate in the process, depending on the themes selected for a particular review. HRSDC is always involved to a degree because of its responsibility for labour market policy and growing OECD interest in social policy. However, this involvement has usually been limited to the first stage of responding to the questionnaire and meeting with the country review team. Former senior officials from HRSDC report that they are not typically consulted on the draft recommendations, and may well disagree with them. In fact, there have been reviews where HRSDC was not even made aware of the draft recommendations. Nonetheless, HRSDC officials have frequently been called to justify policies questioned by the OECD at the final stage, the EDRC meeting.

Based on data obtained from an Access to Information request for documents related to the 2006 Economic Survey and interviews with two former senior HRSDC officials, it is clear that the department is placed on the defensive during the country review process. Meetings were scheduled with HRSDC officials at the first stage, focusing on labour market policy (Employment Insurance and training) and social policy issues (especially with respect to welfare-to-work transitions). While a lot of staff time was clearly taken up by the process, there is a sense in the e-mails between officials of what can only be described as OECD fatigue. Assistant deputy ministers whom the OECD wanted to meet were not available. Moreover, reference was made in e-mails to "the same old questions" and "wonderfully leading questions."

A continuing point of contention between the OECD and HRSDC has been the Employment Insurance (EI) program, specifically, the fact that benefits are more "generous" in high-unemployment regions. (In Orwellian fashion, UI became EI, or Employment Insurance, as part of Unemployment Insurance reform, denoting a supposed shift from "passive" income support to active labour market policies.) This tension continues despite the fact that, as detailed later, the program was changed radically in the mid-1990s in response to earlier OECD recommendations. In a twenty-page response on EI issues – mainly referring to departmental and academic research studies that have been published in annual Monitoring and Assessment Reports – the department questioned continuing OECD support for individual experience rating and more stringent "activation" requirements, as well as the view that levels of recurrent use of EI in high-unemployment regions are excessive. Too great a stress on activation was questioned as being possibly demotivating for participants. The department also took a skeptical view of the frequently expressed OECD view that the EI program creates significant disincentives to inter-regional labour mobility. Research was provided to suggest that EI has less than a 1 percent impact on labour migration within Canada. OECD support for experience rating of employers was challenged on the grounds that it could lead to reluctance to hire on the part of employers.

Officials were questioned on the evidence basis for the 2000 pre-election changes to EI, which increased access to benefits by modifying specific program provisions (eliminating the intensity rule that reduced benefits for frequent users, a form of individual experience rating strongly supported by the OECD). The department's response was that the increase in total benefits would be marginal, and that the intensity rule had proved to be punitive in some high-unemployment areas.

Unlike previous years, the department was given draft recommendations – to limit repeated use of EI through experience rating or more stringent activation requirements. The EI policy evaluation branch suggested that there should be no response, since this was "a nice counter-balance to a lot of feedback we receive from other stakeholders."

By contrast, the Department of Finance is involved at all stages of the review process. Besides being consulted at the first stage, it has input to the draft recommendations, which were circulated to all assistant deputy ministers in the department in 2006. Over fifty pages of closely written notes were submitted in response to the draft 2006 Economic Survey (partly incorporating comments from other departments). Many were directed towards correcting perceived factual inaccuracies. The department did push back against the perceived tenor of some OECD recommendations, defending the specific structure of some tax measures, such as scientific research and development tax credits, and continued government restrictions on foreign investment in the financial and communications sectors. There appears, however, to have been no strong defence of the Conservative government decision in the 2006 budget to cut the GST, and commentary in fact highlighted OECD and Department of Finance agreement that the key priority should be to reduce effective corporate tax rates and eliminate capital taxes.[2] The Bank of Canada is also closely involved and has access to the draft recommendations.

Draft recommendations are, according to a senior Department of Finance officer, rarely a cause of great friction, but are often modified as a result of discussion. The report that goes to the EDRC for formal approval is, then, a negotiated text to some significant degree. Officials from the Department of Finance and the Bank of Canada are always present for the discussion of the draft report by the EDRC. HRSDC has, on occasion, also been asked to participate at the final stage, but usually in a defensive role, to be held to account for lack of compliance with OECD (and, implicitly, Department of Finance) recommendations. Reportedly, when countries are seen to be "offside" on a particular issue, the process can be quite tough. Senior HRSDC officials have been grilled at the EDRC for hours on Canadian Unemployment Insurance policy, a process that undoubtedly has some influence on the advice given to ministers at home, and that strengthens the hand of the Department of Finance in domestic policy discussions.

Effectively, then, the country review process is an intensive policy dialogue between professional economists from ECO, from the Department of Finance and the Bank of Canada in the case of Canada, and the economic ministry representatives on country delegations to the OECD who sit on the EDRC. As such, it largely excludes labour market and social policy specialists from DELSA and from HRSDC who might sometimes bring a different perspective to bear on labour market and social policy issues. Just as the Department of Finance usually wins when there are policy disagreements at home, ECO trumps DELSA in the country review process. HRSDC has proposed that someone from the department be appointed to the Canadian permanent delegation to the OECD, paralleling the economic counsellor position, but this proposal has been rejected by the Canadian government. Even though the focus of the country reviews has shifted from purely macroeconomic to broader labour market and even social policy issues, the breadth of expertise that is drawn upon in the review process has not been correspondingly broadened.

If there is criticism of the country being reviewed in the final public report, it is very likely with the tacit agreement of the Department of Finance. In this sense, OECD advice is a lever that policy officials can bring to bear against ministers to counter political pressure. Country reviews can and do serve an important agenda-setting function, softening the path to implementation of policies that the department of finance would like to implement. *Economic Surveys* also help produce a sense of expert consensus in advance of decisive government action.

In the case of Canada, OECD reviews in the early to mid-1990s helped set the stage for deep government spending cuts to eliminate the deficit, major cuts to the "generosity" of the Unemployment Insurance program, the 2 percent inflation target, and formal debt reduction targets, as detailed below. The most recent review endorses and sets the stage for a major government priority, further reductions in the taxation of capital. Major themes covered in the reviews are identified jointly, and often reflect current government priorities. For example, the 1993 country review contained an extensive review of income security policies, setting the stage for Government of Canada policy papers released in 1994. Senior officials report that policy ideas that don't fly at home can be launched through the country review process, and then presented to ministers as external expert advice.

The OECD and "Structural Reform" of Labour Market Policy in Canada in the 1990s

The OECD Jobs Study of 1994 resulted in a number of country-specific recommendations to the Government of Canada, building on a major thematic review of income security policies in the 1993-94 *Economic Survey of Canada*. The major priority of the OECD was to reform the UI system to reduce perceived disincentives to work and to counter long-term benefit dependency. In the 1993-94 survey, the Canadian UI system was characterized as unusually generous neither in terms of the benefit rate nor the replacement period but rather in terms of low qualification periods in high-unemployment regions (within the context of a regionally differentiated program). The key concern was a pattern of short periods of work and long-run dependency on UI for frequent recipients, especially in these high-unemployment regions. The solution was seen to lie in no, or at least significantly reduced, regional differentiation of program parameters, and the introduction of experience rating, in terms of either employer premiums or penalties for repeat users.

Building on restrictive UI program changes in 1993 and 1994, there was a major legislative reform to the Canadian UI program in 1996. In summary, work requirement periods to qualify for benefits were changed from weeks to hours and substantially increased (from a low of ten weeks to as much as 920 hours in high-unemployment regions), excluding many part-time, mainly female workers, younger workers, and some seasonal workers. Both the income replacement level and the duration of benefits were also significantly reduced. Workers quitting jobs "without cause" were disqualified, penalties were imposed on repeat users, and maximum insurable earnings were frozen for a decade so that the effective replacement rate for average to higher-paid workers was cut by almost one-third in inflation-adjusted dollars. No one would dispute that the "generosity" of the system was significantly reduced, and this was the explicit goal of reform. A study by Timothy Sargent (2005) for the Department of Finance found that the "generosity" of the system had been cut in half.

In late 1994, the newly elected government released three major policy framework papers under the overall title *Agenda: Jobs and Growth*. The so-called Purple Paper ("A New Framework for Economic Policy") prepared by the Department of Finance and the Green Paper prepared by HRSDC (especially the supplementary paper, "From Unemployment Insurance to Employment Insurance") clearly echoed and endorsed the mainstream and OECD Jobs Study view that unemployment could not be lowered below the "natural" or structural rate of unemployment without sparking off wage-driven inflationary pressures. The main determinant of the "natural" or "non-accelerating inflationary rate of unemployment" (NAIRU) was seen to be labour market institutions – specifically wage-setting institutions (minimum wages and collective bargaining) that keep wages "too high" for the relatively unskilled, and systems of income support for workers that allegedly create "disincentives to work," raise the "reservation wage" of unskilled labour, and encourage dependency on income support as opposed to acceptance of jobs at prevailing (low) wages for the unskilled.[3]

In the Purple Paper, the NAIRU was estimated to be "at least 8 percent," in line with OECD estimates published in *Economic Surveys*. Put simply, the dominant view was that Canadian unemployment was high and had to be kept high through macroeconomic policy to keep inflation low and stable. Unemployment could thus be permanently lowered only by making wages more flexible, which in turn required labour market reforms with a major focus on reducing UI generosity. The close linkage of Department of Finance and OECD thinking is evident in a paper presented by departmental economists to Working Party 1 of ECO in 1996, detailing how the Canadian NAIRU had been reduced by the UI cuts as well as reductions in minimum wages and union bargaining power (Sargent and Sheikh 1996).

A series of research studies prepared for HRSDC by academic economists were drawn upon to reach the key Green Paper conclusion that the UI system had raised the Canadian structural unemployment rate and had to be made much more "insurance-like" and much less generous. Many of these studies were also much more nuanced than the OECD view, however, and questioned whether the UI system had indeed raised structural unemployment in Canada to anywhere near the degree suggested by both the OECD and the formal Government of Canada policy papers (Jackson 1994). In the "structural rigidities" perspective, all of the focus is put on the supply side of the job market rather than on aggregate demand. Many prominent Canadian academic economists argued at the time that continued high unemployment in Canada in the early to mid-1990s was mainly the result of persistent macroeconomic slack resulting from excessively tight monetary policy in the early and late 1980s, followed by fiscal stringency (Fortin 1996, 2001). There was little evidence of wage-driven inflation in the late 1980s, when unemployment had briefly fallen to or below the perceived NAIRU. Moreover, many of the studies also suggested that any empirically identifiable impacts of the UI benefit structure on the incidence and duration of unemployment were very small. Last but not least, the OECD and Government of Canada policy papers largely ignored the benefits of the existing UI program in terms of macroeconomic and community stabilization, income security and income redistribution, and income benefits needed to support efficient job search and labour mobility.

The important point is that the OECD view of the key role of UI in raising structural unemployment in Canada was fully shared by the Department of Finance and the Bank of Canada, and probably by most officials at HRSDC. The written response to the OECD questionnaire by HRSDC in 2006 notes that the 1996 Employment Insurance Act "represented the most fundamental restructuring of the EI program in twenty-five years and was consistent with the recommendations for labour market reforms contained in the 1994 OECD Jobs Study." The key goals of reforms were, as urged by the OECD, stated to be "improving incentives to work and reducing dependency" and making the program "more insurance-like." An internal study provided to the OECD team in response to a question on the impact of EI reform on structural unemployment suggested that EI reform had cut the "natural rate" of unemployment.

The conventional wisdom that informs Canadian Unemployment Insurance policy has been developed and refined through many interactions between the OECD and Canadian government economists and senior officials. There has clearly been a good deal of OECD/Canadian government analytical discussion of the issue, and the OECD's advice served as an important source of external validation and support for a very politically contentious change in policy. In fact, UI reform under the Mulroney government of 1984-2003 had been derailed by very strong opposition to the somewhat similar recommendations of the Forget Task Force, and the UI cuts in the mid-1990s proved to be hugely controversial and politically damaging to the Liberal Party in high-unemployment regions in Atlantic Canada and Quebec (the minister responsible for their introduction was defeated in his own constituency).

That said, UI reform deviated from the OECD prescription in several significant ways. First, the UI program still retained a regionally differentiated structure, with lower qualifying periods and longer benefit periods in high-unemployment regions, and no experience rating was introduced for employer premiums. The OECD has, post reform, strongly criticized a regionally differentiated structure in almost all country reviews, arguing that this raises structural unemployment and constitutes a serious disincentive to inter-regional labour mobility. Second, since 1996, some incremental and modest changes have been made to the program that the OECD clearly views as ill-informed and politically motivated backsliding. The intensity rule (which reduced benefits for frequent claimants) was eliminated in 2001, and so-called pilot projects have been used to increase access to benefits and benefit duration in high-unemployment regions (Gray 2006). Every OECD country review of the past decade has criticized the Government of Canada for not going far enough in the original reform, and for backsliding since.

Further, the OECD prescription – in line with the approach in HRSDC's Green Paper – was to shift from so-called passive income support, to "active" employment measures such as training and skills development for the unemployed, and "activation" measures such as intensive counselling and assistance in job search. The government did not so much shift from passive to active labour market spending, however, as cut both as part of the drive for rapid deficit reduction. Following UI reform, most active labour market measures for the unemployed were cut and devolved to the provinces, with little monitoring of results for effectiveness (Haddow 1998). OECD country reviews have been somewhat critical of this relative neglect of active measures and of monitoring for policy effectiveness. The 1998 review recommended that the federal government should not, in fact, leave active labour market policy entirely to the provinces and that excessive devolution to the provinces would undermine labour mobility (OECD 1998d, 8).

The OECD has also been quite critical of lack of government attention to skills training for lower-paid, lower-skilled workers, especially in recent years. The 2000 review flagged lack of sufficient attention in Canada to support for lifelong learning, and a lengthy section in the 2003 report noted the need for recognition and portability of skills, and problems of literacy and numeracy. The 2004 report argued for a focus not just on post-secondary education (which has been viewed as very important to growth of a knowledge-based economy) but also on the basic skills of those at the low end of the workforce. Canada's lagging performance relative to other OECD countries in terms of literacy and numeracy and both public and employer training for the less skilled has been comprehensively documented. These themes were reiterated at length in the 2006 review.

In the same vein, the OECD has long urged reforms to provincial social assistance policies. As early as the 1993-94 report, which focused on the Canadian income security system, the OECD drew attention to the so-called welfare trap – the fact that many persons leaving social assistance for low-paying jobs are worse off because of high effective marginal tax rates created by the loss of income and in-kind benefits (such as prescription drugs and housing and child care support) with rising employment income. The proposed solution has been some kind of income supplementation system for those leaving welfare for work. This was finally introduced in extremely modest form in the 2006 federal budget, adding to some provincial initiatives. Canada has lagged well behind the US and the UK in terms of income supplementation, however, relying much more on the punitive stick of very low welfare benefits to create incentives to work, as opposed to the carrot of top-ups to low wages. It is fair to say that the OECD, in a somewhat nuanced way, supports at least a mix of sticks and carrots, and could be seen as ahead of Canadian practice in welfare reform.

Moreover, again contrary to the OECD's advice, the savings from UI reform were not used to significantly reduce payroll taxes for an extended period of time. In the OECD's view, payroll taxes like the UI premium work against job creation since they increase the wedge between worker income and employer costs, and increase the effective minimum wage (since payroll taxes on very low wage workers cannot be passed back to workers). Over the period from 1996 to 2005, over $50 billion accumulated in the UI account through higher-than-needed premiums, effectively reducing the accumulated federal public debt by that amount. It was only in 2005 that the UI account was roughly balanced on an annual basis.

To conclude, the OECD has had significant influence on Canadian labour market policy, helping to define the conventional wisdom that led to deep UI cuts. However, it has had less influence in other, related areas. To some degree, shared HRSDC/OECD views on the role for active labour market policy as outlined in the Jobs Study were sidelined by the Department of Finance, which resisted new program spending until very late in the Liberal mandate.

OECD Influence on Macroeconomic and Fiscal Policy

As noted above, in the early to mid-1990s, the OECD, the Department of Finance, and the Bank of Canada all subscribed to NAIRU economic orthodoxy, with the implication that monetary policy should tighten as needed to keep unemployment at its "natural" rate in order to meet the inflation target. There is, in country reviews, barely a hint of disagreement over the conduct of Canadian monetary policy. *Economic Surveys* almost always commend the Bank of Canada for its past actions, and urge caution moving forward. Canada's formal inflation targets (1-3 percent, then the midpoint of 1-3 percent) agreed between the Department of Finance and the Bank of Canada were strongly endorsed by the OECD, which has consistently urged stable inflation as a key economic policy goal.

If there has been a hint of disagreement, it lies in the direction of the OECD's urging even greater caution about the potential menace of inflation. The Bank of Canada was quicker than the OECD to abandon NAIRU orthodoxy, and now formally maintains that judgment of whether or not the economy is operating at capacity involves analysis of a wide range of capacity indicators and not just the unemployment rate. OECD country reviews and documents published estimates of the NAIRU until the late 1990s, and the 2000 review noted that the Bank of Canada had de-emphasized the output gap as a guide for monetary policy. There are indications that Department of Finance officials may even have seen labour market rigidities as less of a problem than did the OECD in the mid-1990s (Sargent and Sheikh 1996).

It is worth noting that, in recent years, the Canadian unemployment rate has fallen well below OECD estimates of the NAIRU, with no sign of wage-driven inflation. The 1995 review estimated the Canadian NAIRU at 8.5 percent, while the rate has fallen well below 7 percent in recent years. Low inflation combined with very low unemployment compared with the previous twenty-five years strongly suggests that the monetary policies urged on Canada by the OECD were unduly restrictive in the late 1980s and into the 1990s, and that much of Canada's high-unemployment problem was caused by restrictive fiscal and monetary policies rather than by supposed labour market rigidities. This was precisely the argument of leading Canadian academic economists such as Pierre Fortin, Lars Osberg, and Tom Courchene, all former presidents of the Canadian Economics Association, whose critiques of macroeconomic policy were never taken seriously in OECD *Economic Surveys*.

On fiscal policy, the OECD strongly urged cutting public spending to reduce the deficit and then pay down debt through the 1990s. In the period since the early 1990s, the federal government rapidly eliminated the deficit and then, from 1997, began running large surpluses, which have substantially cut the accumulated debt as a share of GDP from 71 percent in 1997 to less than 40 percent today. The extent of fiscal discipline imposed was by far the greatest of any major OECD country, including countries with worse deficit and debt positions at the start of the 1990s (Stanford 2004). In fact, between 1992 and 2002, total government program spending in Canada fell by 10 percentage points of GDP compared to an OECD average of just 1 percentage point. Of this reduction, about half came from federal program spending cuts. Again, if there was any disagreement, the OECD position was to urge even tougher fiscal restraint. Country reviews applauded the deep spending cuts imposed in the mid-1990s, especially on UI and transfers to the provinces for social spending, and failed to note that fiscal consolidation in Canada was far more tilted towards spending cuts than towards tax increases compared with the US under President Clinton or the OECD norm. Economic surveys paid almost no attention to the social impacts of deep cuts to the UI and social assistance programs, notably a sharp increase in poverty levels for the working-age population and a fall in real incomes for much of the population for an extended period.

With the deficit gone, the OECD urged that priority should be given to paying down debt through surpluses. The formal position of the Liberal government was that, as surpluses opened up, half would go to restoring public spending, with the other half divided between tax cuts and debt reduction. The Department of Finance agreed more with the OECD view, however. In a note to the minister of finance on the 2000 Economic Survey of Canada, which called for modification of the 50/50 rule to put more emphasis on debt and tax reduction, the deputy minister said that there was "little of direct concern to the Department" (Department of Finance Canada 2000). In the 2001 Economic Survey the OECD again called for paying down debt, with a formal debt reduction target, followed by selective tax cuts (OECD 2001d, 13). Any spending increases, it argued, should be very narrowly focused. In the event, this proved closer to the actual course of policy than the Liberal election promise of a 50 percent allocation of surpluses to reinvestment in programs, and the government adopted a formal medium-term debt reduction goal (25 percent of GDP) in 2003.

Further, the OECD has urged that there be less emphasis on broadly distributed cuts to personal income taxes than those implemented between 2000 and 2005, and more focus on corporate income tax cuts and to personal income tax rates on high earners to improve tax competitiveness vis-à-vis the US (OECD 1997c, 2000b). The most recent Economic Survey (2006o) urged further corporate tax cuts combined with corporate income tax base–broadening measures so as to lower marginal effective tax rates on capital. Department of Finance research submitted to the OECD team similarly highlighted the need for further corporate tax cuts, going beyond the deep cut in the federal corporate tax rate from 28 percent to 21 percent since 2000.

OECD advice on fiscal and monetary policy has been consistently even more tilted towards the economic orthodoxy of low inflation, sound public finance, and low taxes than the Department of Finance and Bank of Canada – despite the fact that no other OECD country accepted the OECD's advice on fiscal policy to the same degree. Over the course of the 1993-2005 period, cheered on by the OECD, the fiscal capacity of Canadian governments and public spending of all levels of government fell very sharply relative to GDP, as economic resources were directed towards debt reduction and tax cuts. Canada became a much more unequal society. Between 1989 and 2001, the income share (after taxes and transfers) of the top 20 percent of families rose from 16.8 percent to 23.9 percent of the total; while median real wages and real family incomes for the bottom 60 percent of families stagnated. The income share of the top 1 percent soared, following closely the trend towards ever higher "top tail" driven inequality in the US. The difference in social spending and public services between Canada and the US narrowed considerably (see Jackson 2004b).

This ultra-orthodox economic agenda was implemented despite all the evidence to be found in abundance in OECD reports that Canada is a relatively low tax/low social expenditure country, and that there is no link between low taxes/low social spending and good economic performance. As the OECD grudgingly recognized in the new Jobs Strategy, a group of high tax/high social spending countries have, indeed, actually done very well in terms of economic growth and employment.

A Kinder, Gentler OECD?

As detailed in Chapter 8, in 2006 the OECD released a major reassessment of the 1994 Jobs Strategy. The result of joint work by DELSA and ECO, it recognized that good employment outcomes can be reached through different policy packages. While still tilting strongly in favour of the neoliberal/

Anglo-Saxon model of highly deregulated labour markets and flexible (i.e., highly unequal) wages that is to be found in Canada, the report recognized that the "social democratic" or "inclusive liberal" model to be found in some small Northern European countries can achieve at least equally impressive results in terms of high employment and low unemployment rates. The latter model is characterized by a much more equal distribution of wages, achieved mainly through widespread collective bargaining; by more generous benefits for unemployed workers; by high levels of investment in skills; by active labour market policies; and by high levels of social investment (financed by relatively high taxes) – in short, the precise opposite of OECD prescriptions for Canada over the previous decade.

The TUAC view is that even the revised Jobs Strategy should have been much stronger in favouring the social democratic model. The positive impacts of a more regulated labour market on substantive social outcomes such as low levels of poverty, a relatively equal income distribution after taxes and transfers, and greater equality in the job market are relatively discounted. The report still tilts in favour of deregulated Anglo-Saxon–style labour markets, while acknowledging the need for modest social investment to achieve more equitable outcomes after the fact. The close link between different labour market models and key social outcomes is discounted in even the most progressive OECD work, partly due to unwillingness to face up to the social consequences of highly "flexible" wages and more insecure jobs, and partly because the labour market choices we make as democratic societies are deeply value-laden and interest-laden, and are inherently political issues rather than simply technical issues.

Unfortunately, the new Jobs Strategy will not explicitly or directly inform future economic reviews of member countries. Instead, the process of multilateral surveillance and monitoring through country reports will, moving forward, be informed by another major OECD study conducted by ECO for the EDRC, *Going for Growth* (OECD 2007e). This puts forward a new "structural reform" agenda with country-specific recommendations that yet again draws attention to supposed labour market rigidities. In the case of Canada, the UI program is, once again, targeted for reform as a key priority. OECD/Government of Canada interaction appears destined to continue to reinforce the neoliberal agenda embodied in the conventional economic wisdom.

Notes

1 This chapter is based partly on the experience of the author as Senior Economist with the Canadian Labour Congress, who has, in that capacity, met with OECD country review teams in Canada and has participated extensively in OECD and Trade Union Advisory Committee (TUAC) to the OECD meetings since 1989. TUAC regularly convenes meetings between trade union economists and senior officials of the Economics Department (ECO) and the Directorate for Employment, Labour and Social Affairs (DELSA), as well as with members of the Economic Policy Committee (EPC) and the Economic and Development

Review Committee (EDRC). Interviews were conducted with senior officials from the Department of Finance and Human Resources and Social Development Canada who have had long experience with the role of the OECD in shaping Canadian public policy, as well as with a member of the 2006 Canadian delegation to the OECD and colleagues at TUAC. In addition, written records of OECD/Government of Canada interaction mainly relating to the 2006 Economic Review of Canada were obtained through Access to Information requests A-2006-00129/jl and A-2006-000238/i.e (although considerable material was deleted due to restrictions on information release).

2 It is hard to summarize commentary since a great deal of the released information was withheld and blanked out.

3 For a detailed analysis of the NAIRU theory in a Canadian context, see Jackson (2000).

10
Lost in Translation? OECD Ideas and Danish Labour Market Policy
Holly Grinvalds

This chapter examines in some detail the labour market reforms of Denmark, a country thought to be a non-complier with the Organisation for Economic Co-operation and Development's Jobs Strategy (see Chapter 8). It shows that, while the current flexicurity model in Denmark is less the result of the power of OECD ideas than domestic political factors, the OECD did indeed help pave the way for labour market reforms. It did so by helping to introduce the concept of structural unemployment into Danish discourse, which shifted attention from macroeconomic policy strategies for fighting unemployment to the deficiencies of labour market policy. At the same time, the norm of consensus in Danish politics, the convention of including social partners in labour market policy making, as well as a common desire to preserve the standard of living for the unemployed, all prevented OECD ideas from having a more direct impact on reforms. Instead, much of the specific content of labour market policy was the result of domestic negotiations.

This chapter builds the case for thinking about the travel and influence of ideas not as a process of transfer but as a process better described as translation. Similar to linguistic translation, foreign ideas cannot be immediately used or applied by policy makers; they need to be interpreted, modified, and negotiated in ways that depend on local context and players. This does not mean, however, that the influence of ideas is lost. Through the process of translation, "translators" can be affected (Czarniawska and Joerges 1996, 24); what they know and what they perceive to be in their interest may change. If we look for the influence of OECD ideas in policy change that closely reflects OECD recommendations, then we may underestimate this power of ideas.

The process of ideational influence is examined in three parts: idea transfer, idea acceptance, and idea impact. "Policy transfer" is commonly understood as a process whereby "knowledge about policies, administrative arrangements or institutions is used across time and space in the development of policies, administrative arrangements and institutions elsewhere" (Stone 1999, 51).

In this study, however, "transfer" refers to the movement of OECD ideas into the domestic policy debate. As we can assume that OECD member states are aware of the goings-on at the OECD, transfer is evident when an idea is debated or commented on in the national media, interest group publications, government documents, or parliamentary debates. Acceptance occurs when individuals (e.g., senior bureaucrats, ministers) or groups (e.g., political parties, labour or employer unions) become advocates. Once an idea has been accepted, the interests, knowledge, and actions of policy actors may be affected, which in turn shapes the policy-making process. Evidence of impact is found in actual policy changes or in interviews and documents that tell us why some reforms were made and others not.

The OECD's Ideas
The OECD has long been providing recommendations on labour market policy. Reports from the 1980s focused on the detrimental effects of narrow wage structures and the need for training and education to encourage adaptation to new technologies and economic structures (OECD 1986a, 1986b, 1987b). By the late 1980s and early 1990s, the concepts of "active" labour market policies, "activation," and "active" society were prevalent, particularly in reports from the Education, Employment, Labour and Social Affairs Directorate (DEELSA) (OECD 1988a, 1989a, 1990a). Country-specific recommendations were published in the Economic and Development Review Committee's annual *Economic Surveys* of Denmark. Its 1989-90 survey provided a detailed assessment of Danish labour market policy. Working from a supply-side perspective, the survey argued that "the malfunctioning of the labour market is at the core of the macroeconomic imbalances in the Danish economy," and that the problem of Danish unemployment is not only cyclical but "structural" in nature (OECD 1990b, 64).

Several explanations for high structural unemployment were discussed. One focused on Denmark's "generous" unemployment benefits, which, according to the report, allowed employers to abuse the system by laying off workers in times of low production, only to rehire them when production increased (OECD 1990b, 67). Generous benefits were said to prolong job search activity thus lengthening spells of unemployment, particularly among lower-paid workers (OECD 1990b, 68).

Excessive wages were seen as the second factor, creating low profitability for firms and reduced demand for workers, particularly low-skilled and younger workers (OECD 1990b, 74-75). An "insider" and "outsider" bargaining system was said to reinforce this wage structure. According to the OECD, insiders have little incentive to consider the needs of outsiders, such as the effect of wage hikes on hiring practices. In this regard, the OECD recommended that employers and employees shoulder a larger share of the cost of employment benefits (OECD 1990b, 74).

The chapter also focuses on active labour market policies. According to the OECD, while Denmark spent more than any other OECD country on passive and active measures,[1] there were a number of problems, including the "artificial nature" of job offers and the lack of program assessments (OECD 1990b, 82). In addition, the "career" of the unemployed – the time spent moving from benefits to training to job offers – was seen as unduly long (OECD 1990b, 83).

Idea Transfer

Employment became a major issue in Denmark following the 1973 oil crisis (OECD 1994b, 37). Unemployment averaged 9 percent through the 1980s and peaked at 12 percent in 1993 (Green-Pedersen 2001, 53-70). At first, many believed that the crisis would soon pass, so the initial response was to stimulate domestic demand and improve competitiveness (Green-Pedersen 2001, 56). Labour market reforms aimed at maintaining the qualifications of the unemployed and their right to benefits.

By the early 1980s, faith that the crisis would soon pass was fading. The Conservative-Liberal government, which took office in 1982, embraced a supply-side approach, which was not out of step with the OECD's own structural adjustment agenda (Andersen 2002, 64-65). They were not alone: many political actors, including labour unions and employer associations, began to see economic problems in structural terms, which, in the early 1980s, led to a reconceptualization of industrial policy, and by the late 1980s, labour market policy as well (Kjær and Pedersen 2001, 219-48; Torfing 1999, 5-28). An "overheating" of the economy in 1987, characterized by simultaneous high domestic demand, wage inflation, and unemployment, helped entrench structural unemployment as an "institutional truth" (Andersen 2002, 63).

The label of structural unemployment was, however, not unambiguous, and there was much debate over its cause and the best possible solution for it. In this debate, some, though certainly not all, referred to ideas from the OECD. The OECD's key link was with the Ministry of Finance but an economic advisory council, thinks tanks, the employers federation, and the business-oriented press also played a role as conduits for OECD-inspired ideas. The linkages of international diffusion were thus not limited to state organs but penetrated society.

Government Ministries

The evolution of perceptions of unemployment is captured in reports by government ministries. Two policy prescriptions were prominent: to cut benefits, supposedly increasing the incentive for employment, and further education for the labour force to deal with a skills "mismatch." The earliest reports on structural unemployment were published by the Ministries of

Labour and Education (Ministry of Labour and Ministry of Education Denmark 1986; Ministry of Labour Denmark 1987). As one might expect, particularly from the Education Ministry, the reports emphasized the role of education and training (particularly technical training), while a change in the benefit scheme was not considered. Here the OECD was referred to only as a source of statistics.

Following the 1987 public sector–led wage surge, a different perspective appeared in a report jointly prepared by the Labour, Education, Finance, Tax, Social, and Economic Affairs Ministries. The 1989 *White Paper on the Structural Problems of the Labour Market* voiced concern for many of the labour market issues highlighted in OECD reports: the narrow dispersion of wages, the generosity and financing structure of unemployment benefits, the lack of control over testing for willingness to work, as well as concerns about training and education. This report cited the OECD to a much greater extent, including an *OECD Economic Studies* paper on labour market flexibility (Kau and Mittelstädt 1986) and the *New Framework for Labour Market Policies* (Government of Denmark 1989, 58-59).

By the early 1990s, reference to, and use of, OECD work became even more extensive, especially by the Ministry of Finance. The ministry's annual *Medium Term Economic Survey* of the Danish economy, in chapters dedicated to labour market issues, cited the OECD frequently, either as a source of comparative statistics or as support for the ministry's own analysis. In the 1993 report, for example, the ministry indicated that its conclusions on cyclical and structural estimates of unemployment were "supported by the OECD's analyses of the structural unemployment in Denmark" (Ministry of Finance Denmark 1993, 186).

According to interviews with finance ministry officials, this increased use of OECD research and ideas was facilitated by a reorganization of the ministry and a shift in the attitudes of ministry personnel towards the OECD. As in other OECD countries, a permanent delegate to the OECD is seconded from the Ministry of Finance. This Finance attaché attends meetings of interest to the ministry, particularly those of the Economic and Development Review Committee (EDRC), which is responsible for the country-specific *Economic Surveys*. In the late 1980s, organizational change in the ministry encouraged greater interaction between this attaché and the rest of Finance, by moving the attaché from the budget to the economic policy division of the ministry, a division fast becoming more active in labour market issues (Interview B 2006). In this way, labour market policy discussions in the economic committees of the OECD were more smoothly inserted into the Finance Ministry's labour market policy analysis.

In addition to the attaché, the Ministry of Finance also sent non-permanent or ad hoc delegates to meetings such as those of the Economic Policy Committee and Working Party 1 that examine structural policy (Vinde 1998).

What was learned in these committees was then fed into the work and analysis of the Ministry of Finance. For example, one civil servant recalled that OECD analysis was used extensively when preparing the *Medium Term Economic Surveys* of the ministry. Furthermore, the same division doing the survey would also prepare papers for political discussions in cabinet committees, which allowed for a "very fruitful interaction between analytical evidence and policy" (Interview A 2005).

Finally, some members of the Ministry of Finance also took short leaves to work in the OECD Secretariat. According to Marcussen's interviewees, this short stay – two to five years – at the OECD was highly regarded, and was viewed as a career-enhancing experience (Marcussen 2002, 205).

These organization linkages and alterations were accompanied by changes in the general disposition of personnel towards the OECD. According to one civil servant, when he began his career in the 1970s, Finance personnel mainly sought to deflect OECD critiques and that of fellow member states (Interview B 2006). This defensive posture gave way over the course of the 1980s. The new generation of ministerial staff in the early 1980s believed that the ministry should be held accountable for any poor policies at home. As they moved into more senior positions, this resulted in increasing use of the OECD as "inspiration" for ministry work. One member of this new generation recalls that when he was promoted to supervisor of the OECD Finance attaché, he encouraged the attaché to allow more critical reviews of Danish policy (Interview B 2006). Since each member state can amend and must approve the wording of its country-specific *Economic Survey,* civil servants hoping to make certain reforms can use OECD publications as a way to legitimize an issue that currently gets little traction at home. Marcussen has called this active participation regarding OECD recommendations the "boomerang hypothesis" (2002, 208).

Think Tanks and Research Centres

Danish ministries were not the only relevant actors to utilize OECD research and analysis. Two particularly important actors in labour market policy debates, the Danish Economic Council (Det Økonomiske Råds, or DØR), an economic advisory body funded by the Danish government but otherwise independent, and the Centre for Labour Market and Social Research (CLS) at the University of Aarhus, both utilized the OECD.

DØR, in its twice annual report on the Danish economy, was among the first in Denmark to express concern over benefit levels and wage structure. Similarities between DØR's recommendations and the OECD's own advice are striking. For instance, the report refers to the "international debate becoming known as the 'insider-outsider' problem" (Danish Economic Council 1988, 60). To solve this problem, the report argued for "increased wage differentials possibly combined with wage subsidies to unskilled workers or

[their] employers" (Danish Economic Council 1988, 145). Further recommendations included changes to the unemployment benefit system to reduce
the replacement rate to increase employment incentives, as well as altering
the financing of benefits such that employers and employees would share
more of the cost with the state (see Danish Economic Council 1988,
143-45).

The work of CLS is regarded as being "inspired by a series of leading
scholars from the OECD, England and America." Their research also supported the claim that Denmark was experiencing structural unemployment
(Torfing 2004, 147). Though the centre was established only in 1993, two
important articles on structural unemployment were published that year by
the centre's researchers, Nina Smith (1993) and Niels Westergaard-Nielsen
(1993). Smith argued for increased wage flexibility and training to fight the
"insider-outsider" problem. Westergaard-Nielsen agreed that the wage structure was problematic, but as lower wages were not politically feasible, he
focused on increased training and reform of the financing of the unemployment benefit system (see Torfing 2004, 147).

The use of OECD work by these non-governmental actors demonstrates
that the reach of the OECD goes beyond member state governments to civil
society. Both formal and informal relationships facilitate this interaction.
At the formal level, the OECD has contact with "prominent think tanks,"
in addition to government ministries, social partners, and the Central Bank
when it undertakes its several-day fact-finding mission prior to drafting the
EDRC country review (Interview C 2005; Interview D 2005; Interview E
2006). Another formal way for Danish economists to have contact is as
consultants to the OECD (Interview E 2006).

These formal relations are supplemented with informal ones facilitated
by virtue of their shared economic perspectives and research agendas and
by the Danish background of some OECD officials. As a member of the Secretariat from DØR explains: "You will see a lot of examples [indicating] that
the OECD has taken some of the ideas in our reports. Of course we go to the
OECD reports and get ideas ... We are colleagues" (Interview D 2005). Danes
who work at the OECD appear to provide an important link with domestic
economists. Given Denmark's small population and the fact that many
economists circulate between the Ministry of Finance, DØR, and the OECD,
OECD ideas can move easily and quickly in Denmark.

The Social Partners
In addition to serving member state governments, the OECD has formal
relations with labour and employer organizations through the Trade Union
Advisory Committee (TUAC) and the Business and Industry Advisory Com-
mittee (BIAC). LO (Danish Confederation of Trade Unions) and DA (Danish
Employers' Confederation) are members. TUAC and BIAC are umbrella

organizations with consultative status at the OECD. They have regular meetings with OECD committees and working groups, including the Council at
the Ministerial Level, and with the Secretariat under the Labour/Management
Programme, which serves "as a forum for pre-consultation between trade
union and management experts on future matters in the OECD's programme
of work" (Vinde 1998, 49-50; TUAC).

There is little evidence that LO played a role in transferring OECD ideas
in the late 1980s and early 1990s. Its own research centre, the Economic
Council of the Labour Movement, had been preoccupied with macroeconomic business cycle analysis. To the extent that its research dealt with structural
policy analysis, it was mainly in the area of business and industry (Torfing
2004, 146). Furthermore, LO's position on labour market policy – which will
be looked at in greater detail later – differed greatly from the OECD's. In
particular, LO did not want to see benefits lowered or wages cut.

In contrast, DA shared many of the same perspectives as the OECD on
labour market issues, and therefore did make use of its analysis. In a book
produced by the Rockwool Foundation, which brought together several key
figures from union and employer organizations, Poul Erik Pedersen, Administrative Director of DA, wrote a piece on why "labour markets must adapt
to international conditions" (1992, 97-111). He referenced extensively the
OECD's *Labour Market Policies for the 1990s* (1990c) and the *Economic Surveys*
for Denmark from 1989/90 (1990b). These reports were used to support an
argument for shifting from passive to active labour market measures and for
lowering wages for youth (Pedersen 1992, 106-8).

Media and Parliament

Major OECD reports are likely to receive headlines in Denmark, making the
news media another mechanism of OECD transfers (Marcussen 2002, 195-
201; Torfing 2004, 159). Ritzaus Bureau, the largest Danish news agency,
provides a regular column on OECD reports and meetings in its upcoming
events, enabling the Danish press to keep on top of OECD developments.
In his survey of three major daily newspapers in Denmark from 1996 to
2000, however, Marcussen argues that, though the OECD is well covered,
the quality and frequency of this coverage varies from paper to paper (2002,
195-201). *Børsen,* a business newspaper, may mention the OECD daily, and
will have a reporter permanently assigned to the OECD to follow up on
stories. In contrast, *Aktuelt* (a Social Democratic Party paper) and *Information*
(a small left-wing paper) mentioned the OECD less frequently, and were
typically less critical of the information fed from the news agencies (Marcussen 2002, 195).

In the early 1990s, the OECD was frequently cited in the Danish press on
labour market policy matters. The release of a Danish *Economic Survey,* or
even an OECD Working Paper received headlines in the major dailies (see

Bendixen 1993; Skovgaard 1993; Vestergaard 1993). In many cases, it was not the media per se that transferred OECD ideas into debate, but guest authors such as the economic affairs minister or an economist at the Central Bank (see Petersen 1990; Jensen 1991). For those outside the informal and formal OECD networks discussed above, these media reports may be their first or only link with the OECD. For example, press references to OECD reports are found to play a key role in keeping information-overloaded parliamentary members abreast of the research published by multiple international organizations (Marcussen 2004a, 202).

In summary, there is much evidence that prior to the major labour market reforms beginning in 1993, OECD ideas were transferred into policy debates, particularly by such key players as the Ministry of Finance, the Danish Economic Council, classical economists, DA, and the (primarily business-related) media. These groups employed OECD ideas as support for their arguments and as templates or inspiration for their own analyses. Many mechanisms of transfer were at work. In the Finance Ministry, transfer was facilitated by the multiple delegates who visit the OECD each year, organizational change in the ministry, and an increasingly positive attitude towards and familiarity with the OECD among senior civil servants. An informal professional network linked the OECD with Danish economists who shared their analytical perspective. DA drew upon OECD ideas as a result of its membership in BIAC, and the news media was aided by the inclusion of OECD goings-on in the daily reports of Denmark's largest news agency.

Overall, the main conduits for OECD ideas were primarily individuals who spoke the language of economics and were imbued with the values of the profession. The policy transfer literature has not explored in much depth the relationship between the *transferor* and *what* is transferred. However, research on when political actors make use of social science research shows that a significant determining factor is the perceived quality of the research – its technical quality, objectivity, and cogency – even if it contradicts or challenges prevailing policies (Weiss and Bucuvalas 1980, 250). Indeed, Danish interviewees who acted as conduits indicate that they perceive OECD research and analysis to be high in quality, objective, and rigorous. Furthermore, scholars of social learning argue that learning is more likely in a setting that is less politicized and more insulated, where people meet repeatedly and where there is a high level of interaction among participants (Checkel 1999, 549). When individuals engage in deliberative arguments rather than giving and receiving lectures and demands, and when the persuader is "an authoritative member of the in-group to which the persuadee belongs," learning is also more likely (Checkel 2001, 549, 563). As interviewees indicate, OECD meetings, whether in Paris or Copenhagen, changed just these kinds of conditions and forged good working relationships, which could account for the transfer of ideas that is observed.

The Acceptance and Impact of OECD Ideas

Despite much political debate, few policy changes were made prior to the major reforms of 1993.[2] The primary reason for the lack of progress was the lack of consensus among the major labour market policy players: the government, LO, and DA. In particular, the Conservatives had committed themselves to undertake major reforms only if they could secure the cooperation of the trade unions (Torfing 2001, 301) and/or the Social Democrats. This proved difficult to do. This section looks at those obstacles to reform, how they resulted in the appointment of a commission on labour market policy in 1992, and how the negotiations of that commission played out.

Roadblock 1: Disagreement among the Political Parties

The Conservative-Liberal government of the late 1980s accepted many of the OECD's ideas about labour market reform. In 1988, Conservative Prime Minister Poul Schlüter announced a "new social vision for Denmark" in which activation would be combined with lower benefits. In his opening speech to Parliament in 1991, Schlüter argued that the benefit system and the wage structure needed serious reconsideration (Folketing 1991, 12). He would not rule out active labour market policies, especially for youth, but he warned against the possible high costs of such an endeavour and the delay this might cause in finding a permanent solution to unemployment (Folketing 1991, 10-11). As one government official recalled, "the bourgeois government had not fallen in love with activation, but they also could not stand to see people hanging out on the street corner" (Torfing 2004, 127).

The Conservative-Liberal government operated with a two-pronged position on unemployment. It saw the need to maintain the qualifications of the workforce until the next upswing in the economy, but it also believed that lower compensation would push people into jobs. This vision was not shared by the Social Democrats, who, while in favour of training and education measures for the unemployed, were against the idea of lowering benefits or wages. Reacting to Schlüter's opening speech, the leader of the Social Democrats, Svend Auken, attacked the idea that lower benefits would do anything to change the unemployment rate, arguing that in the early 1970s, when benefits were just as high, unemployment was low (Folketing 1991, 135-36). This division meant that a major reform could not get off the ground, as every proposal offered by the Conservative-Liberal government included cuts to benefits, something the Social Democrats would not support.[3]

Roadblock 2: Disagreement between the Ministry of Finance and the Ministry of Labour

Another roadblock to labour market reform came in the form of division between the Ministry of Finance and the Ministry of Labour. In effect, the conflict between LO and DA paralleled a similar divide within the bureaucracy. Many officials in the Ministry of Finance felt that their counterparts in the Ministry of Labour confined its mission to facilitating negotiations with the social partners and implementing the agreement (Interview B 2006). Others point out that the Labour Ministry respected the role of unions in policy making, and also perceived the maintenance of the living standards of the unemployed to be one of its main purposes (Torfing 2004, 91).

For the most part, this conflict arose because the concept of structural unemployment, and the accompanying OECD-inspired solutions, had taken a firm hold in the Ministry of Finance. As one Finance official said of OECD reports on the labour market, "it is evident that they were supported by the Danish experience from the 1980s. The reports had the effect that it was difficult to formulate a contrary perspective" (Torfing 2004, 159, my translation). The Ministry of Finance's focus on structural policy had many consequences for the internal workings of the ministry, its position within the central administration, and the workings of other ministries. Finance changed from a comparatively small player in labour market policy into what is referred to today as a "super-ministry" (Torfing 2004, 87). Policy matters that earlier came under the purview of the Labour or Social Affairs Ministries were redefined as matters of "structural policy" and thus a matter for the Ministry of Finance.

Also at this time, the Ministry of Finance hatched a plan to establish a government commission on unemployment (Interview B 2006). The plan's proponents believed that a commission that brought together the social partners and various government ministries would succeed in working out a deal for labour market reform. If the social partners could agree to a reform, then the Social Democrats would be obliged to honour that agreement and support the reforms. A commission would also give the Ministry of Finance greater influence in the process, as Finance and Labour would help form the commission's secretariat (Interview B 2006). On 3 December 1991, Parliament agreed to such a commission that would investigate the "structural problems of the labour market."

The Zeuthen Commission, as it came to be known, consisted of representatives from both employer and employee associations and an independent chair, Hans Zeuthen, head of Statistics Denmark. In a break with past practices, the commission also included eight experts in labour market and social policy. Their role was to draw on their expertise and non-partisan status to facilitate negotiations between the government and the social partners. Political parties were not formally represented in the committee, but civil servants who participated in the committee as members of the secretariat would represent the interests of their minister, and the policy experts were appointed by the political parties.

The committee's work was supported by a secretariat. Formally, the government was not part of the committee and participated only through this secretariat. Nevertheless, interviews with committee members tell how "the secretariat exerted strong influence on the work in the committee because it prepared the main part of the technical analysis" (Schmidt-Hansen and Kaspersen 2004, 21) and participated in discussions. Furthermore, while the secretariat was made up of several ministries – Finance, Labour, Social Affairs, Economic Affairs, Tax, Education, and the Prime Minister's Office – it was headed by a top civil servant from Finance, who helped to negotiate key compromises (Interview E 2006; Interview G 2006; Interview H 2005).

The Zeuthen commission's formal title was the "Commission on Structural Problems of the Labour Market," and this use of the term "structural" is significant. Despite the roadblocks to reform, there was one thing on which the main political players agreed: the problem of unemployment was structural and the solution therefore required a reform of labour market policies. "Structural unemployment," defined as "that part of unemployment which is not reversed by subsequent economic upturn" (OECD 1994a, 32), is, by definition, impervious to macroeconomic policies. Its solution requires a focus on the structural aspects of the economy. By the early 1990s, the government, LO, and DA had all accepted that unemployment was "structural," and the commission would seek reforms appropriate to this problem definition.

At the same time, the concept of structural unemployment is so broad that the government, LO, and DA came to the commission with very varied solutions. For example, when asked why LO agreed to join the commission, a representative replied that it was necessary in order to prevent the bourgeois government from lowering benefit levels, changing the wage structure, and altering the financing of the benefit system (Interview G 2006). LO hoped to focus instead on education and training of workers.

Wages and Benefits

While the OECD interpretation of structural unemployment had an important influence in Denmark, the OECD's recommendations for reform had little impact. The lowering of benefit levels, for example, was not only not implemented but was not even on the Zeuthen Commission's agenda. The commission's mandate was to assess current activation policies, such as work offers and training offers, and to evaluate two models for reforming the financing of the benefit system (Udredningsudvalget 1992a). The most likely reason benefit levels were not part of its mandate was that the government knew that LO and the Social Democrats would not accept it (Interview B 2006; Interview H 2005). Nor was the lowering of wages, particularly for low-skilled workers, on the agenda of the commission as this too was not politically feasible.

The OECD had recommended that if employees and employers paid a larger share of the cost of unemployment benefits, then the "insider-outsider" problem, which contributed to compressed wages, might be alleviated. This issue of financing reform was, in fact, incorporated into the mandate of the Zeuthen Commission, but it was very controversial. Neither DA nor LO wanted to reform the financing system. It was the government that was interested in change, as it was paying the bulk of unemployment benefit costs (Schmidt-Hansen and Kaspersen 2004, 21). Since DA and LO were not in favour, the experts' views assumed a greater importance. At least one expert was strongly in favour of reforming the financing system, arguing for a more "performance-related" system, which would penalize employers who use it to manage periods of low demand or to support seasonal work (Interview E 2006; Interview H 2005). The DA and LO representatives were not convinced, however (Interview E 2006).

Needless to say, this controversial proposal for reforming the benefit system was not accepted. Instead, a small earmarked tax on all workers was levied in 1993. In principle, this tax can be reduced if the costs of active and passive unemployment measures decrease, offering some incentive to "insiders" to consider the needs of "outsiders" (Torfing 1999, 16). It is unlikely, however, that a small earmarked tax of this kind is what the OECD had in mind for combating this problem.

Activation

Activation was the second major issue for the commission, but, unlike reforms to the financing of benefits, "a stronger focus on activation policy was well within everybody's opportunity field given the common understanding of unemployment as a structural problem" (Schmidt-Hansen and Kaspersen 2004, 22). All members of the commission agreed that the current system was using job and training offers primarily as means to requalify the unemployed for another round of passive benefits. As a result, offers were given late in the course of unemployment and the duration of an offer was determined more by rules of benefit requalification than by the needs of the unemployed (Udredningsudvalget 1992a, 51). The commission concluded that "it is therefore not sufficiently possible [in the current system] to adapt [activation] efforts to the wishes and needs of unemployed individuals." Furthermore, "the present activation system does not make good use of the 9.3 billion crowns at its disposal for such measures" (Udredningsudvalget 1992a, 51, my translation). The goal of the reforms was to make the system more "offensive" by creating individual action plans, activating individuals sooner, and generally improving the quality and flexibility of the job and training offers through a decentralization of decision-making powers, which created a larger role for the social partners.

For several reasons, the role played by OECD ideas in the commission's negotiations concerning activation was not particularly significant. OECD ideas about activation appear to have been overshadowed by other OECD ideas about cutting benefits and cutting wages. Interviewees more quickly recalled the OECD's position on benefits and wages than the ones on active measures (Interview H 2005; Interview I 2005). One interviewee recalled OECD economists' saying that active measures were "at best harmless" but for the most part a "waste of money" (Interview H 2005). Overall, the OECD's positive support for active measures had not gotten through.

In fact, other sources were more influential than the OECD in the Danish debate on activation. The Zeuthen Commission report drew lessons from Swedish and German activation and training systems (Udredningsudvalget 1992b). Others have suggested that the activation ideas were inspired by a discourse on marginalization coming from "professional groups and left-wing sociologists" (Torfing 1999, 22). The Danes' own experience with youth activation a couple of years prior to the Zeuthen Commission may have contributed in part to a willingness to see all working-aged persons activated.

In summary, although OECD ideas made their way into domestic debates, they did not play a large role when it came time for serious negotiations inside the Zeuthen Commission. One major exception to this was the concept of structural unemployment, which can be credited in part with helping to pave the way for reform by providing a common problem conceptualization and a focus on a particular (though varied) set of labour market reforms as possible solutions.

The Zeuthen Commission Legacy

The process of labour market reform in Denmark spanned the 1990s decade. The Zeuthen Commission marked a shift of labour market policy paths, however. Activation became a central pillar of the flexicurity model in Denmark, and unemployment benefits remained high. The financing of the benefit system was not radically altered, and control of the activation system was decentralized. For the story of OECD ideas, therefore, the critical juncture came during the later 1980s and early 1990s, as the labour market policy players reassessed their understanding of the labour market and negotiated these reforms.

Not only did the Zeuthen Commission lay the foundation for the present system but it also made clear which policy solutions for fighting unemployment were feasible and which were not. In other words, "it made it possible for the Government in office and coming Governments to avoid critical issues that lay outside the consensus zone" (Schmidt-Hansen and Kaspersen 2004, 22). As a result, the legislative process became largely a technical matter of transferring policy proposals into legal text, in which the social partners were not involved (see Torfing 2004, 255-66).

Perhaps the best evidence that the Zeuthen Commission set Denmark on a new track is that the new labour market reforms were implemented not by the Conservative-Liberal government that struck the commission but by the Social Democratic–led government that followed it. In January 1993, the Conservative-Liberal government resigned suddenly and the Social Democrats took power. By this time, the Social Democrats had a new leader, Poul Nyrup Rasmussen, who brought in a new party platform, shifting the party closer to the centre (Marklund and Norlund 1999, 41). As a result, the Social Democrats received the support of the centre parties and were able to govern with a majority in Parliament, one of the first in many years. With a majority government, Parliament became a less important venue for the negotiation of labour market reforms, and the Social Democrats, for the most part, were able to implement the first round of such reforms without renegotiating the Zeuthen proposals.

Conclusion

Despite a growing scholarly interest in transnational governance, few studies have examined the influence of the OECD on domestic policy making in member states. Those studies that have, most notably *The OECD and European Welfare States* (Armingeon 2004; but also see Lodge 2005), found little evidence of the OECD's influence. This does not square with studies that describe the OECD as a creator and disseminator of ideas; a forum for the benchmarking and surveillance of government activities; or a venue for policy learning and the socialization of civil servants (Marcussen 2001). This chapter suggests that it is not an either/or proposition. Rather, we may not understand the complexities of the OECD's influence if we limit our analysis to a comparison of OECD recommendations and domestic policy. Instead, we need to trace the flow of ideas through the processes of idea transfer, idea acceptance, and idea impact. Such an approach can reveal how ideas are translated in the domestic context.

In this study, we found that idea transfer is mediated by a number of factors: the OECD's ability to facilitate policy learning depends on the degree to which actors view the OECD as a reliable source of information or as part of the "in-group"; the organization of the state can hinder or enhance the flow of ideas in and out of it; and networks of professionals can help OECD ideas permeate civil society. The impact of ideas is also heavily constrained by domestic factors. As Peter Hall has argued, ideas are not immediately comprehensible and will need to be judged and interpreted using "the existing stock of knowledge that is generally conditioned by prior historical experience" (Hall 1989b, 370). Ideas will need to show economic, political, and administrative viability (Hall 1989b, 371).

At the same time, ideational scholars have argued that periods of uncertainty or crisis caused by the failure or discrediting of old ideas can open up windows of opportunity for policy learning and the re-evaluation of one's interests (Blyth 2001; Checkel 1999; Flockhart 2004; Hall 1993). In this chapter, we can see both dynamics of uncertainty and certainty at work. Persistent unemployment paired with a crisis of wage inflation discredited old thinking about labour market policy and opened up a space for new knowledge about structural unemployment and structural reforms to take effect. At the same time, other norms – consensus politics, the role of social partners, and maintaining high living standards for the unemployed – remained constant, and were the standards by which OECD ideas were judged. As a result, unemployment benefits were not radically lowered and wage disparity was not altered. It was a process of translation rather than full and wholesale transfer; and, as is the case with translations, some of the ideas that are translated into the local context will have the effect of changing the translator in the process, while other ideas, not well suited, will get lost in translation.

Notes

1 "Active" is defined as "measures which aim at reducing structural unemployment by increasing the flexibility of the labour market and the qualification of the labour force" (OECD 1990a, 81-82).

2 A notable exception to this was the Youth Allowance Scheme introduced in 1991. This reform was significant, even though it affected only a narrow range of the working population, because it was the first true attempt at "activation" of the unemployed.

3 For a summary of the multiple attempts at major reform, see Green-Pedersen (2002b, 120-22).

Part 3: Governance and the Social

11

The OECD Guidelines for the Licensing of Genetic Inventions: Policy Learning in Response to the Gene Patenting Controversy

Lisa Drouillard and E. Richard Gold

The Organisation for Economic Co-operation and Development's recently adopted Guidelines for the Licensing of Genetic Inventions were developed in response to health policy debates concerning the exercise of patent rights over human gene sequences. Controversies about gene patents have prompted a number of high-profile calls for governments to consider changes to their patent acts and patent office administration. A range of legislative and administrative reforms have been suggested that might address the problems related to gene patents, including the inclusion of statutory research and clinical use exemptions to improve freedom to operate and access to medical care; ethical limits to patents through the inclusion of *ordre public* or morality clauses; increased scrutiny of the review of gene patent applications at patent offices; and new or broadened avenues for third-party opposition to the granting of patents. Following requests from member states, the OECD followed a policy path quite typical of the organization, one directed not at legislative change or reforms within patent offices but at institutions that license genetic inventions. This approach might be seen as a reflection of a rescaling of policy development mechanisms bypassing debates related to national patent reform initiatives. Indeed, policy development in this transnational forum may have been easier than at a national level. The move towards defining the terms of "good citizenship" for those holding patents for genetic inventions can be characterized as the result of policy learning or social learning. The process and location of policy development facilitated a shift in national policy dialogue capable of breaking a significant impasse in the debates about gene patenting. The Guidelines typify the kind of governance benchmark and tool of inquisitive regulation described in the introductory chapter of this volume.

Controversies about the ethical, social, and economic consequences of gene patenting reflect two decades of debates within academic and policy circles. These concerns include the introduction of commercial values into the way we view the human body, ensuring equitable access to genetic technologies that are useful to improving health, and the effects of patents on the culture of collaboration, peer review, and validation in scientific communities. The economic concerns relate to the fear that by granting patents over basic scientific findings, we may be creating economic monopolies over basic knowledge that is so important to health research. These controversies relate not only to the patenting of genetic material itself but also to related technologies as well as the manner in which those with patent rights actually use those rights (ALRC 2004a). Because of their complexity and international scope, these controversies landed at the OECD for resolution. This chapter describes the policy problems that led to the participation of the OECD and analyzes the result of that intervention.

The gene patenting debate has given rise to discussion of a variety of possible policy responses, ranging from mechanisms internal to patent legislation to better procedures and/or resources at patent offices and courts, and to better supervision of how patent holders exercise their rights. What all of these options have in common is that they view patent law and licensing policy as economic and social policy levers. On the one hand, patent law can be understood – wrongly, we later argue – as a lever to induce private investment in the creation and dissemination of new goods and services that themselves may increase wealth and social welfare, including in the health sector (ALRC 2004b). On the other hand, patent law is also seen as generating the negative social, ethical, and health policy impacts raised above. Parsing through these concerns is no easy matter, especially given the paucity of evidence on how patents affect research, product development, or access to new technologies. Our analysis is complicated further by the tendency of health and industrial policy analysts to share, borrow, or merge arguments about the impact of gene patents on health care and on innovation in the biotechnology sector. While the common language used to characterize the gene patenting problem has intensified the push to find a clear policy response, it has also generated confusion over the policy objectives, the nature of the problem to be addressed, and appropriate strategies to mitigate identified problems.

While the issue of patenting in human genetics is clearly narrower in scope and impact than some of the social policy issues addressed in this volume, we can certainly characterize gene patenting as a "wicked policy problem," in both its complexity and its reach (Zeitlin 2003, 3). Even at the smallest scale of decision making – that of the researcher or licensing professional making a strategic decision regarding the patenting and licensing of a human genetic invention – there is significant impact on how we as a society value commercial control of important health resources and on the manner in which scientific collaboration proceeds. At the scale of the regional economy, policy on patenting in health biotechnology reflects relatively short-term imperatives to manage the costs of new health care technologies and support emerging and existing biotechnology industries whose intellectual property is often seen as their principal asset. National governments must weigh the risks and benefits of intervening in disputes between patent holders, health researchers, and health care providers that involve a heady mixture of concerns ranging from the need to maintain both equality of access to new health technologies and a common standard of care across regions, to the need to advance regional and sectoral economic development, to the need to support policy objectives that encourage innovation. Looking internationally, governments must weigh the impact of real and perceived boundaries of intellectual property policy arising from international trade agreements (such as the World Trade Organization Agreement on Trade-Related Aspects of Intellectual Property Rights). Efforts to address these issues within the OECD have prompted a broad review of the systemic impact of gene patents on the cycle of innovation and product development in health technologies, the equality and access domains for basic scientific knowledge, and the public trust in health science and commercialization models.

These complexities enable us to characterize the gene patenting problem as one resulting from an elaborate division of labour within and between governments and government departments. The way chosen to address this type of problem was to find a mechanism – the OECD's consultative processes – that enabled policy makers to coordinate the varied understandings of the underlying problem by bringing together actors across sectors, disciplines, and divisions of society and government. Given the solution selected, this case study offers insight into the analytical strength of theories of learning, governance, and policy development studied in relation to the OECD as an international organization. It also supports the contention that, while one step removed from economic or health policy decision making, international agencies have become "a platform for debate and a carrier of policy ideas across borders" (Marmor et al. 2005, 338).

Policy Learning and Consensus within the OECD
Following direction from its member states, the OECD's main policy response to concerns about gene patents focused on the development of Guidelines for the Licensing of Genetic Inventions (hereafter the "Guidelines") rather than on patent legislation or patent office practice. These set out principles and best practices to assist patent holders and their private and public sector licensees to negotiate licence agreements with respect to genetic inventions. The Guidelines take it for granted that gene patents are necessary to encourage innovation while attempting to mitigate social and economic harms through persuasion of those holding rights over these patents. Follow-up policy research at the OECD has continued to focus on

patent holder behaviour and studying the merits of various models of collaboration that encourage better access to or pooling of intellectual property
in biotechnology (OECD 2006p, 3).

The OECD's approach to these issues is of interest in light of the selection
of policy instruments, the process of problem identification, and the forum
for dialogue within the OECD. What is notable here is how the policy process
generated responses to two distinct, although generally conflated, sets of
policy problems related to health care: (1) how to improve access to new
health technology, and (2) how to stimulate (or remove barriers to) biotechnology innovation. This response is of particular interest in the context of
ongoing and unsettled debates about classifying the "problem" of gene
patents as well as the identification of evidence needed to prompt the adoption of one of the various policy solutions.

In this chapter, we analyze the policy processes and environment that
underlay the development of the Guidelines as a policy tool in a challenging
context, and identify similarities between this case study and models of the
policy learning in the literature on international organizations and policy
transfer that is well characterized by the work of Hemerlijck and Visser
(2003). Here, policy learning is manifested through a transfer up from member states and their experts to consensus-based guidelines, and also through
a dialogue within a suitably multidisciplinary forum within the OECD (the
Working Party on Biotechnology) and back out to states and stakeholders.
The case study strongly reflects a theme raised in Chapter 1, on the OECD
in historical perspective: both that the organization serves better as a place
for constructive argument rather than negotiation, and that social learning
in this context is an effective means of getting at desired policies. Discussion
of the direction of policy learning (transnational, from member states to
international policy, or diffusion of "best practices" out) is really of secondary importance to the role the organization played in this instance in creating
peer relationships critical to learning through argument. Within this context,
we can understand the OECD's successes in identifying and characterizing
the "problem" of gene patents and locating solutions as the outcome of a
dialogue among a diverse set of stakeholders that may not have engaged
with each other in a national context. The consideration of alternatives to
the Guidelines and subsequent policy developments also sheds light on the
role of the OECD in forging consensus among divergent interests through
reliance on experts, governments, and social partners in the issue identification process.

While aggressive licensing practice in medical genetics was recognized in
the literature as a symptom of an imbalance in the gene patent bargain, the
development of licensing guidelines could not have been easily anticipated
from the lead-up to the OECD's engagement in the process. To understand
how this result came to the fore, we review the policy development process

leading to the Guidelines, the sense of crisis in the delivery of health care engendered by gene patents, the need for collaboration across sectors and jurisdictions to address the problem, and the engagement of a broad group of stakeholders in reviewing available evidence and rationales for policy action.

Analytical frameworks of policy learning and policy transfer are useful in characterizing the development of these Guidelines as a policy tool (Hemerlijck and Visser 2003; Stone 2001). The policy learning framework maps very well onto the policy development processes witnessed in response to gene patenting controversies in the emphasis on crises and failures as triggering devices for policy change. As Hemerlijck and Visser noted (2003, 9), such crises are "unusual events that can be interpreted as a crisis." In this case, the crisis arose out of a coincidence of a very public controversy over terms of licensing for a particular clinical genetic test and a related surge in academic publications on the possible effects of gene patents on innovation in health research. In a number of member states, policy makers in health departments viewed the licensing practices of particular gene patent holders as jeopardizing access to patient care, equality of standards of care, and the sustainability of the public health care system. Given that the increase in gene patenting and in commercially oriented licensing of genetic inventions by universities was the logical outcome of policies aimed at encouraging the patenting and commercialization of university and public sector health research in many OECD countries, the crisis was also understood as, at best, the unanticipated consequence of policy and, at worst, a policy failure. Added to this, researchers and health care providers feared negative effects from the continued expansion and replication of this commercially oriented licensing, creating a substantial fear of imminent danger. In light of the above, some have characterized policy makers' efforts to address the issue of gene patents through patent reforms and other measures as "responding more to high-profile media controversies, than to systemic data about the issues" (Caulfield et al. 2006, 1094).

Bridging the study of welfare reform and health policy, Marmor and colleagues (2005) noted that the same complexities that led to the need for new approaches in studying economic and social policy development prompted similar analytical challenges to the study of health policy. They described the growing need for international comparative health policy research and lesson drawing as follows:

The confluence of economic, demographic and ideological factors that led to extensive debate about the future of the welfare state also created pressures to reform health care systems. Fiscal strains and declining political support for an active role of the state undermined support for welfare state expansion and that strain also affected health policy. There was indeed growing pressure to seek for new policy solutions abroad. The pressure also gave rise to a new body of research within national research communities as well as international agencies like the World Bank, OECD, WHO and European Union. (Marmor et al. 2005, 344)

They note, however, that most health policy research in these international organizations has so far consisted of merely descriptive studies of health systems that pay too little attention to the institutional and cultural factors that are critical to the successful reception and implementation of new ideas.

The OECD's response to the gene patenting debate moved beyond a mere description of the gene patent problem in different national contexts to a more substantive, interdisciplinary analytical approach to shaping behaviour at an institutional level. This may be due in part to the location of the policy debate: outside traditional fora dedicated solely to either health policy or to industrial policy to a forum in which both were intermixed. The emphasis in the policy learning literature on transnational policy networks as the locus of productive exchange and argument, as described in Stone's overview (2001), is also strongly supported by this case. She notes that "in many issue areas, governments and international organizations no longer have the ability to design and/or implement effective public policies." Transnational and multidisciplinary networks provide structural framework for policy-oriented learning (Stone 2001, 12).

The analysis of evidence and policy alternatives played out in the space provided by a division of the OECD directed at supporting the development of biotechnology policy in an interdisciplinary manner. This enabled the participation of industry through the Business and Industry Advisory Committee (BIAC), experts in the fields of intellectual property law, clinical and research genetics, and representatives from both health and industry departments from member states. The resulting analysis focused on practical issues of common concern and led to the decision to pursue a modest but workable policy alternative to those highlighted in most national reports and policy debates.

During the lead-up to the decision to draft guidelines, member states and experts were convened to present evidence regarding the potential negative impact of gene patents on research (which remains, as it was then, inconclusive) and views on the need for policies that would curtail the unwanted behaviour of perceived outliers in the licensing arena. The goal was to assist research institutions and health providers in ensuring that their interface with commercial enterprises supported both their business plans and their broader mandates.

The OECD's approach to engaging stakeholders in problem identification and instrument choice characterized key elements of policy learning: engaging a diversity of actors with different interests, and setting up a dialogue that required sustained deliberation in a context where stakeholder domains are deliberately eroded. While we describe below the composition and interests of the participants who engaged in selecting licensing guidelines as the policy instrument of choice, it is worth noting that not only were the participants in the OECD discussions diverse in their interests but they also implicitly recognized that a breakdown of public trust in the intellectual property regime would be detrimental to the interests of all parties. The OECD workshop report, *Genetic Inventions, Intellectual Property Rights and Licensing Practices: Evidence and Policies* (2004), reflects the complexity of this concern and its function in galvanizing the support of diverse actors for policy action in the context of a basic conservatism about adjustments to the patent system:

> OECD member countries wish to address public concerns about systematic gene patenting. Lack of trust in the patent system and its application to genetic inventions stems from many sources. While companies and patent offices are sometimes accused of not acting in the public interest, such concerns increasingly extend to the actions of scientists, doctors, universities and government agencies. At the same time, OECD member countries recognize the role the patent system has played in developing a vibrant biotechnology industry, which contributes to the advancement of science and public health. (OECD 2002d, 3)

. The combination of perceived crisis, policy failure, the search for promising alternatives, and the uncertainty under which policy makers must make decisions represented, as suggested by the literature, the key drivers for policy action over gene patents. The conditions that prompted action here evoke the policy learning model described by Hemerlijck and Visser, who note that "it takes major external shocks to change core beliefs, decision-making routines, and existing distributions of resources and capabilities ... crisis situations function as important catalysts for non-routine policy learning" (2003, 10).

Action in response to both the debates related to the ethics of gene patenting and the perceived negative impacts on health care generally required a triggering crisis. In this case, the crisis that prompted action was essentially an unrepresentative but high-profile use of a gene patent (Caulfield et al. 2006, 1092). Because of this, some commentators have challenged much of the policy response that has followed from the gene patenting debate as being prompted by the "hard case that makes bad law" (ALRC 2004a). Closer consideration of the case, the controversy, the review of evidence, and the resulting policy direction will help determine the extent to which the OECD's response manifests a reaction to anecdotal evidence of a problem in gene

patenting or a measured response prompted by a policy crisis characterized
not merely by a tangible impact on health care systems but also by a coales-
cing of concerns from a broad mix of stakeholders.

Access and Anti-Commons
While academic debates over the effects of gene patents on research and
health care reach back to at least the mid-1980s, policy debates started later
in reaction to the convergence of several key factors, including the following: high-profile controversies about the behaviour of particular patent
holders; increased political unease about the impact of gene patents on
health care; the emergence of preliminary data on the impact of gene patents
on innovation in biomedicine; and the widespread acceptance of a powerful
characterization of the problem embodied in early studies (Gold 2003). A
recent overview of the gene patenting debate identifies as key policy drivers
the international controversy associated with Myriad Genetics' decision to
enforce its patents over two breast cancer genes and a surge in policy literature studying the emergence of an "anti-commons" in biomedical research
(Caulfield et al. 2006, 1091). While the emphasis on Myriad Genetics is
overstated, both controversies arise over and over in policy documents.

The debate among the leading academic contributors to the gene patenting debate is representative of how the issue has been framed in various
policy fora and national reviews of the impact of patenting on health care
and innovation. First, these policy discussions begin with the assumption
that intellectual property systems are necessary to encourage research and
development into new health technologies and, by extension, that patenting
supports health innovation and advancements in improving health outcomes (Gold et al. 2002). Second, there is a widespread and clearly registered
alarm in the policy community over the surge in the number of human gene
patents and related applications, and how this could result in the "tragedy
of the anti-commons" that would deter biomedical research (Heller and
Eisenberg 1998, 699).

The "anti-commons" problem, characterized at a theoretical level by Michael Heller, was first applied to biomedicine by legal scholars Heller and
Rebecca Eisenberg (1998). This problem views the increasing number of not
only private but also widely distributed rights over basic biomedical information – which include not only gene sequences but also fundamental
knowledge about the biochemistry of the human body and its pathogens – as
imposing such a high transaction cost that biomedical research founders.
This could result, it was theorized, in "stifling life-saving innovations further
downstream in the course of research and product development." Heller
and Eisenberg's work was cited extensively in the academic literature, and
the characterization of the gene patenting controversy as the "anti-commons

problem" became common parlance in policy documents as well (CBAC 2006; ALRC 2004a; Nuffield Council on Bioethics 2002).

Policy responses to such complex issues would not move forward without a powerful example demonstrating the real impact of the anti-commons problem. The one that arose through the media – but certainly not the only example – was that of Myriad Genetics. Because the company was perceived to be unwilling to provide full access to the breast and ovarian cancer genes over which it held patents, the policy community saw Myriad Genetics as exemplifying the kind of behaviour among patent holders that was at the root of a more generalized and growing anti-commons problem. This perception drove the public and policy makers to view gene patents as presenting a very immediate problem for patient care, and generated a policy crisis that captured sustained attention from a diverse group of policy makers.

There are two interesting features of the linkage between Myriad Genetics and the anti-commons problem. The first is that perceptions about the behaviour of key players were at least as important as the facts related to the case. Myriad Genetics was presumed to have acted in certain ways – largely because of its failure or inability to make known its side of the story – when the reality is far from clear. Other actors may have actually better exemplified the problem than Myriad Genetics, but due to the failure of the public record to describe what actually occurred, the company became the primary villain. Second, the perceived problem attributed to Myriad Genetics was not, in fact, an anti-commons problem but a problem of blocking patents. The chief concern over Myriad Genetics was not that it represented a large number of widely held patents that presented high transaction costs to researchers – the company held all the relevant patents – but that the company simply refused to license the use of the breast and ovarian cancer genes to those who wished to either research them or deliver services based on them. Thus, Myriad Genetics represents a conflation of two very different concerns over gene patenting: refusals to license and the anti-commons problem. Nevertheless, the conflation stuck and the anti-commons problem came to be widely used as a descriptor of the problems that gene patents presented for health systems.

Recent academic literature and debates within government advisory bodies such as the Canadian Biotechnology Advisory Committee come to a general conclusion that policy makers responded more to high-profile media controversies than to systemic evidence about the anti-commons problem (Caulfield et al. 2006; CBAC 2006). Following on this concern, researchers have studied how gene patents shape researcher behaviour and have attempted to gauge the extent of the anti-commons problem empirically (Walsh 2004; Stern and Murray 2005). The conclusions drawn from this research have generally discounted the impact of the anti-commons problem as a significant threat to research freedom or to innovation in biotechnology, except in the field of clinical genetics. While the value of the evidence generated in such studies cannot be discounted, these analyses miss a more important point: how and why these events triggered policy responses across jurisdictions. They also miss an opportunity to assess how the definition of the anti-commons problem galvanized policy attention. Attention to these questions may help us understand how the widespread adoption of this analogy and problem identification confounded policy makers both in their efforts to identify the core issues that needed to be addressed and in the evidence that would be required to support policy measures.

It is this dialogue, and not so much the facts behind the Myriad Genetics case, that resulted in the development of the Guidelines. The analysis of the context of the crisis, the conflict, debate and merging of diverse policy interests, and the impact of policies within member states that could be drawn upon by the OECD are more relevant factors that map the OECD's policy response onto models of policy learning in transnational networks.

Gene Patents and Health Care Administration

Health care administrators' concerns over gene patents have focused on the ability to introduce genetic products and services into the health care system in an efficient and economical manner that protects patient privacy and other interests. They fear that gene patents may prevent them from doing so by removing their ability to decide when, how, and to whom new services are offered. This concern was magnified significantly by the perception that Myriad Genetics had decided to employ a business model involving its patents over breast and ovarian cancer gene mutations (BRCA 1 and BRCA 2 genes) that limited further diagnostic and therapeutic research into breast and ovarian cancer (Gold 2002). Myriad Genetics' model (employed by others as well) was to conduct all large-scale (and more expensive) diagnostic testing through its laboratories in the United States.[1] This presented what seemed to be a clear case of conflict between patent holders and public laboratories over health research and health care. Myriad Generics made matters worse by issuing letters to four Canadian provincial governments telling those governments that they were funding public laboratories that were violating the company's patents. In Europe, a number of public research centres and laboratories as well as genetics societies filed oppositions to Myriad Genetics' European patents. Some Canadian laboratories and provincial governments chose, perhaps because of the lack of such a procedure, to ignore the company's threats and to continue to offer the tests (OECD 2002d, 17).

In the wake of these controversies, a number of national policy reports in Canada, the United Kingdom, and Australia raised concerns about the effects of gene patents (as opposed to other health products and services) on health research and health care (Ontario Ministry of Health and Long-Term Care

2002; ALRC 2004a; Nuffield Council on Bioethics 2002; Cornish et al. 2003). These reports identified a number of reasons why gene patents and associated techniques intruded more into health administration than do patents in other areas. Essentially, health care administrators do not have the flexibility to introduce new genetic tests in the most efficient and least costly manner. For example, the patent holder can use its power to require that all tests be conducted in its laboratories even though less expensive or better-quality laboratories exist elsewhere. By doing so, they not only increase costs but create concerns over privacy and the integration of the genetic tests with ancillary health services, such as genetic counselling and follow-on care.

In light of these controversies and concerns, a number of policy reports called for revision of patent legislation, such as the introduction of an opposition period and additional protection to health care providers from infringement actions, as well as measures to improve patent office administration, such as the tightening of utility and description requirements by patent offices and the restriction of broad-based patents (Ontario Ministry of Health and Long-Term Care 2002).

Gene Patents and Innovation
Before the policy crisis and its underlying events emerged, many concerns had been raised about the potential negative impacts of the surge in patenting in genetics on downstream innovation. The standard rationale for the patent system – one that is far from universally accepted – is that it provides an incentive to conduct research that has a practical outcome. The patent system is considered successful if it encourages researchers to conduct research they otherwise would not have undertaken more than it discourages other researchers from working in the field. The concern registered was that granting patents on human genes was not having this effect in many cases (Gold 2006). Some evidence indicates that researchers and laboratories have moved away from developing new genetic testing procedures or verifying existing procedures because of the existence of patents (Merz et al. 2002). Other studies show that there is little evidence of such an effect. It is simply a difficult empirical question to test. Nonetheless, the uncertainty over researchers' freedom to operate continues to be a concern. Given that health research policy in many OECD countries encourages institutions to patent research results, concerns about anti-commons problems may increase in tandem with the success of health research commercialization policies.

National Responses
A number of national government reports issued between 2001 and 2004 sought to address the above policy concerns. The Ontario government issued a report in January 2002 entitled *Genetics, Testing and Gene Patenting: Charting New Territory in Health Care,* which put forward several options for the federal

government (which has jurisdiction over patents and competition law) to consider. These included a number of statutory and administrative safeguards employed in other jurisdictions, such as: (1) changing patent law to allow researchers to conduct clinical research using patented genes (the "research exception" or "experimental use" provisions); (2) clarifying the standards that the patent office uses to assess inventions for patentability in genetics; (3) limiting patents to genetic inventions with a clear and narrow purpose; (4) using existing medical use exceptions to include the provision of genetic tests; (5) adopting an *ordre public* and morality clause; (6) introducing a post-grant opposition process to enable an inexpensive and reliable method of challenging issued patents; (7) tailoring the compulsory licensing provisions within the Patent Act to the provision of genetic tests; and, (8) evaluating whether a specialized patent court is necessary (Gold 2006).

The Australian Law Reform Commission (ALRC) undertook the most comprehensive review of patents over genetic inventions, but this review did not generate a report until after work on the Guidelines was initiated (it was released in 2004). It is worth noting that it too placed a strong emphasis on the need for adoption of a clear research exception, changes in patent office policy that would shift the burden on patent applicants to demonstrate that their genetic inventions are useful, and measures to improve the training of patent examiners. It also recommended that model licence agreements to facilitate fair licensing be developed.

The response in Europe was quite different, given that many of the safeguards considered in the reviews undertaken in Canada and Australia, such as research exemptions, opposition procedures, and public order and morality provisions in the patent system were already in place. European institutions challenged Myriad Genetics' patents using the European Patent Office's existing opposition procedures, and based their opposition on failure to meet the EPO's patentability criteria related to the novelty, inventiveness, and description of the invention in the company's patents. However, the impetus for France's Institut Curie, a cancer research centre in Paris, to lead a group of research institutions and genetics societies in successfully opposing Myriad Genetics' European patents was described as an opposition to the company's "abuse of power," rather than to the technical validity of the patent (Lecubrier 2002). Nonetheless, the existing opposition procedures provided a window for responding to concerns about the public health impact of these patents. France, Germany, and Belgium also responded to the challenges of gene patents through legislation. France has enacted a compulsory licensing scheme that applies to diagnostic procedures such as genetic tests. Germany grants limited patents to very narrow and particular uses of gene patents (Shiermeier 2000). Belgium created a statutory research exemption in response to the Myriad Genetics controversy (Caulfield et al. 2006).

The United States has for some time debated the introduction of new legislation that would reform its patent system by adding an opposition process, among other changes. The motivations for this, however, reach beyond concerns about the biotechnology sector alone. Measures to advance patent reform in the US followed the publication of joint reports by the National Academy of Science and the Federal Trade Commission on the impact of current practices of patent protection on innovation in a number of high-technology industries. Prior to the publication of these reports and to the concrete measures to advance patent reform, the US National Research Council and the National Institutes of Health (NIH) undertook both research and policy measures to address concerns raised early on about the potential negative impact of their research commercialization policy. In February 1996, the US National Research Council convened a workshop on patenting and licensing in biomedical research. At the same time, the NIH invited legal scholar Rebecca Eisenberg to chair a working group to recommend policies that NIH might pursue to ensure maximum social value from NIH-funded inventions. The working group fed into the development of a set of guidelines issued in 1999 for sharing of NIH-funded biomedical research resources. Compliance with those guidelines subsequently became an explicit consideration in the granting of NIH grants and contracts, and is now regarded, at least by some in technology transfer offices, as federal policy. The NIH guidelines encourage grant and contract recipients to license or otherwise share research tools with all biomedical researchers who request them (NIH 2005).

In 2000, the NIH drafted best practice guidelines for all genomic inventions that are based largely on how the NIH's own technology transfer office licensed inventions from NIH laboratories. The final guidelines were published in the Federal Register in April 2005 and recommend that recipients of NIH funding strongly consider broad and non-exclusive licensing of genomic inventions, with allowances for cases when exclusive licensing is needed to induce large investment in post-discovery commercial development (Pressman et al. 2006). While the final NIH document was launched well into the development of the OECD Guidelines, the participation of US delegates in the OECD initiative aided in the sharing of approaches to shaping licensing behaviour. The NIH approach provided a promising lead on a form of incremental policy response that was targeted primarily at the question of access to genetic inventions and mitigating the negative impacts of commercialization policy on research in genetics.

OECD Reaction to the Gene Patenting Controversy

In January 2002, the OECD's Working Party on Biotechnology organized a forum to discuss member states' emerging concerns about gene patents. The forum's mandate was to study and address issues related to genetic inventions, intellectual property rights, and licensing practices. The organization was also asked to convene a workshop to investigate concerns about the impact of patenting and licensing of genetic inventions on access to information, products, and services for researchers, clinicians, and patients. Practitioners from industry, government, public research organizations, and the legal community were engaged to address the following issues:

- the challenges raised by the proliferation of patents on genes and gene fragments, and by the licensing strategies of firms, research bodies, and others
- studies and empirical data that could shed light on the economic impact of the present system of intellectual property protection for genetic inventions, particularly studies that explore how patenting and licensing practices have influenced the research process, new product development, and the clinical diffusion and use of novel treatments and diagnostics
- the advantages and disadvantages of various policy measures, within and outside the intellectual property regime, which could be used to address any systemic breakdowns in access to genetic inventions. (OECD 2002d)

The workshop also sought to articulate recommendations to governments, firms, and funding agencies about how intellectual property rights for gene-based inventions could be best managed in the public interest.

In the lead-up to the workshop, it was recognized that member states were challenged to address concerns about gene patenting that were based largely on anecdotes, and that the impact of particular licensing arrangements was very difficult to study in light of the sensitive proprietary information involved in investigating licensing negotiations. Available evidence was presented related to the impact of gene patents on access to research results among university researchers and on access to diagnostic tests for patients and clinicians, and the impact of intellectual property in human genetics on the diffusion of information and technology generally. While researchers reported having to adapt to a more crowded patent landscape in genetics, licensing professionals seemed already to be developing methods to simplify approaches to gaining the access researchers required by simplified licence and transfer agreements, and methods to mitigate the problem of stacking of royalties. New players such as patient groups were also becoming more involved in decisions about patenting and licensing, such that they could exercise more control over access to end products, such as diagnostic tests (OECD 2002d).

In light of the breadth of interests represented in this debate, the discussion of policy responses strongly emphasized the need to strike a balance between the protection of patented inventions and the promotion of better access for researchers generally (in both the public and private sector) and for health systems. The discussion also stressed the unsustainable costs and time dedicated to legal disputes over patent rights, and the slow and imperfect response of the courts in addressing circumstances of perceived imbalances in the maintenance of the right to reward for innovation in genetic science without hampering either research or commerce. While the need for greater capacity and proficiency within patent offices was raised, it was recognized that improvements in patent office administration would not significantly affect the economic and social impacts of the patent system where problems were identified. The workshop report noted: "If indeed DNA patents are found to lead to systematic and serious access problems, final authority about whether the patent system functions for the greatest public good rests with the government" (OECD 2002d).

Legislative and regulatory proposals were considered in order to improve the balance of interests in the patent regime for human genetics, as well as measures to encourage self-regulation. The mechanisms discussed generally mirrored those legislative and regulatory safeguards detailed in the national reports on gene patenting described previously.

In the discussion, it was recognized that legislative approaches to address the problems identified would likely be enacted slowly and bluntly. As patent systems are obliged under the limitations of international trade agreements to remain technology-neutral, the changes suggested, such as clearer research exemptions and opposition proceedings, would be applied to all areas of technology instead of being crafted in a way that more nimbly addresses challenges in a fast-moving field like biotechnology. Likewise, judicial decisions on oppositions would be time-consuming and limited in their scope of response to the criteria that could be used to invoke a challenge or opposition – that is, patents could most easily be challenged based on claims that the patent application did not adequately meet technical patenting criteria. Even where provisions for appeal on the basis of public order and morality do exist, successful opposition invoking these provisions have been few and far between (Gallochat 2004). Options calling for the creation of new regulatory authorities were regarded as costly and cumbersome (OECD 2002d).

Reforms to patent office administration to improve the quality of patents in genetics and biotechnology and thereby limit the need for challenges and appeals concerned with poor quality or overbroad patent applications were regarded by workshop participants as a quicker method of addressing some problems and more targeted to issues related to genetics. The OECD workshop report did note, however, that such reforms do not carry as much weight as legislative changes in terms of wide public legitimacy as a policy response. The development of best practice guidelines for licensing through a consultative process might be able to help with the problem of public legitimacy, and may be a tool that is suitably flexible to the needs and circumstances of a broad range of member states, although it was recognized that mechanisms relying on self-regulation may also raise concerns from a public legitimacy standpoint (OECD 2002d).

Evidence Considered in Weighing Policy Alternatives
It was recognized at the OECD workshop in 2002 that the evidence available about patent holder behaviour in human genetics was neither robust nor reliable. It did appear clear that the rise in DNA-based patents was a trend that was increasing and evident across all major patent jurisdictions, and that these patent applications were becoming more complex. It was also recognized that public institutions played a very strong role in shaping this trend, as the percentage of DNA patents held by universities and public research institutions was relatively high (1999 data showed that university and public or non-profit research organizations accounted for 42 percent of gene patent assignees) (Cook-Deegan 2002 in OECD 2002d). If manoeuvring thickets of patent rights over DNA was causing significant constraints for health researchers, public sector entities played a significant role in shaping that landscape. The need to sort through relevant patents was becoming time-consuming and expensive for all players.

Evidence related to the behaviour of patent holders and the licensing practices of owners of genetic inventions was presented using data from both private sector firms and research organizations in biopharmaceuticals in Germany and the United States, and from an international comparative study of markets for technologies in biopharmaceuticals (Strauss et al. 2002 in OECD 2002d). These studies were presented with the understanding that the evidence, while informative, was incomplete, given that it was based primarily on surveys and interviews with licensing professionals. As such, the evidence presented focused on the extent to which firms and organizations perceived that their freedom to operate was being limited by the increasing number and complexity of patents in genetics. As such, these studies could gauge perceived limitations on freedom to operate, and the impact this perception had on shaping researchers' behaviour, but the data could not say definitively whether the patents or terms of licensing were themselves limiting flexibility or access to new technologies (OECD 2002d). As this was true of data from individual firms and research organizations, the aggregate impact of patents in genetics was that much more difficult to gauge.

Evidence on whether, and to what extent, access to patented clinical genetic tests had been unreasonably restricted, and regarding clashes between patents and ethical considerations, was presented by legal experts who study the impact of gene patents, private sector lawyers concerned about access, and ethicists concerned about the impact of the patent in genetics on public trust in the patent system. The debates emphasized the particular public importance of genetic tests for predisposition to disease and the ethical implications of limitations on clinical access to these tests that were emerging from patents. There were, however, instances where the cost of developing a clinical diagnostic test was such that high licence fees were seen as necessary in order to recoup research costs, particularly for smaller firms engaged in research and product development in clinical genetics. It was questioned whether the licensing model being employed was in fact the best way of securing financial rewards for the investments made in health research. Furthermore, public health authorities also raised the issue that significant public investments in early-stage research used in the development of clinical genetic tests had seemingly no impact on the ability of public hospitals and laboratories to secure access to these technologies once they had been commercialized. While the studies presented to the OECD highlighted the breakdown in reasonable licensing terms, it was also recognized that information about the negotiation of licensing terms and why these may fail was also absent (OECD 2002d).

Licensing Guidelines as a Policy Outcome
In light of these debates and the evidence presented, member states mandated the development of guidelines for the licensing of genetic inventions. By concentrating on licensing practices only, the approach was to narrow the scope of the OECD's policy intervention and not to attempt to address all concerns related to gene patents. While morally binding on member states, the Guidelines are not legally binding (except to the extent determined by any particular country). The Guidelines assist parties by giving them a starting point in negotiations but are open to parties' choosing to follow different practices where those parties feel it appropriate.

Since the Guidelines represent the joint wisdom of all OECD countries, they are written in a purposive fashion using general language. It is for each country to determine, given the nature of its industry, health care system, and traditions, how best to transform the moral obligation to implement the Guidelines into policy within that country. Implementation of the Guidelines is likely to take the form of a mixture of a change to law, dissemination and acceptance of the Guidelines through industry and university organizations, judicial decisions, and administrative action in granting agencies and technology transfer offices.

The success of the Guidelines initiative remains heavily dependent on the supporting policies and institutions within member states that may, at a minimum, bring about their acceptance as best practice. The Guidelines' strength as a policy tool – their adaptability as a mechanism encouraging incremental change and recognition of common objectives of stakeholders – can be seen as a weakness by stakeholders who viewed the recent gene patenting controversy as an opportunity to advance broader patent system reforms. In light of the fact that the OECD approached the problem of gene patents from the supply side, rather than implementing measures that would establish domains of access to existing patented technologies (such as encouraging statutory exemptions from infringement for researchers), also prompts the legitimate criticism that the approach was inconsequential to the immediate policy problems identified in the policy and academic literature – existing barriers to access to genetic diagnostic tests.

Conclusion: Genetic Testing and the OECD Response – High-Profile Anecdotes or Motivating Crisis?

In light of the criticisms and limitations noted above, it is clear that the Guidelines provide only a partial response to the issues that prompted policy makers to search for mechanisms to address the gene patenting controversy. The immediate policy problem that prompted the intervention was addressed in some jurisdictions by existing patent system provisions for opposing patents (Europe), was possibly mitigated in other jurisdictions by the decision of some governments to ignore patent holders' claims and call for patent reforms to address the underlying problem (Canada), and were avoided in other jurisdictions (Australia), perhaps in light of the cautionary tales provided by the reactions in other states. This partial resolution to the driving policy crisis led some advisory bodies treating the issue of gene patenting (CBAC 2006; ALRC 2004a) to be cautious in embracing policy measures that would address this problem through legislative or regulatory changes. Instead, measures were suggested that would improve administrative processes in patent examination and in the use of existing patent system safeguards, such as patent abuse provisions. Furthermore, the apparent weakness in the evidence regarding a generalized anti-commons problem in genetics research, in light of continued study of the issue, has been as significant for the debate as the initial currency given to that analogy in industry and health policy circles. Evidence of an anti-commons problem has been considered the go/no-go trigger for policy responses to concerns about the effects of gene patents on the research community.

The success of the OECD Guidelines lies primarily in defining the policy problem and the most feasible location of policy change. The policy dialogue that prompted the development of the Guidelines recognized not only the weakness in the evidence of the anti-commons problem but also the methodological limitations of the study of researcher and patent holder behaviour. Concerns about a generalized anti-commons problem in the research realm was accepted as a subordinate problem, or perhaps only one among a number of concerns about the negative impact of the exercise of patent rights in human genetics. Where overlapping patent rights were accepted as a concern in light of the preliminary evidence given, there was a recognition that the increasing transaction costs and time spent by researchers (in both the public and private sectors) navigating patent thickets were significant enough to warrant some kind of response. This contrasts with the requirement of evidence accepted by some policy researchers who have posited that "anti-commons or restricted access-type failures require not that one strategy [of access] be unavailable, but that the entire suite be simultaneously ineffective" (Caulfield et al. 2006, 1093).

Similarly, by moving forward with a modest but pragmatic policy tool that might improve the sharing of research results on reasonable licensing terms, and improve the ability of public research organizations to manage their sizable proportion of patents over human gene sequences in a way that supports better research and health system access to innovations in genetics, the Guidelines provided a mechanism for beginning to address a problem for health researchers and health care systems generated by the gene patenting controversy, while the disputes between the patent holder and laboratories internationally continued to play out. In doing so, the initiative involved some recognition from member states that the approaches taken in response to Myriad Genetics, such as challenging the offending patent legally or using the technology without a licence, did not represent sustainable policy, given the burdens of legal risk this might place on the public sector. In identifying best practices in licensing genetic inventions, the Guidelines defined the triggering crisis as bad practice. This may offer some satisfaction to negatively affected stakeholders, even if it offers no immediate solution to existing conflicts.

Last, the Guidelines target a particular problem that affects public trust in both the genetics research enterprise and in the patent system generally. In identifying an approach to licensing that provides an avenue for protecting research results through the patent system while encouraging access to the invention through non-exclusivity, lower royalty rates, and avoidance of reach-through rights, the Guidelines provide public research organizations with the tools to manage their intellectual property rights in a manner more congruent with their mandates as public institutions. From early on in the gene patent controversy, Heller and Eisenberg identified government commercialization policy as a key factor directing researcher behaviour in a manner that foretold the emergence of an anti-commons problem. Patents were merely a symptom. This characterization of the problem has been confirmed by other researchers even where they have focused on the narrower problem of evidence of the anti-commons effects of patents alone (Walsh et al. 2004; Cho et al. 2003). Given that governments across the OECD countries have been actively engaged in crafting policy to encourage commercialization of health research, and particularly in light of the fact that the number of patents held by universities is often taken as the principal measure of success of those policies, policy mechanisms that can advance the university's mandate to patent *and* share research results reasonably have

become critical. While one might question the public interest in the underlying commercialization policy in light of the evidence of a negative effect
on sharing of health research, the acceptance of the need for such policies
in light of the desire to move health research more quickly from bench to
bedside is virtually universal across governments in OECD countries. As
such, it is helpful that the Guidelines address concerns related not so much
to the exercise of gene patents generally but to situations where applications
or patent rights for technologies of significant public interest were not made
available on terms acceptable to both health systems and industry departments, and to public and private sector stakeholders. Reconciling government
policy with respect to the commercialization of health research and the need
for accountability to public investment in health research that might be
sold back to hospitals and universities once commercialized is a key nuance
of the Guidelines that may ultimately contribute to their usefulness as a
policy tool.

The development of the Guidelines as a policy process within the OECD
is instructive with regard to the functioning of the OECD as an international
organization and its role as a forum for policy learning and policy transfer.
With respect to the participation of member states, experts, and other parties such as BIAC within the organization, this case provides some supporting
evidence of the benefits of engaging a broad group of stakeholders in order
to generate fulsome policy debate. The recognition of common concerns
related to gene patenting raised by these diverse interests intensified the
interest and commitment in generating some form of policy solution to the
problems identified by health and industry departments in member states.
The conflict in the views on appropriate strategies to mitigate these problems, and on the priority that should be given to stimulating innovation
through patent protection versus the need for sustainable access to new
technologies for health systems, helped to generate a more nuanced policy
response that could accommodate multiple public interest objectives. The
divergence of interests and views may also have helped to raise the bar of
evidence required to move forward with policy initiatives without minimiz-
ing the legitimacy of concerns over impacts and behaviours that are difficult
to test empirically.

One last matter of interest to theorists of policy learning is the tension
between the dynamics of policy transfer literature and that focused on social
learning in a transnational network. The impact of the US National Institutes
of Health's work on licensing guidelines as funding criteria is certainly of
interest, but the significance of the US government's or experts' role in supporting such a policy model for the OECD is hard to determine. Where one
might be quick to characterize the OECD Guidelines initiative as a policy
transfer from the US to a transnational forum, such an analysis discounts
the significance of OECD members' building upon a health department

policy in developing an IP governance tool. Perhaps just as important is the question of the construction of peer relationships between policy decision makers in industrial and health policy that allowed for such a transfer. Just as the problem of gene patents rose in profile in light of the concerns related to both innovation and health access, so the use of the OECD as a forum that created a dialogue between health and industry policy was an important factor in moving towards a workable response. Similarly, the case study highlights the use of the OECD as a site of transnational governance capable of advancing policy in areas where overlapping national, regional, and sectoral jurisdictions may work against the progress of policy development on a national level.

Notes

The views expressed in this chapter are those of the authors and are not intended to represent those of the Government of Canada.

1 Indeed, prior to the Myriad Genetics case, the approach of Miami Children's Hospital in licensing the test for Canavan's disease in the late 1990s prompted research participants and non-profit groups that had funded the research to lobby for a change in the patent holder's approach to licensing and the cost charged for the diagnostic test (Borchardt 2000). The impact of licensing of tests for Haemocratosis on laboratory practice is also well studied (Merz et al. 2002).

12

The OECD's Social and Health Policy: Neoliberal Stalking Horse or Balancer of Social and Economic Objectives?

Bob Deacon and Alexandra Kaasch

This chapter focuses on the ideas promulgated by the Organisation for Economic Co-operation and Development (OECD) in the domain of social and health policy. We argue that the ideas underlying the OECD's social and health policies are not primarily neoliberal but rather appear to balance the economic imperatives of the international financial organizations with the social concerns of the United Nations social agencies. In this field, the OECD takes more account of, and reflects the different experiences and policy priorities of, the diverse countries making up its membership. The United States, with its exceptional residual and privatized social policy, does not drive the OECD in this policy field. Social policy advice emerging from the OECD Directorate for Employment, Labour and Social Affairs (DELSA) is as often supportive of elements of conservative corporatism and social democracy as it is of liberalism. To be sure, not all of the OECD directorates sing to the same social and health policy songbook, and some of its advice to developing countries does not match that offered to more developed countries. We take issue, however, with the conclusions of Armingeon and Beyeler (2004), who characterized the OECD's social policy advice as neoliberal. Their conclusion was derived from a study of the social policy advice buried within the country review mechanisms emanating from the Economics Department. Our conclusions are based upon a more detailed analysis of the work of the Department of Education, Labour and Social Affairs (DELSA) and other allied departments.

The OECD and Competing Global Social Governance Institutions

Looking at global social and health governance, we are faced with an architecture of global governance that "is characterized by a high degree of diversity and complexity ... [and a] heterogeneous and at times contradictory character" (Koenig-Archibugi 2002, 62).[1] There are a number of competing and overlapping institutions (intergovernmental and international non-governmental organizations, business organizations, broader civil society organizations, etc.), including the OECD, all of which have some stake in shaping global social policy understood as global influences upon national and supranational policies. The struggle between them for the right to shape policy and for the content of that policy is what passes for an effective system of international social governance (Deacon 2007). The fragmentation and competition may be analyzed according to different groupings of contestations, the first and most damaging of which is that the World Bank and, to a lesser extent, the International Monetary Fund (IMF) and the World Trade Organization (WTO) are in competition for influence with the rest of the UN system. The World Bank's health, social protection, and education policy for countries is not always the same as that of the World Health Organization (WHO), International Labour Organization (ILO), or United Nations Educational, Scientific, and Cultural Organization (UNESCO), respectively. While the world may be said to have one emerging ministry of finance in the shape of the IMF (with lots of shortcomings) and one ministry of trade in the shape of the WTO, it has at least, before even considering the OECD, two ministries of health (the World Bank and the WHO), two ministries of social security (the World Bank and the ILO), and two ministries of education (the World Bank and UNESCO). Moreover, the UN social agencies (WHO, ILO, UNICEF, UNESCO) are not always espousing the same policy as the UN Development Programme (UNDP) or the UN Department of Economic and Social Affairs, while the Secretary General's initiatives, such as the Global Compact or the Millennium Project, may bypass the social development policies of the UN's Department of Economic and Social Affairs.

The OECD sits somewhere alongside or between this World Bank/IMF/WTO and UN contest. At first glance, it is a rather small international organization (in terms of member states) but, due to its important outreach activity, the OECD represents a *global* social policy actor. In terms of the OECD work on social and health policy, it is to DELSA that we turn first. Formed in 1974, it now comprises employment, social policy, health, and migration sections. The social policy section split into social policy and health in 2003-2004, reflecting a considerable rise in the number of OECD health policy analysts. An independent education policy directorate was formed in 2002. These increases in the size and range of activities of DELSA and allied departments are reflected in the inclusion of social policy issues in the country review mechanisms.[2] Whereas in the 1990s the Economics Department did not even send a draft of the country reviews to DELSA for its consideration, it now does so, albeit with a rather short deadline for revisions. At the same time, other directorates, namely, Fiscal Affairs and Financial and Enterprise Affairs, touch on the domain of social and health policy, sometimes offering a rather different emphasis in their policy advice. Policy coordination and synergy is not always achieved across these departments.

DELSA work on social protection includes statistical and analytical work on labour markets, social security benefits, pensions, social assistance, and children's allowances. For health, it translates into substantial statistical work in deriving indicators for health care systems, collecting data, and reporting data back to the member states (Health Quality Indicators Project, the System of Health Accounts, OECD Health Data) and analytical work within the OECD Health Project. Social policy is also included in the OECD's outreach work. Certainly, as we shall later discuss, its social policies for developing countries have been adopted wholesale by the UN as the Millennium Development Goals (MDGs). Whereas we cannot testify to a predominantly neoliberal emphasis in OECD social policy advice to developed countries, this is not so clearly the case in its outreach work to developing countries.

From Social Policy as a Burden to Social Policy as an Investment?

In terms of social policy ideas, DELSA achieved at the outset a high profile for the topic of social policy through the conference it convened in 1980, and the subsequent report, entitled *The Crisis of the Welfare State*. While pushing the matter of social welfare higher up the agenda, it concluded that social policy in many countries creates obstacles to growth (OECD 1981). The continued association of the OECD with the "welfare as burden" approach by some commentators stems from that publication. Further work on social expenditures in OECD countries followed from this initiative. The interest in this, and the enthusiasm of Ron Gass, then director of the Social Affairs Directorate, led to the first meeting of social affairs ministers in 1988. OECD work in this field continued and became widely used among scholars. Publications followed and continue, on pensions (1988b, 1993c, 2005d), on health expenditure and policy (1990d, 2004f), and on labour markets and "active social policy" (1994c, 2005e). More recently, work has been undertaken on migration (2006q), on balancing care and work (2002e, 2003h, 2004g, 2005f, 2006r), and on long-term elderly care. With the more recent creation of the Directorate of Education, work already undertaken in this field (OECD 1998e) is likely to increase (see Chapter 13).

In 1991, the concern of the Council of the OECD about the burden of taxes on employment to sustain welfare expenditure gave rise to further work on social policy by DELSA under its new director, Tom Alexander. Wishing not simply to repeat the "welfare as burden" mantra, and learning perhaps from parallel work of the OECD Development Centre, which, in its review of the dynamic Southeast Asian economies, concluded that "limited but effective action by the state ... [has led to] rapid return to growth" (OECD 1993c, 41), the social affairs official responsible for the draft of the impending ministerial conference fashioned the *New Orientations for Social Policy* report, which asserted that "non inflationary growth of output and jobs, and political and social stability, are enhanced by the role of social expenditures as investments in society" (OECD 1994c, 12). This and other sentiments, such as "restrictions on social expenditure could be counter productive if the objectives of social policy are sacrificed. Jeopardising the quality of life ... may be the most costly route of all" (OECD 1994c, 13), were adopted with minimal change as they progressed from the office in the Social Affairs Directorate, through middle- and high-rank meetings of government ministers, to the 1992 ministerial conference itself. These "new" orientations reflect the fact that, in contrast to the US-influenced IMF and World Bank, the economic and social policy of the OECD represents a much more balanced set of economic and social considerations, more typical of mainstream European social and economic policy. Indeed, the OECD's subsequent review, *A Caring World*, concluded that "one of the effects of globalization could be to increase the demand for social protection ... a more useful blueprint for reform would be to recognise that globalization reinforces the need for some social protection" (OECD 1999a, 137). Mark Pearson, currently head of the Social Policy Division (DELSA), held the pen in this report as he did in the most recent "big social policy idea" report of the OECD, *Extending Opportunities* (2005e). This view that social expenditures are important for investment and stability continued to be reflected in the focus of the 2007 OECD Council, which addressed growth with equity. The chair's summary of the meeting noted that "investing in human capital and skills, including training and life-long learning, is critical in helping countries and citizens adjust (to globalization)" (OECD 2007f).

Social Protection Policy: DELSA Holding the Line on Public Pensions while Activating Others to Work?

The attempt by the OECD to balance economic efficiency and social protection of necessity has led it to recommend policy changes that have been seen by some defenders of the European Social Model (as represented by the work-based welfare states of Germany and France) as evidence that the OECD is a neoliberal stalking horse located in Paris. This is most clearly the case in relation to the OECD's frequent calls to loosen up labour markets, but it is also discerned by its critics in its insistence that the main purpose of education is to enhance employability, its proposals to add a private tier to pension schemes, and its exhortation to consider the options for mixed funding in health care.

Thus, with regard to labour markets, Farnsworth reminds us that the OECD Jobs Study (OECD 1994a) "recommends that governments: tackle inflation, increase wage and employee flexibility, eliminate impediments to the creation and expansion of enterprise, relax regulations on employment, increase employee skills and reform social protection systems to ensure they do not impinge on labour markets" (Farnsworth 2005, 223).

Indeed, this emphasis in the work of the OECD on social protection continues. Even within the core issues of labour markets, however, the most recent OECD report on this topic (OECD 2006s) argued that strong trade unions and employment protection laws can go hand-in-hand with low levels of unemployment. In 2003, OECD activities on social policy included ongoing work on employment-related social policies under the heading of "Making Work Pay." The summary report of *Extending Opportunities: How Active Social Policy Can Benefit Us All* argues: "Instead of relying on taxes and public transfers alone, OECD countries need to look for other ways to deal with the social challenges of today. In this volume, the policies that aim to do this are called active social policies because they try to change the conditions in which individuals develop, rather than limiting themselves to ameliorate the distress these conditions cause" (OECD 2005e, 2006v).

Recent work on sickness, disability, and work in Norway, Poland, and Switzerland concluded that "a key challenge is helping sick and disabled people find work or keep their job. Most people who start claiming disability benefits will not work again, but many want to work and could work if given the right training and support. Helping persons with health problems or disability to work will improve their integration into society as well as their incomes. In the long term, such a policy will raise the prospect of higher overall economic output of a country, thereby helping to meet the challenge of ageing populations" (OECD 2006u, 2006v).

Activation policies include giving children a good start in life by enabling people to reconcile work and care and encouraging welfare-to-work programs. The Babies and Bosses program of the OECD, reviewed in Chapter 14, even suggests that social democratic Sweden is regarded as a star pupil of the OECD in this policy field, reinforcing our view that the OECD does not draw good practice lessons only from social policies associated with "liberal" welfare states.

The study by Henry and colleagues of the OECD's education policy in the context of globalization concludes that globalization has encouraged a convergence in education policies internationally around "an ascendant neo-liberal paradigm of policy in which education has been largely (though not solely) framed as human capital investment and development. Such a paradigm serves to legitimate a set of educational values feeding off and feeding into the broader culture of rampant individualism and consumerism unleashed by the victory of capitalism over communism. Educational purpose has, in large measure, been reduced to a student's calculus of job opportunities or to the state's calculus of maximum return on minimum input" (Henry et al. 2001, 175).

They assert that "the OECD has been a key player in sponsoring such a set of values" (see also Chapter 13). Their analysis of OECD policy and the work of the associated Centre for Educational Research and Innovation (CERI) stops with the publication of its *Pathways and Participation in Vocational and Technical Education* (OECD 1998e). It will be interesting to see how OECD educational policy develops now that it has an independent Directorate of Education. The new strategic objectives of the directorate agreed upon at a meeting of ministries of education in 2003 are all-encompassing: to assist members and partners in achieving high-quality lifelong learning for all, contributing to personal development, sustainable economic growth, and social cohesion. In terms of the impact of globalization on higher education, CERI is collaborating with UNESCO in developing guidelines for cross-border tertiary education.

In terms of pension policy, the OECD (DELSA) does seem to strike a middle ground between that of the World Bank, with its strong push for defined contribution, fully funded, individualized privatized pensions, and that of the ILO, with its continued defence of the public intergenerational solidarity-based pay-as-you-go (PAYG) defined benefit systems. Its recent reviews of pension systems are sound analyses of the costs and benefits of country schemes with a comparative analysis of the pensions citizens might expect from the contributions they make. The latest version draws attention to the fact that "people in OECD countries will have to save more for their retirement as a result of the major pensions reforms carried out across the OECD in recent years. In France, Germany, Italy, Japan and Sweden, for example, future benefits will be cut by between 15 and 25 percent and in Mexico and Portugal by over 30 percent from what they would have been entitled to before the reforms" (OECD 2007g).

The earlier report *Ageing Societies and the Looming Pension Crisis* (OECD 2002f, 2) had pointed to the need to reform (not replace) state PAYG schemes to ensure their sustainability by such means as extending working lives and eliminating early retirement provisions rather than drastic cuts in entitlement. At the same time, it pointed to problems in private pension schemes, such as the consequences of stock market slump. Here the OECD has been active in promulgating guidelines for the better management of private pension schemes (2002g).

This balancing act between public and private continues, but critics of the OECD might find some support for their view that at heart it is a neoliberal stalking horse by noting that other directorates take a different view. In a working paper of the Economics Department, Casey argues that "a higher share of retirement income from private sources makes it less likely that reductions in replacement rates of public pensions leads to an increase in poverty among the elderly" (Casey et al. 2003, 31). This in effect supports the case for adding a private tier to the pension mix. Moreover, the Directorate for Financial and Enterprise Affairs (rather than DELSA) publishes a

Pension Market in Focus newsletter, which reports regularly on a range of meetings designed to inform policy actors about the better management of private pension funds.

Indeed, tensions between DELSA and the Directorate for Financial and Enterprise Affairs are self-evident in their outputs. People involved argue that the best way of getting a coherent line is to have one pension division. Meanwhile, and rather to underline the point about a possible division of opinion on social protection between two directorates, a background paper by Willem Adema of DELSA (2006), prepared for a meeting with the German Corporation for Technical Collaboration in China in June 2006 on "Formulating Standards for Urban Subsistence Security," addresses the positive role of public social assistance, including social pensions, in meeting the needs of households.

With an eye to outreach work, the latest *Pension Market in Focus* newsletter produced by the Directorate for Financial and Enterprise Affairs reported on meetings in Chile (the "home" of private pensions) on pension privatization in Latin America held jointly with the International Organization of Pension Supervisors (IOPS). The involvement of the private sector IOPS rather than the longer-established public sector–oriented International Social Security Association (ISSA) is unsurprising, given the private sector orientation of the finance directorate. In the same vein, the newsletter reported on a meeting of the OECD's Working Party on Private Pensions held in Beijing in September 2006 as a "continuation of its outreach work. An ongoing project is planned with the Ministry of Labour ... providing international experience into how to develop the occupational pension fund market" (OECD 2006t, 16).

OECD Health Policy Capitalizes on WHO Shortcomings and Acknowledges the Value of Diverse Approaches to Health Systems?

In health policy, too, an evenhanded approach is evident. This is not to say that OECD work does not include elements usually looked at very critically by some social policy scholars. A closer look at what is actually being said about issues like raising financing pressure, private health insurance, or co-payments/user fees, however, reveals that the OECD is well aware of the dangers of certain reform directions. It does not suggest that the market would fix the problems. In particular, the outcome of the OECD Health Project was a typically thorough and professional OECD piece of work undertaken in collaboration with professional bodies and the WHO.

It is important to note that OECD health work has recently increased substantially. This is a direct consequence of the unhappiness expressed by a number of OECD member countries with the attempt by the WHO to develop an index and rank order of health service performance. The World Health Report of 2000, *Health Systems: Improving Performance* (WHO 2000), was an ambitious report in which the WHO set out to compare and evaluate health systems within countries on the basis of five criteria: level of health of population, distribution in health outcomes, responsiveness of service, distribution of responsiveness, and fairness of financing. These five criteria were weighted and averaged into one index, which was then compared with health input data (such as health expenditures) to calculate an efficiency for the particular health care system. The report was criticized not so much for its findings but for the claims that its methods were suspect and did not stand technical comparison with those of the OECD or the World Bank or of independent scholars (Häkkinen and Ollila 2000). As a direct consequence, Australia and the Netherlands chaired a new ad hoc OECD Committee on Health that commissioned the OECD to undertake a comparative evaluation of health systems. At the same time, the European Union Directorate for Health decided to outsource its health policy analysis to the OECD. This work was reported to the first OECD meeting of health ministers in 2004, and resulted in a further increase in health work.

The major part of the OECD work on health is done within DELSA – more concretely, in the new Health Division (previously part of the Social Policy Division). Due to the interdisciplinary character of health, some research also takes place in other departments. Working relations between the Health Division of DELSA and the Directorate for Financial and Enterprise Affairs appear to be constructive, and there is rather less evident tension between the health policy publications of the two directorates than in pension policy, as noted above. Despite the location of the Health Division within DELSA, publications on health are not primarily characterized by social and redistributive starting points, but employ medical, technical, and/or economic definitions of health (OECD 2000c). This does not automatically imply, however, that social policy objectives are not addressed within the OECD's policy models. Overall, the approach to health systems is socioeconomic. Health systems are described as important to OECD economies *and* the well-being of citizens. They are considered an important element of social cohesion *and* as the largest service sector among OECD economies.

This mixture becomes particularly clear in the report *Towards High Performing Health Systems* (OECD 2004f), the product of a three-year project on health, culminating in a meeting of OECD health ministers in May 2004. The report names, among other things, universal coverage for a core set of health services and accessibility of those services to the population as important elements of health care systems. The focus is on the challenges health systems face and related reforms, less on their structure or organization in general. Accordingly, the work of the OECD concentrates on issues like the level and mix of resources; institutional and incentive characteristics; regulation and self-regulation of health systems; the impact on public finances; and the ability to meet the challenges of medical advances, aging populations, and rising expectations. The background to this work is an interest in measuring, assessing, and improving performance of health systems (Or 2002, 7).

More concretely, the OECD Health Project's work program addressed issues of rising costs and *efficiency,* outcomes of health expenditure and *effectiveness,* and issues of access and *equity.* Subprojects were carried out on waiting time, emerging technologies, private health insurance, and long-term care. On the issue of financing, the report states: "A rising spending in GDP ratio is not necessarily problematic from a policy perspective. Indeed, social welfare may well be improved by increasing spending, particularly if demand for health-care services tends to rise more rapidly than income and if the cost of technical change is more than compensated with improvements in the quality of care and resulting health outcomes ... Nevertheless, policy makers must make decisions regarding the value of spending in the health sector versus competing priorities for scarce resources" (OECD 2004f, 86).

On how to achieve equity, the report argues clearly for comprehensive access to health services. Accordingly, user fees are considered as a problem regarding equity. And while private health insurance is of particular interest in OECD health work, it is not considered as the panacea to national health care financing problems: "Increasing the private share of health financing also raises issues as to financing equity ... at least to some degree, private health insurance tends to be a more regressive source of financing than most public or social insurance systems. It is, however, more progressive than out-of-pocket payments, in that it provides individuals with a means of pooling health-care costs" (OECD 2004f, 88).

The report further provides an interesting discussion about reducing the burden of public households with the means of private health insurance. According to this, private health insurance cannot be the way to solve the public system's financing problems due to the nature of private insurance: "private health insurance has not led to significant reductions in public spending on health ... and entails trade-offs with equity that are costly to offset" (OECD 2004f, 17). It might be used only in certain cases. Despite this, there are suggestions on how to reform the private sector (OECD 2004f, 84). Other publications, for example, by Colombo and Tapay and a policy brief on *Private Health Insurance in OECD Countries* (Colombo and Tapay 2004), offer a far from wholehearted endorsement of private health insurance, repeating many of the points above about the impact on equity and its failure to reduce public spending.

Understanding and Characterizing OECD Social and Health Policy: Don't Focus on the Economic and Development Review Committee

Even though we have argued that, compared with the ideologically driven World Bank, the OECD should be regarded as a source of evenhanded, technically competent knowledge on aspects of social and health policy, it still finds itself tarred with that neoliberal brush. To some extent, this might be due to the fact that its highest-profile activity, the country appraisal mechanism, is under the control of the Economics Department, and this gives emphasis to the OECD labour market policies that are clearly in favour of flexibility. Certainly, the recent review of the social policy advice given by the OECD to thirteen European countries paints a picture that is nearer the neoliberal end of the range than the one painted above (Armingeon and Beyeler 2004). Thus:

> OECD recommendations are to cut budgets, eliminate labour market rigidities, strengthen competition, free international trade, rationalise production, exploit all new technologies, refrain from demand management, strengthen the personal responsibility of individuals and families and reduce generous social security benefits ... In addition to suggestions concerning labour market policies and social security benefits, the OECD's general advice regarding health policy has been to allow for more competition. In education policy the principal suggestion is to improve education – particularly vocational training – and to better target higher education towards the labour market. Pension policy recommendations generally consist of a double strategy; increase the average age of retirement and add funded or private pension systems to public pay-as-you-go systems. (Armingeon 2004, 228)

In sum, in contradiction to our assessment above, Armingeon (2004, 229) concludes: "Hence the OECD has a coherent ideational strategy, which resembles the general liberal advice to reduce state intervention in society and the economy and to free markets from public regulations as long as these are not indispensable for the functioning of the economic exchange."

As an account of the work of the Economics Department and in particular the Economic and Development Review Committee (EDRC) mechanism, this may be valid. But it is not valid as an account of the social and health policy analytical and advisory work of the OECD as a whole. Indeed, we would venture to suggest that relations between DELSA and the EDRC process are now slowly changing and we might expect more impact of DELSA on the EDRC in future. In the 1990s, drafts of the EDRC were not circulated for comment to DELSA and other departments. Now they are, albeit with a limited time for comment and with some shift in social policy advice, as noted earlier.

Neither should the EDRC reports be regarded as the most important source of OECD advice on social and health policy making in OECD countries. The EDRC reports have to be acceptable to the countries being commented upon and are signed off by the country concerned. In this process, it is the ministry of finance that takes the lead, and it is to be expected that the reports might emphasize treasury thinking. At the same time, many OECD Social and

Health Policy reports, driven by the concerns of professionals in the Social Policy and Health Policy sections of DELSA, are published more independently under the auspices of the Secretary-General. Moreover, when major social and health policy reports are submitted to and agreed upon by the Council of Ministers, these are often accepted with minor changes as they are being read by the more sympathetic health and social affairs ministries. In this sense, to focus on the EDRC to determine OECD social and health policy is like focusing upon the ministry of finance within a country to determine national social and health policy.

A further indication that, in terms of social and health policy, the OECD is not a stalking horse for neoliberalism is the relatively little attention paid to changing the OECD's social policy by the Nordic countries, in contrast to the enormous trust funds they have established to influence World Bank social policy and development thinking (Deacon 2007). By the same token, the United States is also not a major player. Its representative on the DELSA committee is from the relatively unimportant Human Services department of the federal government, which is not interested in pensions, rather than the US Treasury, which has intervened to influence World Bank pension policy (Wade 2002). It is fair to conclude that in terms of the influence upon the social and health policy of ministries of social affairs, the OECD works through the dissemination of best practice, where "best" is defined by an *inclusive* range of possible criteria from which countries can choose. More generally, the dissemination strategy of the Social Policy and Health Policy sections is directed at think tanks and the academic community. It is the progressive Brookings Institution that OECD social policy professionals are as likely to talk to in Washington as the US government.

The Role of the OECD in Development: MDGs as Progress or Residualism?

Finally, the role of the OECD in relation to social and health policy in developing countries needs discussion. As explained in Chapter 5, the OECD discussions about social policy for developing countries take place in a different location and often arrive at different conclusions and recommendations. Even if it is possible to characterize the OECD in terms of its views on national social policy for *developed* countries as evenhanded and concerned as much with universalism, public provision, and equity as with targeting and market efficiency, this is not always the case with regard to its views on social policy in a *development* context. Certainly, from the standpoint of social policy ministries of the OECD, many would be very worried if some of the content of the goals and targets in social development policy designed initially by the OECD for the global South were to be applied to social policy in the North.

We examine the UN's adoption of the Millennium Development Goals as goals and targets to be met with the support of Official Development Assistance (ODA) in this context. These goals and targets were first articulated within the OECD's Development Assistance Committee (DAC). The OECD DAC report *Shaping the Twenty-First Century: The Contribution of Development Co-operation* (1997d) set a number of specific targets for development policy. This led to a joint venture between DAC, bilateral donors, and the World Bank to establish indicators of progress towards their achievement. The OECD DAC targets, later adopted as the MDGs, focus on the poorest of the poor in poor countries, include halving of the number of people in extreme poverty, making basic education available to all, and enabling access for all to reproductive health services, with concomitant reductions in maternal and infant mortality rates and gender inequality. The two positives in this approach are the inclusion in the agreed-upon measures of poverty of one indicator of inequality (the poorest fifth's share of national consumption), which suggests that redistribution policies are not forgotten entirely, and the fact that measurable and attainable targets and the monitoring of them are in place. The other side of the coin remains the limited goals of the MDGs in terms of public service provision of only universal *primary* education and universal *reproductive* health, compared with the broader agenda of the Copenhagen 1995 UN summit, which had been more concerned with equitable access to services (Deacon 2007, 75). This leaves ample scope for the privatization of the rest of social provision while international attention is focused on these issues of basic service delivery only.

This distinction between what the OECD might be saying to *developed* countries and *developing* countries becomes also clear when looking at *Policy Insights No. 11* from the OECD Development Centre. Drechsler and Jütting (2005) discuss the potential of private health insurance (PHI) for the poor in developing countries. There, the "promotion" of PHI is much less carefully undertaken than in relation to developed, OECD member countries. Even though it is acknowledged that the contribution of PHI towards universal health coverage is limited, it is argued that there is "the need to move away from excessive reliance on point-of-service payment to pre-payment and risk-sharing. Private health insurance (PHI) offers a potential alternative to insure against the cost of illness and lately has been receiving increasing consideration from policy makers around the world."

It is stressed, however, that PHI cannot go without an efficient institutional and regulatory framework to prevent market failure. While the willingness to accept private health insurance is thus certainly greater in the development context, it is nevertheless important to note that this does not necessarily (only) mean for-profit private health insurance: "If PHI is carefully managed and adapted to local needs and preferences, it can be a valuable tool to complement existing health-financing options. In particular non-profit group-based insurance schemes could become an important pillar of the health-financing system, especially for marginalized individuals who do not have access to formal insurance. The introduction of PHI is not an end in itself, but ideally an element in a process towards achieving universal coverage" (Drechsler and Jütting 2005).

Returning to the concern that the MDGs initially sponsored by the OECD DAC are a form of residual or neoliberal social policy, it needs to be said that within the framework of DAC, much subsequent work by social development professionals from member ministries of international development has sought to widen the social development agenda to include a more universal approach to social protection and social services. This network of social development professionals (POVNET) is currently working on social protection and social policy, one of the first fruits of which is a new statement on Comprehensive Social Policies for Development (STAKES 2006), which is anything but a neoliberal social policy agenda (Wimann et al. 2006, 12-15). These earlier criticisms that the OECD says one thing to the global North and another to the global South may be in need of revision. It is noteworthy that the new DELSA Health Policy Division has established an inclusive set of relations across the organization, including those with the OECD DAC, and this might be helping to forge North/South policy coherence. The Social Policy Division does not have such a relationship and so moves towards a less neoliberal social policy approach in DAC are to be attributed to POVNET rather than the Social Policy Division within DELSA.

The OECD as a Global Social and Health Policy Actor: Offering Choices but Leading the Debate?

How then might we come to a conclusion about the role of the OECD as a global social policy actor? We have placed the OECD between or alongside a number of other international organizations and other global social policy actors. Chapter 13 shows that the OECD to some extent has replaced UNESCO in the education field. A closer look at the field of health has revealed recent attempts of the OECD to take on the role of an international health organization, at least for its member states. This means that the OECD is learning from the shortcomings of the WHO, perhaps becoming *the* health organization for the developed states with unknown future implications for the health policy of developing countries. In terms of social policy more generally and social protection in particular, it is to the OECD that one turns for an evenhanded, comprehensive approach concerning developed countries, although in this field the ILO remains a key global player in the South.

Regarding its interaction with regional actors like the EU, the OECD appears not only as a rather "European" organization but also as a global leader/initiator or "first mover" (Dostal 2004), particularly in health policy:

the EU's Open Method of Coordination has been developed from how the OECD was perceived, and the European Commission has provided financial means for the OECD Health Project in order not to duplicate work.

Is there *awareness* in the wider community of the OECD as an important global social policy actor? For health – perhaps because of OECD work in this field – our impression from document analysis and interviews is that other global actors (such as WHO, ILO, and the World Bank) do not consider the OECD an important actor in the field, while those who work for the OECD suggest otherwise. Porter and Webb suggest, however, that authors of academic articles often do not seem to see the need to properly reference the sources beyond the mere use of the OECD label. The publications have gained a reputation of authoritative statements of knowledge in many policy areas (Porter and Webb 2004, 7). This contrasts sharply with the flawed attempt of the World Bank to promote itself in these policy domains as *the* knowledge bank. An evaluation of World Bank research in the period 1998-2005 finds that in the Bank new research methods have been promoted "without adequate evaluation"; in some cases, "the degree of self-reference rises almost to the level of parody" (Deaton 2007). This is not a judgment that is level at the OECD.

Inside the OECD, the potential drivers of the work program are the Secretary-General, the member states, the Secretariat, or different directorates or divisions. In this context, it is important to understand the degree of autonomy that the OECD DELSA has to initiate and float new policy and research agendas. A significant example is the case of the Babies and Bosses work program, which was driven from within DELSA against the initial objection of ministers. Another example is the choice of private health insurance as a major topic in health policy (no matter the divergent recommendations), which as a result has become an area of interest in both the Health Division in DELSA and the Development Center despite the general independence of the directorates and the non-coordinated work between them. Overall, we agree with Busch (2006, 12) that the "OECD secretariat and its subdivisions enjoy considerable autonomy in carrying out their tasks."

The actual importance of the respective directors-general of the organization comes into focus here. At the time of the WHO ranking debacle, we were informed that the then director-general was particularly interested in strengthening the OECD's role in health policy. This would underline the Secretariat's role to define problems, point out issues of importance to member states, and propose solutions or areas of research need accordingly (Busch 2006, 14). More comprehensive work on an issue, particularly more legal instruments, is, however, very dependent on the member states' interest in the issue – or dependent on the success of the respective directorate or division in convincing member states about the issues in question.

The relationship with particular member states – from the perspective of people working in DELSA – was said to be one in which specific criticisms of countries was avoided and was dependent on the willingness of a particular country to be criticized. Critical comment was more indirect, not focusing on the particular situation in the country in question, but pointing to alternative possibilities. Using particular countries as positive or negative examples is not part of the DELSA strategy. Here it is trying to avoid the mistake the WHO made with its *World Health Report 2000*. For the field of social policy and health, we would support Busch's interpretation (2006, 17) that the directorate is concerned about how its work is perceived by member states, and thus is very careful to point out best practices connected to a particular state that should be adopted by others. In this sense, the OECD stands in sharp contrast to the one-size-fits-all fast track one-policy-message approach that came to be associated with the World Bank and the IMF. This does seem to be in contrast to the OECD activity in education, which is much more about ranking and pointing out the advantages of particular national systems (Chapter 13).

The influence of the OECD in the field of social and health policy is, according to those working within DELSA, as much indirectly through the networks of epistemic communities as directly through advice to governments. Informants within DELSA report that informing and influencing key academics is an important aspect of their dissemination strategy. Challenging the assumptions of "intergenerational accounting," selling the idea of "actuarial neutrality," and criticizing the notion of "notional defined contributions" are part of the work of scholars working on pensions in DELSA. Phoning scholars known to be advisors to government is important. The OECD social and health policy professionals are significant players in the global scholarly community, respected for their academic integrity and non-ideological position.

In terms of the substance and policy orientation of OECD advice in this field, we have argued, contrary to the thesis of McBride and colleagues (Chapter 8) and Ruckert (Chapter 5), that the OECD stands for a considered attempt to reconcile the economic imperatives and macroeconomic concerns of the international financial organizations with the social solidarity concerns of the UN social agencies. Moreover, OECD social and health policy takes account of and reflects the different experiences and policy priorities of the diverse countries making up the OECD membership. It also advances in specific ways, through argument and research, the social and health policy agenda, and is responsible for some policy innovation. We have taken issue with the conclusions of Armingeon and Beyeler (2004), who characterized the OECD's social policy advice as neoliberal. Their conclusions derived from their study of the social policy advice within the country review mechanisms do not stand up compared with our conclusions based upon analysis of the work of DELSA and allied departments. Social policy advice emerging from the OECD is as often supportive of elements of conservative corporatism and social democracy as it is of liberalism.

Notes

1 See also Hein and Kohlmorgen (2003).
2 See, for example, the recent *Economic Survey of the Russian Federation* (OECD 2006x), which called for substantial improvement in the Russian health care system.

13
OECD Education Policies and World Hegemony
Kjell Rubenson

"The OECD has become a kind of 'éminence grise'" of industrialised countries' education policy (Rinne et al. 2004, 456; see also Henry et al. 2001; Vickers 1994). In Gramscian terms (Adamson 1980; Boggs 1976), the Organisation for Economic Co-operation and Development has achieved hegemony over educational discourse through its capacity to manufacture the "common sense" of society. The OECD is able to set agendas that become taken for granted and govern national policy actors' approach to educational reforms.

This chapter argues that the OECD has reached this position by fostering a connection between the economic and educational spheres. More specifically, it investigates how shifts in the dominant political economy have affected the OECD's educational policy discourse.

Education at the OECD

The OECD's long-standing involvement in educational matters may be surprising since the OECD Convention does not include any reference to education (Papadopoulos 1994). The closest reference is in Article 2(b), which mentions vocational training. However, the general Preamble to the Convention presents economic strength and prosperity as essential for individual freedom and general well-being, and Papadopoulos (1994, 11) discerns an implied role for education in the OECD charter relating to its contribution to economic growth and, through this, an increase in general well-being.

Notwithstanding this comment, George Papadopoulos, drawing on over thirty years of working at the OECD, acknowledges that gaining a standing for education within the organization and integrating it into its core activities was never easy (Papadopoulos 1994, 12). Another former employee suggests that it was only in the mid-1990s that education "really found recognition throughout the offices of 'the Chateau'" (Istance 1996, 94). Tracing the changing organizational placement of education within the OECD indicates a growing understanding of the centrality of education to the overall mission of the OECD. Initially, education was located in the Office for Scientific and Technical Personnel, which addressed issues concerning shortages of scientific and technological manpower. Later, in 1968, in recognition of the wider importance of education to the mandate of the OECD, the Centre for Educational Research and Innovation (CERI) was established. Then, in 1970, the Office for Scientific and Technical Personnel was transformed into the Educational Committee.

Education was first housed within the Directorate for Scientific Affairs and in 1975 became part of the new Directorate for Social Affairs, Manpower and Education, which, in 1991, was renamed the Directorate for Employment, Labour and Social Affairs (DELSA). It consisted of two major committees, the Educational Committee and the Committee for Employment, Labour and Social Affairs. Papadopoulos (1994) sees the shifting location of education as reflecting the decreased importance of science policy and scientific manpower and, as concerns grew over escalating unemployment, a movement for education and training towards OECD's core interest in manpower and employment policies. Perceptions of the consequences of this shift vary (Henry et al. 2001). Some, including Papadopoulos, see in it a new impetus to education's social mission, while others maintain that it resulted in a short-term focus on labour market and employment to the detriment of long-term educational concerns (Henry et al. 2001, 10). Finally, in 2002, education became a separate Directorate, possibly a sign of the central importance given to education in an emerging knowledge economy and knowledge society.

The Educational Directorate comprises two core programs, the Education Policy Committee (which replaced the Education Committee on 1 January 2007) and the Centre for Educational Research and Innovation. These are governed by intergovernmental bodies involving all member countries and are largely supported by core funding coming from the OECD base budget (so called Part I program funding) (Papadopoulos 1994, 15). Some of their activities are partly or fully funded under Part II program funding, however, which is targeted to specific activities and where the contributions are coming directly from countries and/or institutions. In addition to the two core programs, there are presently three more specialized programs: Institutional Management in Higher Education (IMHE), which has institution-based membership; the Programme on Educational Building (PEB), with more limited country membership; and the highly visible and influential Programme for International Student Assessment (PISA).

Work on educational matters follows the standard OECD model, with committees and working groups forging national and international networks. Plenary bodies set the general lines of work and review the results, usually on the basis of the conclusions of specially convened intergovernmental conferences of senior officials, occasionally with the participation of ministers (Papadopoulos 1994, 13). The more detailed implementation of the programs is done within more specialized meetings of country representatives and experts. The Educational Directorate's influence on national education policies does not emanate from budgetary power or the ability to issue sanctions. Paradoxically, lack of legislative power may have allowed the organization to develop into a semi-autonomous educational think tank (Istance 1996). Papadopoulos (1994, 13) notes that the OECD's catalytic role starts with the identification of key emerging policy issues facing individual countries: "These are issues which are somewhat ahead of actual country developments and thinking, but not so far ahead as to appear unrealistic or irrelevant." Drawing on international experts, the OECD Secretariat develops a position paper addressing how and why the challenges have arisen, their implications, and the need for further studies within the OECD. This form of policy research uniquely combines the collective policy experience of member countries with insights from academic research. A semi-autonomous think tank capable of sophisticated long-term planning is also partly an inter-national civil service and a shared state apparatus (Dostal 2004). This combination of characteristics has positioned the OECD to gain hegemony over the educational agenda.

The OECD and Control of the Educational Agenda

The OECD's long-term ability to control educational discourse and influence national policy agendas rests on two pillars: bureau-shaping strategies focusing on hegemony over knowledge management (Dunleavy 1991) and an extensive interface between national bureaucracies and their counterparts at the OECD (Dostal 2004; Henry et al. 2001; Rinne et al. 2004; Vickers 1994). The elaborate and ongoing interactions between national civil servants and their counterparts at the OECD provide the former with a rich milieu for policy learning (Dostal 2004). So, for example, Lampinen (2000) suggests that the strong influence over Finnish education policies derives from the attendance of Finnish civil servants and decision makers at various OECD educational meetings.

Compared with other supranational organizations, particularly the United Nations Educational, Scientific, and Cultural Organization (UNESCO), the OECD's capacity to authoritatively provide expert comparative knowledge has afforded the organization a discursive advantage. In the field of education, the OECD provides a supranational information management system that is made up of three main components: (1) synthesized formulations of central policy issues, (2) policy examinations of individual countries or groups of countries (so-called country reviews), and (3) yearly publication of statistics and indicators (Papadopoulos 1994; Rinne et al. 2004). Country reviews traditionally focused on an individual country and looked broadly at its educational policies. However, the OECD has increasingly also engaged in thematic reviews, where a specific form of education or issue, such as school to work or adult learning, is studied across countries.

Country reviews are undertaken at the request of national ministries, which identify high-priority policy fields and issues to which the review will give particular attention. The emphasis is negotiated within the Secretariat, and examiners are chosen for their expertise (research, practice, and/or policy) in the emphasized areas (Papadopoulos 1994). No other international organization has developed the practice of peer review to the same extent as the OECD in its country reviews (Pagani 2002a). Although focusing on specific fields and issues, reviews also assess the general functioning of a country's education and training system. While this may result in uneven coverage of particular issues, all central areas are at least partially addressed. National authorities prepare a report that is made available to a group of experts appointed by the OECD. The experts prepare a final report, the so-called Country Notes, which assesses accomplishments and shortcomings and makes recommendations (Papadopoulos 1994). The report is presented at a "confrontation-meeting" where senior national policy makers, often including the minister, representatives from the OECD, and the examining committee, review the findings. The review is published in the OECD's series *Reviews of National Policies for Education*. Since the early 1990s, the OECD monitors whether or not its recommendations have been implemented. It also began launching "thematic reviews" that focus on particular issues and/or sectors of education, such as higher education or adult learning (Henry et al. 2001). This has enabled the organization to sharpen its analysis of major policy issues and engage in "evidence-based" recommendations of appropriate policy options.

Educational reviews differ from economic policy reviews in that there is a more limited role for the Secretariat and greater responsibility for the independent experts (Papadopoulos 1994, 26). This may help explain why leading international scholars, such as A.H. Halsey, Mauritz Kogan, Martin Trow, Torsten Husen, and Martin Carnoy, have been so willing to repeatedly participate as experts and act as "rapporteurs" and chief authors of the Country Notes. The fact that one of the leading sociologists of education, A.H. Halsey, with a lifelong concern with equality of opportunity, took part in country reviews during three decades, the last in 1990 (Smith and Smith 2006), assured that equity issues continued to be a central issue in the Country Notes. However, final reports from thematic reviews are prepared by the Secretariat, which allows it to adapt the message to the organizational discourse (Dostal 2004, 445).

The emergence of the OECD's statistics and indicators program has, over the last decade, become central to the organization's hegemonic influence over the educational agenda and the national policy discourse (Henry et al. 2001). It forms the basis for much educational benchmarking, and it has become particularly important as governments embraced the principles of evidence-based educational policy making (Schuller 2005). The OECD started a project assembling and analyzing education "inputs and outcomes" only reluctantly, and after heavy pressure from the United States (Henry et al. 2001; Papadopoulos 1994). The US proposal was met with deep suspicion from the staff of CERI, who found the whole idea unprofessional (Heyneman 1993, 375). There was keen support for the project from several other member states, however, which were responding to political pressure from the accountability movement.

The history of the indicator project shows how OECD member countries, out of national political interest, can influence the OECD agenda. The American insistence that the OECD get involved with indicators originated in a report from the US 1983 National Commission on Excellence in Education. In order to assess the US position in the international market, it expressed the need for international comparisons of both students' learning achievement and efficiency of education systems (Cusso and D'Amico 2005, 206). Despite an apprehensive start, the OECD indicators project may, as Walberg and Zhang (1998) suggest, have become the most ambitious international education research project ever undertaken. From an agenda-setting perspective, the OECD, through its indicator program, displaced UNESCO as the key agency for educational statistics. In response to growing demand for benchmarking of students' learning achievements in different countries, the OECD launched the Programme for International Student Assessment (PISA). This replaced the International Association of Education Achievement (IEA) as the principal agency in assessing student learning achievements. PISA has become an important vehicle for the OECD to extend its influence into non-member countries also. The 2006 PISA involves fifty-one countries, of which twenty-four are not OECD members. The statistical production provides the OECD with the necessary instrument for developing a more normative analysis of education policy and strengthens its vision of the socioeconomic role of education (Cusso and D'Amico 2005). The indicators are a key element in the organization's effort to tie educational outcomes more closely to economic outcomes. Building on experience from the indicators program and PISA, there is presently a joint effort by DELSA and the Educational Directorate to launch a new indicators activity, the Programme for the International Assessment of Adult Competencies (PIAAC). Its purpose is to provide the statistical and analytical basis needed to address policy issues such as the types of skills most needed, the extent to which there are mismatches between available skills and economic and social requirements, and the mechanisms through which skills are acquired and lost. "Among other issues, PIAAC will enable countries to assess: how their education and training systems perform in the production of key competencies; the effects this has on their labour markets, social development and long-term macro-economic performance; and which policies and institutional settings are associated with success in bringing about efficient school-to-work transitions, enhancing the labour market situation of adults at-risk of socio-economic distress, and enabling learning throughout the life-cycle" (COM/DELSA/ EDUC 2005, 6).

PIACC may enable the OECD to seamlessly extend its overriding economic discourse into education and, at the national level, strengthen the ties between labour and education ministries.

The OECD's knowledge management system plays various roles in national educational policy making. Individual countries pay close attention to the OECD's yearly publications on educational statistics, *Education at a Glance*. For example, in relation to the 1996 publication, the Canadian Council of Ministers of Education stated (CMEC 1996): "'[the] OECD's work complements our efforts in Canada to develop indicators that will inform policy decisions,' said Mr. John Carlyle, Deputy Minister of Education in Manitoba and co-chair of the Canadian Education Statistics Council (CESC), a joint initiative of the Council of Ministers of Education, Canada, and Statistics Canada. The 43 indicators included in the report provide a rich, comparable, and up-to-date array of information."

Pagani (2002a) notes that when the press picks up on a story, it increases the pressure to act. In Germany, the low achievement of German pupils on the PISA tests resulted in an outcry in the national press and the creation of a parliamentary commission on educational achievement (Schmidt 2004).

Vickers (1994) suggests that in Australian policy making, the information provided by the OECD has had two key functions. Sometimes it has offered the government new ways of conceptualizing a problem, the so-called enlightenment function; in other cases, it has been used to legitimate an already chosen policy direction. The OECD's 1985 country review of Australian youth policy is an example of the former "in that it introduced a new way of understanding the youth unemployment problem; one which contrasted sharply with the interpretations that hitherto had dominated local discussion" (Vickers 1994, 9). The alternative legitimation function is illustrated by how then minister of education Dawkins used information from the OECD to push through a fundamental reconstruction of the Australian higher education system. Even though the OECD never directly made specific recommendations concerning the Australian higher education system, the minister used OECD rhetoric when linking national wealth and human resources to argue that the only way to secure the living standards of Australians was by reforming higher education and making it more responsive to the economy.

An analysis of Finnish responses to country reviews reveals a similar pattern (Rinne et al. 2004). In the 1982 country review, the OECD, in line with its thinking on recurrent education, recommended a closer integration between general education and the first stage of tertiary-level vocational education. It held that Finland should consider creating a vocational university system. The Finnish authorities initially dismissed both ideas, but a decade later, the government engaged in extensive reforms in accordance with the recommendations. The OECD report can be seen as having had an enlightenment function. At other times, such as the 1995 review of higher education in Finland, solutions to the Country Notes analysis had already been identified in the government's own background report. Here the OECD recommendations had the function of legitimating an already chosen policy direction. The latter is also visible in the 1989 review of education in Sweden, where the OECD argued for a further decentralization of responsibilities for adult education, as well as for the creation of regional centres rather than giving increased support to existing providers. The suggestions corresponded to the dominant thinking within the OECD but were contrary to the tradition within Swedish adult education. The recommendations provided support for the Swedish government's general decentralization agenda, however, and reforms of Swedish adult education were closely aligned with the recommendations the OECD had provided a decade earlier.

Given provincial jurisdiction in Canada, there has been little interest in asking for country reviews of its educational system. The only one, in 1976, included strong criticism of Canadian education, particularly the federal/provincial relationship in education, and the government did little to circulate the findings. However, Canada has frequently responded positively to the OECD's request to participate in thematic educational reviews that focus on the relationship between education and the economy. Recently, Canada participated in the Thematic Review of Adult Learning. Again, the OECD examiners critically raised the issue of the federal/provincial relationship in the area of education and training. They elaborated on how the lack of a forum for a national dialogue hampered the Canadian skills strategy (OECD 2002h, 44). When the Canadian Council of Learning (CCL) was established by the federal government in 2004, the minister stated that the CCL was being created in response to the OECD's criticism of the lack of a national structure for addressing lifelong learning.

During the last decade, there has been strong criticism of the OECD's agenda for education because it is seen to foster an educational discourse fuelled by a neoliberal ideology, with a sole focus of serving the market's need for human capital (Henry et al. 2001; Olssen and Peters 2005; Rinne et al. 2004; Rubenson 2006a). In this respect, the OECD merely reflects the fact that neoliberalism has come to comprise the raison d'être of politics in most OECD member countries, particularly in the Anglo-Saxon nations. "It has narrowed the discourse of political, economic, and social debate, transforming what it means to be liberal, social democratic, or even progressive conservative by asserting itself against social entitlements, rights, and citizenship" (Clement and Vosko 2003, viii). The central presuppositions include the self-interested individual, free market economics, and a commitment to laissez-faire (Olssen and Peters 2005, 314). The impact of the dominant political economy on the OECD's educational agenda will be explored through a comparison of the dominant discourse during two distinct political economic eras at the OECD. To understand the political economic impact on educational policies, one has to pay close attention to how the developments in the economics discipline have profoundly influenced the OECD's educational agenda.

Political Economy, Economics of Education, and the OECD's Educational Agenda

Economic Growth and Investment in Education during the Keynesian Era

Work on education and economic growth began with a focus on scientific and technical personnel in the mid-1950s. *Forecasting Manpower: Needs for the Age of Science* (OECD 1960) maintained that more refined comparative statistics were a prerequisite for an effective examination of educational policies affecting the supply of scientists and engineers (Papadopoulos 1994, 26).

The new OECD data revealed for the first time the full extent of the educational gap between North America and Europe. Until then, Europe had been primarily preoccupied with the technological gap it had vis-à-vis the Soviet Union and how to bridge it. The OECD data helped point to another challenge for Europe – how to catch up with North America in the new competitive economic environment created by the liberalization of trade. This "became part of the hidden, and at times, explicit agenda of the education and science policies of the more advanced among the European OECD countries, which was not without its influence on the relevant OECD programmes themselves" (Papadopoulos 1994, 28).

Educational staff at the OECD were quick to note the new opportunities that the economic growth objective provided: "The rapid shift in programme priorities toward the economics of education ... was in fact an inspired intentional move designed to secure a lasting place for education within the new Organization" (Papadopoulos 1994, 37). This quote exemplifies how educationists at the OECD from the very beginning have actively legitimated an organizational role for education by invoking economic issues as well as economic theory.

What took place indicates how the OECD responds to external conditions and the process by which it gains control over the agenda. In 1959, the Secretariat assembled a small working group of economic experts that, on the basis of the best possible academic knowledge of the time, helped prepare a brief entitled *Prospects of Long Term Economic Growth*. Then a small study group was given the task of clarifying the theoretical and practical issues surrounding economic development and education. Referring to the task force report, the Secretariat presented a strong argument that was acceptable to economists as well as educationists and that could be sold to finance policy makers. The outcome was a high-profile OECD conference on economic growth and investment in education in Washington, DC, in the fall of 1961.

The OECD study group, which included some of the leading economists on both sides of the Atlantic, played a major role in the development of a new field in the economics of education that contributed to the human investment revolution in economic thought (Sobel 1982). The enthusiastic recognition of human capital theory came about because it provided a framework for incorporating the economics of education, the economics of discrimination, and the economics of poverty into an applied branch of microeconomics termed "the economics of human resources" (Sobel 1982, 56). The concept also provided an umbrella for the conservative elements, interested primarily in growth, and the reformists, who saw in educational expansion the possibility of equalization of opportunity, income, and, ultimately, power. Human capital theory could explain economic development as well as inequality in earnings (Schultz 1961, 2). Schultz contended that the best way of achieving even greater future income equality was by increasing the availability of free or low-tuition education.

The OECD quickly became the prophet of this doctrine and produced a series of policy reports (OECD 1961a, 1964, 1965a, 1965b, 1966b) that inspired many countries to develop strategies to expand education in the name of economic prosperity. In Canada, the Economic Council of Canada, under the chairmanship of J. Deutsch, repeatedly linked education and national economic growth. Increased investment in human resources to improve knowledge and skills was proclaimed as the most important ingredient for attaining the goal of faster and better sustained productivity and growth. The Ontario Minister of Education, W.G. Davies, maintained in a 1966 speech that the human capital approach was one of the major factors that influenced the organization of the province's community college system: "Dr Deutsch ... placed most of the problems facing the developing economy of this province and this country at the doorsteps of education. I said this imposed quite a large load on education and that we would do our best to respond ... there is a very direct relationship between what we are attempting to do within the field of education and the economy, and just as importantly, the social development of this province and of course this nation" (Davis 1978, 162).

Similarly, official documents arguing for and resulting in an expansion of secondary and post-secondary education in Sweden make extensive reference to OECD documents on educational investment (SOU 1965, 1966).

Today's educationalists are concerned that economics has come to colonize the educational agenda. This was all but absent at the beginning of the human capital era, however. Few perceived any conflicts between economic efficiency and social and economic equality. The narrow manpower issues of the early 1950s had given way to a focus on the right of all individuals to have access to education. This brought into focus the broader role of education in a democratic society (Papadopoulos 1994). Issues around educational opportunity, social and economic inequalities, and untapped ability had come to the foreground, and, under the leadership of the OECD, leading sociologists and educationalists were brought together to study barriers to educational equality. Just before the Washington conference on investment and education, the OECD organized a meeting on ability and educational opportunity (OECD 1961b). A.H. Halsey, who acted as rapporteur, noted: "The new alliance between education and economics holds out the promise of a richer life for millions who would otherwise exist far below their potential human stature. The challenge to governments and their economic and educational advisers to pursue this promise is a noble one" (OECD 1961b, 45).

Developments within the economics of education had provided a space for sociologists and educationalists to explore how reforms of the educational system could combat the effects of social class and other inequalities on educational opportunities. The economic theories did not, as is the case today, raise the "relevance" criterion, but focused on how a larger proportion of the population could get access to a more extensive education, more or less of what already existed for the fortunate sections of the population.

Initially, economic growth data appeared to confirm the human capital thesis and justify the rapid expansion of the educational system (Papadopoulos 1994, 65). By the late 1960s, however, the labour market faced increasing difficulty in absorbing graduates, economists started to talk about an oversupply, and, despite vastly increased public spending on education, not much had been achieved in the struggle against economic, social, and, more specifically, educational inequalities (Husen 1979; Karabel and Halsey 1977). Consequently, interest in the economics of education and human capital faded quickly, and interest in education as a broader policy tool began to take a backseat (Rinne et al. 2004). When the human capital argument returned, it was to be in a new guise.

The 1970s and 1980s saw slow economic growth, rising public deficits, heightened inflation, and increasing unemployment. In this context, the OECD again turned its attention to education as the generator of economic growth. This was now an era of global capitalism, characterized by increased economic competition and rapid advances in information technology. A neoliberal framework had replaced the Keynesian creed. As early as the mid-1970s, the OECD had become an advocate of supply-side labour market reforms (Dostal 2004, 447).

DELSA's preoccupation with welfare and labour market reforms, set within the neoliberal paradigm, profoundly affected education at the OECD. In 1982, CERI's mandate was changed in order to more strongly "emphasize a specific OECD approach to educational problems in relating them to the economic and social objectives of Member countries" (Henry et al. 2001, 64). The intention was to more closely link educational activities to other work within the OECD. The 1984 Ministerial meeting called for a re-examination of the role of education, with a focus on how it could better respond to future economic requirements (Papadopoulos 1994, 174). This led CERI to embark on an extensive program of comparative analytical studies at the enterprise level to explore training and skills implications of new technology and work organization (see CERI 1989). The centre of the discussion had shifted from a preoccupation with the educational system to a focus on the world of work. This change followed the shift that had occurred in the economics of education.

Instead of addressing economy-wide growth patterns, as had been the case in the 1960s, second-generation human capital was grounded in a microeconomic outlook focused on the individual firm. Economists argued that technological change functions as a mediating factor promoting demand for education. Education in turn promotes technological change and ultimately results in productivity gains (Welch 1970; Bartel and Lichtenberg 1987). Thus, *education must be viewed not only as an investment but also as a factor of production*. For Welch, the incentive for acquiring a college education was based on considerations of changing technology, *and if technology becomes stagnant, this incentive is reduced and may disappear* (Welch 1970, 41). His and others' work (Bartel and Lichtenberg 1987; Wozniak 1984) highlighted the role of education in developing workers' innovative capacity and adaptability to new technology. In response to the new economic and political context, and strongly influenced by recent developments in economic theory, the OECD's 1989 highly influential report *Education and the Economy in a Changing Society* noted that national differences in economic performance could be attributed to educational effectiveness and a country's learning capabilities (1989b). The report pointed out that "'education' is becoming less clearly distinct from that which is 'the economy'" (OECD 1989a, 19), and that,

"'Education and the Economy' has become a catch-phrase for a vague but urgent dissatisfaction with the status quo" (OECD 1989b, 17).

The new political economic imperative ruptured the broad consensus about educational policy that had characterized the 1960s and 1970s. Within the new economic imperative, the relationship between education and the economy, particularly work, became the key issue, and a major battleground emerged between competing ideologies and interests. The OECD no longer called for a general expansion of public education but wanted drastic reforms to the very nature of public education. Concerns for equality of opportunity were replaced by calls for flexibility and responsiveness to labour market needs (OECD 1989b). Education was no longer promoted as a common good but as an instrument in global competition (Marginson 1997). The stress shifted to the role of education in developing individuals' capacity for continuous learning, creativity, and self-reliance, thereby promoting their quality and flexibility in the labour market.

The OECD's long-term interest in educational equality did not vanish under the new economic/political paradigm, but the focus gradually shifted so that it was more exclusively on human resources with regard to employment and employability (Henry et al. 2001, 68). The conceptualization of equity has moved from supporting a liberal or social democratic position to a market liberal understanding of equity.

The new OECD rhetoric on education and the economy is strongly reflected in Canadian policy documents from the mid-1990s, which express a strong need to establish closer ties with the labour market and speak *of adapting education to the real requirements of the labour market, of making it more relevant, and of easing the transition into the workplace* (Gouvernement du Québec 1996, 54). It was this sentiment that had also governed the drastic university reforms in Australia and Finland. Increased private sector involvement in educational matters was promoted by the OECD to foster educational sector responsiveness to the demands of the economy. The Canadian Jobs Strategy (CJS) launched in 1985, and its 1989 replacement, the Labour Force Development Strategy (LFDS), were Canadian attempts to achieve market sensitivity and private sector involvement. In the United Kingdom, the government introduced new qualification and skills programs under the auspices of local skills councils (Taylor 2006).

In the K-12 system, the new policy perspective raised complex questions about how to make the curricula more relevant while simultaneously reducing school failure. While recognizing that initial education is ultimately about the promotion of individual growth, the OECD notes *the need for more adequate introduction to jobs, careers, and the world of work in schools and familiarization with and command of information technologies* (OECD 1989b, 30). To achieve this, the OECD recommends the development of active exchange between schools and local enterprises and employers. Improved school-to-work transition is also seen as a way to combat high youth unemployment rates. Establishment of content-and-performance standards was promoted as another strategy to combat school failure (OECD 1995b).

The second generation of human capital theory shifted the focus to the quality and nature of initial education but also expanded the understanding of education; *education is not simply synonymous with schooling* (OECD 1989b, 38). Responding to the concern for a rapid and continuous transformation of working life, adult education and training became closely tied to the second generation of human capital (OECD 1989b). A third major change from the first to the second generation of human capital thinking in education was the direct inclusion of welfare-to-work considerations. Adult education and training was seen as part of an active labour market policy aimed at shifting unemployed people off welfare and into the labour market. The OECD approach was formed around its understanding of the changing structure of the labour market as outlined in the Jobs Study report (OECD 1994a, 1996e). In accordance with a neoliberal agenda, the OECD recommended what has come to be labelled a low-skills approach to the knowledge economy (Brown et al. 2001). This strategy assumes a bifurcated labour market and argues for job creation in the private sector in two streams – skilled, high-wage jobs and low-wage jobs. The latter would provide employment for the large group of low-skilled unemployed workers (Cruikshank 2002). Similarly, there would be two streams of training, one for high-skill jobs and another for the low-skill sector. The latter would focus on getting the clients job-ready and would promote short welfare-to-work programs.

Comparisons of the 1961 and 1989 OECD reports on education and the economy, and the analytical work that informed them, reveal the decisive impact of the dominant political economy and economics of education theory on the OECD's educational agenda. For the OECD to successfully launch a policy agenda, however, it is not enough for the Secretariat to align itself with the dominant political economy. The idea also has to speak to a current problem in ways that make sense to the system. This dilemma will be illustrated by the case of two generations of lifelong learning at the OECD.

Two Generations of Lifelong Learning

Generation 1: Recurrent Education
The first generation of lifelong learning originated in the unprecedented enrollment expansion in secondary and higher education across the industrialized world. The problem of oversupply of graduates forced the OECD to examine the relationship between education and economic development and to note the inability of the system of educational planning to link manpower forecasts and the output of educational graduates. The OECD,

and particularly CERI, developed the concept of recurrent education, which became central to OECD educational activities during much of the 1970s. "It represents the nearest OECD ever came to advocating an explicit strategy of its own for the long term development of educational systems in advanced industrial societies" (Papadopoulos 1994, 112).

The idea of recurrent education grew out of a Swedish Parliamentary Commission on Higher Education (U68 1969a, 1969b) and was launched internationally in 1969 at the Versailles Conference of the European Ministers of Education by Swedish Minister of Education Olof Palme. This is another example (see the US and the indicators program above) of a member country trying to transplant its national policy into a supranational discourse using the OECD platform.

The fundamental principle, as outlined by the OECD, is that "recurrent education is a comprehensive educational strategy for all post-compulsory or post-basic education, the essential characteristic of which is the distribution of education over the total life-span of the individual in a recurring way, i.e., in alternation with other activities, principally with work, but also with leisure and retirement" (CERI 1973, 16).

In 1975, the OECD endorsed recurrent education as a strategy for the long-term planning of educational provision. In the general rhetoric on recurrent education, proponents claimed that it would yield economic gains, benefit the labour market, lead to increased equality, and stimulate the students' search for knowledge. Behind the "poetry," however, there were pragmatic issues related to the educational crisis that largely shaped the philosophy. Thus, recurrent education was promoted as a response to the question of how to fit together student profiles, the competencies of the labour force, and the needs of the labour market (Lindensjö 1981). This would be achieved partly by spreading the long period of education in youth over the individual's whole life cycle, but the total period would not necessarily have to be longer than in the traditional system.

These bold ideas were never implemented or even given serious consideration in national or further international policy debates, and interest in developing the educational system in accordance with the principle quickly disappeared. Recurrent education, as presented by CERI, was not well anchored in the broader OECD policy agenda and had no political or economic appeal to policy makers. Nor was it supported by educationalists or industrialists. In short, in the case of recurrent education, the OECD's agenda-setting effort lacked the support of the required national "policy window"; further, it was not well anchored in the overall program of the OECD.

Generation 2: Lifelong Learning

The 1989 OECD report *Education and the Economy in a Changing Society* quickly became a bible for ministers of education and also for their colleagues holding labour portfolios. It is difficult to find any policy document from this era where educational policy is not discussed in the context of the challenges and threats of global competition and new technologies. In the OECD's search for an overarching strategy to address the new challenges, the principle of recurrent education made its comeback, now labelled as lifelong learning. The OECD's new position on lifelong learning was presented in the report *Lifelong Learning for All* (OECD 1996d), prepared for the 1996 Council of Ministers meeting. Reflecting the closer ties between the economy and education at the OECD as well as in member countries, the 1996 Ministerial declaration on lifelong learning was a joint communiqué with the OECD ministers of labour.

The OECD did not attempt to revive the concept of recurrent education but instead promoted the more encompassing but less specific idea of lifelong learning. By 1996, the OECD had embraced the notion that learning is not necessarily intentional and structured, and can take place in formal or informal institutional settings (Tuijnman and Broström 2002, 102). Informed by the new microeconomic perspective on human capital, the OECD's central interest in out-of-school learning focused on the workplace. Radical ideas, such as restructuring of university education or deferring of entrance to post-school education so as to accommodate demanding periods of work experience, had given way to an emphasis on self-directed learning, the need for schools to foster the ability and readiness to learn, and the idea that learning takes place throughout one's whole life. With human resources at the forefront of the OECD's renewed interest in lifelong learning, it is unsurprising that adult learning finally became a major issue within the OECD.

The concept of lifelong learning, as promoted by the OECD, is well suited to a neoliberal agenda. The heightened emphasis on the individual's responsibility for learning is embedded in a changing understanding and articulation of the very concept of lifelong learning. It signals a move away from education to a focus on learning (Griffin 1999): "The emphasis on 'learning' rather than 'education' is highly significant because it reduces the traditional preoccupation with structures and institutions and instead focuses on the individual ... the realisation of lifelong learning depends to a large degree on the capacity and motivation of individuals to take care of their own learning" (Tuijnman and Broström 2002, 103).

Persons must make adequate provisions for the creation and preservation of their own human capital (Marginson 1997). The Third Way, while advocating an understanding of the good society that promotes a balance between state, market, and civil society, reflects the hegemonic influence of neoliberal thinking also found in left-leaning governments (Ryner 2002).

The success of the OECD's second generation concept of lifelong learning is easily understood. First, it is fully linked to the dominant political and economic agendas both within the OECD and in member countries. Second, the concept, as presented by the OECD, had its strongest support in the business community. In fact, the European Round Table of Industrialists had promoted it since 1984. In its approach to lifelong learning, the OECD has achieved a total symbiosis between learning and production, and education is finally fully integrated into the main OECD agenda.

In understanding the hegemonic position that the OECD has achieved in lifelong learning, one has to appreciate that the organization's position on lifelong learning has rivals. From the early 1970s, UNESCO promoted a very different understanding of the concept stemming from concerns with the processes of modernization and the democratic processes in society (Faure 1972). Its concept was situated within a humanistic tradition arguing that lifelong education would promote a better society and quality of life and enable people to adapt to and control change. The concept was one of personal development; the catchwords were that people were "making themselves" rather than "being made." Individuals were expected to work towards achieving the central goals of democracy and humanism, and the total development of self, through self-evaluation, self-awareness, and self-directed learning. In the competition over the agenda between the two supranational organizations, UNESCO has lost out (Rubenson 2006b). The UNESCO discourse on lifelong learning has been totally replaced by the OECD's second generation thinking, and today's national policy debates are almost exclusively driven by the OECD paradigm of lifelong learning with the EU as its prophet (European Commission 2000).

Concluding Remarks

This chapter has focused on how the OECD, through its power of discursive closure (Dostal 2004, 445), has acquired the capacity to set agendas for education that become taken for granted as a "rule of ideas." Its success in having its discourse on education and the economy become commonsense thinking is reflected in Tony Blair's words that "education is the best economic policy we have" (Martin 2003, 567). This hegemony is a result of the specific structure of the OECD policy networks, which can be likened to the veins of the body, and the organization's international knowledge management capacity, which constitutes the blood flowing through what Dostal (2004) has labelled as a shared state apparatus.

The expansion of the indicators program and the thematic reviews appear to be of growing importance among the OECD's members as the knowledge management instruments available to manufacture a consensus on its discourse. They are also fundamental in the organization's efforts to more strongly integrate education into the core of labour market and economic agendas. Education at the OECD provides an interesting case in understanding the OECD's role in transnational governance and how its knowledge-managing capacity gave it discursive control. First, education policy traditionally is very closely related to national culture and the nation state. Second, the OECD Convention does not include any direct reference to education as a concern for the organization. Third, there is fundamental tension between the economic world view that informs work at the OECD and education as a public good embedded in the humanistic tradition. Thus, when trying to assess whether or not the OECD's educational agenda is moving to embrace an "inclusive" form of liberalism, it must be noted that the educational establishment has always been suspicious of Friedmanesque neoliberalism. This is also true of those from the broader field of education, including economics of education, working within the Secretariat. Therefore, even after the organization embraced the neoliberal world view, issues around inclusiveness, equity, and opportunity structures remained on the agenda but were mainly addressed in a narrower scope and related to employability and/or labour market structures. This would suggest that education may have shifted from a liberal/social democratic value system to a form of inclusive liberalism (see the introductory chapter to this volume) by the middle of the 1980s. This may also explain why there does not seem to be any obvious political economic movement over the last five years in the Education Directorate.

The special narrowness in approaching equity within education may be understood as inclusive liberalism in the sense that it does invoke a form of inclusiveness, but it also has strong neoliberal features. This can be exemplified with reference to the conclusion from the OECD's review of adult learning policies and practices in seventeen countries that provides an in-depth analysis of factors found to contribute to increased participation. The adult learning thematic review was designed to contribute towards making lifelong learning a reality for all and to increase employability among the low-skilled (OECD 2005g). The purpose was to better understand factors affecting adults' access to and participation in education and training, and to enhance policies and approaches to increase incentives for adults to undertake learning. The purpose of the project clearly had an inclusiveness agenda constructed around employability of low-skilled adults. The final report prepared by OECD staff from DELSA and the Education Directorate highlights several crucial conditions for increasing participation in adult education among low-skilled adults. An overall conclusion is that governments can play a useful role by: (1) creating the structural preconditions for raising the benefits of adult learning; (2) promoting well-designed co-financing arrangements; (3) improving delivery and quality control; and (4) ensuring policy coordination and coherence. These recommendations may at first sound Keynesian. The OECD finds, however, that because of inconclusive evidence about the overall quantitative impact of market failures, adult learning policy ought to focus primarily on schemes with large leverage potential. The OECD therefore concludes (OECD 2005g, 11): "Regulatory and institutional arrangements that are conducive to enhancing investments by firms and individuals, while limiting public financing, are key within this type of strategy." This message is textbook neoliberalism and shows that not only is the perspective on inclusiveness set within a narrower parameter, employability, but that the policy agenda is constructed within a neoliberal framework. This is particularly remarkable as, despite the claim of evidence-based policy making, I find the OECD's conclusion to be diametrically opposed to the policy lesson that can be drawn from the available statistics on participation in adult learning that have been collected as part of the OECD's indicators program on adult literacy (see OECD 2000d, 2005g, 2005h). The available data reveal that the high participation and, compared with other countries, low inequalities in the Nordic countries can be directly linked to a state that sets a very demanding equity standard and has developed an institutional framework to support this ambition (Rubenson 2006a).

The example of the Thematic Review of Adult Learning suggests how the introduction of thematic reviews has equipped the OECD with a particularly effective instrument through which to present a policy agenda that is allegedly evidence-based but where the evidence is viewed through the dominant ideological glasses. In this case, they have a neoliberal tint.

14
Babies and Bosses: Gendering the OECD's Social Policy Discourse
Rianne Mahon

This chapter focuses on the Babies and Bosses thematic study, a "meditative activity" reflecting on how to promote the reconciliation of work and family life as part of the OECD's broader active social policy agenda. The reconciliation agenda was designed, in part, in response to a development in a growing number of member states – the shift from the male breadwinner to the adult earner family – that has given rise to a set of new social needs (care for very young children and the frail elderly) previously met by caregiver-housewives. At the same time, reconciliation policies are understood to contribute to the solution of other problems, such as child poverty, demographic change, and the need to modernize social security systems.

There are, however, different ways of reconciling work and family life. What sort of perspective does the OECD – or, more specifically, the Social Policy Division of the Directorate for Employment, Labour and Social Affairs (DELSA)[1] – offer? As Chapter 12 argues, in the social policy field, the OECD is no longer singing exclusively from the neoliberal hymn book. This shift is certainly reflected in the analytical grid used in the *Babies and Bosses* series, which takes an "inclusive liberal" approach. While the latter shares key features with neoliberalism, the OECD's reconciliation agenda also addresses lacunae in the neoliberal model. The "gendering" in the title of this chapter is also intended to capture the dimension of policy learning on the part of the DELSA staff. While the *Babies and Bosses* series started with measures to reconcile the paid and unpaid work of women, by the end it had begun to embrace elements of a more egalitarian model, in which men and women share care work within the family. While the gendering began when the team was carrying out its research on Japan, it was its exposure to Swedish debates that led the research team to the notion of equal sharing of domestic care work. While holding fast to its inclusive liberal principles, it did draw the lesson that effective reconciliation requires measures aimed at changing men's roles as well as women's.

The OECD's "Inclusive Liberalism" Turn

What kind of organizational discourse framed the Babies and Bosses thematic study? In the broadest terms, the frame stems from the OECD's mandate, which, as Chapter 2 suggests, centres on the definition of "standards of appropriate behaviour for states that seek to identify themselves as modern, liberal, market-friendly, and efficient." Yet these standards have undergone some important modifications. O'Connor and colleagues (1999, 43-65) have identified three variants of liberalism – classic, new or social liberalism, and neoliberalism. To these can be added a fourth – inclusive liberalism. All variants of liberalism share an emphasis on the individual and, as C.B. Macpherson (1977) so cogently argued, all retain a profound allegiance to a capitalist market economy. In this context, while social policies may mitigate the adverse effects of capitalist development, they need to be consistent with the operation of market incentives or, for those seen as legitimately outside the market, must operate within clear boundaries. Nor should social policies go so far as to challenge capitalist social relations: equality of opportunity, perhaps, but not equality of condition. These common features should not, however, be allowed to obscure significant differences among the varieties of liberalism.

The Keynesian ideas that formed the core of the OECD's original discourse drew in a particular way on the vein of social liberalism opened by nineteenth-century thinkers like John Stuart Mill. In contrast to classical liberalism, Keynesian liberalism saw a positive social policy role for the state, sustaining full employment across the business cycle by protecting (male breadwinner) workers against income risks such as unemployment, ill health, and old age. By the 1960s, this had come to include active labour market policy – measures strongly advocated by the OECD – as a means of improving the inflation/unemployment trade-off. Since the late 1970s, however, Keynesian liberalism has been challenged by the spread of neoliberalism.

Neoliberalism shares with classical liberalism a celebration of market individualism and minimal government. Privatization, contracting out, and public/private partnerships are all part of the neoliberal toolkit. The OECD was an early convert to the neoliberal supply-side paradigm. This became evident in its social policy stance in the 1980s (Deacon et al. 1997). Throughout the 1980s, the OECD helped to spread the neoliberal view of social policy as an obstacle to growth. This persisted in the 1990s in the reviews prepared by the Economic Department (Armingeon and Beyeler 2004).

While the Jobs Strategy, discussed elsewhere in this volume, continued on a neoliberal course, towards the end of the 1990s, DELSA began to admit a positive role for the "right sort" of social policies, beginning with *A New Orientation for Social Policy* (OECD 1994c), elaborated in *A Caring World* (OECD 1999a), and further developed in *Extending Opportunity: How Active Social*

Policy Can Benefit Us All. In making this shift, DELSA was by no means alone. Craig and Porter (2004) have drawn attention to important themes – "opportunity" and "empowerment" or the activation of capacities and the legitimation of social investments designed to promote them – that began to appear in the 1990s in the social policies of a number of OECD countries and in the discourses of international organizations, including the OECD's DELSA. They have labelled this emergent social policy discourse "inclusive liberalism." Although Craig and Porter ultimately see inclusive liberalism as but another version of neoliberalism, there is a good case for seeing it as a distinct form of liberalism.

To be sure, neoliberalism and inclusive liberalism have some important elements in common, but they draw on different elements of the liberal tradition. Just as neoliberalism would apply elements of classic liberalism to a twenty-first century context, inclusive liberalism draws on social liberalism, albeit in a different way from its Keynesian predecessor. For inclusive liberals, the task is not to roll back the welfare state but rather to redesign it, replacing the consumption-oriented policies of the Keynesian era with measures that support the development and use of human and social capital. Here it finds its inspiration in an earlier social liberalism, which "included the positive freedoms of *opportunity and personal development*" (O'Connor et al. 1999, 50, emphasis added). Accordingly, inclusive liberalism stresses individual capacity for development and accepts a role for the state in creating conditions for all to develop their capabilities, while emphasizing individual responsibility to take advantage of these opportunities. These themes have informed the OECD's social policy agenda, at least since 1998.

The call for redesign, not dismantling, the welfare state was clear in the new social policy agenda announced in the final communiqué to the 1998 meeting of social and health ministers: "A truly 'caring world' is one in which social and health policies adapt and respond sensitively to the *opportunities* and needs of individuals and their families, while remaining sustainable, and *empower them to develop their full potential* and *to contribute fully to society*" (OECD 1999a, 144, emphasis added). These themes also appear in the next official iteration, *Extending Opportunities,* which called for active social policies because "this shift away from the reactive, compensatory approach of the past gives greater emphasis to *investing in people so as to maximise their potential to become self sufficient, autonomous members of society*" (OECD 2005e, 6, emphasis added). In the final communiqué of the 2005 meeting, OECD social policy ministers similarly underlined that "social policies must be proactive, stressing *investment in people's capabilities and the realisation of their potential,* not merely insuring against misfortune" (OECD 2005i, emphasis added).

Both neoliberalism and inclusive liberalism stress the centrality of employment, while rejecting Keynesian demand-side measures. Rather, emphasis is on the supply side, by removing barriers to work, especially work disincentives that arise from tax/benefit systems. For inclusive liberals, however, such reforms need to be accompanied by training and other forms of assistance, including support services, designed to develop individual capacities. Thus, for instance, *Extending Opportunities* would remove barriers to employment through "welfare to work" (workfare) and "welfare in work," which means the redesign of tax and benefit systems to make work pay. In addition, measures are needed to ensure adequate wages, while "the reassessment of the OECD Jobs Strategy should identify policies which will help end labour market exclusion." And "if government provides the resources to overcome barriers, then individuals have a responsibility to take advantage of this opportunity" (OECD 2005e).

Both neoliberalism and inclusive liberalism advocate the "flexibilization" of labour markets and accept that this means greater inequality (at least in the here and now). In this respect, they differ from that version of social liberalism that would tackle the source of growing income inequality at its root.[2] Inclusive liberals do, however, aim for equality over the life cycle. In fact, there is a clear generational dimension to DELSA's active social policy agenda, which would shift social expenditure from the current focus on the elderly to investments in children, youth, and prime-age adults. Adjustments to pensions and related policies, in turn, are seen as helping to make room for investments in early childhood development to give children the best possible start, a theme that appears in both the 1998 and the 2005 final communiqués.

Of particular importance is the gender dimension to social policy redesign, one that has become increasingly visible in the OECD's agenda. The OECD/DELSA has embraced the adult worker family. Lone parents, now employable, should be included in workfare programs. DELSA recognizes that this also entails public support for child care as part of a broader package of employment supports. As the 1998 final communiqué noted, "family friendly policies, including improved access to affordable and quality childcare, access to parental leave, greater flexibility in work arrangements and training opportunities can provide the key to better employment opportunities for families with young children, especially lone parents" (1999a, 145). Yet lone parents are not the only focus of inclusive liberalism's social investment in the family.

Support for the adult worker family norm is considered especially important for a number of reasons. The adult earner family makes it possible to redesign "overly generous" social insurance programs originally built to sustain the male breadwinner in his role: pensions and unemployment insurance schemes can be fully individualized. More broadly, women's withdrawal from the labour market is now seen as a waste of human capital, no longer affordable in light of population aging. At the same time, women's labour force participation cannot be allowed to come at the expense of fertility rates. For DELSA, then, the state has an important role to play in the "reconciliation of work and family life."

The embrace of the adult earner family need not lead to greater gender equality, however. In general, while inclusive liberals see a positive role for the state to play in helping the adult worker family reconcile work and family life, the measures envisaged usually focus on making it possible for women to combine workforce participation with unpaid care work in the home, without changing men's roles. As we shall see, in the first three volumes of *Babies and Bosses*, the DELSA team noted but did not challenge the inequitable division of care labour between men and women. By the time the fourth volume was released, however, the team had come around to the view that shared parental leave offered the best possibility for maintaining women's human capital and labour force attachment while giving children "the best possible start." This was reflected in the documents prepared for the 2005 meetings, which clearly suggested that fathers increase their share of parental leave (OECD 2005a, 5). It was reiterated, albeit in a more muted fashion, in the final ministerial communiqué. In the next section, we shall argue that this shift reflected lesson drawing on the part of the team, especially as it was exposed to Swedish debates.

Developing the Reconciliation Agenda: Babies and Bosses

Policy documents like *A Caring World* can be important in shaping a directorate's organizational discourse as well as in setting a new agenda for member states, especially when sanctioned by ministerial meetings. On their own, however, they are insufficient, because the OECD lacks the capacity to issue directives. Thus, the production and dissemination of the results of research on what the member states are actually doing constitutes a critical part of the OECD's toolkit. Prior to the launch of the Babies and Bosses study, DELSA had commissioned little research on the reconciliation of work and family responsibilities. Reporting through the Working Party on Social Policy of the Employment, Labour and Social Affairs Committee, *Babies and Bosses* marked DELSA's first major information-gathering exercise in this area.[3]

Babies and Bosses combine elements of "meditation" (exploring a new area) and "inquisition" (Jacobsson 2006), with the emphasis on the former. The four volumes examine reconciliation policies and practices in thirteen member country case studies. Five of the countries would be considered "liberal" (Australia, Canada, Ireland, New Zealand, and the United Kingdom); three Nordic social democracies (Denmark, Finland, and Sweden); and Austria the clearest example of a continental corporatist regime. The Netherlands and perhaps Switzerland also share certain core features with this model (Esping-Andersen 1999). Portugal has many of the core traits of the Southern

European variant (Ferrera 1998), while Japan is considered a hybrid (Esping-Andersen 1997).

The research design suggests that this was not intended to foster "fast policy transfer," where agreed-upon indicators could be used to draw up league tables, comparing the "laggards" with those coming closest to "best practice." The team, headed by Willem Adema,[4] felt that reconciliation was a relatively new and complex policy field. As adequate indicators had yet to be identified, it would be inappropriate to attempt a quantitative comparison of all member countries. Instead, it developed sets of limited – three- or four-country – comparisons, which allowed for a greater attentiveness to country-specific concerns and institutional patterns. In turn, this appears to have allowed for some "policy learning."

Nevertheless, the analytical grid employed clearly reflected DELSA's inclusive liberal turn. In line with the new social policy agenda, *Babies and Bosses* clearly presented women's increased labour market participation as a solution to a range of common problems – poverty, low fertility/aging, and, more broadly, the modernization of social policy. It recognized that adoption of policies to reconcile work and family life involves the "potential escalation of public intervention," but accepted that "this may not be a bad thing" (OECD 2002e, 22), especially if "properly" done.

One key message was that member states should eliminate incentives for mothers to stay at home. In some countries, the solution was seen to involve the elimination of spousal allowances from government and/or employer social insurance schemes, while other countries were encouraged to move from family to individual taxation. Of particular concern was the exemption of lone parents from the obligation to seek work. Such "barriers to employment" should be eliminated.

In line with the activation emphasis, *Babies and Bosses* is in favour of public support for non-parental child care arrangements, especially for children under three. *Babies* recognized that, on their own, markets may not be capable of delivering the number of spaces needed at a price parents can afford. There is thus a role for government to compensate for market failure. For the authors of *Babies*, however, public sector monopolies are to be avoided – even though *Babies'* authors recognize that wage rates and employment conditions in the Nordic system tend to be better than in the countries relying on private sector provision (OECD 2002e, 2005i). Private provision is to be preferred, as it "is geared towards serving customer demand ... and may also be conducive to innovative practices" (OECD 2002e, 88). In addition, *Babies* showed a preference for family child care for under-threes to reduce costs and "improve choice."

Consistent with the frame, demand-side subsidies are also to be preferred to investment in the supply side, in part for reasons of equity: from DELSA's perspective, in the context of scarcity, supply-side subsidies only benefit those who are able to get a place and do nothing for parents who cannot find one. If governments subsidize parents, then the latter presumably can find some form of care, especially if the government helps to improve the flow of information. The main reason, however, has to do with efficiency: demand-side subsidies put pressure on providers to keep costs low and to meet parental demands for such things as more flexible opening hours. *Babies and Bosses* did recommend that public subsidies be used only for purchase of quality child care. Its view of quality assurance, however, reflects a New Public Management perspective, where child care providers are seen as a group pursuing its own self-interest at the expense of children and parents unless checked by market-like mechanisms.

Babies and Bosses was keen to promote family-friendly policies in the workplace. Its advice in this regard reflects the preference for labour market flexibilization common to neoliberalism and inclusive liberalism. At the same time, and more in line with the softer view articulated in the revised Jobs Strategy, it admits that states also have to get involved to promote other objectives, including gender equity. Thus, *Babies 4* noted that the growth of temporary work in Finland and Sweden, which contributed to the fall in fertility rates, was blamed on the "stringent employment protection" measures still in force in those countries. Here Finland and Sweden are compared unfavourably with Canada and the United Kingdom. Yet temporary work in Sweden (14.6 percent) is just a bit higher than it is in Canada (12.5 percent), according to the OECD's own figures (OECD 2005f, 64).

Babies was quite critical of Japan for the highly gendered split between regular and irregular employees. Instead of recommending the abolition of "insider" privileges typical of neoliberalism, however, it enjoined the Japanese government to "enforce more actively gender equity and equal pay for equal work legislation" (OECD 2003h, 13), reflecting inclusive liberalism's preference for "flexicurity." *Babies 4* also recognized the positive role that collective bargaining can play in systems where collective agreements cover a large part of the labour market. Where unions are weaker, however, governments are enjoined to offer "tailored" family-friendly advice to individual firms, especially small and medium enterprises (OECD 2005f, 29).

Babies and Bosses is also favourably disposed to the expansion of part-time work as a cheaper solution to the care of very young children. At the same time, it clearly began to recognize that part-time work contributes to the channelling of women into low-paid, non-standard jobs. Thus, the first volume noted that "many households in Australia and the Netherlands distribute paid work along the 'one and a half' earner model in terms of hours of paid employment, while in terms of contribution to household income a 'one and one quarter' model appears a better description" (OECD 2002e, 28). The second volume recognized that "not all part time work is equal, and its value as a reconciliation solution depends in part on it not becoming a trap for those (mainly women) workers in low-paid, dead-end jobs" (OECD 2003h, 19).

The *Babies and Bosses* volumes clearly recognized that it is women whose lives are being changed in this new "family-friendly" world, not men. In fact, men's patterns have not changed in most of the countries examined. The first volume noted that "men do not appear to have changed their behaviour markedly ... Indeed, male behaviour remains largely traditional in all three countries:[5] take up rates of parental leave among men are low, and although the gender gap in unpaid housework is smaller in Denmark than in the other two countries, caring remains primarily a female activity" (OECD 2002e, 14). The point is reiterated in *Babies 4*, which noted that "in all four countries, women spend more time providing care for children than men; they overwhelmingly take more parental leave than men, and they are most likely to reduce working hours after childbirth" (2005f, 29).

When the first volume was produced, the authors saw little possibility of changing men's behaviour. Thus the vision of shared care through the reduction in working time for *both* parents, which has been on the agenda in the Netherlands, "is likely to remain illusory for the near future, as it would require a fundamental change in male labour market behaviour, evidence for which is lacking" (OECD 2002e, 15). The second volume noted that "everywhere, take-up of existing family-friendly measures is predominantly a female affair, as illustrated by the proportion of eligible fathers taking up parental leave ... traditional gender notions appear difficult to change" (2003h, 21). The Japanese government is, however, lauded for having set targets (10 percent leave taken by men), as this may help change societal attitudes. That understanding is reiterated in the third volume, but the change became more even more pronounced in the fourth volume.

This "gendering" was clear from changes in the table of contents. Whereas the first two volumes organized the key chapter that summarized the main findings (Chapter 1) around more technical aspects concerning reconciliation, the third and fourth volumes concluded with sections that focused on "promoting gender equity." Whereas the chapter on labour markets in the first volume spoke of "labour market outcomes" in general terms, in the second it highlighted the experience of "mothers in employment," reflecting the learning provoked by the Japanese experience. A similar section in the third volume was preceded by a section on "gender differences in employment outcomes" and followed (3.4) by one on gender earnings differentials. The fourth volume also included a section on gender differences in pay.

An important output of the Babies and Bosses project was the identification of indicators and the construction of an online database on family outcomes and policies, which will permit comparison of the performance of all member countries. The indicators include gender pay gaps for full- and part-time workers, temporary employment and sectoral/occupational concentration by gender, time used for work, care and daily household chores, and take-up of parental leave benefits by mothers and fathers.[6] Such data can prove useful for those advocating gender equality even if, for the most part, *Babies and Bosses'* recommendations do little to tackle the root causes, especially the growth of non-standard employment and, with it, deepening inequality in the labour market.

The main exception was its position on parental leave. This gendering really began with the second volume,[7] and the lesson was reinforced by the (temporary) addition of feminist scholar Janet Gornick to the Babies and Bosses team in 2003. Well known for her quantitatively based comparative analyses of policies pertaining to the reconciliation of work and care, Gornick was hired to help the team develop a set of indicators. During the five months spent there, she engaged in frequent discussions of gender equity issues with the other members of the team.[8] She participated, moreover, in the Portuguese country visit, where gender equity was also being avidly discussed (OECD 2004g, 17).[9] The combination of Gornick's arguments and exposure to the Portuguese debates may have prodded Babies and Bosses to adopt a more proactive stance towards fathers' sharing of the unpaid care work. The report noted that "in itself, the Portuguese policy stance may not change workplace culture overnight, but, without this policy signal to fathers, changes towards more gender equitable workplaces will be even more difficult to accomplish" (OECD 2004g, 26). It took the Swedish experience, however, to drive the point home.

Learning from Sweden?

Clearly the Babies and Bosses team's engagement with the Swedish experience reinforced and deepened the lessons it had begun to learn. Like the earlier (Gornick) example, however, it also testifies to the importance of the dialogue – between researchers at the OECD and in member states, as well as between OECD staff and key national civil servants – that the OECD governance system facilitates. Not surprisingly given the nature of the exercise, there was also the potential for learning (or for lesson reinforcement) on Sweden's part. In fact, what motivated the key Swedish official to advocate Sweden's participation in the Babies and Bosses exercise was the hope of using international comparisons to facilitate policy learning, and thus facilitate another round of incremental reforms designed to deepen the Swedish model. As we shall see, however, the willing pupils proved to be the DELSA team itself, while the Swedish government buried its "inconvenient" advice because the OECD supported what many in the Swedish gender equity policy community wanted to hear, but not the government of the day.

Although the fourth volume had yet to be published at the time of the 2005 meeting of ministers of social affairs, Sweden, and the Nordic model more generally, had already been singled out as an example of best practice, albeit with the caveat that it was likely to prove too expensive for most member countries. Thus, in Sweden "a combination of flexible use of paid parental leave, affordable high quality childcare, extensive out of school care, and entitlement to shorter hours for both parents when children are young has helped parents in squaring their work and care commitments, contributed to comparatively high fertility rates, high employment rates among mothers with children, and low child poverty, although at significant budgetary costs" (OECD 2005a, 13).

As *Babies 4* would go on to document, the Swedish model for reconciliation is embedded in a universal welfare state that provides support throughout the life course. It clearly has done better than most in terms of women's labour force participation rates (77 percent, with a small 3 percent gender employment gap); poverty rates ("particularly low" at 4 percent), fertility rates (which hold up well compared with the OECD average, despite the dip that occurred in the 1990s), and the generational profile of social expenditure (net expenditure of families at 3.5 percent of GDP). Yet while Sweden pioneered *parental* leave (1974) and its child care system has been singled out as a best practice example, it was clear that gender equality had yet to be achieved. Swedish women still take the lioness's share of parental leave, and they are the ones who reduce their hours while their children are still in preschool. Moreover, while the gender wage gap is relatively low, at least among the lower-income deciles,[10] a product of decades of "solidaristic wages bargaining,"[11] there is a marked occupational segregation by gender and, as the OECD found, a powerful "glass ceiling."

This situation was not unknown in Sweden, of course, which had seen a resurgence of feminist activism in the late 1980s and 1990s (Mahon 1996). In response, from 1994, successive social democratic[12] governments moved to incorporate feminist demands. These included equal access to positions of official power, equal pay for equal work, and measures to combat violence against women, supported by a conception of gendered relations of power that had to be changed if progress was to be made. The government's response to the feminist agenda included the adoption of a gender mainstreaming program, aimed at re-educating top civil servants as well as cabinet ministers.

One of the civil servants, who may already have been open to these ideas but who clearly learned to think in feminist terms, was Ilija Batljan. In 1996, Batljan[13] joined the Swedish Ministry of Health and Social Affairs, not long after the Social Democrats returned to office ready to establish its feminist credentials. From 2000 to 2005, Batljan held the important post of Director and Chief Analyst at the Ministry of Health and Social Affairs. Just as importantly, from our perspective, he also served as vice chair of the OECD's Employment, Labour and Social Affairs Committee from 2001 to 2004, from which position he interacted with the DELSA social policy officials on a regular basis. Batljan was thus part of the discussions that led to the launching of Babies and Bosses, and it was also he who convinced the Swedish government to participate in the review.[14] His eagerness to participate had a lot to do with the growing sense, shared by others, that new initiatives were needed to break through the barriers to gender equity.

Batljan's concern grew out of his involvement (as chair) in the working party on fertility (2000-2001). The government appointed the working party in 2000 in response to the drop in fertility that Sweden had experienced in the 1990s. The report concluded that "a well developed system of family support, aimed at combining work and family life, is a necessary but not sufficient condition" (DS 2001,13, my translation) for families to choose to have their ideal number (2) of children. Full employment and access to secure employment are also crucial, as was made clear by the experience of the 1990s – high, for Sweden, unemployment and, even when unemployment dropped, the spread of temporary work that hit hardest at women in their key childbearing years. Parents wanted to establish themselves in the labour market before starting families.

One of the report's key messages to couples choosing to have the number of children they wanted was the importance of sharing the unpaid care work in the home. As Batljan subsequently noted, "Gender equitable access to education and the labour market, when not combined with the preconditions for reconciling work and family and with gender equity in the home leads to very low fertility rate" (SOU 2005, 20, my translation).

The implication was that changes were needed *in the domestic sphere,* to achieve a genuine sharing of care work, as well as in the labour market (among other things, the restoration of full employment and the elimination of precarious work). This grew out of the report's findings that although upon entering the labour market men's and women's wages were quite similar, the gap grew as they moved into their late 20s – prime childbearing years – and continued. There was also evidence that women were being discriminated against in getting jobs, especially with smaller firms. In one study, one-third of employers admitted that they asked whether women planned to have children, while another showed that two-thirds of women and one-fifth of men had been asked whether they planned to start a family (DS 2001, 194-95). The uneven division of parental leave also feeds into the pattern of occupational segregation noted by the Babies and Bosses team. Thus, the report of the working party on fertility concluded, "Sweden does rather well in an international context with regard to gender equity but there are still gaps ... that can create barriers when women and men decide to have children. A strong indication of the limits to gender equity is the clearly negative impact that childbirth has on women's income in comparison with men who have children and with women who have not had children" (DS 2001, 272, my translation).

The Fertility Report was not alone in concluding that the division of unpaid labour within the home had to change in order for gender equity and other social goals to be achieved, and that there was a role for public policy in bringing this about. Some, like Claes Bergström, the Gender Equity Ombudsman (*JämO*) called for a complete individualization of parental leave. There was also significant support for this option among the Left party (one of the Social Democrats' coalition partners) supporters: as many as one-quarter favoured complete individualization (*Dagens Nyheter*, 25 October 2005). The Social Democratic Women's Federation (SSKF) and Social Democratic Youth (SSU), and LO (the highly influential Swedish blue-collar trade union central), favoured a version of the Icelandic solution – allocation of one-third to each parent, while leaving it to families to decide how to share the remainder. This would represent an incremental step, involving the increase of the "daddy month" from two to five months. As the data provided by the government-appointed Thorwaldsson commission showed, the original quotas had helped increase fathers' share from a very modest 10 percent in 1994, following the introduction of the first one-month quota, to nearly 19 percent in 2004 (SOU 2005, 148). The commission recommended the increase, combined with a rise in compensation rates (floor and ceiling),[15] in order to bring parents' behaviour in line with their (gender-equitable) attitudes.

On this issue, the government had the advantage that it faced a divided opposition. The Liberals were for raising the ceiling, including an equity bonus (90 percent for months equally divided), and strengthening employment protection for those on leave (*Dagens Nyheter*, 16 September 2005), and 40 percent of its supporters favoured increased quotas. The rural-based Centre party agreed to raise the ceiling and the floor, with its women's wing wanting a father bonus for months shared. In contrast, the neoliberal Conservative party favoured a reduction in total compensation levels to 76 percent and in length of leave to one year, and the addition of a child care tax cut of 3,000 Swedish crowns for the lowest-paid parent if the other parent took some of the leave. They were also calling for measures to make it easier to hire domestic help – for child care or other work. Both the Conservatives and the socially conservative Christian Democratic Party favoured the introduction of a municipal care allowance, with the right to three years' leave.[16]

The Babies and Bosses team was well aware of the Swedish debate. There were several references to the Batljan report in *Babies 4*, and the report's influence was visible in the way a new concern with conditions under which parents could choose to have their ideal number of children (the magical two) appeared in the fourth volume. The main impact, however, was to cement the lesson that the reform of parental leave represents an important means for inducing fathers to take an equitable share. Among others, the team met with representatives from JämO's office and those involved in the Thorwaldsson commission, which had yet to issue its report.[17] The team's conclusion is of interest:

> A Swedish government committee is reviewing different aspects of the parental leave system, and it could consider different options to achieve a more gender equitable use of parental leave, including, for example, granting a bonus to parents who equally share parental leave entitlement, increasing the duration of leave period that are non-transferable between parents and/or increasing information to both parents about fathers' rights to parental leave. In Sweden, as in most other countries, the policy debate about a more equitable sharing of the care burden during the early months has yet to start in earnest. (OECD 2005f, 211)

In other words, even Sweden had a way to go to establish conditions for women's full integration into the labour market – an integration that, it now understood, required changing men's participation in domestic care work. Thus, one of the team's three recommendations to the Swedish government was to find some way to reduce the gender difference in the use of parental leave, although it would have liked to have added, "and reduce the total leave to one year."[18]

Ironically, it was *Babies and Bosses'* support for measures to increase shared parental leave that led the government of the day to bury the report. *Babies 4* was released when the government of the day had decided not to accept Thorwaldsson's recommendations, in light of polls showing that 60 percent of Swedes did not want to increase quotas and as few as 30 percent of the Social Democrats' supporters were in favour of expanding them (*Dagens Nyheter*, 10 February 2005). Although the report's authors had taken care not to specify what measures should be taken, Prime Minister Persson, backed by Minister of Social Affairs Berit Andnor (Batljan's boss), did not want the report to be used by those within its own ranks – SSU and the SSKF – or among its coalition partners who were pushing for change.

Conclusion

The OECD's inclusive liberal turn – at least in the area of social policy – is clearly reflected in its reconciliation agenda, considered central to the organization's broader social policy agenda. Although this agenda shares with neoliberalism an emphasis on "employability," it recognizes a positive role for government in enabling individuals to develop their capabilities. Just as the original social liberalism included women among those to be empowered, so too does DELSA's inclusive liberalism. The gendering of the OECD's social policy agenda comes in part from the way women's labour force participation has come to be seen as critical to solving the problems of child poverty, the labour supply problems linked to fertility decline and population aging, and the need for early childhood development as the first step towards lifelong learning for the "knowledge economy." In this context, active measures to help mothers reconcile work and family life can be readily justified.

Why has DELSA broken with the neoliberalism that marked its social policy discourse in the 1980s? As Noel (2006, 320) argues, part of the explanation lies in the wider context: data showing the overall increase in income inequality during the last two decades of the twentieth century (a trend visible across the OECD too); the impact of the East Asian financial and economic crisis of July 1997; anti-globalization protests and the growth of the World Social Forum; and victories of parties of the Left in key European countries. In this sense, the turn towards inclusive liberalism on DELSA's part represents an attempt to "re-embed" the global capitalist economy in light of reactions to a decade of aggressive neoliberalism (Craig and Porter 2004).

This chapter has also argued that the Babies and Bosses thematic study began to push the organizational discourse beyond this to embrace the idea of shared care. This reflects a process of policy learning on the part of the Babies and Bosses team. Although the latter employed a consistently "inclusive liberal" analytical grid throughout the four volumes, the research process was structured in a way that allowed for learning on DELSA's part. The research design – the choice of more in-depth, small series comparisons, rather than a largely quantitative comparison of all thirty OECD member countries – reflected the relative newness of the area and the DELSA staff's recognition that suitable indicators had yet to be developed. It gave the team a chance to learn from each country's experience. It took the very marked gender inequalities in Japan to drive home the point that reconciliation too often involved changes in women's lives, to enable them to juggle paid work and domestic care, while men's lives remained the same. It was also the newness of the area for the OECD that led it to enlarge the epistemic community, drawing one of the leading feminist scholars working in this area. Her presence, in turn, prepared the team to hear the Portuguese and, more importantly, the Swedish debates on shared parental leave as essential for gender equity. Previously established connections with a key Swedish official further facilitated this process.

Through exposure to Swedish debates, the Babies and Bosses team began to confront one of the sources of gender inequality – the unequal division of care labour in the family – but what about the other, the labour market itself? To be sure, tackling the unequal division of domestic care would contribute towards diminishing gender discrimination in the labour market.

We need to ask also, however, about the labour market itself. It is not by accident that most OECD countries have seen the spread of "non-standard" jobs – temporary, part-time, self-employment – over the last decades, and with this, growing inequality of income. While *Babies and Bosses* recognizes that temporary jobs and some forms of part-time work contribute to gender (and, we would add, class) inequality, the solutions it envisions are limited. Governments can offer "encouragement, promote the virtues of family-friendly policies, or otherwise try ... to raise awareness of the issue" (OECD 2003h, 21). They can also provide consultants who can help firms make their workplaces family-friendly.

More broadly, DELSA advocates "flexible" labour markets, albeit the "flexicurity" version. This leaves intact a deeply inegalitarian post-industrial employment structure. In addition, like the rest of the OECD, DELSA strongly supports the current liberalization of flows of goods and capital without questioning the neoliberal terms on which this is based. Under these conditions, however, employers are driven to boost competitiveness by all means available, and, not surprisingly, this results in limited interest on their part in the general adoption of equality-promoting family-friendly policies. To be sure, some employers may be prepared to develop family-friendly packages, possibly including personal services such as housecleaning as well as child care and flex-time, for female employees possessing substantial "human capital." This does little, however, for the majority of women – and men – left to fend for themselves in "liberalized" labour markets.

Notes

1 Established in 1974 as the Directorate for Education, Employment, Labour and Social Affairs (DEELSA), it became DELSA when Education formed its own directorate. For simplicity's sake, I refer to it simply as DELSA.

2 For an alternative design, see Herzenberg et al. (1998). Among international organizations, the International Labour Organization (ILO) perhaps comes closest to articulating this position.

3 The "Starting Strong" thematic study of early childhood education and care was launched in 1999 by the directorate when it was DEELSA, but this study was handled by the Education and Training Policy Division, now part of the Education Directorate.

4 Over the course of the study, the team involved a variety of researchers, but it was Adema who provided the strong element of continuity, working under the general direction of Mark Pearson, head of the Social Policy Division and co-author (with Adema) of *A Caring World*.

5 Australia, Denmark, and the Netherlands.

6 These indicators are available online: http://www.oecd.org/els/social/family.

7 I thank Adema for this point, which he made in his comments on the first draft of this chapter on 25 January 2007.

8 This was disclosed by Gornick in an e-mail interview in 2005.

9 This point was also made by Willem Adema in an interview in Paris on 15 May 2006.

10 Sweden is rightly criticized for its "glass ceiling" but the solution (quietly) suggested – greater availability of low-wage domestic service – while pushed by the bourgeois parties, goes against the grain of the Swedish model (OECD 2005c, 205).

11 For more on this, see, *inter alia*, Mahon (1987, 1996).

12 The bourgeois coalition government (1991-94) had a contradictory position but the Liberal leader, who held an important cabinet post, did manage to introduce some important initiatives, including the first "daddy month" (i.e., for fathers only) into the parental leave system.

13 A short biography of Batljan can be found at http://www.oecd.org/speaker/0,2879,en_21571361_30968861_31722056_1_1_1_1,00.html.

14 As he indicated in an interview in Nynäshamn on 4 May 2006. This was also corroborated by Barbara Martin-Korpi, the key person in charge of early childhood education and care policy in the Ministry of Education, when I interviewed her in Stockholm on 18 April 2006.

15 The generally favourable (currently 80 percent) compensation rate – at times higher for time taken by the father – was supposed to make it more feasible for higher-paid fathers to take leave without undue burden on family budgets, but the ceiling on payments, which had affected 17 percent in 1995, had been frozen such that by 2004, 40 percent of the labour force – and 50 percent of male workers – earned incomes above the ceiling (SOU 2005, 176).

16 Several bourgeois-dominated municipalities in the greater Stockholm area were in fact using the room available to them to experiment with a version of this.

17 This information is derived from an interview with Willem Adema in Paris on 16 May 2006.

18 This preference comes out strongly in the background documents to the 2005 meeting of ministers of social affairs (OECD 2005a, 5).

Conclusion

Stephen McBride and Rianne Mahon

Globalization has enhanced the importance of international organizations such as the Organisation for Economic Co-operation and Development; at the same time, the OECD has played an important part in fostering the liberalization of trade and investment flows that paved the way for economic globalization. New techniques of domestic governance have also put a premium on the kind of comparative policy performance assessment that the OECD supplies. Nonetheless, there has been surprisingly little written that documents or analyzes the OECD's role. Our object in inviting contributions to a volume on the OECD's role in global governance was to fill an important gap in the literature.

As the organization focuses on policy areas traditionally regarded as domestic but increasingly regarded as requiring international collaboration, we felt that it was important to combine the perspectives of scholars with a starting point in international political economy with those of scholars who have focused on the role of the state in the domestic sphere. We sought no uniformity of theoretical approach. This volume thus brings together neo-Gramscians, social constructivists, political economists, and public policy analysts. All, however, recognize the importance of transcending methodological nationalism if we are to understand the complex, multi-scalar dynamics of transnational governance. Moreover, all recognize the role played by knowledge or ideas as a critical instrument of soft regulation. The preceding chapters show that this approach has yielded fruitful results.

We do not try to recreate here a summary of the findings of the individual chapters. The initial request from the editors, subsequently refined by interactions among the contributors, identified a number of themes that have been collectively addressed. The identification of the types of transnational governance activities with which the organization was engaged and the role(s) it has sought to fill, either at the behest of member governments or through the exercise of its own initiative or autonomy, constituted one such theme. Moreover, as the chapters reveal, the OECD's discourse and policy advice has shifted over time and may be undergoing further evolution. Capturing some of the dimensions of change was thus a second theme explored throughout this volume. Relations between the OECD and its member states formed another obvious point of inquiry. We were interested in both how much autonomy this international organization enjoys from its members and to what extent, and in what ways, it is able to obtain compliance with its various recommendations and decisions.

Although the OECD is composed of states, we also wanted to examine its relations with organizations of civil society and with other international organizations and non-member states. Labour and business representation had long been a feature of its internal structure, and there were signs that, in the aftermath of the failed Multilateral Agreement on Investment, the OECD was devising a new strategy of consultations with representative civil society organizations – past and present OECD activity in this area seemed a promising avenue to explore. Finally, the extent to which the OECD faces new challenges in the era of globalization merited attention.

The chapters show that the OECD is at the centre of a complex web of influences and meetings that involve knowledge production, broadly conceived. Knowledge here covers a wide range of meanings and includes basic data collection, problem definition and conceptualization, and comparative policy analysis, leading to detailed recommendations and ideological rationalizations for the measures that states should, in the OECD's view, be taking. To the extent that it is able to present its work in a neutral, technical guise, it tends to be more effective, appealing to other international organizations, national governments, and other political forces. Yet the OECD's role in knowledge production is political as well as technical. Summarizing this insight, Porter and Webb refer to the "incremental reinforcement of particular practices through the OECD's ability to confer authority on them by portraying those practices as unproblematic, apolitical, and relatively routine ways of doing things that are known to be best due to the appearance of consensus that the OECD creates."

The OECD occupies a position in the system of multi-level governance that has modified nation-state predominance even in policy areas that are clearly domestic. Thus national decision makers must take into account commitments made under global economic agreements, such as the World Trade Organization agreements, and regional ones, such as the European Union and North American Free Trade Agreement. Membership in the OECD also involves commitments to certain norms and practices, though enforcement is left more to peer pressure than in some of the other agreements. OECD membership also involves national decision makers (not just or even principally politicians but also public servants, extending some way down the bureaucratic hierarchy) in relatively intense and constant interaction, discussions, reports, assessments, and evaluations of the policy practices of their own and other governments. The networks that evolve include other international organizations, appointed experts, and representatives of civil society organizations. Knowledge production and dissemination are central to their activities. In these fora, participants undoubtedly learn, and borrow some policy ideas directly, from their counterparts. In addition, the OECD, considered as an organization, is in the business of drawing lessons, generalizing them, and packaging them for presentation to member states. Depending on the subject matter, the OECD's policy recommendations might include a diversity of models or approaches that work or might tend towards a one-size-fits-all universal model. The data the OECD assembles, moreover, are critical to its surveillance function.

In analyzing the OECD's role, a number of contributors found useful the distinction drawn by Bengt Jacobsson (2006) between "regulatory," "mediative," and "inquisitorial" activities. For the most part, the OECD lacks enforcement capacity and must rely on various forms of moral suasion to achieve its ends, though some of its decisions are considered binding on its members and, perhaps equally important, are conditions that prospective new members must meet in order to join the club. Thus Wolfe concludes Chapter 1 by positing that the OECD's most effective role is not one of rule making but rather one of "influencing policy by identifying norms and principles for negotiations that take place in the many other international organizations that use its ideas." Such influence reflects the broad principles of liberalization, open markets, and trade that constitute a bedrock of what the OECD is about. This means that activities described as "mediative" and "inquisitorial" are central tools for the OECD in its production and dissemination of knowledge.

The OECD has undergone expansion in the global era and the addition of more members is expected. In addition, it works closely with non-member states and proffers advice and recommendations. The gradual incorporation of other states, especially important developing states or those that are in transition to becoming liberal-democratic capitalist polities, offers the prospect of extending the OECD's influence beyond the rich, northern bloc of countries that have traditionally constituted its core membership. As the global economy becomes increasingly integrated, such a strategy may be viewed as essential to ensuring the organization's continued relevance. At the same time, one of the issues faced by the OECD as it seeks to expand its membership beyond its traditional base as a "rich countries' club" is whether its consensus-building techniques can serve as effectively with a larger and more diverse membership base. If they manage to do so, then the OECD will attain a more global reach. If not, then much of the effectiveness of the OECD would be at risk. Moreover, even if the strategy is generally successful, it may be at the cost of losing a venue where the richest and most economically advanced countries can map out their own positions before these are pursued in broader multilateral arenas.

Collectively, our chapters trace the OECD's application of meditative and inquisitorial techniques to a wide variety of policy areas. In the process, the dynamic relationship between the OECD and member governments is delineated. One aspect of that relationship, which is touched on in several chapters, is the role of the United States within the OECD. The OECD's predecessor was founded at the instigation of the US, and the Americans remain well represented within the organization at both staff and political levels. The US also exerts indirect influence because of the hegemony of the largely American-centred economics discipline. Nevertheless, the OECD is based in Europe, and among its European members are found a broader range of ideas than the neoliberal model that the US has done so much to spread. There is some evidence that the issue of US influence may overlap with that of differences between the economic and social policy portfolios of the OECD, with the neoliberal American model having made a stronger impact on the former and being less apparent in the latter.

More specifically, as we flagged in the introduction, in this volume are different readings of the OECD's current ideological stance. Historically, it is clear that for the early part of its existence the OECD reflected the broadly Keynesian principles of the postwar consensus. In the late 1970s, it made a transition to the new hegemonic ideas of neoliberalism. How dominant are neoliberal doctrines within the organization today? Contributors vary in their assessments. Those focusing on economic policy in general, economic development issues, and labour market policy are more likely to detect undiluted neoliberalism than those focusing on social policy, health, public sector management, and new areas such as cities. The latter tended to find new ideological currents of "inclusive" or "innovative" liberalism. The most obvious exception to this rule of thumb is education, which may be explained by the intrusion of economic logic into the education file. Traditionally understood, education is akin to social policy. Nevertheless, in the context of neoliberal economics, education, reconfigured as human capital development, becomes a key tool of economic competitiveness and is analyzed by the OECD in those terms (Chapter 13).

The contestation within the OECD is interesting in that it indicates an active process of creating hegemonic ideas that has links to the documented intra-organizational differences within the OECD (between its Economics Department and the Directorate for Employment, Labour and Social Affairs [DELSA], for example). This is not solely a closed "in-house" process. The Secretariat's interaction with member states, which often hold conflicting views, outside experts, and civil society organizations also contributes to the development of these ideas.

A review of the individual findings and insights led to a compilation of general findings. Given the early stage of research on the OECD's role in transnational governance, the general findings of this volume may be treated as hypotheses to be explored in future research as much as firm conclusions. These are:

- The closer an issue area is to the OECD's central economic mandate, the more likely OECD discourse and recommendations are to reflect the dominant ideological paradigm, which, for the moment, remains neoliberalism.
- Conversely, the further an issue is from the organization's central economic mandate, the more likely OECD discourse and recommendations are to reflect other varieties of liberalism.
- The apparent exception of education may be explained by its reconceptualization by the OECD as a vital economic function.
- The OECD is able to reach far into domestic policy areas precisely because its edicts and recommendations are non-binding on member states. It relies instead on instruments of soft regulation – the production and dissemination of knowledge, the publication of comparative data, and peer review.
- The actual impact of OECD policy advice appears to be most extensive in member states that were already aligned with the basic direction of OECD advice and less extensive in member states operating within a different ideological and institutional framework. This suggests path-dependency of national models that limits OECD influence on those member countries that conform least to the dominant paradigm. Thus, the liberal welfare states (in terms of Esping-Andersen's 1990 original typology) proved most compliant with the OECD's turn, after 1975, to a neoliberal paradigm, and the social democratic and continental conservative models, while influenced by it, proved less compliant. Nevertheless, even when countries continue to deviate from OECD-defined best practice, the organization may have played a role in providing new definitions of problems to be tackled.
- The broadening of the OECD's membership raises the possibility of either extending the OECD's core values (sometimes described as liberal democracy plus liberalized markets) or undermining the ability of the exclusive OECD club to develop consensus solutions based on similarity of economic development levels and shared values.
- Recognition of national variation and context, and rejection of a single universal model by OECD agencies, is more apparent in some areas than in others. Remoteness from the core economic mandate of the OECD appears to be the most important factor that allows for recognition of diversity of policy approaches.

- Internal tensions and contestation are features of the OECD. Among other things, these features raise the possibility of a further paradigm shift in the organization, from neoliberalism to some other form of liberalism. If this occurs, it is unlikely to be the result of internal processes alone.

In illuminating the OECD's influential role in global governance, the chapters in this volume help us understand the role of knowledge and knowledge construction in both its technical and political/ideological dimensions. Collectively, the contributors have advanced our understanding of an organization that has been subject to too little analysis. While it is true that much remains to be done before the role of this complex international organization can be fully integrated into accounts of global and transnational governance, it is also true that there is no longer any excuse for leaving it out of the picture, as has been done so often in the past.

Abbreviations

ALRC	Australian Law Reform Commission
ANPED	Northern Alliance for Sustainability
APEC	Asia-Pacific Economic Cooperation
BIAC	Business and Industry Advisory Committee
BIT	bilateral investment treaty
CCL	Canadian Council of Learning
CERI	Centre for Educational Research and Innovation
CESC	Canadian Education Statistics Council
CF&P	Center for Freedom and Prosperity
CIEC	Conference on International Economic Cooperation
CIME	Committee on International Investment and Multinational Enterprises
CJS	Canadian Jobs Strategy
CMEC	Canadian Council of Ministers of Education
CSE	consumer subsidy equivalents
DAC	Development Assistance Committee
DELSA	Directorate for Employment, Labour and Social Affairs
DØR	Det Økonomiske Råds
DSM	dispute settlement mechanism
EC	European Community
ECSS	Executive Committee in Special Session
EDRC	Economic and Development Review Committee
EEB	European Environmental Bureau
EEC	European Economic Community
EPC	Economic Policy Committee
EPOC	Environmental Policy Committee
EU	European Union
FDI	foreign direct investment
FIRA	Foreign Investment Review Agency
FSA	Financial Services Agreement

GAB	General Arrangements to Borrow
GATT	General Agreement on Tariffs and Trade
GOV	Directorate on Governance and Territorial Development
GST	Goods and Services Tax
HIPC II	Enhanced Heavily Indebted Poor Countries
HRSDC	Human Resources and Social Development Canada
HTC	Harmful Tax Competition
ICGN	International Corporate Governance Network
IDT	international development target
IEA	International Energy Agency
IFI	international financial institution
IGO	intergovernmental organization
ILO	International Labour Organization
IMF	International Monetary Fund
IMHE	Institutional Management in Higher Education
INGO	international non-governmental organization
IOPS	International Organization of Pension Supervisors
IPE	international political economy
ISSA	International Social Security Association
LEED	Local Economic and Employment Development
LFDS	Labour Force Development Strategy
MAD	Mutual Acceptance of Data
MAI	Multilateral Agreement on Investment
MDG	Millennium Development Goal
MDRI	Multilateral Debt Relief Initiative
MEI	multilateral economic institution
MFN	Most Favoured Nation
MNC	multinational corporation
NAIRU	non-accelerating inflationary rate of unemployment
NATO	North Atlantic Treaty Organization
NCP	national contact point
NGO	non-governmental organization
NIE	new institutional economics
NIEO	New International Economic Order
NPM	New Public Management
ODA	Official Development Assistance
OECD	Organisation for Economic Co-operation and Development
OEEC	Organisation for European Economic Co-operation
PEB	Programme on Educational Building
PHI	private health insurance
PIAAC	Programme for the International Assessment of Adult Competencies
PISA	Programme for International Student Assessment

PRS	Poverty Reduction Strategy
PSE	producer subsidy equivalents
PUMA	Public Management Committee
RTA	regional trade agreement
SAPs	structural adjustment policies
TDPC	Territorial Development Policy Committee
TSA	transnational structure of authority
TUAC	Trade Union Advisory Committee
UNCTAD	United Nations Conference on Trade and Development
UNDP	United Nations Development Programme
UNESCO	United Nations Educational, Scientific, and Cultural Organization
WHO	World Health Organization
WP 3	Working party on Policies for the Promotion of Better Payments Equilibrium
WTO	World Trade Organization
WWF	World Wide Fund for Nature

References

Abrahamsen, Rita. 2004. The power of partnerships in global governance. *Third World Quarterly* 25 (8): 1453-67.

Adamson, W.L. 1980. *Hegemony and revolution: A study of Antonio Gramsci's political and cultural theory.* Berkeley: University of California Press.

Adema, Willem. 2001. Net social expenditure. Labour Market and Social Policy Occasional Paper No. 52. Paris: OECD.

–. 2006. Social assistance, policy development and the provision of a decent level of income. OECD Employment and Migration Working Papers, No. 39. Paris: OECD.

Agell, Jonas. 1999. On the benefits from rigid labor markets: Norms, market failures and social insurance. *Economic Journal* 109 (453): 143-64.

Alderson, Arthur S. 2004. Explaining the upswing in direct investment: A test of mainstream and heterodox theories of globalization. *Social Forces* 83 (1): 81-122.

ALRC (Australian Law Reform Commission). 2004a. Genes and ingenuity: Gene patenting and human health. Report No. 99. Sydney: Government of Australia.

–. 2004b. Gene patenting and human health. Discussion Paper 68. Sydney: Government of Australia.

Amin, Ash, Angus Cameron, and Ray Hudson. 2002. *Placing the social economy.* London: Routledge.

Andersen, Jørgen Goul. 2002. Work and citizenship: Unemployment and unemployment policies in Denmark, 1980-2000. In *Changing labour markets, welfare policies and citizenship,* ed. Jørgen Goul Andersen and Per H. Jensen, 59-84. Bristol, UK: Policy Press.

Anderson, K. 2001 The politics of retrenchment in a social democratic welfare state: Reform of Swedish pensions and unemployment insurance. *Comparative Political Studies* 34 (9): 1063-91.

Anheier, Helmut, et al. 2001. Concepts of global civil society. In *Global civil society 2001,* ed. Helmut Anheier, 3-22. Oxford: Oxford University Press.

Anker, Richard, et al. 2003. Measuring decent work with statistical indicators. *International Labour Review* 142 (2): 144-77.

Armijo, Leslie Elliott. 2001. The political geography of world financial reform: Who wants what and why? *Global Governance* 7 (4): 379-96.

Armingeon, Klaus. 2004. The OECD and national welfare state development. In *The OECD and European welfare states,* ed. Klaus Armingeon and Michelle Beyeler, 226-42. Cheltenham: Edward Elgar.

Armingeon, Klaus, and Michelle Beyeler, eds. 2004. *The OECD and the European welfare states.* Cheltenham: Edward Elgar.

Aubrey, Henry G. 1967. *Atlantic economic cooperation: The case of the OECD.* New York: Praeger for the Council on Foreign Relations.

Aucoin, Peter. 1995. *The new public management: Canada in comparative perspective.* Montreal: Institute for Research on Public Policy.

Auer, Peter. 2004. Institutions and policies for labour market success in four small European countries. In *Challenging the market: The struggle to regulate work and income*, ed. Jim Stanford and Leah F. Vosko, 75-94. Montreal and Kingston: McGill-Queen's University Press.

Baker, Dean, Andrew Glyn, David Howell, and John Schmitt. 2004. Unemployment and labour market institutions: The failure of the empirical case for deregulation. Working Paper No. 43. Geneva: International Labour Office.

–. 2005a. Labour market institutions and unemployment. In *Fighting unemployment: The limits of free market orthodoxy*, ed. David Howell, 72-119. Oxford: Oxford University Press.

Baker, A., D. Hudson, and R. Woodward. 2005b. Introduction: Financial globalization and multi-level governance. In *Governing financial globalization: International political economy and multi-level governance*, ed. A. Baker, D. Hudson, and R. Woodward, 3-23. London: Routledge.

Bakker, Isabella. 2003. Neo-liberal governance and the reprivatization of social reproduction: Social provisioning and shifting gender orders. In *Power, production and social reproduction*, ed. Isabella Bakker and Stephen Gill, 66-82. Toronto: Palgrave Macmillan.

Barnett, M.N., and M. Finnemore. 1999. The politics, power and pathology of international organizations. *International Organization* 53 (4): 699-732.

Bartel, A., and F. Lichtenberg. 1987. The comparative advantage of educated workers in implementing new technology. *The Review of Economics and Statistics* 69 (1): 1-11.

Barzelay, Michael. 1992. *Breaking through bureaucracy: A new vision for managing government.* Berkeley: University of California Press.

Bayne, Nicholas. 1998. International economic organizations: More policy making, less autonomy. In *Autonomous policy making by international organizations*, ed. Bob Reinalda and Bertjan Verbeek, 195-210. London: Routledge.

Beer, Andrew, Graham Haughton, and Alaric Maude. 2003. *Developing locally: An international comparison of local and regional economic development.* Bristol, UK: Polity Press.

Belot, Michèle, and Jan C. van Ours. 2004. Does the recent success of some OECD countries in lowering their unemployment rates lie in the clever design of their labor market reforms? *Oxford Economic Papers* 56 (4): 621-42.

Bendixen, Grit. 1993. Dagpenge-system for Slapt og Rundhåndet. *B.T.* (2 March), Section 1: 14.

Bennett, Colin J. 1991. What is policy convergence and what causes it? *British Journal of Political Science* 21 (2): 215-33.

Bernstein, Steven. 2001. *The compromise of liberal environmentalism.* New York: Columbia University Press.

Bevir, Mark, R.A.W. Rhodes, and Patrick Weller. 2003. Traditions of governance: Interpreting the changing role of the state. *Public Administration* 81 (1): 1-17.

BIAC. 2006a. *Annual report 2006.* Paris: BIAC.

–. 2006b. About BIAC. http://www.biac.org/aboutus.htm.

Bieler, Andreas. 2001. Questioning cognitivism and constructivism in IR theory: Reflections on the material structure of ideas. *Politics* 21 (2): 93-100.

Bieler, Andreas, and Adam D. Morton. 2004. A critical theory route to hegemony, world order, and historical change: Neo-Gramscian perspectives in international relations. *Capital and Class* 82: 85-113.

Bienefeld, Manfred. 2000. Structural adjustment: Debt collection device or development policy? *Ferdinand Braudel Center Review* 23 (4): 533-87.

Blagescu, M., and R. Lloyd. 2006. *2006 Global Accountability Report: Holding power to account.* London: One World Trust.

Blair, David J. 1993. Trade negotiations in the Organization for Economic Co-operation and Development. London: Kegan Paul International.

Blyth, Mark. 2001. The transformation of the Swedish model: Economic ideas, distributional conflict and institutional change. *World Politics* 54 (1): 1-26.

Boggs, C. 1976. *Gramsci's Marxism.* London: Pluto Press.

Bonoli, G. 2003. Social policy through labor markets understanding national differences in the provision of economic security to wage earners. *Comparative Political Studies* 36 (9): 1007-30.

Borchardt, John K. 2000. Children's parents sue hospital over genetics patent. *The Scientist* 1 (1): 20001122-2.

Boston, Jonathan, John Martin, June Pallot, and Pat Walsh. 1996. *Public management: The New Zealand model.* Auckland: Oxford University Press.

Boston, Jonathan, Paul Dalziel, and Susan St. John. 1999. *Redesigning the welfare state in New Zealand: Problems, policies, prospects.* Auckland, New Zealand: Oxford University Press.

Boyle, Nigel, and Ravi Roy. 2003. National policies and globalization: Varieties of neo-liberal youth labour market policy under Thatcher and Blair. In *Global turbulence: Social activists' and state responses to globalization,* ed. Marjorie Griffin Cohen and Stephen McBride. Aldershot, UK: Ashgate.

Bradford, Neil. 2002. Why cities matter: Policy research perspectives for Canada. CPRN Research Report F/23. Ottawa: Canadian Policy Research Networks.

–. 2007a. Placing social policy? Reflections on Canada's new deal for cities and communities. *Canadian Journal of Urban Research* 16 (2): 1-26.

–. 2007b. Whither the federal urban agenda? A new deal in transition. CPRN Research Report F/65. Ottawa: Canadian Policy Research Networks.

Brenner, Neil. 2004. *New state spaces: Urban governance and the rescaling of statehood.* New York: Oxford University Press.

Brenner, Neil, and Nik Theodore. 2002. Cities and geographies of "actually existing neo-liberalism." In *Spaces of neo-liberalism,* ed. Neil Brenner and Nik Theodore, 2-33. Oxford: Blackwell.

Brown, P., A. Green, and H. Lauder. 2001. *High skills: Globalization, competitiveness and skill formation.* Oxford: Oxford University Press.

Brusse, Wendy A. 1997. Liberalising intra-European trade. In *Explorations in OEEC history,* ed. Richard T. Griffiths. Paris: OECD.

Brunsson, Nils, and Bengt Jacobsson, ed. 2000. *A world of standards.* Oxford: Oxford University Press.

Bryan, Dick, and Michael Rafferty. 2000. Globalization as discipline: The case of Australia and international finance. In *Globalization and its discontents,* ed. Stephen McBride and John Wiseman. London: Macmillan.

Busch, Per-Olof. 2006. The OECD Environment Directorate. The art of persuasion and its limitations. Global Governance Working Paper No. 20. Amsterdam: Global Governance Project.

Cammack, Paul. 2004. What the World Bank means by poverty reduction, and why it matters. *New Political Economy* 9 (2): 189-211.

Camps, Miriam. 1975. "First World" relationships: The role of the OECD. Atlantic Papers 2/1975. New York: The Atlantic Institute for International Affairs and the Council on Foreign Relations.

Casey, Bernard. 2004. The OECD Jobs Strategy and the European Employment Strategy: Two views of the labour market and of the welfare state. *European Journal of Industrial Relations* 10 (3): 329-52.

Casey, Bernard, et al. 2003. Policies for an ageing society: Recent measures and areas for further reform. Economics Department Working Paper No. 369. Paris: OECD.

Caulfield, Timothy, Robert Cook-Deagan, F. Scott Kieff, and John P. Walsh. 2006. Evidence and anecdotes: An analysis of human gene patenting controversies. *Nature Biotechnology* 24 (9): 1091-94.

CBAC (Canadian Biotechnology Advisory Committee). 2006. *Human genetic materials, intellectual property and the health sector.* Ottawa: Canadian Biotechnology Advisory Committee.

Center for Freedom and Prosperity. 2004. Coalition for Tax Competition letter to Senator Judd Gregg and Representative Frank Wolf. http://www.freedomandprosperity.org/ltr/ctc-gregg-wolf/ctc-gregg-wolf.shtml.

–. 2006. Letter to the Honorable Joshua B. Bolten. http://www.freedomandprosperity.org/ltr/ctc-bolten/ctc-bolten.shtml.

CERI (Centre for Educational Research and Innovation). 1973. *Recurrent education: A strategy for lifelong learning.* Paris: OECD.

–. 1989. *The human factor in economic and technological change: Towards an enterprising culture.* Paris: OECD.

Chang Ha-Joon, ed. 2002. *The rebel within: Joseph Stiglitz and the World Bank.* London: Anthem Press.

Checkel, Jeffrey T. 1999. Social construction and integration. *Journal of European Public Policy* 6 (4): 545-60.

–. 2001. Why comply? Social learning and identity change. *International Organization* 55 (3): 553-88.

Clarke, Susan, and Gary Gaile. 1998. *The work of cities.* Minneapolis: University of Minnesota Press.

Clement, W., and L. Vosko, ed. 2003. *Changing Canada. Political economy and transformation.* Montreal and Kingston: McGill-Queen's University Press.

CMEC (Canadian Council of Ministers of Education). 1996. OECD releases education indicators report. Press Release, 9 December 2006. http://www.cmec.ca/releases/prsrlse.htm.

Cohn, Theodore H. 2002. *Governing global trade: International institutions in conflict and convergence.* Aldershot: Ashgate.

Colombo, Francesca, and Nicole Tapay. 2004. Private health insurance in OECD countries: The benefits and costs for individuals and health systems. In OECD Health Working Papers No. 15. DELSA/ELSA/WD/HEA(2004)6. Paris: OECD.

COM/DELSA/EDUC. 2005. International assessment of adult skills: Proposed strategy. 24 October 2005. Paris: OECD.

Cornish, Llewelyn, et al. 2003. *Intellectual property rights (IPRs) and genetics: A study into the impact and management of intellectual property rights within the healthcare sector.* Cambridge: Public Health Genetics Unit.

Cox, Robert W. 1983. Gramsci, hegemony, and international relations: An essay in method. *Millennium: Journal of International Studies* 12 (2): 162-75.

–. 1986. Social forces, states and world orders: Beyond international relations theory. In *Neorealism and its critics,* ed. Robert O. Keohane, 204-54. New York: Columbia University Press.

–. 1987. *Production, power and world order: Social forces in the making of history.* New York: Columbia University Press.

–. 1992. Global perestroika. *Socialist Register* 28: 26-43.

–. 1999. Civil society at the turn of the millennium: Prospects for an alternative world order. *Review of International Studies* 25 (1): 3-28.

–. 2005. Global perestroika. In *The Global Governance Reader,* ed. Rorden Wilkinson. New York: Routledge.

Craig, David, and Doug Porter. 2004. The Third Way and the Third World: Poverty reduction and social inclusion strategies in the rise of "inclusive" liberalism. *Review of International Political Economy* 11 (2): 387-423.

–. 2006. *Development beyond neo-liberalism? Governance, poverty reduction and political economy.* London: Routledge.

Crockett, Andrew. 1989. The role of international institutions in surveillance and policy coordination. In *Macroeconomic policies in an interdependent world,* ed. Ralph C. Bryant et al., 343-65. Washington, DC: International Monetary Fund.

Cronin, Bruce. 2001. Productive and unproductive capital: A mapping of the New Zealand system of national accounts to classical economic categories, 1972-95. *Review of Political Economy* 13 (3): 309-27.

Cruikshank, J. 2002. Lifelong learning or re-retraining for life: Scapegoating the worker. Proceedings of the 21st annual conference of the Canadian Association for the Study of Adult Education, 30 May to 1 June, Toronto.

Curzon, Gerard. 1965. *Multilateral commercial diplomacy: The General Agreement on Tariffs and Trade and its impact on national commercial policies and techniques.* London: Michael Joseph.

Cusso, R., and S. D'Amico. 2005. From development comparatism to globalization comparativism: Towards more normative international education statistics. *Comparative Education* 41 (2): 199-216.

Czarniawska, Barbara, and Bernward Joerges. 1996. Travels of ideas. In *Translating organization change*, ed. Barbara Czarniawska and Guje Sevón, 13-47. Berlin and New York: Walter de Gruyter.

DAC (Development Assistance Committee). 1996. *Shaping the twenty-first century: The contribution of development co-operation.* Paris: OECD.

Danish Economic Council. 1988. *Dansk Økonomi Juni 1988.* Copenhagen: Danish Economic Council.

Davis, W.G. 1978. The community colleges. The CAATs in Ontario. In *Coming of age*, ed. R. Kidd and G. Selman. Toronto: Canadian Adult Education Association.

Deacon, Bob. 2007. *Global social policy and governance.* London: Sage.

Deacon, Bob, M. Hulse, and P. Stubbs. 1997. *Global social policy: International organizations and the future of welfare.* London: Sage.

Dean, Mitchell M. 1999. *Governmentality: Power and rule in modern society.* Thousand Oaks, CA: Sage.

Deaton, Angus (chair). 2007. An evaluation of World Bank research, 1998-2005. Washington, DC: World Bank, http://go.worldbank.org/U6VB00O7X1.

Deibert, R.J. 2000. International plug 'n play? Citizen activism, the Internet, and global public policy. *International Studies Perspectives* 1 (3): 255-71.

Demirgüç-Kunt, Asli, and Ross Levine. 2001. Financial structure and economic growth: Perspectives and lessons. In *Financial structure and economic growth*, ed. Asli Demirgüç-Kunt and Ross Levine. Cambridge, MA: MIT Press.

Department of Finance Canada. 2000. Memorandum from Deputy Minister to Minister, 4 September 2000. Obtained through Access to Information Request .A-2006-000238/i.e.

Devos, Serge. 1991. The Trade Committee of the OECD: Thirty years and a hundred meetings. Trade Committee TD(91)100. Paris: OECD.

Dharam, Ghai. 2003. Decent work: Concept and indicators. *International Labour Review* 142 (2): 113-46.

Djelic, Marie-Laure, and Kerstin Sahlin-Andersson, ed. 2006a. *Transnational governance: Institutional dynamics of regulation.* New York: Cambridge University Press.

–. 2006b. Introduction: A world of governance: The rise of transnational regulation. In *Transational governance: Institutional dynamics of regulation*, ed. Marie-Laure Djelic and Kerstin Sahlin-Andersson, 1-28. New York: Cambridge University Press.

–. 2006c. Institutional dynamics in a reordering world. In *Transnational governance: Institutional dynamics of regulation*, ed. Marie-Laure Djelic and Kerstin Sahlin-Andersson, 375-98. New York: Cambridge University Press.

Dolowitz, David P., and David Marsh. 2000. Learning from abroad: The role of policy transfer in contemporary policy-making. *Governance* 13 (5): 5-24.

Dostal, Jörg M. 2004. Campaigning on expertise: How the OECD framed EU welfare and labour market policies – and why success could trigger failure. *Journal of European Public Policy* 11 (3): 440-60.

Drake, William J., and Kalypso Nicolaidïs. 1992. Ideas, interests, and institutionalization: "Trade in services" and the Uruguay Round. *International Organization* 46 (1): 37-100.

Drechsler, Denis, and Johannes Jütting. 2005. Private health insurance for the poor in developing countries? Policy Insights No. 11. OECD Development Centre.

Driscoll, Ruth, and Allison M. Evans. 2005. Second-generation poverty reduction strategies: Opportunities and emerging issues. *Development Policy Review* 23 (1): 5-25.

DS. 2001. Barnafödandet: *Fokus – från Befolkningspolitik till ett Barnvänligt Samhälle.* Ds 2001: 57. Stockholm: Regeringskansliet.

Dunleavy, P. 1991. *Democracy, bureaucracy, and public choice.* New York: Harvester.

Economist. 2006. Flexicurity: a model that works. 7 September.

Egan, Daniel. 2001. The limits of internationalization: A neo-Gramscian analysis of the Multilateral Agreement on Investment. *Critical Sociology* 27 (3): 74-97.

Eichengreen, Barry. 1989. Hegemonic stability theories of the international monetary system. In *Can nations agree? Issues in international economic cooperation*, ed. Richard N. Cooper et al., 255-99. Washington, DC: Brookings Institution.

Esping-Andersen, Gøsta. 1990. *The three worlds of welfare capitalism.* Cambridge: Polity Press.

–. 1997. Hybrid or unique? The Japanese welfare state between Europe and America. *Journal of European Social Policy* 7 (3): 179-89.

–. 1999. *Social foundations of postindustrial economies*. New York: Oxford University Press.

European Commission. 2000. *A memorandum on lifelong learning*. Luxembourg: Office for Official Publications of the European Commission.

Evans, Mark. 2004. Policy transfer in a competition state: Britain's "New Deal." In *Policy transfer in global perspective*, ed. Mark Evans, 64-79. Aldershot: Ashgate.

Falk, Richard. 1999. *Predatory globalization: A critique*. Cambridge: Polity Press.

Farnsworth, Kevin. 2005. International class conflict and social policy. *Social Policy and Society* 4 (2): 217-26.

Faure, Edgar. 1972. *Learning to be*. Paris: UNESCO.

Ferrera, Maurizio. 1998. The four "Social Europes": Between universalism and selectivity. In *A new social contract? Charting the future of European welfare*, ed. M. Rhodes and Y. Meny. London: Macmillan.

Financial Times. 2005. NGOs voice doubts on next OECD chief. 30 November, 4.

Finnemore, Martha. 1996. Norms, culture and world politics: Insights from sociology's institutionalism. *International Organization* 50 (2): 325-47.

Fischer, Stanley. 1988. International macroeconomic policy coordination. In *International economic cooperation*, ed. Martin Feldstein, 11-43. Chicago: University of Chicago Press.

Flockhart, T. 2004. "Masters and novices": socialization and social learning through the NATO Parliamentary Assembly. *International Relations* 18 (3): 361-80.

Folketing. 1991. Folketings Forhandlinger. No. 1 1991-1992. Copenhagen: Schultz Information.

Forman, S., and D. Segaar. 2006. New coalitions for global governance: The changing dynamics of multilateralism. *Global Governance* 12 (2): 205-25.

Forrest, Anne. 2001. Connecting women with unions: What are the issues? *Relations Industrielles* 56 (4): 647-73.

Fortin, Pierre. 1996. The great Canadian slump. *Canadian Journal of Economics* 29 (4): 761-87.

–. 2001. Interest rates, unemployment and inflation: The Canadian experience in the 1990s. In *The review of economic performance and social progress*, ed. Keith Banting, Andrew Sharpe, and France St. Hillaire, 113-31. Ottawa: Centre for the Study of Living Standards.

Fratiani, Michele, and John Pattison. 1991. International institutions and the market for information. In *The political economy of international organizations: A public choice approach*, ed. Roland Vaubel and Thomas D. Willett, 100-22. Boulder, CO: Westview Press.

Financial Stability Forum. 2006. 12 key standards for sound financial systems. http://www.fsforum.org/compendium/key_standards_for_sound_financial_system.html.

Fuhrer, Helmut. 1996. A history of the Development Assistance Committee and the Development Co-operation Directorate. In *Dates, names and figures*. Paris: OECD.

Gallochat, Alain. 2004. Provisions d'ordre public et moralité etles brevets génétiques. Policy paper prepared for Health Canada.

Gensey, Guy. 2003. The liberalization of trade in financial services: Exercising domestic regulatory authority. PhD dissertation, Dalhousie University.

Gertler, Meric. 2001. Urban economy and society in Canada: Flows of people, capital and ideas. *Isuma: The Canadian Journal of Policy Research* 2:3 (Autumn): 119-30.

Giddens, Anthony. 2000. *The Third Way and its critics*. Cambridge: Polity Press.

Gill, Stephen. 1990. *American hegemony and the Trilateral Commission*. New York: Cambridge University Press.

–. 1993. Epistemology, ontology, and the Italian school. In *Gramsci, historical materialism, and international relations*, ed. Stephen Gill, 21-49. Cambridge: Cambridge University Press.

–. 2000. Grand strategy and world order: A neo-Gramscian perspective. Lecture delivered at Yale University on 20 April.

–. 2003. *Power and resistance in the new world order*. New York: Palgrave Macmillan.

Gills, Barry K., ed. 2000. *Globalization and the politics of resistance*. London: Palgrave Macmillan.

Gold, E. Richard. 2002. Gene patents and medical access. *Intellectual Property Forum* 40: 20-27.

–. 2003. From theory to practice: Health care and the patent system. Special edition of the *Health Law Journal* 21.

–. 2006. Uptake of OECD Guidelines for the Licensing of Genetic Inventions. In *Human Genetics Licensing Symposium report*, 68-86. Ottawa: Health Canada.

Gold, E. Richard, Timothy Caulfield, and Peter Ray. 2002. Gene patents and the standard of care. *Canadian Medical Association Journal* 167 (3): 256-57.

Goldenberg, Eddy. 2006. *The way it works: Inside Ottawa*. Toronto: McClelland and Stewart.

Golub, Stephen S. 2003. Measures of restrictions in inward foreign direct investment for OECD countries. OECD Economic Studies No. 36. Paris: OECD.

Gordenker, Leon, and Thomas George Weiss. 1996. Pluralizing global governance: Analytical approaches and dimensions. In *NGOs, the UN and global governance*, ed. Leon Gordenker and Thomas George Weiss, 17-47. Boulder, CO: Lynne Rienner.

Gottschalk, Ricardo. 2005. The macro-content of PRSPs: Assessing the need for a more flexible macroeconomic framework. *Development Policy Review* 23 (4): 419-43.

Gouvernement du Québec. 1996. *The state of education in Québec, 1995-1996*. Québec City: Gouvernement du Québec.

Government of Denmark. 1989. *Hvidbog om Arbejdsmarkedets Strukturproblemer.* Copenhagen: Government of Denmark.

Graefe, Peter. 2006. The social economy and the American model: Relating new social policy directions to the old. *Global Social Policy* 6 (2): 197-219.

Gramsci, Antonio. 1971. *Selections from the "Prison Notebooks,"* ed. and trans. Q. Hoare and G. Nowell-Smith. New York: Lawrence and Wishart.

Gray, David M. 2006. Has EI reform unravelled? C.D. Howe Institute Backgrounder No. 98. Toronto: C.D. Howe Institute.

Green-Pedersen, Christoffer. 2001. Minority governments and party politics: The political and institutional background to the "Danish miracle." *Journal of Public Policy* 21 (1): 53-70.

–. 2002a. The role of different social democratic responses. *Governance* 15 (2): 271-94.

–. 2002b. *The politics of justification: Party competition and welfare-state retrenchment in Denmark and the Netherlands from 1982 to 1998*. Amsterdam: Amsterdam University Press.

Gregg, Paul, and Alan Manning. 1997. Labour market regulation and unemployment. In *Unemployment policy: Government options for the labour market*, ed. Dennis Snower and Guillermo de la Dehesa, 395-429. Cambridge: Cambridge University Press.

Gregory, Holly J. 2000. *The globalization of corporate governance*. New York: Weil, Gotshal and Manges. First published in *Global Counsel* 5 (September-October 2000). http://rru.worldbank.org/Documents/PapersLinks/globalisation_of_corporate_governance.pdf.

Griffin, C. 1999. Lifelong learning and social democracy. *International Journal of Lifelong Education* 18 (4): 329-42.

Griffith-Jones, Stephany, Ricardo Gottschalk, and Xavier Cirera. 2000. *The OECD experience with capital account liberalization*. Brighton: Institute of Development Studies, University of Sussex.

Griffiths, Richard T. 1997. "An act of creative leadership": The end of the OEEC and the birth of the OECD. In *Explorations in OEEC history*, ed. Richard T. Griffiths, 235-56. Paris: OECD.

Gurría, Angel. 2007a. What policies for globalising cities? Rethinking the urban policy agenda. Opening remarks by Angel Gurría, OECD Secretary-General, Madrid, 29 March 2007.

–. 2007b. Summary and conclusion by Angel Gurría, OECD Secretary-General, Madrid, 30 March 2007.

Haas, Peter. 1992. Introduction: Epistemic communities and international policy coordination. *International Organization* 46 (1): 1-35.

Haddow, Rodney. 1998. How Ottawa shrivels: Ottawa's declining role in active labour market policy. In *How Ottawa spends, 1998-99*, ed. Leslie A. Pal, 99-126. Toronto: Oxford University Press.

Häkkinen, Unto, and Eeva Ollila. 2000. The World Health Report 2000. What does it tell us about health systems? Analyses from Finish experts. In *Themes from Finland//2000.* Helsinki: STAKES (National Research and Development Centre for Welfare and Health).

Hall, Peter A. 1989a. *The political power of economic ideas: Keynesianism across nations.* Princeton, NJ: Princeton University Press.

–. 1989b. Conclusion: The politics of Keynesian ideas. In *The political power of economic ideas: Keynesianism across nations,* ed. Peter Hall, 361-93. Princeton, NJ: Princeton University Press.

–. 1993. Policy paradigms, social learning, and the state: The case of economic policymaking in Britain. *Comparative Politics* 25 (4): 275-96.

Hall, Peter A., and David Soskice, eds. 2001. *Varieties of capitalism: The institutional foundations of comparative advantage.* Oxford: Oxford University Press.

Hambleton, Robin, Hank V. Savitch, and Murray Stewart. 2002. Globalism and local democracy. In *Globalism and local democracy: Challenge and change in Europe and North America,* ed. Robin Hambleton, Hank V. Savitch, and Murray Stewart, 1-19. New York: Palgrave.

Hansen, Hans Krause, Dorte Salskov-Iversen, and Sven Bisley. 2002. Discursive globalization: Transnational discourse communities and new public management. In *Towards a Global Polity,* ed. Morten Ougaard and Richard Higgott, 107-24. London: Routledge.

Hartman, Y. 2005. In bed with the enemy: Some ideas on the connections between neoliberalism and the welfare state. *Current Sociology* 53 (1): 57-73.

Hayden, A. 2000. Netherlands sets example: Shortest hours, fewest jobless. *CCPA Monitor* 7 (2): 21.

Hein, Wolfgang, and Lars Kohlmorgen, ed. 2003. *Globalisation, global health governance and national health politics in developing countries: An exploration into the dynamics of interfaces.* Hamburg: Deutsches Übersee Institut.

Helleiner, Eric. 1994. *States and the reemergence of global finance.* Ithaca, NY: Cornell University Press.

Heller, Michael A., and Rebecca S. Eisenberg. 1998. Can patents deter innovation? The anticommons in biomedical research. *Science* 280 (5364): 698-701.

Hemerijck, Anton, and Jelle Visser. 2003. Policy learning in European welfare states. Unpublished manuscript, University of Amsterdam.

Henderson, David. 1996. The role of the OECD in liberalising trade and capital flows. *World Today* 19 (1): 11-28.

–. 1999. *The MAI affair – A story and its lessons.* London: Royal Institute of Economic Affairs.

Henry, M., B. Lingard, F. Rizvi, and S. Taylor. 2001. *The OECD, globalization and education policy.* London: Pergamon.

Herzenberg, Stephen, John A. Alic, and Howard Wial. 1998. *New rules for a new economy: Employment and opportunity in post-industrial America.* Ithaca, NY: ILR.

Heyneman, S.P. 1993. Quantity, quality and source. Presidential Address. *Comparative Education Revue* 37 (4): 372-88.

Hobson, John M. 2000. *The state and international relations.* Cambridge: Cambridge University Press.

Hodson, Dermot, and Imelda Maher. 2001. The open method as a new mode of governance: The case of soft economic policy co-ordination. *Journal of Common Market Studies* 39 (4): 719-46.

Hoekman, Bernard. 1993. New issues in the Uruguay Round and beyond. *Economic Journal* 103 (421): 1528-39.

–. 1995. Assessing the general agreement on trade in services. In *World Bank Discussion Papers 307 – The Uruguay Round and the developing economies,* ed. Will Martin and L. Alan Winters, 327-65. Washington, DC: World Bank.

Hood, Christopher. 1998. *The art of the state: Culture, rhetoric, and public management.* Oxford: Clarendon Press.

Hooghe, Liesbeth, and Gary Marks. 2001. *Multi-level governance and European integration.* Boulder, CO: Rowman and Littlefield.

Houde, Marie-France, and Katia Yannaca-Small. 2004. Relationships between international investment agreements. OECD Working Papers on International Investment 2004/1. Paris: OECD.

Howell, David. 2005. Introduction. In *Fighting unemployment: The limits of free market orthodoxy*, ed. David Howell, 3-34. Oxford: Oxford University Press.

Husen, T. 1979. *Schools in question: A comparative study of school and its future in western societies*. Oxford: Oxford University Press.

ILO (International Labour Organization). 1999. Report of the Director-General: Decent work. International Labour Conference, 87th Session, 1-17 June, Geneva.

–. 2003. *Decent work: For a globalization with decent jobs*. Conclusions of the presentations and debates at the 3rd World Social Forum, 28 January, Porto Alegre, Brazil.

IMF (International Monetary Fund). 2001. Strengthening country ownership of Fund-supported programs. Policy Development and Review Department. http://www.imf.org/external/np/pdr/cond/2001/eng/strength/120501.pdf.

Institute of International Finance. 2002. Policies for corporate governance and transparency in emerging markets. http://www.iif.com/data/public/NEWEAG_Report.pdf.

Interview A. 2005. Interview by Holly Grinvalds. Tape recording. 7 December. Copenhagen.

Interview B. 2006. Interview by Holly Grinvalds. Written notes of telephone conversation. 16 October.

Interview C. 2005. Interview by Holly Grinvalds. Tape recording. 28 September. Paris.

Interview D. 2005. Interview by Holly Grinvalds. Tape recording. 1 December. Copenhagen.

Interview E. 2006. Interview by Holly Grinvalds. Written notes of telephone conservation. 5 October.

Interview G. 2006. Interview by Holly Grinvalds. Written notes of telephone conversation. 11 October.

Interview H. 2005. Interview by Holly Grinvalds. Tape recording. 9 December. Copenhagen.

Interview I. 2005. Interview by Holly Grinvalds. Tape recording. 8 December. Copenhagen.

Istance, D. 1996. Education at the Chateau de la Muette. *Oxford Review of Education* 22 (1): 91-96.

Iu, Justin, and Jonathan Batten. 2001. The implementation of OECD corporate governance principles in post-crisis Asia. *Journal of Corporate Citizenship* 4: 47-62.

Jackson, Andrew. 1994. The economic impacts of Unemployment Insurance – The case for the defence. CLC Research Paper No. 3. Ottawa: Canadian Labour Congress.

–. 2000. The perverse circularity of NAIRU-driven economic policy in Canada. *Canadian Business Economics* 8 (2): 1-17.

–. 2004a. Measuring and monitoring economic and social well-being: Comments from a labour perspective. Statistics, Knowledge and Policy: OECD World Forum on Key Indicators, 10-13 November, Palermo.

–. 2004b. Paul Martin's economic record: Living standards of working families and prospects for future prosperity. In *Hell and high water: An assessment of Paul Martin's record and implications for the future*, ed. Todd Scarth, 73-91. Ottawa: Canadian Centre for Policy Alternatives.

Jacobsson, Bengt. 2006. Regulated regulators: Global trends of state transformation. In *Transnational governance: Institutional dynamics of regulation*, ed. Marie-Laure Djelic and Kerstin Sahlin-Andersson, 205-25. New York: Cambridge University Press.

Jacobsson, Bengt, and Kerstin Sahlin-Andersson. 2006. Dynamics of soft regulation. In *Transnational governance: Institutional dynamics of regulation*, ed. Marie-Laure Djelic and Kerstin Sahlin-Andersson, 247-66. New York: Cambridge University Press.

Jensen, Anne E. 1991. Strukturpolitik en Svær Opgave. *Berlingske Tidende,* 16 July, Section 1: 6.

Jessop, Bob. 2003. *The future of the capitalist state*. Cambridge: Polity Press.

Johnston, Donald J. 1998. Why territorial development matters. *OECD Observer* (210, February/March): 4.

Johnston, D. 2001. Message from the OECD Secretary-General, Donald J. Johnston: OECD Forum 2001 – Building partnerships for a sustainable future. http://www.oecd.org/document/39/0,3343,en_2649_34493_33619943_1_1_1_1,00.html.

Josling, Timothy E., Fred H. Sanderson, and T.K. Warley. 1990. The future of international agricultural relations: Issues in the GATT negotiations. In *Agricultural protectionism in the industrialized world,* ed. Fred H. Sanderson, 433-64. Baltimore: Johns Hopkins University Press.

Jubilee Debt Campaign. 2006. *Tightening the chains or cutting the strings: The status of HIPC conditionality in 2006.* Jubilee Debt Campaign Report. http://www.jubileedebtcampaign. org.uk/download.php?id=314.

Kaldor, Mary H., Helmut K. Anheier, and Marlies Glasius, eds. 2007. *Global civil society 2006/7.* London: Sage.

Kanter, James. 2006. OECD setting the stage to admit new members. *International Herald Tribune,* 10 May. http://www.iht.com/articles/2006/05/10/business/oecd.php.

Kapur, Devish. 1998. The IMF: A curse or cure. *Foreign Policy* 111: 114-30.

Karabel, Jerome, and A.H. Halsey. 1977. *Power and ideology in education.* Oxford: Oxford University Press.

Kau, Friedrich, and Axel Mittelstädt. 1986. Labour market flexibility. *OECD Economic Studies* 6 (Spring): 7-44.

Keck, M., and K. Sikkink. 1999. Transnational advocacy networks in international and regional politics. *International Social Science Journal* 51 (159): 89-101.

Kenny, Michael, and Randall Germain. 1998. Engaging Gramsci: International relations theory and the new Gramscians. *Review of International Studies* 24: 3-24.

Keohane, Robert O. 1978. Review: Economics, inflation, and the role of the state: Political implications of the McCracken Report. *World Politics* 31 (1): 108-28.

Kettl, Donald F. 2005. *The global public management revolution,* 2nd ed. Washington, DC: Brookings Institution.

Key, Sydney J. 1999. Trade liberalization and prudential regulation: The international framework for financial services. *International Affairs* 75 (1): 61-75.

Kipping, Matthias, and Lars Engwall, eds. 2002. *Management consulting: Emergence and dynamics of a knowledge industry.* Oxford: Oxford University Press.

Kjær, Peter, and Ove K. Pedersen. 2001. Translating liberalization: Neo-liberalism in the Danish negotiated economy. In *The rise of neo-liberalism and institutional analysis,* ed. John L. Campbell and Ove K. Pedersen, 219-48. Princeton, NJ: Princeton University Press.

Klammer, Ute, and Katja Tillmann. 2001. Flexibilität und soziale Sicherung – eine vielschichtige Herausforderung für politische Gestaltung. In *Flexicurity: Soziale Sicherung und Flexibilisierung der Arbeits- und Lebensverhältnisse,* ed. U. Klammer and K. Tillmann, 513-17. Düsseldorf: Hans Böckler Stiftung.

Klugman, Jeni, ed. 2002a. *A sourcebook for poverty reduction strategies. Volume 1, Core techniques and cross-cutting issues.* Washington, DC: World Bank.

–, ed. 2002b. *A sourcebook for poverty reduction strategies. Volume 2, Macroeconomic and sectoral approaches.* Washington, DC: World Bank.

Kobrin, S.J. 1998. The MAI and the clash of globalizations. *Foreign Policy* 112: 97-109.

Koenig-Archibugi, M. 2002. Mapping global governance. In *Governing globalization,* ed. David Held and Andrew McGrew, 46-69. Cambridge: Polity Press.

Koromzay, Val. 1991. Monetary and fiscal policies. In *Economic policies for the 1990s,* ed. John Llewellyn and Stephen J. Potter, 163-82. Cambridge, MA: Blackwell.

Kristensen, Thorkil. 1967. Five years of OECD. In *European Yearbook 1965,* vol. 13. The Hague: Martinus Nijhoff.

Krugman, Paul R. 1991. *Has the adjustment process worked?* Washington, DC: Institute for International Economics.

Kuhn, Peter. 1997. Canada and the "OECD hypothesis": Does labour market inflexibility explain Canada's high level of unemployment. Canadian International Labour Network Working Paper No. 10. http://www.ciln.mcmaster.ca/papers/cilnwp10.pdf.

Kurtz, J. 2002. NGOs, the Internet and international economic policy making: The failure of the OECD Multilateral Agreement on Investment. *Melbourne Journal of International Law* 3 (2): 213-46.

Lairson, Thomas D., and David Skidmore. 1997. *International political economy: The struggle for power and wealth.* New York: Harcourt Brace.

Lampinen, O. 2000. *Suomen Koulutujärjestelmän Kehitys*. Tampere, Finland: Guademus. Quoted in R. Rinne, J. Kallo, and S. Hokka, Too eager to comply? OECD education policies and the Finnish response. *European Educational Research Journal* 3 (2): 463.

Lecubrier, Aude. 2002. Patents and public health. *European Molecular Biology Organization Report* 3 (12): 1120-22.

Lehtonen, Markku. 2007. Environmental policy integration through OECD peer reviews: Integrating the eeonomy with the environment or the environment with the economy? *Environmental Politics* 16 (1): 15-35.

Ley, Robert, and Pierre Poret. 1997. The new OECD members and liberalization. *OECD Observer* 205: 38-42.

Lindensjö, B. 1981. *Högskolereformen. En studie i offentlig reformstrategi*. Stockholm Studies in Political Studies in Politics 20. Stockholm: Stockholms Universitet.

Llewellyn, John, and Stephen J. Potter, ed. 1991. *Economic policies for the 1990s*. Cambridge, MA: Blackwell.

Lloyd, C. 2002. Regime change in Australian capitalism: Towards an historical political economy of regulation. *Australian Economic History Review* 42 (3): 238-66.

Lodge, M. 2005. The importance of being modern: International benchmarking and national regulatory innovation. *Journal of European Public Policy* 12 (4): 649-67.

Macdonald, Laura. 1994. Globalising civil society: Interpreting international NGOs in Central America. *Millennium: Journal of International Studies* 23 (2): 267-85.

Macdonald, Laura, and Arne Ruckert, ed. Forthcoming. *Post-neo-liberalism in the Americas: Beyond the Washington consensus*. New York: Palgrave/Macmillan.

Macpherson, Crawford Brough. 1977. *The life and times of liberal democracy*. Oxford: Oxford University Press.

Mahon, Rianne. 1987. From Fordism to new technology, labour markets and unions. *Economic and Industrial Democracy* 8 (1): 5-60.

–. 1996. Women wage earners and the future of Swedish unions. *Economic and Industrial Democracy* 17 (4): 545-86.

–. 2005. The OECD and the reconciliation agenda: Competing blueprints. Revision of a paper prepared for "Challenges and Opportunities Faced by European Welfare States: The Changing Context for Child Welfare," 7-8 January, University of Oxford, UK.

Manning, Nick. 2004. Mutual admiration? OECD advice to the UK. In *The OECD and European welfare states*, ed. Klaus Armingeon and Michelle Beyeler, 197-211. Cheltenham: Edward Elgar.

March, James G., and Johan P. Olsen. 1998. The institutional dynamics of international political orders. *International Organization* 52 (4): 943-69.

Marcussen, Martin. 2001. The OECD in search of a role: Playing the idea game. Paper prepared for presentation at the European Consortium for Political Research, 6-11 April, Grenoble, France.

–. 2002. *OECD og Idéspillet – game over?* Copenhagen: Hans Reitzels Forlag.

–. 2004a. Multilateral surveillance and the OECD: Playing the idea game. In *The OECD and European welfare states*, ed. Klaus Armingeon and Michelle Beyeler, 13-31. Cheltenham: Edward Elgar.

–. 2004b. The Organization for Economic Cooperation and Development as ideational artist and arbitrator: Reality or dream? In *Decision making within international organizations*, ed. Bob Reinalda and Bertjan Verbeek, 90-107. London: Routledge.

–. 2004c. OECD governance through soft-law. In *Soft law in governance and regulation: An interdisciplinary analysis*, ed. Ulrika Morth, 103-28. Cheltenham: Edward Elgar.

Marginson, Simon. 1997. *Markets in education*. St Leonards, Australia: Allen and Unwin.

Marjolin, Robert. 1989. *Architect of European unity: Memoirs, 1911-1986*. London: Weidenfeld and Nicolson.

Marklund, Staffan, and Anders Nordlund. 1999. Economic problems, welfare convergence and political instability. In *Nordic social policy: Changing welfare states*, ed. Mikko Kautto et al., 19-54. London and New York: Routledge.

Marmor, Ted, Richard Freeman, and Kieke Okma. 2005. Comparative perspectives and policy learning in the world of health care. *Journal of Comparative Policy Analysis* 7(4): 331-48.

Martens, Kerstin, and Carolin Balzer. 2004. Comparing governance of international organizations – The EU, the OECD and educational policy. Paper presented to the European Consortium for Political Research, 13-18 April, Uppsala, Sweden.

Martin, I. 2003. Adult education: Lifelong learning and citizenship: Some ifs and buts. *International Journal of Lifelong Learning* 22 (6): 566-79.

Martin, Paul. 2005. Address by Prime Minister to the Conference of the Federation of Canadian Municipalities. 5 June, St. John's, NF.

McBride, Stephen. 1992. *Not working: State, unemployment and neo-conservatism in Canada.* Toronto: University of Toronto Press.

–. 2005. *Paradigm shift: Globalization and the Canadian state,* 2nd ed. Halifax: Fernwood Publishing.

McBride, Stephen, and Russell Williams. 2001. Globalization, the restructuring of labour markets and policy convergence: The OECD "Jobs Strategy." *Global Social Policy* 1 (3): 281-309.

McBride, Stephen, Kathleen McNutt, and Russell A. Williams. 2007. Tracking neo-liberalism: Labour market policies in the OECD area. In *Neo-liberalism, state power and global governance,* ed. Simon Lee and Stephen McBride, 79-93. Dordrecht, Netherlands: Springer.

McCracken, P.W. 1977. *Towards full employment and price stability: Report to the OECD by a group of independent experts.* Carnegie-Rochester Conference Series on Public Policy, vol. 11. Paris: OECD.

McKeen-Edwards, Heather, Tony Porter, and Ian Roberge. 2004. Politics or markets? The determinants of cross-border financial integration in the NAFTA and the EU. *New Political Economy* 9 (3): 325-40.

Merz, John F., Antigone G. Kriss, Deborah G.B. Leonard, and Mildred K. Cho. 2002. Diagnostic testing fails the test. *Nature* 415 (6872): 577-79.

Millstein, Ira M. 2000. Corporate governance: The role of market forces. *OECD Observer* 221/222 (Summer): 27.

Ministry of Finance Denmark. 1993. *Finansredegørelse 1993.* Copenhagen: Ministry of Finance Denmark.

Ministry of Labour and Ministry of Education Denmark. 1986. *Debatoplæg om Vækst og Omstilling.* Copenhagen: Ministry of Labour.

Ministry of Labour Denmark. 1987. *Arbejdsmarkedspolitikken Sommeren 1987: Så Langt Er Vi Kommet.* Copenhagen: Ministry of Labour Denmark.

Moravcsik, Andrew M. 1989. Disciplining trade finance: The OECD export credit arrangement. *International Organization* 43 (1): 173-205.

Morgan, Clara. 2007. Constructing international student assessment: The role of the OECD. PhD dissertation, School of Public Policy and Administration, Carleton University.

Mouelhi, Mia, and Arne Ruckert. 2007. Ownership and participation: The limitations of the Poverty Reduction Strategy Paper (PRSP) approach. *Canadian Journal of Development Studies* 28 (2): 277-92.

Murphy, Craig. 2000. Global governance: Poorly done and poorly understood. *International Affairs* 76 (4): 789-803.

–. 2005. Global governance: Poorly done and poorly understood. In *The Global Governance Reader,* ed. Rorden Wilkinson, 90-103. New York: Routledge.

Nestor, Stilpon. 2001. Corporate governance trends and developments in the OECD area: Where do we go from here? *International Financial Law Review* Supplement: The IFLR guide to corporate governance.

Nielsen, Klaus, and Stefan Kesting. 2003. Small is resilient: The impact of globalization on Denmark. *Review of Social Economy* 61 (3): 365-87.

Noaksson, Niklas, and Kerstin Jacobsson. 2003. *The production of ideas and expert knowledge in OECD: The OECD Jobs Strategy in contrast with the EU Employment Strategy.* Stockholm: University of Stockholm, Stockholm Centre for Organizational Research.

Noboru, Seiichiro. 2004. *A strategy for enlargement and outreach.* Report by the chair of the Heads of Delegation Working Group on the Enlargement Strategy and Outreach. Paris: OECD.

Noel, Alain. 2006. The new global politics of poverty. *Global Social Policy* 6 (3): 304-33.

Nuffield Council on Bioethics. 2002. The ethics of patenting DNA. Discussion paper. London: Nuffield Council on Bioethics.

O'Brien, Robert, Anne Marie Goetz, Jan Aart Scholte, and Marc Williams. 2000. *Contesting global governance: Multilateral economic institutions and global social movements*. Cambridge: Cambridge University Press.

O'Connor, Julia, Ann Shola Orloff, and Sheila Shaver. 1999. *States, markets, families: Gender, liberalism and social policy in Australia, Canada, Great Britain and the United States*. New York: Cambridge University Press.

Odell, John S. 1982. *US international monetary policy: Markets, power and ideas as sources of change*. Princeton, NJ: Princeton University Press.

OECD. 1960. *Convention on the Organization for Economic Cooperation and Development*. Paris: OECD.

–. 1961a. *Economic growth and investment in education*. Paris: OECD.

–. 1961b. *Ability and educational opportunity*. Paris: OECD.

–. 1962. Decision of the Council on Relations with International Non-Governmental Organizations. OECD Doc C(62)45 (1962). Paris: OECD.

–. 1964. *Economic aspects of higher education*. Paris: OECD.

–. 1965a. *Economic models of education*. Paris: OECD.

–. 1965b. *The residual factor and economic growth*. Paris: OECD.

–. 1966a. *The balance of payments adjustment process*. Paris: OECD.

–. 1966b. *Financing of education for economic growth*. Paris: OECD.

–. 1977. *Towards full employment and price stability: A report to the OECD by a group of independent experts*. Paris: OECD.

–. 1978. *From Marshall Plan to global interdependence: New challenges for the industrialized nations*. Paris: OECD.

–. 1981. *The crisis of the welfare state*. Paris: OECD.

–. 1986a. *Flexibility in the labour market: The current debate*. Paris: OECD.

–. 1986b. *Labour market flexibility. A report by a high-level group of experts to the Secretary-General*. Paris: OECD.

–. 1987a. *National policies and agricultural trade*. Paris: OECD.

–. 1987b. *Structural adjustment and economic performance*. Paris: OECD.

–. 1988a. *Employment outlook*. Paris: OECD.

–. 1988b. *Reforming public pensions*. Paris: OECD.

–. 1989a. *Employment outlook*. Paris: OECD.

–. 1989b. *Education and the economy in a changing society*. Paris: OECD.

–. 1990a. Modelling the effects of agricultural policies. OECD Economic Studies No. 13. Paris: OECD.

–. 1990b. *Economic surveys 1989-90 Denmark*. Paris: OECD.

–. 1990c. *Labour market policies for the 1990s*. Paris: OECD.

–. 1990d. *Health care systems in transition*. Paris: OECD.

–. 1991. Economic policy-making since the mid-1960s. *OECD Economic Outlook* 50: 1-11.

–. 1993a. *Exchange control policy*. Paris: OECD and Centre for Co-operation with European Economies in Transition.

–. 1993b. *National treatment for foreign controlled enterprises*. Paris: OECD.

–. 1993c. *Economic integration, OECD economies, dynamic Asian economies and Central and Eastern Europe*. Paris: OECD.

–. 1994a. *The Jobs Study: facts, analysis, strategy*. Paris: OECD.

–. 1994b. *The OECD Jobs Study: evidence and explanations. Part 1: Labour market trends and underlying forces of change*. Paris: OECD.

–. 1994c. *New orientations for social policy*. Paris: OECD.

–. 1994d. *Annual report of the OECD*. Paris: OECD.

–. 1995a. *Governance in transition: Public management reforms in OECD countries*. Paris: OECD.

–. 1995b. *Introduction to the OECD Codes of Liberalization*. Paris: OECD.

–. 1995c. Emerging markets and the liberalization of capital movements. *OECD Economic Outlook, No. 58*. Paris: OECD.

. 3

–. 1995d. *A multilateral agreement on investment: Report by the Committee on International Investment and Multinational Enterprises and the Committee on Capital Movements and Invisible Transactions*. Paris: OECD.

–. 1996a. Meeting of the Council at Ministerial Level Paris, 21-22 May. Communiqué. http://www.g7.utoronto.ca/oecd/oecd96.htm.

–. 1996b. The relationship between the MAI and the WTO agreements: Note by the chairman. OECD Meeting DAFFE/MAI/EG4/A(96)2. Paris: OECD.

–. 1996c. *Ireland: Local partnerships and social innovation*. Paris: OECD.

–. 1996d. *Lifelong learning for all*. Paris: OECD.

–. 1996e. *The OECD Jobs Study: Implementing the strategy*. Paris: OECD.

–. 1997a. OECD challenges and strategic objectives: 1997. Note by the Secretary-General. OECD Doc C(97)180. Paris: OECD.

–. 1997b. *Implementing the OECD Jobs Strategy: Member countries' experience*. Paris: OECD.

–. 1997c. *Economic survey of Canada*. Paris: OECD.

–. 1997d. *Shaping the twenty-first century: The contribution of development co-operation*. Paris: OECD DAC.

–. 1998a. *Survey of OECD work on international investment*. Paris: OECD.

–. 1998b. *Integrating distressed urban areas*. Paris: OECD.

–. 1998c. The OECD Jobs Strategy: Progress report on implementation of country-specific recommendations. Working Paper No. 196. Paris: OECD.

–. 1998d. *Economic survey of Canada*. Paris: OECD.

–. 1998e. *Pathways and participation in vocational and technical education*. Paris: OECD.

–. 1999a. *A caring world. The new social policy agenda*. Paris: OECD.

–. 1999b. *Principles of corporate governance*. Paris: OECD.

–. 1999c. *Implementing the OECD Jobs Strategy: Assessing performance and policy*. Paris: OECD.

–. 2000a. *Making poverty reduction work: OECD's role in development partnership*. Paris: OECD.

–. 2000b. *Economic survey of Canada*. Paris: OECD.

–. 2000c. *A system of health accounts*. Paris: OECD.

–. 2000d. *Literacy in the information age*. Paris: OECD.

–. 2001a. *Devolution and globalisation: Implications for local decision-makers*. Paris: OECD.

–. 2001b. *Local partnerships for better governance*. Paris: OECD.

–. 2001c. *Cities for citizens: Improving metropolitan governance*. Paris: OECD.

–. 2001d. *Economic survey of Canada*. Paris: OECD.

–. 2002a. Peer pressure as part of surveillance by international institutions. Record of discussion led by Niels Thygesen, Chairman, Economic Development Review Committee, Tuesday, 4 June. Paris: OECD.

–. 2002b. *Forty years' experience with the OECD Code of Liberalization of Capital Movements*. Paris: OECD.

–. 2002c. *Territorial review: Canada*. Paris: OECD.

–. 2002d. *Genetic inventions, intellectual property rights and licensing practices*. Paris: OECD.

–. 2002e. *Babies and bosses: Australia, Denmark and the Netherlands*, vol. 1. Paris: OECD.

–. 2002f. *Ageing societies and the looming pension crisis*. Paris: OECD.

–. 2002g. *Regulating private pension schemes: Trends and challenges*. Private Pensions Series No. 4. Paris: OECD.

–. 2002h. *Thematic review of adult learning – Canada: Country notes*. http://www.oecd.org/pdf/M00032000/M00032160.pdf.

–. 2003a. *OECD economic surveys: Canada 2003*. Paris: OECD.

–. 2003b. *Experiences from the regional corporate governance roundtables*. Paris: OECD.

–. 2003c. *Public sector modernisation*. Policy brief. Paris: OECD.

–. 2003d. *Annual report 2003*. Paris: OECD.

–. 2003e. *Fighting corruption: What role for civil society? The experience of the OECD*. Paris: OECD.

–. 2003f. TDPC high-level meeting: Policy fact sheets. Paris: OECD.

–. 2003g. *The sources of economic growth in OECD countries*. Paris: OECD.

–. 2003h. *Babies and bosses: Austria, Ireland and Japan*, vol. 2. Paris: OECD.

–. 2004a. *Getting to grips with globalisation: The OECD in a changing world.* Paris: OECD.

–. 2004b. *OECD economic surveys: United States 2004.* Paris: OECD.

–. 2004c. *Overview of the OECD: What is it? History? Who does what? Structure of the organization?* Paris: OECD.

–. 2004d. OECD territorial review of Montreal. Policy brief. Paris: OECD.

–. 2004e. *2004 employment outlook.* Paris: OECD.

–. 2004f. *The OECD health project. Towards high-performing health systems.* Paris: OECD.

–. 2004g. *Babies and bosses: New Zealand, Portugal and Switzerland,* vol. 3. Paris: OECD.

–. 2005a. *Public sector modernisation: The way forward.* Policy brief. Paris: OECD.

–. 2005b. *Modernising government: The way forward.* Paris: OECD.

–. 2005c. *Civil society and the OECD.* Paris: OECD.

–. 2005d. *Pensions at a glance: Public policies across OECD countries.* Paris: OECD.

–. 2005e. *Extending opportunities: How active social policy can benefit us all.* Paris: OECD.

–. 2005f. *Babies and bosses: Canada, Finland, Sweden and the United Kingdom,* vol. 4. Paris: OECD.

–. 2005g. *Promoting adult learning.* Paris: OECD.

–. 2005h. *Learning a living. First results of the Adult Literacy and Life Skills Survey.* Paris/Ottawa: OECD/Statistics Canada.

–. 2005i. Extending opportunity: How active social policy can benefit us all. Final communiqué. Paris: OECD.

–. 2006a. China and the OECD. Policy brief special edition, May 2006. Paris: OECD.

–. 2006b. *Methodology for assessing the implementation of the OECD principles on corporate governance.* Paris: OECD.

–. 2006c. *Labour and the OECD: The role of TUAC.* Paris: OECD.

–. 2006d. Civil society and parliamentarians. http://www.oecd.org/document/22/0,2340,en_2649_34495_2435158_1_1_1_1,00.html.

–. 2006e. Relations with BIAC and TUAC. http://www.oecd.org/document/53/0,2340,en_2649_34489_1910965_1_1_1_1,00.html.

–. 2006f. *OECD communications guiding principles.* Paris: OECD.

–. 2006g. OECD global forums: Global forum on development. http://www.oecd.org/document/26/0,2340,en_36335986_36339065_37105434_1_1_1_1,00.html.

–. 2006h. *Annual report 2006.* Paris: OECD.

–. 2006i. *Policy framework for investment.* Paris: OECD.

–. 2006j. *Competitive cities in the global economy: Horizontal synthesis report.* Paris: OECD.

–. 2006k. *Boosting jobs and incomes – Policy lessons from reassessing the OECD Jobs Strategy.* Paris: OECD.

–. 2006l. Jobs and incomes: The restated OECD Jobs Strategy. *DELSA Newsletter* 3: 1-8.

–. 2006m. Boosting jobs and incomes – Lessons from reassessing the OECD Jobs Strategy. Speech by Angel Gurría, Secretary-General of the OECD, to the G8 employment and labour ministers, 9-10 October, Moscow.

–. 2006n. *2006 employment outlook.* Paris: OECD.

–. 2006o. *About economic surveys and the EDRC.* Paris: OECD. http://www.oecd.org/document/51/0,2340,en_2649_34111_34627763_1_1_1_1,00.html.

–. 2006p. *Guidelines for the licensing of genetic inventions.* Paris: OECD.

–. 2006q. *International migration outlook.* Paris: OECD.

–. 2006r. *Babies and bosses – Reconciling work and family life: A synthesis of findings for OECD countries.* Paris: OECD.

–. 2006s. *Live longer, work longer.* Paris: OECD.

–. 2006t. *Pension Markets in Focus.* October 2006, issue 3. Paris: OECD.

–. 2006u. *Sickness, disability and work: Breaking the barriers – Norway, Poland and Switzerland.* Paris: OECD.

–. 2006v. Too many workers leave the labour market through sickness and disability benefits, says OECD. http://www.oecd.org/document/32/0,3343,en_2649_201185_37635040_1_1_1_1,00.html.

–. 2006w. *OECD Code of Liberalisation of Capital Movements.* Paris: OECD.

–. 2006x. *Economic survey of the Russian Federation.* Paris: OECD.

–. 2007a. *Agricultural policies in non-OECD countries: Monitoring and evaluation 2007, highlights.* Paris: OECD.

–. 2007b. OECD Council Resolution on Enlargement and Enhanced Engagement. Adopted by the Council at Ministerial Level on 16 May 2007. Paris: OECD.

–. 2007c. Competitive cities: A new entrepreneurial paradigm in spatial development. Summary in English. Paris: OECD.

–. 2007d. *Linking regions and central governments: Contracts for regional development.* Paris: OECD.

–. 2007e. *Economic policy reforms: Going for growth.* Paris: OECD.

–. 2007f. Chair's summary of the OECD Council Meeting, 15-16 May, Paris.

–. 2007g. *Pensions at a glance: Public policies across OECD countries.* Paris: OECD.

–. n.d. Comments received from Web consultations. Paris: OECD.

OECD Watch. 2005. Five years on: A review of the OECD guidelines and national contact points. http://www.oecdwatch.org/docs/OECD_Watch_5_years_on.pdf.

Ohlin, Goran. 1967. The Organization for Economic Cooperation and Development. *International Organization* 22 (1): 231-43.

Olssen, M., and M.A. Peters. 2005. Neo-liberalism, higher education and the knowledge economy: From the free market to knowledge capitalism. *Journal of Education Policy* 20 (3): 313-45.

Ontario Ministry of Health and Long-Term Care. 2002. *Genetics, testing and gene patenting: Charting new territory in healthcare.* Toronto: Government of Ontario.

Or, Zeynep. 2002. Improving the performance of health care systems: From measures to action (a review of experiences in four OECD countries). Labour Market and Social Policy – Occasional Papers No. 57. DEELSA/ELSA/WD(2002)1. Paris: OECD.

Orloff, A.S. 1993. Gender and the social rights of citizenship. *American Sociological Review* 58 (3): 303-28.

Orr, Marion, ed. 2007. *Transforming the city: Community organizing and the challenge of political change.* Lawrence: University of Kansas Press.

Ougaard, M. 2004. *Political globalization: State power and global forces.* Basingstoke, UK: Palgrave.

Pagani, Fabrizio. 2002a. Peer review: A tool for co-operation and change. Unclassified study SG/LEG(2002)1. Paris: OECD.

–. 2002b. Peer review as a tool for co-operation and change: An analysis of an OECD working method. *African Security Review* 11 (4): 15-24.

Papadopoulos, G. 1994. *Education 1960-1990. The OECD perspective.* Paris: OECD.

Patterson, L., and C. Briar. 2005. Lone mothers in liberal welfare states: Thirty years of change and continuity. *Hecate* 31 (1): 46-59.

Peck, Jamie. 2002. Political economies of scale: Fast policy, interscalar relations, and neo-liberal workfare. *Economic Geography* 78 (3): 331-60.

Pedersen, Poul Erik. 1992. Arbejdsmarkedet Må Tilpasses de Internationale Betingelser. In *Arbejde og Ledighed i 1990erne,* ed. Gunnar Viby Mogensen, 97-112. Copenhagen: Spektrum.

Peters, B. Guy, and Jon Pierre, ed. 2001. *Politicians, bureaucrats and administrative reform.* London: Routledge.

Petersen, Niels Helveg. 1990. Debat: Strukturfejl i Dansk Økonomi. *Politiken,* 29 May, Section 2: 7.

Pierson, Paul. 1994. *Dismantling the welfare state? Reagan, Thatcher, and the politics of retrenchment.* Cambridge: Cambridge University Press.

Plumptre, Wynne A.F. 1977. *Three decades of decision: Canada and the world monetary system 1944-75.* Toronto: McClelland and Stewart.

Polèse, Mario, and Richard Stren. 2000. Understanding the new sociocultural dynamics of cities: Comparative urban policy in a global context. In *The social sustainability of cities: Diversity and the management of Chang,* ed. Mario Polèse and Richard Stren, 3-39. Toronto: University of Toronto Press.

Pollitt, Christopher, and Geert Bouckaert. 2000. *Public management reform: A comparative analysis.* New York: Oxford University Press.

Pontusson, Jonas. 2005. *Inequality and prosperity: Social Europe vs. liberal America*. Ithaca, NY: Cornell University Press.

Poret, Pierre. 1998. Capital market liberalization: OECD approach and rules. Paper presented at the 10th international conference of the International Banking and Finance Institute.

Porter, Tony. 2005. *Globalization and finance*. Cambridge: Polity Press.

Porter, Tony, and Michael Webb. 2004. The role of the OECD in the orchestration of global knowledge networks. Paper presented at the 45th annual convention of the International Studies Association, 17-20 March, Montreal.

Premfors, Rune. 1998. Reshaping the democratic state: Swedish experiences in a comparative perspective. *Public Administration* 76 (1): 141-59.

Prempeh, Edward O. 2006. The anticapitalism movement and African resistance to globalization. *Studies in Political Economy* 77: 85-104.

Pressman, Lori, et al. 2006. The licensing of DNA patents by US academic institutions: An empirical survey. *Nature Biotechnology* 24 (1): 31-39.

Putnam, Robert D., and Nicholas Bayne. 1987. *Hanging together: Cooperation and discord in the seven-power summits*. Cambridge, MA: Harvard University Press.

Putnam, Robert D., and C. Randall Henning. 1989. The Bonn summit of 1978: A case study in coordination. In *Can nations agree? Issues in international economic cooperation*, ed. Richard N. Cooper et al., 12-140. Washington, DC: Brookings Institution.

Reimann, K.D. 2006. A view from the top: International politics, norms and the worldwide growth of NGOs. *International Studies Quarterly* 50 (1): 45-67.

Rinne, R., J. Kallo, and S. Hokka. 2004. Too eager to comply? OECD education policies and the Finnish response. *European Educational Research Journal* 3 (2): 454-85.

Risse, Thomas. 2000. "Let's Argue!" Communicative action in world politics. *International Organization* 54 (1): 1-39.

Rose, Richard. 1991. What is lesson-drawing? *Journal of Public Policy* 11 (1): 3-33.

Rosenau, James N., and Ernst Otto Czempiel, eds. 1992. *Governance without government*. Cambridge: Cambridge University Press.

Robertson, D. 2000. Civil society and the WTO. *World Economy* 23 (9): 1119-34.

Robinson, Andrew. 2006. Towards intellectual reformation: The critique of common sense and the forgotten revolutionary project. In *Images of Gramsci: Connections and contentions in political theory and international relations*, ed. Andreas Bieler and Adam D. Morton, 75-87. New York: Routledge.

Robinson, William I. 2004. *A theory of global capitalism: Production, class, and state in a transnational world*. Baltimore: Johns Hopkins University Press.

Rubenson, Kjell. 2006a. The Nordic model of lifelong learning. *Compare: A Journal of Comparative Education* 36 (3): 327-41.

–. 2006b. Constructing the lifelong learning paradigm: Competing visions from the OECD and UNESCO. In *Milestones: Towards lifelong learning systems*, ed. Søren Ehelers. Copenhagen: Danish University of Education Press.

Ruckert, Arne. 2006. From the Washington to the post-Washington consensus: Towards an inclusive-neo-liberal regime of development. *Labour, Capital, and Society* 39 (1): 35-67.

–. 2007. Reproducing neoliberal hegemony? A neo-Gramscian analysis of the poverty reduction strategy paper in Nicaragua. *Studies in Political Economy* 79: 91-118.

Rugman, Alan M. 1998. The political economy of the Multilateral Agreement on Investment. http://www.g7.utoronto.ca/annual/rugman1998/rugman1.htm.

Rupert, Mark. 1995. *Producing hegemony: The politics of mass production and American global power*. Cambridge: Cambridge University Press.

Ryan, P. 2003. The state of the welfare state. *Review of Income and Wealth* 49 (1): 135-45.

Ryner, M.J. 2002. *Capitalism restructuring. Globalisation and the Third Way*. London: Routledge.

Sahlin-Andersson, Kerstin. 2000a. National, international and transnational construction of new public management. Stockholm Centre for Organizational Research (SCORE) Working Paper 2000-4. Stockholm: University of Stockholm, SCORE.

–. 2000b. Arenas as standardizers. In *A world of standards*, ed. Nils Brunsson and Bengt Jacobsson, 100-14. Oxford: Oxford University Press.

Sahlin-Andersson, Kerstin, and Lars Engwall, ed. 2002. *The expansion of management knowledge: Carriers, flows, and sources.* Stanford, CA: Stanford Business Books.

Salzman, James. 2000. Labour rights, globalization and institutions: The role and influence of the Organization for Economic Cooperation and Development. *Michigan Journal of International Law* 21: 769-848.

–. 2005. Decentralized administrative law in the Organization for Economic Cooperation and Development. *Law and Contemporary Problems* 68 (3-4): 189-224.

Salzman, James, and Julio Bacio Terracino. 2006. Labor rights, globalization and institutions: The role and influence of the Organization for Economic Cooperation and Development. In *Social issues, globalization and international institutions: Labor rights and the EU, ILO, OECD and WTO,* ed. Virginia A. Leay and Daniel Warner, 311-403. Boston: Martinus Nijhoff.

SAPRIN (Structural Adjustment Participatory Review International Network). 2003. The policy roots of economic crisis and poverty. http://www.saprin.org/SAPRI_Findings.pdf.

Sargent, Timothy C. 2005. An index of Unemployment Insurance disincentives. Working Paper No. 95-10. Economic and Fiscal Policy Branch. Ottawa: Department of Finance Canada.

Sargent, Timothy C., and Munir A. Sheikh. 1996. *The natural rate of unemployment: Theory, evidence and policy implications.* Economic Studies and Policy Analysis Division. Ottawa: Department of Finance Canada.

Sarfati, Hedva. 2003. Welfare and labour market reforms: A new framework for social dialogue and collective bargaining? *European Journal of Industrial Relations* 9 (3): 265-82.

Savoie, Donald J. 1994. *Thatcher, Reagan, Mulroney: In search of a new bureaucracy.* Toronto: University of Toronto Press.

Sawyer, Malcolm. 2004. The NAIRU, labour market "flexibility," and full employment. In *Challenging the market: The struggle to regulate work and income,* ed. Jim Stanford and Leah F. Vosko, 33-50. Montreal: McGill-Queen's University Press.

Schäfer, Armin. 2006. A new form of governance? Comparing the open method of coordination to multilateral surveillance by the IMF and the OECD. *Journal of European Public Policy* 13 (1): 70-88.

Shiermeier, Quirin. 2000. Germany gives green light to gene patents. *Nature* 407: 934.

Schmidt, G. 2004. Reactions of participating countries as reflected in the press. *European Education* 35 (4): 58-69.

Schmidt-Hansen, Ulrich, and Lars Bo Kaspersen. 2004. *Consensus and conflict: The preliminary results from studies of the political decision-making process within employment, pension and integration politics in Denmark.* Copenhagen: Department of Sociology, University of Copenhagen.

Schmitt, John, and Jonathan Wadsworth. 2005. Is the OECD Jobs Strategy behind US and British employment and unemployment success in the 1990s? In *Fighting unemployment: The limits of free market orthodoxy,* ed. David Howell, 156-96. Oxford: Oxford University Press.

Schneider, Ronald. 2003. Reassessing the Jobs Strategy: A new road map against unemployment. *OECD Observer* 259: 30-31.

Scholte, Jan Aart. 2002. Civil society and governance in the global polity. In *Towards a global polity,* ed. M. Ougaard and R.A Higgott, 145-65. London: Routledge.

–. 2004. The WTO and civil society. In *Trade politics: International, domestic and regional perspectives,* ed. B. Hocking and S. McGuire. London: Routledge.

Scholte, Jan Aart, with A. Schnabel, ed. 2002. *Civil society and global finance.* London: Routledge.

Schricke, Christian. 1989. La CEE et l'ocde à l'heure de l'acte unique. *Revue Générale de Droit International Public* 93 (4): 801-30.

Schuller, T. 2005. Constructing international policy research: The Role of CERI/OECD. *European Educational Research Journal* 4 (3): 170-79.

Schultz, T. 1961. Investing in human capital. *American Economic Review* 51 (1): 1-17.

Schwab, Klaus. 2004. *Global competitiveness report 2004-2005.* Executive Summary. Geneva: World Economic Forum.

Setterfield, Mark. 1996. Using the NAIRU as a basis for macroeconomic policy: An appraisal. In *The unemployment crisis: All for nought?* ed. Brian K. MacLean and Lars Osberg, 56-75. Montreal: McGill-Queen's University Press.

Sewell, J.W. 1997. Foreword to *Perspectives on aid and development policy, essay no. 22*, ed. C. Gwin and J.M. Nelson. Washington, DC: Overseas Development Council.

Shonfield, Andrew. 1976. International economic relations of the western world: An overall view. In *International economic relations of the western world, 1959-1971; Vol. 1: Politics and trade*, ed. Andrew Shonfield, 1-140. London: Oxford University Press.

Simpson, Jeffrey. 2004. Martin's lack of focus is eroding his credibility. *Globe and Mail*, 18 February.

Sinclair, Scott. 2000. *GATS*. Ottawa: Canadian Centre for Policy Alternatives.

Skovgaard, Lars Erik. 1993. Gode År for Folk med Fast Job. *Politiken*, 3 March, Money: 3.

Slaughter, Anne-Marie. 2004. *A new world order*. Princeton, NJ: Princeton University Press.

Smilie, Ian, and Henri-Bernard Solignac Lecomte, ed. 2003. *Ownership and partnerships: What role for civil society in poverty reduction strategies?* Paris: OECD.

Smith, G., and T. Smith. 2006. A.H. Halsey: Oxford as a base for social research and educational reform. *Oxford Review of Education* 32 (1): 105-26.

Smith, Nina. 1993. Nye Tendenser og Resultater i Arbejdsmarkedsforskningen – Konsekvenser for den Økonomiske Politik. *Nationaløkonomisk Tidsskrift* 131 (1): 1-20.

Smythe, Elizabeth. 2001. Repoliticizing globalization in Canada: From the MAI to Seattle. *Journal of Canadian Studies* 36 (1): 141-65.

Soederberg, Susanne. 2006. *Global governance in question: Empire, class, and the new common sense in the managing of North-South relations*. London: Pluto Press.

Sobel, Irvin. 1982. The human capital revolution in economic development. In *Comparative education*, ed. Philip G. Altbach, Robert F. Arnove, and Gail P. Kelly, 54-77. New York: Macmillan.

SOU. 1965. *Vuxenutbildning I gymnasium och fackskola*. SOU 1965: 60. Stockholm: Government of Sweden.

–. 1966. *Yrkesutbildningen*. SOU 1966: 3. Stockholm: Government of Sweden.

–. 2005. *Reformerad föräldraförsäkring – kärlek, omvårdnad, trygghet*. SOU 2005: 73. Stockholm: Government of Sweden.

STAKES (National Research and Development Centre for Welfare and Health [Finland]). 2006. Comprehensive social policies for development in a globalizing world. http://www.stakes.fi/social-policies-for-development.

Stanford, Jim. 2003. Revisiting the "flexibility hypothesis." Paper presented at the annual meeting of the Canadian Economics Association, 30 May – 1 June, Carleton University, Ottawa.

–. 2004. Paul Martin, the deficit and the debt: Taking another look. In *Hell and high water: An assessment of Paul Martin's record and implications for the future*, ed. Todd Scarth, 31-55. Ottawa: Canadian Centre for Policy Alternatives.

Stern, Scot, and Fiona Murray. 2005. Do formal intellectual property rights hinder the free flow of scientific knowledge? An empirical test of the anti-commons hypothesis. National Bureau of Economic Research Working Paper No. W11465, July 2005.

Stiglitz, Joseph E. 1998. Towards a new paradigm for development: Strategies, policies, processes. 9th Raúl Prebisch Lecture, 19 October, Geneva. http://siteresources.worldbank.org/CDF/Resources/prebisch98.pdf.

–. 2002. *Globalization and its discontents*. New York: W.W. Norton.

Stiglitz, Joseph, and Andrew Charlton. 2005. *Fair trade for all: How trade can promote development*. Oxford: Oxford University Press.

Stone, Diane. 1999. Learning lessons and transferring policy across time, space and disciplines. *Politics* 19 (1): 51-59.

–. 2001. Learning lessons, policy transfer and the international diffusion of policy ideas. Centre for the Study of Globalization and Regionalization (CSGR) Working Paper No. 69/01, University of Warwick. Coventry, UK: CSGR.

–. 2003. Transnational transfer agents and global networks in the "internationalization" of policy. Paper prepared for workshop on Internationalization and Policy Transfer, 11-12 April, New Orleans.

–. 2004. Transfer agents and global networks in the "transnationalization" of policy. *Journal of European Public Policy* 11 (3): 545-66.

Stone, Frank. 1984. *Canada, the GATT and the international trade system.* Ottawa: Institute for Research on Public Policy.

Sullivan, Scott. 1997. *From war to wealth: 50 years of innovation.* Paris: OECD.

Svensson T., and P. Öberg. 2002. Labour market organizations' participation in Swedish public policy-making. *Scandinavian Political Studies* 25 (4): 295-315.

Taylor, Peter. 1994. The state as container: Territoriality in the modern world-system. *Progress in Human Geography* 18 (2): 151-62.

Taylor, R. 2006. Lifelong learning and the Labour government. *Oxford Review of Education* 31 (1): 101-18.

Therrien, Jean-Phillipe. 2002. Debating foreign aid: Right versus left. *Third World Quarterly* 23 (3): 449-66.

Therrien, Jean-Phillipe, and Carolyn Lloyd. 2000. Development assistance on the brink. *Third World Quarterly* 21 (1): 21-38.

Tobin, Jennifer, and Susan Rose-Ackerman. 2003. Foreign direct investment and the business environment in developing countries: The impact of bilateral investment treaties. William Davidson Institute Working Papers Series, No. 587. Ann Arbor, MI: William Davidson Institute, University of Michigan.

Torfing, Jacob. 1999. Workfare with welfare: Recent reforms of the Danish welfare state. *Journal of European Social Policy* 9 (1): 5-28.

–. 2001. Path-dependent Danish welfare reforms: The contribution of the new institutionalisms to understanding evolutionary change. *Scandinavian Political Studies* 24 (4): 277-309.

–. 2004. Det Stille Sporskifte i Velfærdsstaten: En Diskursteoretisk Beslutningsprocesanalyse. Aarhus, Denmark: Aarhus Universitetsforlag.

TUAC (Trade Union Advisory Committee). 2005. *Governing the global economy: What role for the OECD?* Paris: TUAC.

–. 2006. About TUAC. http://www.tuac.org/about/cabout.htm.

Tuijnman, A., and A.-K. Broström. 2002. Changing notions of lifelong education and lifelong learning. *International Review of Education* 48 (1-2): 93-110.

U68. 1969a. *Mål för högre utbildning.* Stockholm: Swedish 1968 Education Commission.

–. 1969b. *Högre utbildning. Funktion och Struktur.* Stockholm: Swedish 1968 Education Commission.

Udredningsudvalget. 1992a. *Rapport fra Udredningsudvalget om Arbejdsmarkedets Strukturproblemer.* Copenhagen: Udredningsudvalget, Sekretariat.

–. 1992b. *Rapport fra Udredningsudvalget om Arbejdsmarkedets Strukturproblemer,* Appendix Part II, Chapter 11. Copenhagen: Udredningsudvalget, Sekretariat.

UNCTAD (United Nations Conference on Trade and Development). 1997. *Trade and development report 1997.* New York and Geneva: United Nations.

–. 1998. *Trade and development report 1998.* New York and Geneva: United Nations.

–. 2002a. Economic development in Africa: From adjustment to poverty reduction. http://www.unctad.org/en/docs/pogdsafricad2.en.pdf.

–. 2002b. *Experiences with bilateral and regional approaches to multilateral cooperation in the area of long-term cross-border investment, particularly foreign direct investment.* UNCTAD TD/B/COM.2/EM.111/2 Meeting. Geneva: UNCTAD.

UNDP (United Nations Development Programme). 2004. *Human development indicators.* New York: UNDP.

United Nations Division for the Advancement of Women. 2005. *Women 2000 and beyond: Implementation of the Beijing platform for action and compliance with international legal instruments on women.* New York: United Nations.

van Oorschot, Wim. 2004. Balancing work and welfare: Activation and flexicurity politics in the Netherlands, 1980-2000. *International Journal of Social Welfare* 13: 15-27.

Vestergaard, Frede. 1993. Kvinderne er Uskyldige. OECD. Myte om Arbejdsløshed Dementeres. *Weekend Avisen,* 2 July, Section 1: 3.

Vickers, M. 1994. Cross-national exchange, the OECD, and Australian education policy. *Knowledge and Policy* 7 (1): 25-47.

Vinde, Pierre. 1998. *The OECD committee structure: A review.* Paris: OECD.

Wade, Robert H. 1990. *Governing the market: Economic theory and the role of government in East Asian industrialization.* Princeton, NJ: Princeton University Press.

–. 2002. US hegemony and the World Bank: The fight over people and ideas. *Review of International Political Economy* 9 (2): 215-43.

Walberg, J., and G. Zhang. 1998. Analyzing the OECD indicators model. *Comparative Education* 34 (1): 55-70.

Webb, Michael C. 1992. Canada and the international monetary regime. In *Canadian foreign policy and international economic regimes,* ed. A. Claire Cutler and Mark W. Zacher. Vancouver: UBC Press.

–. 2004. Defining the boundaries of legitimate state practice: Norms, transnational actors and the OECD's project on harmful tax competition. *Review of International Political Economy* 11 (4): 787-827.

Weiss, Carol, and Bucuvalas, Michael J. 1980. *Social science research and decision-making.* New York: Columbia University Press.

Weiss, Friedl. 1998. Dispute settlement under the General Agreement on Trade in Services. In *Dispute resolution in the World Trade Organization,* ed. J. Cameron and K. Campbell, 148-70. London: Cameron May.

Welch, F. 1970. Education in production. *Journal of Political Economy* 78 (1): 35-59.

West, J. 2005. Emergence of multi-stakeholder diplomacy at the OECD: Origins, lessons and directions for the future. Paper presented to international conference on Multi-stakeholder Diplomacy, 11-13 February, Malta.

Westergaard-Nielsen, Niels. 1993. Arbejdsmarkedets Structurproblemer. *Nationaløkonomisk Tidsskrift* 131 (1): 21-37.

White, Howard, and Richard Black. 2003. Millennium Development Goals. In *Targeting development: Critical perspectives on the Millennium Development Goals,* ed. Howard White and Richard Black, 1-24. New York: Routledge.

WHO (World Health Organization). 2000. The world health report 2000: Health systems: Improving performance. Geneva: WHO.

Williams, Russell Alan. 2002. Liberalizing "trade in services": Ideas in international political economy. In *Global instability: Uncertainty and new visions in political economy,* ed. Stephen McBride et al., 65-87. Dordrecht, Netherlands: Kluwer Academic Publishers.

Williamson, John. 1990. *Latin American adjustment: How much has happened?* Washington, DC: Institute for International Economics.

Wilkinson, Rorden, ed. 2005. *The global governance reader.* New York: Routledge.

Wilkinson, Rorden, and Steve Hughes, eds. 2002. *Global governance: Critical perspectives.* New York: Routledge.

Wimann, R., T. Voipio, and M. Ylonen, eds. 2006. *Comprehensive social policies for development in a globalising world.* Helsinki: Ministry of Foreign Affairs of Finland.

Winham, Gilbert R. 1986. *International trade and the Tokyo Round negotiation.* Princeton, NJ: Princeton University Press.

Wiseman, John. 1998. *Global nation? Australia and the politics of globalization.* London: Cambridge University Press.

Wolfe, David, and Meric Gertler. 2002. Innovation and social learning: An introduction. In *Innovation and social learning,* ed. David Wolfe and Meric Gertler, 1-25. Basingstoke, UK: Palgrave/Macmillan.

Wolfe, Robert. 1993. The making of the peace, 1993: A review of Canadian economic diplomacy at the OECD. Economic and Trade Policy Branch Working Paper. Ottawa: Department of Foreign Affairs and International Trade Canada.

–. 1998. *Farm wars: The political economy of agriculture and the international trade regime.* New York: Macmillan and St. Martin's Press.

Wood, D. 2000. The international campaign against the Multilateral Agreement on Investment: A test case for the future of globalisation? *Ethics, Place and Environment* 3 (1): 25-45.

Woodward, Richard. 2004. Global monitor: The Organization for Economic Cooperation and Development. *New Political Economy* 9 (1): 113-27.

–. 2006a. Age concern: The future of the OECD. *World Today* 55 (8-9): 38-39.

–. 2006b. Offshore strategies in global political economy: Small islands and the case of the EU and OECD Harmful Tax Competition initiatives. *Cambridge Review of International Affairs* 19 (4): 685-99.

–. 2008. *The Organization for Economic Cooperation and Development*. London: Routledge.

World Economic Forum. 2004. *The global competitiveness report 2004-2005*. Geneva: World Economic Forum.

Wozniak, G. 1984. The adoption of interrelated innovations: A human capital approach. *Review of Economics and Statistics* 66 (1): 70-79.

Yannaca-Small, Katia. 2006. Improving the system of investor-state dispute settlement. OECD Working Papers on International Investment. Paris: OECD.

Zeitlin, Jonathan. 2003. Introduction: Governing work and welfare in a new economy: European and American experiments. In *Governing work and welfare in a new economy*, ed. David Trubek and Jonathan Zeitlin, 1-30. New York: Oxford University Press.

Contributors

Neil Bradford teaches political science at Huron University College, University of Western Ontario. He is also a research associate in Cities and Communities at Canadian Policy Research Networks in Ottawa. His research focuses on urban and community development and strategies for place-based public policy and multi-level governance.

Bob Deacon is Professor of International Social Policy at the University of Sheffield (UK). He is Director of the Globalism and Social Policy Programme (www. gaspp.org) and founding editor of the journal *Global Social Policy*. His recent publications include *Global Social Policy and Governance* (Sage) and, with Paul Stubbs, *Social Policy and International Interventions in South East Europe* (Edward Elgar). He has advised many international organizations on aspects of global social policy.

Lisa Drouillard is a policy manager at Health Canada where she is responsible for policy research and development on issues related to human genetics and health innovation. Her principle policy development experience has been related to the governance of commercialization and uptake of new health biotechnology products.

E. Richard Gold is an associate professor at McGill University's Faculty of Law and founding director of the Centre for Intellectual Property Policy where his research centres on the nexus between innovation, development, and commerce, particularly with respect to biotechnology in the international context. He is also president of the Innovation Partnership, a non-profit consultancy providing advice on and capacity building in the areas of technology transfer, innovation systems, and intellectual property policy and development.

Holly Grinvalds is a PhD student and Teaching Fellow in the Department of Political Studies at Queen's University. Her research interests are comparative welfare state politics; Canadian and Scandinavian public policy, particularly social and labour market policy; policy transfer and diffusion; the role of ideas in the public policy process; and the Organisation for Economic Co-operation and Development (OECD).

Andrew Jackson is National Director of Social and Economic Policy with the Canadian Labour Congress and has academic affiliations with the Institute of Political Economy at Carleton University and the School of Policy Studies at Queen's University. His areas of interest include the labour market and the quality of jobs, income distribution and poverty, macroeconomic policy, social policy, and the impact of globalization on workers. He is the author of *Work and Labour in Canada: Critical Issues* (Canadian Scholars Press).

Alexandra Kaasch is a researcher at Bremen University (Center for Social Policy Research) in Germany and a PhD student at the University of Sheffield (UK). She is a contributor to the *Global Social Policy* digest. Forthcoming publications include "The OECD and Global Health Governance" in K. Martens and A. Jakobi, eds., *Mechanisms of OECD Governance: International Incentives for National Policy Making.*

Rianne Mahon is Chancellor's Professor, Director of the Institute of Political Economy, and a member of the School of Public Policy and Administration and the Department of Sociology and Anthropology at Carleton University in Ottawa. Her earlier work focused on unions and labour market restructuring in Canada and Sweden, while more recently she has written on the politics of childcare. Her current research focuses on "travelling policy ideas" from international organizations to national contexts and from local to national.

Stephen McBride is Director of the Centre for Global Political Economy at Simon Fraser University. He recently co-edited *International Trade and Neoliberal Globalism* (Routledge). His current research deals with the private sector role in international dispute settlement.

Kathleen McNutt is an assistant professor in the Johnson-Shoyama Graduate School of Public Policy at the University of Regina. Recent articles have appeared in *Global Social Policy* and the *Canadian Journal of Political Science*. Her research focuses on policy networks and issues of e-governance.

Leslie A. Pal is Professor of Public Policy at Carleton University's School of Public Policy and Administration. He is the author or editor of books on Canadian public policy, comparative politics, and public management. His most recent book is *Beyond Policy Analysis: Public Issue Management in Turbulent Times* (4th ed., Thomson Nelson). His current research focuses on the role of global policy communities in stimulating and supporting global public management reform.

Tony Porter is a professor in the Department of Political Science, McMaster University, Hamilton. He conducts research on transnational business regulation. His most recent book is *Globalization and Finance* (Polity).

Kjell Rubenson is Professor, Educational Studies, at the University of British Columbia, where he is also Co-Director of the Centre for Policy Studies in Higher Education and Training. His research deals with adult education and postsecondary education and the labour market.

Arne Ruckert is a PhD candidate in the Department of Political Science at Carleton University. He is the author of journal articles and book chapters on the World Bank and the International Monetary Fund's Poverty Reduction Strategy para-- digm. He is co-editor of a forthcoming collection on post-neoliberalism in the Americas (Palgrave/Macmillan). He will take up a SSHRC-funded postdoctoral fellowship at the University of Ottawa in July 2008.

Michael Webb is Professor of Political Science at the University of Victoria. His research interests include International political economy, globalization and governance, and Canadian foreign policy.

Russell Alan Williams is an assistant professor in the Department of Political Science at Memorial University, St. John's, Newfoundland. His research and teaching focuses on the impact of globalization and international political economy on public policy in Canada. He has published a number of pieces on the politics of trade, banking, and labour market policy. He is currently studying Canada's international trade disputes.

Robert Wolfe is a professor in the School of Policy Studies at Queen's University in Kingston, Ontario. He was a foreign service officer for many years, including participation in the Canadian Delegation to the OECD in Paris. His Ottawa assignments included the International Economic Relations Division and the G-7 Summit team. Since joining Queen's University in 1995, Wolfe has published widely on Canadian trade policy, public opinion about trade, and international institutions, notably the World Trade Organization.

Richard Woodward is a lecturer in political economy in the Department of Politics and International Studies at the University of Hull, Quebec. His primary research interests are in the political economy of financial markets with particular reference to the City of London, offshore financial centres, and financial crime. He has written numerous chapters and articles on the OECD and its role in global governance. His first book, *The Organisation for Economic Co-operation and Development*, was published by Routledge in 2008.

Index

international development targets (IDTs), 10, 13, 104-5, 237
international economic cooperation. *See* economic policy cooperation and OECD
International Energy Agency (IEA), 28, 33
International Federation of Agricultural Producers, 83
International Labour Organization (ILO): "decent work" concept, 156-57; international competition in social policies, 227; on OECD as social policy actor, 238-39; pension policy, 231; submission of conventions to parliaments, 7
International Metalworkers Federation, 55
International Monetary Fund (IMF): discussions re Bretton Woods, 34-35; international competition in social policies, 227; paper on country ownership of adjustment policies, 106; role, 8, 121
international monetary system, 33-35
International Non-Governmental Organizations (OECD body), 81
International Organization of Pension Supervisors (IOPS), 232
international organizations: growth of, impact on transnational governance, 5; identity defining, 44-47; nodes in transnational networks, 3; operation of hegemony through these organizations, 98-99; role in promoting neoliberalism, 98; role in transnational governance, 5-6. *See also* multilateral economic institutions (MEIs)
international political economies (IPEs), 5, 78
International Social Security Association (ISSA), 232
International Trade Organization (ITO), 30
investment regimes and the OECD: "best practices" ideologically driven, 118; bilateral investment treaties, 124-25; Codes of Liberalization, 30, 49, 84, 118-19, 121-24, 130-31; current OECD initiatives, 128-31; Declaration on International Investment and Multinational Enterprises (1976), 30, 81; impact of OECD, 131-32; liberalization of global investment regimes, 117-21, 125, 129; neoliberal economic policies, 118; progressive liberalization efforts, 122-23, 125-31; role of OECD in negotiations, 30; "trade in services," concept and liberalization, 122, 125-27. *See also* Multilateral Agreement on Investment (MAI)
Ireland, 264
Israel, 58

Jackson, Andrew, 14
Jacobsson, Bengt, 6, 17, 48, 135-36, 137, 278
Japan, 264-65, 266, 267, 273
Japan Business Federation, 56
Jobs Strategy (OECD): Americanization criticism, 152; compliance and performance by member countries, 158-63; criticism by Employment Directorate (EU) and TUAC, 174; "decent work" concept, 156-57; "flexicurity" cluster of states, 154-57, 159-63; focus on labour market deregulation, 152-53, 155, 157-59, 174; "Four Pillars" of 2006 Jobs Strategy, 165-68; impact on labour market performance, 10, 11, 153-54, 163, 165; neoliberal cluster of states, 154-57, 159-63; neoliberal principles, 155; neoliberalism's entrenchment, 17, 19, 152-54, 157, 163-65, 167-68, 172; policy learning by member countries, 164; policy recommendations for labour market, 158-59; promotion as a "best practices" guide, 152; revision (2006) and partial concessions to inclusive liberalism, 19, 164-68, 173-74, 185-86; Toronto forum on revised Jobs Strategy (2006), 167, 172; vs EU's Employment Strategy, 17-18
Jobs Study (OECD): 10-point action framework, 157-58; approach to education, 254; based on NAIRU, 17, 158, 179-80; basis for Jobs Strategy, 152; "best practices" approach, 158; economic orthodoxy, 17; enhanced flexibility theme, 16, 17. *See also* Jobs Strategy (OECD)
Johnston, Donald, 87-88, 90, 134, 135, 139-40
Jütting, Johannes, 237

Kaasch, Alexandra, 18
Keck, M., 5
Keohane, Robert O., 16-17
Keynesianism: evolution of policy in Keynesian era, 19-20; Keynesianism liberalism, 261; labour market policy, 161; OECD's approach until mid-1970s, 15, 35, 82; OECD's shift away from, toward neoliberalism, 15-17, 19, 35, 50, 82, 279
knowledge networks, transnational (OECD): authoritative reports by OECD, 51-52, 57; expressions of best practices, 48-49; form of global coordination and governance, 73-74; help in defining "modern" state, 7; impact on social policies, 47; influence of OECD models, 48; OECD's contribution to, 43-44; public

Printed and bound in Canada
Set in Stone by Artegraphica Design Co. Ltd.
Copy editor: Frank Chow
Proofreader: Amelia Gilliland
Indexer: Patricia Buchanan